Praise for *Still Here*

"[A] zingy and rigorously researched biography . . . A front row ticket
to the golden age of musical theater, *Still Here* is also an unequivocal
celebration of those who dare to sing a slightly different tune."
—LAUREN MECHLING, *Vogue*

"A marvelous trip back in time to a Broadway that's gone forever: a Broadway before the advent of megamusicals, of body-miking, of the Disney-
fication of Times Square . . . Compulsively readable."
—BROOKE ALLEN, *The Wall Street Journal*

"Sparkling details . . . clink around Jacobs's biography, *Still Here*, like ice
in a rocks glass . . . It would be possible to write a serviceable book about
[Stritch's] life by simply quoting her many one-liners, or by describing
her habit of wearing only tights on stage. But Jacobs . . . doesn't rely on
Stritch's charm to fuel the narrative. Instead, she uses hundreds of interviews and years of research to portray the actress in all her complexity."
—RACHEL SYME, *The New Yorker*

"Alexandra Jacobs incorporates an astonishing amount of research, including countless personal interviews . . . Her portrayal of Stritch is
wholly fleshed out, from the actor's earliest days as a socialite in Detroit
to her time as the reigning grand dame of Broadway . . . *Still Here* will
be a boon to those who revel in hearing about short-lived plays and
musicals like *Time Of The Barracudas* and *Goldilocks* . . . This biography
expertly sketches out the vast other hours of her life, painting a thorough
picture of a woman who lived life on her own terms—in an age when it
was exceedingly difficult to do so."
—GWEN IHNAT, *The A.V. Club*

"Fun . . . Hits all the marks . . . Elaine would have loved Jacobs's bio. It's
the picture she wanted to leave behind."
—JOHN GUARE, *Book Post*

"Stritch famously loved a good time and a good story, so she probably would have enjoyed Jacobs's gossipy text, studded with juicy anecdotes . . . An absorbing story."
—WENDY SMITH, *The Washington Post*

"A fab read . . . *Still Here* will make you feel as if Stritch, brought back to life, is looking into your eyes and singing just for you."
—KATHI WOLFE, *Washington Blade*

"This book, lush with detail and heavy on Broadway history, will appeal to Stritch fans and theater geeks everywhere."
—*Publishers Weekly*

"Jacobs utilizes the massive cache of information [Stritch] left in her wake, including copious interviews and her archives. This meticulous research allows for the conjuring of a surprising and complex realness that serves as a deep and resounding undercurrent to the public persona so widely known . . . The power of Jacobs' biography is the way she sets Stritch's story against the canvas of a shifting century, allowing us to watch as the world expands beyond these limiting boxes for female performers, and cheer as Stritch was able to expand herself."
—KELLY McMASTERS, *Newsday*

"Alexandra Jacobs's engaging new biography, *Still Here*, fleshes out our picture of the raspy-voiced actress and singer . . . Written with the co-operation of the estate, clear-eyed affection, and considerable stylistic flair, *Still Here* offers an intimate . . . portrait of Stritch that leaves intact . . . the mysteries of her personality."
—JULIA M. KLEIN, *The Boston Globe*

"The Stritch presented here is a study in contrasts: she came off as a brassy freewheeler, but she was naïve enough to think Rock Hudson had a crush on her; she was a self-described strong woman, yet the women's movement didn't dent her staunch apoliticality . . . This was the key to her long-lasting appeal: she had an uncanny ability to play to an audi-

ence. This dishy biography will be a ride for the theatrically inclined as Stritch's seventy-year career crosses those of Marlon Brando, Ethel Merman, Noël Coward, Angela Lansbury, Bea Arthur, and, of course, Hal Prince and Stephen Sondheim."
—SUSAN MAGUIRE, *Booklist*

"One of the more surreal, gratifying, and wonderful experiences of my career was when Elaine Stritch played my mother on *30 Rock*. An acting lesson, a therapy session, a chance to know the great La Stritch. This book is your chance."
—ALEC BALDWIN

"Elaine Stritch brought a raw truth to musical theater that had rarely been seen before or since. Her whole self—warts, drinks, and all. In this biography, Alexandra Jacobs shows Stritch's every pore, and we are all better for it."
—SARAH SILVERMAN

"I laughed. I cried. Alexandra Jacobs lovingly pulls back the curtain on 'Stritchy,' a sacred cow of American showbiz, revealing her to be as talented, reckless, flawed, and fabulous as I always hoped she was."
—SIMON DOONAN, author of *Drag* and *Wacky Chicks*

"Alexandra Jacobs's *Still Here* is a delicious, page-turning, and meticulous romp through the distinctive life of a feminist icon. The talented, urbane, smoking-and-drinking queen of Broadway's tough dames lived a life of accomplishment, boldly frank opinions, and just as bold-faced names that defined the Great White Way (and Hollywood) of recent yore. Elaine Stritch balanced theatrical perfectionism, glamorous Manhattan evenings, and behavioral brinksmanship with the never-quite-dismissed lessons of her Catholic background in the Midwest. I learned as much as I was entertained and left smitten: my idea of a pretty terrific book."
—SHEILA WELLER, *New York Times*–bestselling author of *Girls Like Us: Carole King, Joni Mitchell, Carly Simon—and the Journey of a Generation* and *Carrie Fisher: A Life on the Edge*

ALEXANDRA JACOBS

Still Here

Alexandra Jacobs is an editor and a writer at *The New York Times* who has also written for *The New Yorker*, the *Observer*, *Entertainment Weekly*, and many other publications.

STILL HERE

STILL HERE

THE MADCAP,
NERVY, SINGULAR
LIFE OF
ELAINE STRITCH

ALEXANDRA JACOBS

PICADOR   FARRAR, STRAUS AND GIROUX   NEW YORK

Picador
120 Broadway, New York 10271

Owing to limitations of space, all acknowledgments for permission to reprint
previously published material can be found on page 339.

Library of Congress Control Number: 2019020220
Picador Paperback ISBN: 978-1-250-75805-7

Designed by Abby Kagan

Our books may be purchased in bulk for promotional, educational, or business use.
Please contact your local bookseller or the Macmillan Corporate and Premium
Sales Department at 1-800-221-7945, extension 5442, or by e-mail at
MacmillanSpecialMarkets@macmillan.com.

Picador® is a U.S. registered trademark and is used by Macmillan Publishing Group,
LLC, under license from Pan Books Limited.

For book club information, please visit facebook.com/picadorbookclub or
e-mail marketing@picadorusa.com.

picadorusa.com • instagram.com/picador
twitter.com/picadorusa • facebook.com/picadorusa

1 3 5 7 9 10 8 6 4 2

In memory of Peter W. Kaplan, and my father

"I have come for my courage," announced the Lion, entering the room.

"Very well," answered the little man; "I will get it for you."

He went to a cupboard and reaching up to a high shelf took down a square green bottle, the contents of which he poured into a green-gold dish, beautifully carved. Placing this before the Cowardly Lion, who sniffed at it as if he did not like it, the Wizard said:

"Drink."

"What is it?" asked the Lion.

"Well," answered Oz, "if it were inside of you, it would be courage. You know, of course, that courage is always inside one; so that this really cannot be called courage until you have swallowed it. Therefore I advise you to drink it as soon as possible."

The Lion hesitated no longer, but drank till the dish was empty.

"How do you feel now?" asked Oz.

"Full of courage," replied the Lion, who went joyfully back to his friends to tell them of his good fortune.

—L. FRANK BAUM, *The Wonderful Wizard of Oz*

"This time for me! For me! For me! For me! For me! For me! For me!"

—STEPHEN SONDHEIM, *Gypsy*

CONTENTS

STILL HERE

PROLOGUE

On the afternoon of November 17, 2014, hundreds of people made their way through a dark rain toward the Al Hirschfeld Theater on West Forty-Fifth Street in New York City. Settling with a certain expectant jollity into its plush red seats were actors famous and obscure, executives, playwrights, press agents, journalists, out-of-towners, a bronzed billionaire fashion designer who'd pulled up in a limousine, and ordinary civilians arriving on foot with their busted umbrellas.

They had arrived not for a matinee—for this was a Monday, when Broadway stages are by long custom dark—but to pay homage to Elaine Stritch, the indefatigable-seeming entertainer who at eighty-nine had died of stomach cancer four months earlier in Birmingham, Michigan, a leafy suburb northwest of Detroit. Not for Stritch the mealymouthed "passed away"; her preferred euphemism was "left the building." It indicated her fundamentally citified view of life.

Plenty of her contemporaries were present, including Hal Prince, the director and producer whose compactly commanding stance and twenty-one Tonys gave him a Napoleonic air, and Liz Smith, the platinum-haired gossip columnist known as the "grande dame of dish." Some in the audience were puzzled, though, by the absence of Stephen Sondheim, the composer and lyricist whose virtuosic work Stritch was devoted to above all others, whose approval she craved more than anyone else's. (He had a respiratory infection that day, he said later. But he had also refused an earlier invitation to speak, writing simply that he didn't know the honoree well enough, and sending organizers into frenzied analysis of what exactly that might mean.)

There were also others much younger, many of whom had discovered Stritch only after seeing her 2001 one-woman show *At Liberty*: the artful summation of her marathon career conducted with the sole prop of a barstool. Written with John Lahr, then *The New Yorker*'s chief theater critic, its success had led to the recognition she had longed for since arriving in New York almost sixty years before. She was deemed a Living Landmark and joyously heralded by strangers in her regular and often untrousered patrols from the Carlyle on Madison Avenue, the last in a series of venerable hotels she had chosen to call home. So far as that went. "I don't know if I really have any home," she said once. "I don't know how I feel about home. I don't know where home is."

To the end she was both restless and routinized, selfish and generous, straightforward and elliptical. "How do you solve a problem like Elaine Stritch?" asked one of the many celebrities in attendance, the actor Nathan Lane. He was standing at a podium under a Hirschfeld line drawing of the honoree clutching, characteristically, a brandy snifter, made to publicize the 1996 revival of Edward Albee's play *A Delicate Balance*. "How do you hold a fucking moonbeam in your hand?"

The crowd laughed knowingly at the profanity, which Stritch had deployed decades before it was common in polite society. This was one of several ways she had been ahead of her time or even somewhat out of time. She had chosen to live alone when the average woman of her Midwestern, Catholic, upper-middle-class background had become a Mrs. and a mother before age thirty. She had defied stereotypes of gender and age, projecting both feminine and masculine and refusing the slow fade accorded most in her profession (along with plastic surgery). She insisted on being seen and heard, felt and dealt with. She skirted high culture, low culture, and everything in between.

Though it was variously suggested Stritch's voice was infused with gravel, whiskey, or brass—a writer for *People* magazine once compared it to "a car shifting gears without the clutch"—her admirers from the music world had grown to include the longtime director of the Metropolitan Opera, James Levine; the indie rocker Morrissey; and the pop idol Elton John, who had sent half a dozen huge orchid plants to her small private funeral in Chicago with a card reading: "You were a shining star."

Onstage at the Hirschfeld, Stritch's colleagues sang the numbers she'd made her own. Bernadette Peters shrugged and mugged through the goofy and dated "Civilization (Bongo, Bongo, Bongo)," about a jungle native underwhelmed by Western society and its technological advancements. Laura Benanti and Michael Feinstein did the contrapuntal duet "You're Just in Love" from Irving Berlin's *Call Me Madam*, alternately plaintive and twinkling. Betty Buckley got the wistful ballad "I Never Know When (to Say When)," perhaps the sole keepsake from a largely forgotten 1958 musical called *Goldilocks*.

But by far the most affecting performance came toward the event's end, when the lights dimmed and an image of Stritch herself materialized on a big screen, like a glamorous ghost, in what might have been called her prime had she not so forcefully redefined that term. Wearing an ensemble of white blouse and black tights cribbed from Judy Garland's famous "Get Happy" sequence but carried off even more effectively with her long, slim legs, she began the Sondheim song "The Ladies Who Lunch," from the landmark 1970 musical *Company*, which was for so many years her signature anthem.

The Stritch-specter inhabited the dark world of the lyrics completely: cocking her silvery blonde head at the camera, enunciating, clasping her manicured hands as if in prayer, raising and furrowing professionally arched eyebrows, grinning, winking, nodding, jabbing, giving the okay sign, beckoning, pumping a fist, clawing, and throwing both hands up in a V shape that seemed to signify equally victory and defeat.

> So here's to the girls on the go—
> Everybody tries
> Look into their eyes,

And you'll see what they know
Everybody dies.

"Everybody dies," Prince had quoted at the podium, and paused. "I'm not so sure about Elaine."

Indeed, Stritch had been charged with such restless energy, one could be forgiven for believing she might yet emerge for one last encore from behind the Hirschfeld's corrugated curtain. Zelig-like, she had witnessed the Ziegfeld Follies and MTV videos; known the era of blackface and performed for the country's first African American president; and had her saucy one-liners ("another brilliant zinger," per the Sondheim song) committed both to piles of yellowing telegrams and the online echo chamber of Twitter. For decades she had kicked up her heels; for decades more she had made a Sisyphean trudge through the twelve steps of recovery.

Partly because of a consuming love affair with alcohol, partly because she in general found Hollywood "phony" and "a shuck," she had had only middling success in feature films and television. A firmer grasp on those twin brass rings of the entertainment carousel might have afforded her the financial security she was almost pathologically unable to feel, even after her bank account swelled to millions.

But long before the advent of so-called reality TV, the reporter's tape recorder and documentarian's camera had oscillated eagerly toward Stritch, alert to the quality of what is now called "authenticity." This was someone who, it was said often, was incapable of not telling the truth. This didn't mean she didn't sometimes embellish a story or make one up entirely; some whispered that her avowed twenty-four-year commitment to sobriety, openly relaxed in her waning months, was fictitious. But she had an emotional clarity and immediacy, a get-to-the-pointness that eludes most people.

What had propelled this straight-arrow girl from the squarest part of Detroit to the center of Sondheim's urbane artistic circle—or at least to gesticulating insistently on the perimeter? Had she truly beaten her alcohol addiction or merely nudged it to the curb? Was she an under-credited figure in the history of American show business or an adult version of Eloise at the Plaza, tweaking the elevator men and shirking her bills?

The answers would begin there at the Hirschfeld, in the hushed chatter of those gazing up in remembrance and rue, as John Updike put it in "Perfection Wasted," his poem about death, choosing a theater metaphor: "those loved ones nearest / the lips of the stage, their soft faces blanched / in the footlight glow, their laughter close to tears / their tears confused with their diamond earrings." And in the speeches of those onstage.

She had expressly forbidden a memorial, but "we all know that she would want this," said Hunter Ryan Herdlicka, a young actor who'd appeared with and befriended Stritch during her final appearance on Broadway, as the sardonic, wheelchair-couched Madame Armfeldt in Sondheim's *A Little Night Music*. "She lived to be the life of the party and the center of attention."

But Stritch yearned to be not just acknowledged, but understood. She learned after long trial to live in the moment, and to face the future, yet she could not help compulsively examining her past, parsing why a girl from a family who put the convent in conventional had chosen what Oscar Hammerstein II called in *Show Boat* "life upon the wicked stage": the darkened wings, the traveling spotlight, the bouquets, the kissed cheeks and whispered congratulations, and the buckets of champagne chilling in the dressing room.

For his fiftieth birthday, Nathan Lane told the assembled, she'd given him "a beautiful baby picture. Of her." This too got a knowing laugh.

But upon reflection it was a rather poignant anecdote. To share a photograph of oneself as a baby is to ask to be regarded at one's most vulnerable: naked and unspoiled. It is a plea for love.

1.

"THANKS FOR EVERYTHING"

She wasn't exactly born with a silver flask in her fist, but when Marion Elaine Stritch made her first entrance on February 2, 1925, at Harper Hospital in Detroit, at the uncharacteristically early hour of 6:30 a.m., it was into a climate of bustling prosperity.

Considering her later struggles, the date would come to seem apt. It was Groundhog Day, which—because of the hit 1993 movie about a weatherman caught in a time loop, later made into a Tony-nominated musical—would become shorthand for living the same events over and over again, an allegory for addiction. It was also the very thick of national Prohibition, of which it was joked that Punxsutawney Phil, the clairvoyant groundhog of Pennsylvania, was threatening sixty weeks of winter rather than the usual six if he didn't get a drink.

In Michigan the liquor trade had been forbidden since 1917, and the state's proximity to Canada had quickly encouraged bootleggers, some swooshing across Lake St. Clair on ice skates, their bounty behind them on sleds. That was the year Marion's mother, Mildred Isabel Jobe (changed from her father's oft mispronounced "Job"), married her favorite of many beaux, George Stritch. He had acquired a promising new position as a clerk at B.F. Goodrich, in Akron, the Ohio city that had come to be known as the "rubber capital of the world" following the convergence there of Goodyear, Firestone, and the brand-new General Tire. Perhaps Goodrich's most prestigious commission was supplying tires, gas masks, and other equipment used in the Great War, which the United States had just joined.

The young couple had met growing up in Springfield, where George, gray eyed and gangly—"he was all legs," said his eldest granddaughter, Sally Hanley—was raised in humble circumstances. Born on April 7, 1892, according to the marriage certificate, he would eventually become the middle child of five. His father, Henry, was a tailor who'd emigrated from Ireland to Louisville, Kentucky, a decade or so after Garrett Stritch, father to the future cardinal Samuel Stritch, followed the same trajectory. Henry told his offspring that he and Samuel were cousins.

It was the seminal gossip columnist Walter Winchell who first trumpeted in 1947 that Cardinal Samuel Stritch of Chicago was Elaine's uncle, an irresistible piece of publicity repeated by journalists and colleagues throughout her life, though she tried intermittently to correct the record. Eventually she stopped trying. "When you have a lot of relations you don't call anybody cousins anymore—you call them uncle," she said on one occasion. "Or at least they did in that family." After another columnist, Earl Wilson, reported Elaine was the cardinal's daughter, she went to meet the holy man in person. Ushered in by a nun, she sat down on a red-backed seat with a stool under it.

"Elaine, that's my chair," he told her.

"Oh! Sorry."

She then described her problems in the "mad gay life of powder and paint," quoting Noël Coward, and asked what she should do.

"Pray to Our Lady," the cardinal suggested.

George's youngest sister died of tuberculosis in early childhood, and throughout his life he would cry when speaking of her. The remaining children all got jobs as soon as they could: the elder son as a bookkeeper, the two other daughters as stenographers. George worked for a textile mill, for the American Seeding Company, and for the Hunkin-Conkey Construction Company. "I don't think he ever got out of fourth grade," said Frank Moran, Jr., his eldest grandson.

A childhood friend of George, Bobby Clark, had escaped such prosaic labors by developing a tumbling and clowning routine at the local YMCA with an older boy named Paul McCullough. The two of them left town with a minstrel show, graduating to circus, vaudeville, burlesque, musical revues, and—after they were discovered and promoted by the songwriter Irving Berlin—riotous RKO film shorts with titles like *Odor in the Court*. Clark, known for his painted-on glasses, got most of the pratfalls and punch lines ("I rest my case . . . and my feet!"). McCullough was the quieter "straight man," with a toothbrush mustache, a style that did not yet look ominous. Their trademark pantomime was structured around trying and failing to put a chair on a table. (Yes, these were more innocent times.)

George shared Clark and McCullough's sense of humor and their ambition, but also was deeply practical. He needed all these qualities to woo the more cosmopolitan Mildred Jobe. Born on August 13, 1893, or so she told the county court, Mildred was distinctly pretty, buxom, and around five feet tall (the name Pettit was in her mother's lineage), with a long trail of prosperous suitors. "She was a pedestal girl, for sure," Sally Hanley said.

"The way they did dating then, she had a date every night of the week, and the guy that got Sunday night was number one," said another granddaughter, Midge Moran. "And my grandfather moved up from seven to one. So she wanted to marry him and her parents thought she was crazy, because they wanted her to marry the banker. But she didn't. She loved my grandfather."

Mildred never tired of calling attention to her more rarefied breeding and George's good fortune. "She picked him over the rest of them, and she reminded him of that all their lives," said Elaine's youngest niece, Elaine Kelly.

Mildred's father, Louis S. Job, known as L. S., was from Monmouthshire, Wales. He owned racehorses and a number of businesses, among them a bakery and an eponymous tavern on South Fountain Avenue in downtown Springfield, not far from where his family lived, a classy one where roast beef sandwiches were served, there was "a private room for ladies," and men had to stand up at the bar to drink alcohol. The preferred toast over foamy beer tops—"Here's how we lost the farm!"— would become one of Elaine's favorites.

"He was a gentleman's gentleman," Frank Moran, Jr., said, albeit one who would have not been out of place in an Edward Hopper painting. "He'd sit up till the last customer went home, then he'd lock up and go over to the railroad station and chew the rag with the night clerk until the sun came up and the early morning express roared through Spring-field," Elaine wrote in 1955, in a guest column for another of Winchell's competitors, Dorothy Kilgallen, by way of accounting for her own pro-nounced nocturnal tendencies.

Louis's wife, Sarah, nicknamed Sallie, was said to be a descendant of French Huguenots in Virginia, giving her an air of refinement taken on by her only daughter. A son, Howard, eight years older than Mildred, started out as a traveling salesman, married a woman named Onita Albert, and settled in North Carolina, where he became a vice president at Adams-Millis, a hosiery manufacturer.

Mildred had neither need nor expectation of entering a particular profession, even as the women's suffrage movement gathered momen-tum across the country. But she pursued excellence nonetheless: elected president of the class in her finishing school, College of St. Mary of the Springs in Columbus, Ohio, she wrote a prize essay comparing Shake-speare's *A Midsummer Night's Dream* with *The Tempest*; analyzed Sir Wal-ter Scott as a member of the Philomathean Society; and played Liszt on the piano, her specialty, while also learning the trumpet and drums. She also acted in plays and contributed a poem to the 1912 yearbook that began, with unyielding optimism:

> The world ain't half so dreadful
> As lots of people say!
> It's just the way you take it—
> Why life's just what you make it—
> Smile, and the world's your mirror any day.

A subsequent stanza proposed a defense against sour, gossiping people. "Well, if lemons come, just *squeeze* them."

Mildred was the only young lady in her set to have her own horse and buggy, but she rarely if ever drove the family car after she had married, preferring instead to direct from the front passenger seat. ("Okay, George, it's clear on the right . . .") In the miniature theater of the automobile, and with little urging at parties, the couple would continue a custom of singing together in close harmony that they had begun in courtship. "They were lovers from day one, throughout their entire life," Midge Moran said. "It was a love story."

For their honeymoon, the newlyweds traveled to a hotel in Detroit where, nervous about the gangs that had begun to menace the area since Prohibition began, they decided to barricade the door of their room with a dresser. Mildred proceeded to the bathroom, shut this door as well and didn't emerge for an hour or so, whereupon George began to knock.

"Midge, come on out," he called.

"No, I don't want to," she said in a small voice.

"Please."

Finally his young bride emerged, wearing a lacy negligee, a stark contrast to the opaque scapular she used to be given by nuns for baths to prevent her from looking at her body. Tears were running down her face.

"What's the matter?" her groom asked.

"I'm afraid!"

"What are you afraid of?"

"Onita told me what you're going to do to me!"

"Oh, Midge, forget about that. Let's just go to sleep," George said.

Mutual trust and consideration having thus been firmly established, the marriage was consummated the following night.

In the seventy subsequent years together, it would often be said of Mildred that she "ran the show." In October 1918 she gave birth to a daughter, Georgene Frances—named not after her husband, Mildred hastened to tell those who assumed, but because a classmate had had the name and it struck her fancy. George, who had claimed a physical exemption on his draft card the previous year, was with an infant now virtually assured deferment. A month afterward, anyway, the war ended, and not long after he was transferred to B.F. Goodrich's offices in Detroit. The family lived in a series of duplex apartment houses, where they often took in boarders for extra cash. On February 24, 1921, another daughter arrived: Sally Jobe, named for Mildred's mother. Were they hoping a third child would be a boy? "They wanted three boys," Sally Hanley said. "He had names: Michael, William, John. He wanted three boys and they had three girls. And he adored them."

Civic government then could have a benevolent, even jolly air. "Dear Baby, We Hope You Will Grow Up to Be a Fine, Strong Citizen," read the form for the birth certificate typed up after little Marion came in 1925. "We Shall Do All We Can to Make This Possible. Sincerely Your Friend, the Detroit Department of Health." But the clerk botched her surname, foreshadowing a lifetime of misspellings and mispronunciations, to the Germanic-sounding Steich, and left off the "Elaine," a Frenchified version of Ellen or Eleanor, as Marion was of Mary. After nine months, George wrote to amend both, and the middle name was the one that stuck.

Lainey, as she was called, was a blonde and bonny baby, with blue eyes that quickly acquired a mischievous expression. "When Elaine was born, the chandeliers shook, and they never stopped," Georgene became fond of saying, though if there were chandeliers at this juncture they weren't terribly grand.

But after George was promoted at Goodrich the family bought a modest house at 2250 Tuxedo Street for around $9000, dispensed with the lodgers, and hired a live-in African American nanny and cook, Carrie Jones, whom Stritch would later tell of running into at a "black and tan" club downtown when she was a rebellious teenager. Dinner could be a clamorous affair. "They'd be talking and the conversation would be advanced," Elaine Kelly said. "Elaine would get so fed up with all that chitchat that didn't involve her she would pull herself up out of her high chair and stand on it and fold her arms and say 'No! Me!'"

As a toddler, Lainey learned quickly to clap a straw boater hat on her golden curls and imitate Maurice Chevalier to get attention. At age five, during a visit to New York she was buttoned into a taffeta dress and Mary Jane shoes, given a box of chocolates and taken by her uncle Howard to see *The Band Wagon*. Mesmerized by the elegant dancer Fred Astaire and his sister, Adele, singing "We play hoops!" with French accents, she was disappointed later to find that number eliminated from the movie version.

But the Stritch family didn't need to travel east for lavish entertainments. The old vaudeville houses near Detroit's Greektown neighborhood were increasingly being superseded by ambitious construction around Grand Circus Park. There was the Cass Theater, a newly air-conditioned home to "legitimate" plays that hosted Hollywood stars like John and Ethel Barrymore, Boris Karloff, and Bette Davis; and the Shubert Theater, owned by the publisher of the *Detroit Free Press*. This was boom time for elaborate movie palaces—the beaux arts Capitol, the "oriental" Fox, the Spanish gothic United Artists—with glowing neon marquees and grand staircases designed by renowned architects. Particularly sumptuous was the Michigan, open since 1926: a French Renaissance confection by the Rapp brothers from Chicago, with more than four thousand seats and sculptures, ferns, and a pianist in the lobby. When Elaine asserted later that she had moved to New York for "higher ceilings," she was speaking metaphorically.

Americans then were mad for automobiles the way they now are for iPhones, and Detroit, the center of car production, was the fourth-largest city in the country. Along with many of his peers, George was investing in stocks, and despite considerable losses on Black Tuesday in October 1929, he still had the wherewithal to upgrade to a two-story brick house at 18210 Birchcrest Drive; purchased for about $16,000, it had a sunken living room on the left, library on the right, kitchen and dining room in the back, and four bedrooms upstairs.

"Eighteen plus twenty-one ends in zero" was how George taught his girls to remember the number, a warning about settling down too early. Mildred furnished the place traditionally and the family added two little bulldogs: the lethargic Rudy and the peppier Biff, who would jump up on the glass door and bark and scare visitors. Of these there was a constant stream. The area was filling with upwardly mobile families, bracketed reassuringly as it was by institutions representing three stages of adult life: the University of Detroit, the Detroit Golf Club, and Woodlawn Cemetery.

Though many companies floundered in the aftermath of the crash, B.F. Goodrich continued to be on the up-and-up and going places. Net sales in the first six months of 1930 were over two and a half million dollars more than they had been in the same period of the previous year. George got another promotion, to sales manager.

Still, from within their cocoon of material comfort, the sense that money was hard-won and that one's circumstances could change overnight was not lost on the young Stritch girls. "My father was a self-made man so it was laborious" was how Elaine described their circumstances. "It was one step at a time . . . Of course that's what I admired so much about my father. But what I think I secretly wanted to be—you know how Katharine Hepburn would play rich women in movies, and she'd have a scene with her father having a brandy in the library with the guy coming in with the tray? I swear, that's the kind of rich I wanted to be. And it wasn't so much rich, it was that style of living."

She would develop a vexed relationship with money: at intervals parsimonious and profligate, ignorant and canny, generous and withholding. Possessions might be obsessively collected, fiercely guarded, and then renounced overnight.

"Elaine was tight," Frank Moran, Jr., said. "She was so tight she squeaked."

But then again: "Elaine went reckless for years with money, oh my god," Midge Moran said. "She was so reckless with money you couldn't believe."

All happy families may be alike, as Tolstoy wrote, but families with three sisters seem to have extra crackle, inspiring as they have dramatists from William Shakespeare and Anton Chekhov to Wendy Wasserstein and Woody Allen. In Elaine's youth, in one of American pop culture's periodic whimsies, musical groups composed of three sisters happened to be very popular. There were the Boswell Sisters, who sang "The Object of My Affection"; the Pickens Sisters, who moved from Georgia to Park Avenue; the Andrews Sisters ("Don't Sit Under the Apple Tree"); and the Gumm Sisters, the youngest of whom would transmogrify into Judy Garland. The Stritch girls, distinct but loyal, had their own harmony.

Nicknamed Genie by family and close friends, Georgene Stritch was beautiful, studious, and quiet outside the home. "She had a great wit and she was fun—she liked reading, she liked history, she liked literature," her daughter Midge Moran said. "But she was never showy at all. She was not narcissistic." When Elaine was little, she would climb into Genie's bed at night for company, enduring pinches from the older girl as she fidgeted.

Sally Stritch, the middle daughter, was graceful, a little neurotic, and pious. "My mother was a real breast-beater, a very guilty Catholic," Sally Hanley said.

Marianna Sterr, née Walsh, a friend of Elaine since their elementary-school days, regarded Georgene and Sally with awe. "They were lovely. Perfect, perfect ladies," she said. "And *she* was just a little dickens."

Mildred Stritch, the queen of this vest-pocket castle, held her trio of princesses to high standards of deportment and bearing. "My grandmother instilled in all those girls that they were Something," Midge Moran said. Some thought Mildred a too stern disciplinarian and that her youngest in particular suffered from what could be a certain chilliness or focus on externalities. But Elaine could not help but fix her with an adoring gaze. "My mother absolutely fascinated me," she wrote in the 1955 Kilgallen column. "She always looked like nine million bucks. Her hair was always done beautifully, she loved hats and wore them with marvelous aplomb. Her bedroom looked and smelled like a garden. She was terribly feminine and seemed to revel in it."

Few third children are reciprocated with such fascination, even in well-to-do households that have plenty of help. Once, shut out on the porch to play and at a loss for how to amuse herself, Elaine fatally swatted enough flies to spell out her name. "It was her way of supposing her name in lights," according to her friend Julie Keyes.

"And that's what billing is about," Elaine told her. "Dead fucking flies."

She made her first communion on May 21, 1933, at the nearby Gesu Catholic Church with sunlight streaming through kaleidoscopic stained-glass windows bordered by gray stone. A card printed with blue script commemorated the occasion:

> May He bring thee many blessings,
> Keep thee true and pure as now,
> Through the long day of the future
> When life's furrows deck thy brow

Life's furrows were writ large across the nation at the moment, the nadir of the Great Depression. Two months before, Franklin Delano Roosevelt had signed the Cullen-Harrison Act legalizing the sale of beer, and the repeal of Prohibition followed in December. Despite the images of flappers and gangsters merrily tippling from contraband tucked in garters during the 1920s, the use of alcohol among settled, churchgoing upper-middle-class family men could seem seedy and rather shameful; George had concealed a bottle of scotch in his bottom drawer at the Goodrich offices to offer to clients. But now booze was suddenly a sanctified daily indulgence, something to sink into along with the settee cushions with an "aah" at the end of a long day's work.

Though Mildred herself regularly sipped at an old-fashioned, she kept a watchful eye on her husband's intake, having witnessed how drink had held her father in thrall and outright ruined some of his customers. It was in Akron, where she and George had begun their married life, that the group that would become Alcoholics Anonymous began forming in 1935, partly through the efforts of Henrietta Seiberling, a daughter-in-law of Goodyear's founder. Its inaugural tenets included complete abstention from alcohol, the pursuit of spirituality, and regular meetings to share experiences.

"My grandmother was hell-bent," Sally Hanley said. "I always thought that she was an 'adult child of an alcoholic' as they call them in AA." And yet George "didn't abuse alcohol at all. He loved to have a couple of drinks and enjoy himself. But she would be a wreck. She had cocktails, but she was always worried about him."

Once, when George tarried at the office, drinking with his colleagues, Mildred removed her wedding ring, left it on the dresser, and took their three small daughters riding on a Detroit streetcar until it shut down for the night. The ring remained on the dresser for a year in silent, shiny rebuke, and George never stayed out late again.

Elaine found engaging deeply with Mildred difficult. "She was a very straightforward, glamorous woman," she recalled years later. "Meaning she didn't discuss things. She just lived her life moment to moment, day at a time. We didn't have psychological discussions after dinner. If it was a political thing about Roosevelt at the table, Mother would just say 'I don't like him' and that would be the end of her contribution. And it was awfully strong. Or someone's marriage: 'What in god's name he sees in her I will never, never know,' and you never went on with it like 'Mother, you know, I . . .' No! You don't go there at all! She said it, it's finished, and that's law."

George was more interested in discussion, with a fundamental lack of snobbery. When Elaine was twelve years old, the president of General Motors came to dinner. "And I watched my father with him," she remembered. "And then I watched his behavior again the next day with the newsboy who delivered the *Detroit Times*. Same thing. No difference." In Elaine's adult life, her father's democratic impulses warred perpetually with her mother's entitlement.

The Stritches were committed but not strict Catholics. According to Sally Hanley, her grandmother Mildred converted from Protestantism, and only Sally Stritch cared very much about the rituals. "They'd go to Mass on a Monday. Sunday was too busy, for family or something," she said. "They just wrote their own rules."

Georgene, the elder Sally, and Elaine were all enrolled at the all-girls Academy of the Sacred Heart Convent, which bills itself as the oldest independent school in Michigan. Tall and tomboyish, Elaine was cast as the male lead in a school production of *Hansel and Gretel*. "That afternoon I experienced a tiny bit more attention, respect, maybe even admiration," she wrote in notes for an unpublished memoir. "Not only at the convent after the curtain came down but also most definitely at the dinner table the following evening—nobody told me to finish my broccoli."

Outside of school there was a hubbub of social activity largely organized toward the securement of future mates. It began chastely enough, with Ping-Pong tournaments, scavenger hunts, horseback riding, and roller-skating derbies; later there were "frosh frolics" and "loafer leaps," football dances and fraternity cruises.

As George became more established in business, he and Mildred joined the Detroit Athletic Club, commonly referred to as the DAC, downtown across from the Music Hall and with a gently arched natatorium; he also joined the Bloomfield Hills Country Club, with golf on verdant hills, and the Recess Club, in the Fisher Building with its roof tipped in gold. It was at these formal but familiar venues that Elaine began performing in front of a larger audience. Diane Wenger Wilson, another friend since school days, remembers going to the DAC for "family night" on Fridays. "Elaine would get up and sing with the band, even when she was ten, eleven years old," she said. "She had a great deal of pizzazz, even as a youngster."

The attractive, talented, and interpersonally adroit Stritch sisters were becoming boldface names of the community. By the mid-1930s, Georgene's name began to appear in Detroit's then copious society pages as she dived off the springboard of the pool at the Pine Lake Country Club "in a lovely suit of white trimmed with red" (George also sometimes brought home rubber bathing costumes from B.F. Goodrich for the girls and their friends), sang "Happy Birthday" at a surprise party at a classmate's home on Chicago Boulevard, or helped host a "handkerchief shower" for a bride-to-be. Domesticity came naturally to Georgene. "Her mother ran a spotless household; Georgene helped a lot," Sterr said. "I remember being over there and Georgene was vacuuming. A song would come on the radio and Elaine wanted to dance with Georgene. So Georgene would put aside her vacuum cleaner, and away they'd go."

Sally, though, was the really proficient and enthusiastic dancer, studying and eventually teaching at the Arthur Murray Dance Studio at the Hotel Statler on Washington Boulevard, which gave lessons in the rumba, fox-trot, shag, tango, and a hybrid step called the "swinguet." She

performed tap at local functions and practiced ballet in the basement of
18210 Birchcrest, where George had a mirror and barre installed. The
Detroit Free Press's "Chatterbox" columnist cited Sally as among the en-
viable disciples of Sonja Henie, the Norwegian figure skater, one in that
rare breed who, rather than complaining of sore ankles, "give the old
tootsies a pat and then whiz around the rink with an impressive amount
of aplomb."

Elaine was an accomplished dancer as well, but she was more inclined
to hop on a bike—hers or the back of a boy's, without telling her parents where she was going. "My mother always thought she was a bad
influence on me," Sterr said. Their houses were a few blocks apart but
Marianna could cut through two lawns from her backyard to the Stritch
place. To liven up the fifteen-minute walk to school, they'd terrorize the
merchants on Twelfth Street—"you know, run through their stores and
make a fuss." In class, when they were instructed to memorize poetry,
Elaine would stand and theatrically mug her way through stanzas when
the teacher left the room.

"I have a lit-tle sha-dow that goes in and out with me," she recited
once, waggling her hips.

"Elaine! What are you doing?" gasped the teacher upon returning.

"She was a thorn in the nuns' side, I'll tell you," Sterr said. One nun
told Mildred that Elaine was a born leader—the only problem being that
she was leading all the other girls in the wrong direction.

One summer, the two friends were skinny-dipping while staying at
a cottage on Gratiot Beach in Port Huron, when the host's parents, a
Mr. and Mrs. Healy, walked by and saw their clothes and underthings
laid out on the beach. "We were frantic, but they just laughed," Sterr said.
"We had so much fun together—I can't tell you how much fun that girl
was. Those were lovely days. Nothing to think about but what boy you
were going to see . . ." Before they were old enough to date properly,
she and Elaine befriended two contemporaries, Richard and Buddy, and
took to going to church with them, where they'd sit in the balcony pew,
giggling and whispering.

Diane Wenger Wilson remembered a crowd of friends gathering
to listen to programs on the radio (Goodrich distributed the popular

Mantola model) like *The Lone Ranger*, which premiered on a Detroit station, WXYZ, just as Adolf Hitler was being named chancellor of Germany. "We were glued to the radio," she said, though they left Roosevelt's fireside chats to their parents. For a long time, Elaine's favorite song was "I Only Have Eyes for You"; "Are the stars out tonight / I don't know if it's cloudy or bright . . ." She was sent into the hall outside her classroom for imitating Bing Crosby crooning "Pennies from Heaven."

Though not often heard on the radio, among the performers to pass through the Cass and Shubert were George Stritch's old pals from Springfield, Bobby Clark and Paul McCullough, whom a local reviewer called "a couple of super-zanies," adding that "the management might just as well provide a remedy for aching jaws, because the customers will have laughed so repeatedly that their smiles set after a while." Clark and his wife often stayed with the Stritches when he was in town; and once, playing a doctor in a sketch and knowing their youngest was in the audience, he responded onstage to a nurse's knock on the door with the line: "If that's Elaine Stritch I'll be right there." She was thoroughly enchanted.

For a few years, Clark and McCullough were headliners. In the early thirties, they came to Detroit with *Strike Up the Band*, a revision of a 1927 Gershwin musical, and then *Here Goes the Bride*, a new musical comedy written by the naughty *New Yorker* cartoonist and gadabout Peter Arno, based on his experiences in a Reno, Nevada, divorce colony. The book and score proved fatally flawed, but one drama critic had lavished the entire fifteen paragraphs of his column on Clark's performance. "Count on being regaled as you never have been regaled since Mr. Groucho Marx went hunting for his horse in the breakfast room of a Long Island mansion," he wrote, declaring the production "Mr. Bobby Clark's show first, last and all the time. Nothing else matters. There is no need for anything else to matter."

It is one thing to be second banana and another to be regularly squashed underfoot, especially if you suffer from severe depression, as McCullough did. On March 23, 1936, after leaving a Massachusetts hospital where he'd been treated for a nervous breakdown, he stopped in the town of Medford for a shave, grabbed a razor from the barber, and slashed his own throat and wrists, dying two days later.

If Elaine was told about the grisly suicide, she suppressed the memory, at least from the press; or perhaps, like the critics, she only had eyes for Bobby Clark, who returned to the Cass playing opposite Fanny Brice with a traveling production of the Ziegfeld Follies in 1937. Ziegfeld had himself died five years before, and his widow, Billie Burke, who before long would be iridescently immortalized as Glinda the Good Witch in *The Wizard of Oz*, produced the extravaganza, which also featured the stripper Gypsy Rose Lee.

About to turn fifty, Clark was mourning not just his partner but the waning of burlesque, to which he imputed a certain morality. "Remember how the girls in the chorus had to wear opera-length stockings on the stage?" he reminisced to a Detroit journalist. "There couldn't be any profanity, or smut as it is known today. And you know what would have happened to a girl who attempted a striptease act. Nothing less than the patrol wagon."

In fifteen years Elaine herself would be mock-stripping onstage, playing a reporter describing what it was like to interview Lee. She never fantasized about being a Ziegfeld girl parading mutely and smiling in glittering costume and elaborate headdress. She could more readily imagine herself rather delivering punch lines and wisecracks, like the rubber-faced Brice. "As a kid I was not particularly pretty," she said. "I was the girl who sang the songs and told the jokes because I figured the only way to make people love me was to be a million laughs."

Elaine took the lead in a school operetta; played a Hollywood debutante in a "Merry Go Round" revue, and did a trick stunt as a mermaid in a school circus. In a production of *Quality Street*, a play by J. M. Barrie, who'd written *Peter Pan*, she took the role of Valentine Brown, a male suitor, "because I was taller than the other girl that played the heroine." Her voice was also lower than that of most of her friends, a rich alto that lent her songs a maturity beyond her years.

At the Masonic Temple for a musical presentation held by the Junior League, on the cusp of fourteen and wearing a powder-blue chiffon dress, Elaine performed "Thanks for Everything," a hit for Artie Shaw in January 1939: "Thanks for everything / For bringing me moments like this . . ."

The response was overwhelming. Driven back home by her parents, sitting in the back seat, she felt that "a kind of unbelievable excitement was going on inside of me," as she wrote years later. "It topped *Hansel and Gretel*, that's for sure."

She pretended to be asleep as the trees swayed in the wind outside, as if in approval. "My god, Mildred," she overheard her father whisper to her mother. "She can do it. She can really do it."

Elaine couldn't remember later in life whether she'd also had some red wine that evening. "I'm not sure but if I did it wasn't because I was afraid," she wrote. "I sang 'Thanks for Everything' before I knew I needed to drink in order to sing it."

From junior high school on, Elaine's life would be measured out not in coffee spoons like J. Alfred Prufrock's, nor even in wineglasses, but in newspaper column inches.

Early the next year she made her own first appearance in a *Detroit Free Press* gossip feature called "Who Goes Where," written by the anonymous "Passerby," after attending a supper dance held to welcome home a son from prep school in another state. "At Christmas, the girls who came from wealthy families would give lovely parties," Sterr said. "I remember one when they had tables set up through the living room and the dining room and the music room, with maybe six at a table and the girls wearing long dresses and the boys wore tuxedos and then after dinner we would go downstairs. They had a small ballroom with a marble floor, and one wall was all mirrored, and it was like a movie."

The young people were generally served Cokes, but Elaine was intrigued by the similar but mysterious substances that she'd long seen glinting in the grown-ups' glasses, and for that matter in the movies, accented by the musical clink of ice cubes and the curving waft of cigarette smoke above.

One night in the sunken living room of 18210 Birchcrest her father, likely a little tipsy himself, offered her half a whiskey sour. If the Drink Me potion imbibed by Alice in Wonderland had a shrinking effect, this had an opposite, expansive result on Elaine. Swallowing the second half in the pantry, she felt suddenly like "Bette Davis, Ingrid Bergman, Ethel Merman, Gertie Lawrence, and Fanny Brice" in one, as she put it in her one-woman show, taking "a trip to the moon on gossamer wings" (a quote from the Cole Porter song "Just One of Those Things"). "I couldn't get my breath, it was so wonderful."

Sharing liquid courage with one so young might seem reckless parenting in retrospect, but like the Wizard of Oz himself, George was a mere ordinary mortal; in the mid-1930s, many believed that demystifying alcohol in the home would encourage youthful moderation. Devoted to him, Elaine came to associate drinking with affection and authority, as one might do with medicine. Sips and then actual servings of liquor helped expand the contours of her world. Red wine in particular "seemed so elegant, so feminine, so ladylike—and besides, I needed that," she said in her show. "I was scared to death."

Half a bottle of Beaujolais-Villages helped steel her for her first prom, with a date named Bill Rice who was not much more than her five foot seven. Elaine faked a sprained ankle so she could wear ballet slippers rather than high heels with her mother's dress selection, tulle and "with more bows than a symphony orchestra."

Despite a heart-shaped face, a Cupid mouth, thick hair, enviably long legs, and a well-developed bust, she continued to be insecure about her appearance. Her friend Marianna didn't understand this. "She was adorable-looking," Sterr said. "And she had clothes that nobody else had," often bought originally from the Saks Fifth Avenue on Lothrop Road for Georgene or Sally, with their father's charge plate. "Elaine wore her little velvet coats with the fur collars and I had on my little cloth coat," Sterr said.

If the wardrobe wasn't handed down of free will, it might be raided. "In the old houses there would be a little door by the side door. The milkman would come and put the milk in there, and then you'd open the door, get it out, and put it in the icebox," Sally Hanley said. "So Elaine wore her clothes, took Genie's clothes, and put them in the milk chute. The idea was when the boy came to pick her up, she would go around, get Genie's clothes out of the milk chute, and change in the car or whatever and go to the nightclub—places she wasn't supposed to go." Once,

Elaine went to get the hidden bounty, opened the door, and found with a start Georgene's face staring reprovingly up at her.

Elaine loved to recount her capers from those years, some of which sounded like daffy plots for a future situation comedy. When she wanted to date an older boy her parents disapproved of, she had a more age-appropriate one come and pick her up with the undesirable crouched hidden in the back seat. But once George Stritch had an errand. "Oh, would you give me a ride with the dog?" he asked the young man. "Then I'll walk the dog home." Panic ensued as Biff got in the back seat, jumping all over the stowaway, but they got away with it. In Elaine's junior year, she pretended she had a local Halloween party to go to and instead snuck off to rendezvous with a boyfriend in college at Ann Arbor more than an hour away, buying favors at Woolworth as part of her cover-up.

As Georgene matriculated at the University of Detroit, where she would major in history, and with Sally preoccupied by dance and church, Elaine continued refining her act. At the next supper dance, the Passerby found her again; "a vision in white net" entertaining seventy-odd guests with impromptu renditions of Benny Goodman's "Always and Always" and Harold Rome's "Franklin D. Roosevelt Jones," a song about naming one's child after the president, of enduring enough popularity that Judy Garland would sing it in the movie *Babes on Broadway*, wearing blackface, two years later.

Like most American teenagers (a relatively new concept helped along by the automobile's invention), Elaine was concerned less with government affairs than those of the heart. "Dance is this Friday. Date: Rice. Hot damn," she wrote Diane Wenger at her prep school, after returning from an unsuccessful semester away in Albany, New York, at the Kenwood Academy. She was "in gobs of trouble," with half a dozen boys having called "to find out where they stood." After a "honey" of a fight, Rice had told Elaine that he loved her. "And no joke that was 'music to my ears,'" she wrote. "Gosh, he has changed—much more forward (thank God). I really do think the world of him Diane. I think this is it."

Despite the near universal goal of going steady and then entering the covenant of marriage, Elaine continued to play the field, far more energetically than many in her peer group. "She was so popular with the boys, they were scared to ask her to dance," Sterr said. "I found the girls loved her but hated her too because she stole their boyfriends whenever she had the chance. All she had to do was look their way and they'd fall all over themselves. She even did it to me! She had no compunctions."

A few days before Christmas in 1940, the Stritches gave a large party of their own. A rotating music box sat atop the piano in the living room, "tinkling away for all its worth" at Mendelssohn's wedding march, recorded the *Detroit Free Press*'s society columnist, with a male and female figurine in formal dress rotating upon it. As their faces turned to the crowd, it became evident they were miniatures of Georgene Stritch and her beau from the University of Detroit, Frank Sullivan Moran of Grosse Pointe, whom she had known since she was fourteen.

They were married the next month at Gesu at 10:00 a.m., with ostrich feathers on Mildred's hat and Sally as maid of honor in a white wool suit. Recently photographed dancing a new step, the Lions' Lope, with Cotton Price, a running back for the city's football team, the middle sister was now attending the University of Detroit herself and was active in the Junior League of Catholic Women.

Spared returning to the Kenwood Academy because of persistent strep throat, the youngest Stritch sister maintained her frantic dating pace. In Elaine's orbit were more Bills than just Rice, a Bob, a Brad, a couple of Jims, a Chuck, a Darius, a Reid, a Pete, and a Jack Bolton, the brother of Sally's future fiancé, Thomas. Elaine most enjoyed being in a crowd that paid no mind to the legal drinking age, which was twenty-one in Michigan. "Lately it seems we always go places in a huge bunch," she wrote Wenger. "It's really swell." There were trips to see *Gone with the Wind* in a red Chevrolet convertible, a dance where the African American bandleader and jazz singer Cab Calloway performed ("he was just wonderful"), and a friend's wedding to a former star left tackle on the football team where, Elaine confessed, "No kidding Diane, I was plastered. Well, what do you expect when they feed you champagne like water? Went out with Bill that night. As for his condition, I was surprised we got where we were going."

Elaine's own high jinks did not stop her from passing judgment on those whom she perceived as truly out of control. "All of those gals are so damn cheap and wild—no joke, they just act terrible at dances," she wrote of another group. "Helen really went the limit when she had five Tom Collins . . ." Her own set was comparatively decorous. "I'm so in love I could die," another friend confessed. "Promise not to tell anyone but one thing led to another and I kissed him—I couldn't help it." Elaine and her friends exchanged "T.L.'s," short for trade-lasts, or overheard compliments. "Bill said he thought you were a wonderful dancer and had a swell personality," Marianna Walsh wrote to her. "Jimmy said he thought you were one of the best-looking girls he'd ever seen."

On the evening of December 8, 1941, the day after Pearl Harbor, newsboys came pouring along the streets of Detroit, crying out "War is declared! War is declared!" In bed, young Marianna cowered as she heard the shouts. "It scared me to death," she said. "I got up and asked my mother about it and she said, 'Don't worry, it's not here.'"

But ripples were beginning to appear along the smooth surface of the young people's lives. Georgene had become pregnant, and after she gave birth to Frank Jr. in 1942, her husband joined the navy and she moved back to her childhood home. Elaine chafed at the new strictures this setup necessitated. "When people spend a long time in a mossy damp basement to find records they oughta be allowed to play 'em," she scribbled petulantly in red wax crayon on pages torn from a datebook that year. "When people sit home night after night at 18210 without a damn thing to do, they ought to be able to hear a little jive!"

A response—Georgene's?—came in a more careful hand: "If people at 18210 would spend less time on the cuttin' of the rug and more time on delving into the classics they might be invited out more after!"

Elaine retorted: "It is my ardent desire that no individual interested in the classics will ever invite me out—Go to hell!"

Her marriage prospects were being winnowed considerably as the local young men enlisted and were shipped off to training camps. One wrote her from barracks at Camp McCoy in Wisconsin, quarantined due to an outbreak of spinal meningitis and complaining about the beer: "so bad that I have quit drinking. It really has to be bad for that." Others begged for pinup photographs of Elaine as if she were Rita Hayworth.

Elaine wasn't pining for anyone in particular; indeed, a mounting rest-lessness was causing her to disappoint certain suitors. "You certainly sur-prised me when you talked about not being able to find a guy who has what you want," remarked a correspondent stationed at the Army Air Force Technical School in Chicago. "I thought sure as hell that Lee had everything you like."

Lee was James Lee—of all the young men in Elaine's life at this mo-ment, the one most likely to synchronize his plans with hers. Two years older and from nearby Pleasant Ridge, he would attend Harvard after his service, move to New York, and become an actor and then, failing at that, a playwright who would work on *Roots*. Given this literary bent, not particularly common in their set, he was probably the "Jim" who wrote to Elaine, in a firm cursive, that he was reminded of her by "songs mostly" and the movie *You'll Never Know*, calling his love for her "a fluctuating, hot and cold, up and down the toboggan slide affair," and declaring fi-nally, "without you it's just cakes and ale."

If the last sentence was a reference to *Twelfth Night* or W. Somerset Maugham, Elaine may have missed it. Her final marks at the Academy of the Sacred Heart Convent reflected a certain indifference to her school-work. "I passed Caesar on red wine, Cicero on white wine," she told the talk-show host Dick Cavett years later. By senior year she had given up Latin and stopped paying attention to science. Her marks in courtesy, or-der, and penmanship were dismal; she barely passed Christian doctrine and observance of school rules. She did slightly better in history, diction, and composition.

"I heard about you skipping school," Marianna Walsh wrote sternly to her friend. "Too bad you got caught but you just can't get away with that anymore." Marianna remembered George and Mildred buying their youngest daughter a watch as a graduation present.

"Take back the watch," Stritch declared at the DAC. "I want to go to New York." A nun had told her about a finishing school affiliated with the Sacred Heart that she could attend while exploring the dramatic arts. "I wanted to split and go see what was really going on. It was sort of my French foreign legion," Elaine said years later. "I was okay, I was a funny kid, I was laughing all the time, I had a wonderful time and then I grew into total fear and misery for some reason. I was looking for a bunch of people that wanted to get together and do something."

To find herself, she would have to not only diverge from the paths that had been previously trod but in essence disappear entirely into other characters. "One life wasn't enough for me," she proclaimed once. "I wanted to be a nurse, a doctor, a whore, and a queen." Another time, more subdued: "I wasn't too hung up on myself and I wanted to be everyone else I could think of."

It has long been part of the Stritch mythos that she hopped on the Detroiter train all alone, and that a lecture from her father about how she was "not the same after two martinis" sent her caroming straight to the bar car. But in fact she had several companions, and a chaperone who probably did not let her get too out of hand. On September 26, 1943, the women's page of the *Detroit Free Press* announced that a Mrs. Albert F. Wall would be taking her two daughters to the Duchesne Residence School, a Catholic finishing school in New York. Accompanying them would be Mary Bartemeier and Elaine Stritch, aged eighteen. Elaine was in search of an Emerald City, but also a vocation, as practical in its way as stenography.

Having observed her friend's repartee with George, Mildred, Georgene, and Sally for many years, Sterr thought this course of action entirely logical.

"They all seemed to be on stage all the time," she said of the Stritch family. "Each one trying to be wittier than the last."

2.

A HELLUVA TOWN

Moving to New York City is always exciting. Moving to New York City in the autumn of 1943, as a young woman in pursuit of fun, music, nightclubs, and theater with all the trimmings was fantastically auspicious. "The year of miracles," Leonard Bernstein would come to call what lay ahead.

Oklahoma!, the first collaboration between the composer Richard Rodgers and the lyricist and book writer Oscar Hammerstein II, was a smash hit at the St. James Theater on West Forty-Fourth Street—a couple of blocks away from the Algonquin Hotel, where the acidic wit of the Vicious Circle (the group that included the humorist Dorothy Parker and Edna Ferber, the author of the novel *Show Boat*) had been permanently etched. At two even grander hotels, the Pierre and the Plaza, the first American fashion week had been held months before, in defiance of the Nazi occupation of Paris. Its roster of clothing designers included Norman Norell, soon to be a favorite of Elaine's for his simple elegance.

And on the afternoon of November 14, Bernstein, handsome, Harvard-trained, and twenty-five, was an unexpected substitute as conductor of a Carnegie Hall matinee program of Rozsa, Schumann, Strauss, and

Wagner, dispensing with the traditional baton and gesturing passionately with his arms instead. Lenny, as he was nicknamed, was working with a new friend, Jerome "Jerry" Robbins, a promising but difficult dancer and choreographer, on *Fancy Free*, a syncopated ballet about sailors on shore leave, or "at liberty." The piece premiered to twenty-two curtain calls the next spring at the Metropolitan Opera House and would be adapted forthwith into the musical *On the Town*, with book and lyrics by the fledgling writing team Betty Comden and Adolph Green and direction from a veteran of the theater, George Abbott. "New York, New York! It's a helluva town," went its most rousing song.

Even as World War II was turning in the Allies' favor, the atmosphere in the city, as captured by that show, was one of urgency and carpe diem in the face of an uncertain future. And this jibed perfectly with Elaine's impatient personality, though she could not have known how soon she would be mixing with the players of *On the Town*, sequestered as she was in the cosseting fortress of the Duchesne, near the lip of Central Park at 7 East Ninety-First Street.

The gray beaux arts building had been designed by the same architects, Warren and Wetmore, who did Grand Central Terminal. Those who entered encountered a dramatic spiral staircase with low steps, giving the girls who ascended them the feeling of gliding toward heaven, or the third-floor ballroom. Their spotty complexions were flattered by a Tiffany stained-glass skylight, ringed by ornate figures and flowers in a mural painted by Hector d'Espouy.

Aside from the omnipresent nuns, the Duchesne had an ambiance not dissimilar from the Detroit Athletic Club, with clubby common rooms, cozy hallways, and waiter service. The school advertised in women's magazines like *Vogue* and *Harper's Bazaar* that it "offered college age girls cultural advantages of New York"—without, it was implied, any of the rough edges. This was mansion central, off Fifth Avenue, with the teetotaling Hammond family (whose scion Alice had recently married the bandleader Benny Goodman) next door. Across the street Andrew Carnegie's widow, Louise, still occupied their 52,000-square-foot residence.

Checker cabs were big and grand, sometimes with colorful characters at the wheel, embodied by *On the Town*'s Hildy, with room for a convivial five passengers in the back and even retractable roofs. For a nickel Elaine could clamber onto the Fifth Avenue bus, which stopped near the Duchesne, site of her morning instruction, and wheeze past the new Frick Collection museum on Seventieth and through Midtown to Richard Rodgers's office, where she described going a few weeks after arriving in New York to try out for the road company of *Oklahoma!* "Excited and nervous, I spent every cent I had to buy a new suit, new hat and gloves," she told a reporter seventeen years later. "I have a habit of always getting dressed, combed and made up before putting on my skirt. I was so jittery that day that I went off without my skirt. I didn't even miss it until I got off the bus and was in front of the Rodgers office. Then a kind woman approached me and asked if I hadn't forgotten something." How she got out of this scrape went unexplained.

The bus went even farther downtown, all the way to the Dramatic Workshop at the New School at 66 West Twelfth Street in Greenwich Village, where Elaine was to spend afternoons. She had chosen it after auditioning at the old, established American Academy of Dramatic Arts in Carnegie Hall and the Feagin School of Dramatic Radio and Arts, where her contemporary Angela Lansbury went, and which was located in Rockefeller Center, the gleaming commercial plaza.

The Dramatic Workshop was different: it was scrappy, it was experimental, it was bohemian. It had been founded in 1940 by Erwin Piscator from Germany and his wife, Maria Ley-Piscator, a former dancer. The political playwright Bertolt Brecht, author of *The Threepenny Opera* and copious other works, had been groomsman at their wedding.

For the first time, here Elaine was exposed to the harsher realities and shadings of the world outside her sheltered circle in Detroit. With an intense gaze under a widow's peak of graying hair, Piscator's face hinted at profound internal turmoil. He had served on the front lines of his native country's army in World War I and watched friends and comrades die. He loathed militarism and now sought to use his chosen vocation for the advancement of political ideas. "Epic theater" was how his movement came to be known, and his use of spectacle and cinematic effects onstage would foreshadow the grand but dark visions of Harold Prince.

Two of his employees, Stella Adler and Lee Strasberg, would go on to enduring acting schools of their own, influenced by the ideas of Konstantin Stanislavsky, the great Russian director and teacher who'd died in 1938, though they would disagree on how to interpret them. Adler advocated doing research about the character and her circumstances, rather than drawing from one's own past and emotions. Strasberg is often called the father of "Method acting," a form of extreme identification with the character; he long led the Actors Studio, though he was not one of its founding members.

Piscator rather offered history, context, and a sense of shared humanity. Judith Malina, a disciple of his who went on to found, with Julian Beck, an experimental company called the Living Theater, recalled him describing off-the-wall happenings to the mesmerized young American students: actors dressed as firemen hosing down angry audiences with water. "He never partook of the fleshpots of Broadway," she wrote. "Not that he didn't try." As a director Piscator was in charge, paternal, and warm, and this was an ideal match for Elaine, who so trusted her own father. "Piscator would get up and do it with you, take your hand, walk you through a part," she said. "It was gorgeous. It was just like . . . putting your arms around you and telling you that they love you."

He stressed the importance of discipline and well-roundedness. "Whatever field of the theater the student may select, the assumption is that he cannot achieve adequate understanding of his medium unless he has fully absorbed all the elements which, combined, make up a production," read the brochure for the Workshop's 1943–1944 term.

And so, along with such other young aspirants as Marlon Brando, Harry Belafonte, and Shelley Winters, Elaine took as many as twenty-seven hours of classes per week. These included acting, voice and diction, makeup, dance and movement, theater research, march of drama—"a panorama of the history of the theatre from Aeschylus to the present," Malina described this—and styles through the ages, which attempted to elucidate "the baffling differences between Louis XIV, Louis XV, Louis XVI and Napoleon's neo-classicism."

It was a plunge into the deep end for someone whose education in the humanities was erratic at best. Nor was Elaine up-to-date on more current literary figures. "I was a girl raised at the convent and I wasn't reading that D. H. Lawrence," she said. "Come on! F. Scott Fitzgerald? I didn't know who the fuck he was when I came to New York." She was also among the many female students to receive the unwelcome attentions of Henry Wendriner, Piscator's money manager, a short, bald man partial to writing erotic poetry.

Both Mildred Stritch and Erwin Piscator sowed in Elaine a lifelong respect for the "legitimate theater"—whatever subsequent forays she made into musicals, television, movies, talk shows, and cabaret, the straight play remained a lodestar. Even at eighty-three when she could have been at the Carlyle toting up residuals, she would be gamely schlepping to Brooklyn and popping out of a garbage can in Samuel Beckett's *Endgame*.

She first glimpsed a real New York audience from the stage through the mask of a fuzzy animal. It was at the Adelphi Theater on West Fifty-Fourth Street, months before *On the Town* premiered there, in a children's play, *Bobino*, directed by Maria Piscator. Elaine doubled in the roles of a tiger and, she would recall, a cow. "I was so taken with Marlon and he was such a son of a bitch that there was a tossup about who should be the front of the cow and who should be the back of the cow in this damn thing and Marlon wanted to be up front," she said of the young Brando. "I said, 'Oh, that will be all right,' trying to impress him with the fact that I would gladly be the backside of the cow if he was going to be the front."

No doubt she was trying to impress her handsome classmate, but according to *Bobino*'s author, Stanley Kauffmann, who would become better known as a film critic, Brando was not a cow in the play but a giraffe and a clumsy guard. "He had a way of falling that made you know that he'd thought about how to do it a different way from the way every other actor had ever done it, and yet his fall fit into what was going on. It wasn't merely freakish," Kauffmann said on *The Dick Cavett Show* in 1979. Another castmate, Joyce Johnson, remembered Marlon replacing her in the role of a bear. "Brando was not just an actor in a bear suit, he somehow became a bear," she wrote. "When he was on stage, no one could take their eyes off him."

Possibly Brando was tried in yet another part, or possibly Elaine was in hindsight, as it were, superimposing a memory of the plotline of *Gypsy*, where the overlooked child Louise has to play half a cow while her flashier sister, Dainty June, gambols with farm boys.

No matter; she observed astutely how Brando, a year older than she, set himself apart as an actor. It was a technique of indirection diametrically opposed to her own in-your-face style, though both were in their way adaptations to a fundamental feeling of inadequacy. "Whatever the normal emotion would be that most of us would use in life, he'd do the opposite," Elaine said. "Because he had to be different. It was embedded in him that he had to be. Certainly not get in line with anybody. He had to be. His emotion, his reaction would have to be different from the run-of-the-mill. Good actors, Olivier, all of them, would look at a girl when he said, 'I love you.' Marlon looked the other way, or looked up, or looked across. 'You want to go out next Saturday?' It would have to be away from your face. It couldn't be right at you. Because he didn't have the security to do that."

Brando dated widely, proclaiming a preference for women who were foreign or exotic to him. "Marlon reserves his favor for Orientals, Latins, blacks, Polynesians, and Indians, both east and west," wrote his first wife, Anna Kashfi, herself born in Darjeeling, in a 1979 memoir. "When I accused him of choosing 'inferior' women as partners to satisfy his need for superiority feelings, he was incensed. 'My mother was blonde,' he said, thereby exposing—while still denying—the roots of his sexual fancy."

Still, two of his steadiest escorts were Blossom Plumb, a Wasp from Connecticut, and Ellen Adler, Stella's daughter ("the only thing that was foreign about her was the fact that she was Jewish," Elaine remarked).

With her plainspoken Midwestern attitude, Stritch was not really Brando's speed. But "every Saturday night he was taking out the ugliest girl in the class, the one with the buck teeth," she recalled to the gossip columnist Earl Wilson in 1960, "leaning on her elbows" at the King Cole bar at the St. Regis. "It was his idea of generosity. I was the last girl he asked. He made me wait, see?"

At the Duchesne she fretted to the head nun. "Mother Benziger, do you think . . . Oh, if he'd just ask me to go to the movies."

"He will, he will."

One day the school's house phone jangled.

"Elaine! Elaine!" Mother Benziger called exultantly. Marlon was, finally, on the line, and he wanted to ask her young charge out. It proved
a strange first date. He took Elaine to the main branch of the New York
Public Library, where he led her up the stairs between the lions Patience
and Fortitude. He pulled *Wuthering Heights* from a shelf and read pas-
sages from it to her. "He put on a show about how intellectual he was,"
she said. Then they went to have dinner and drinks, and then to a strip
club. "This is a part of life you should know about," Brando told her. There
"a tall redhead took off every stitch of her clothes and I burst into tears,"
she later wrote.

At his Village apartment, Brando changed into silk pajamas, leaving
the shirt unbuttoned. His quarry took one look and fled uptown to confront her grievously blown curfew—or so she told it.

As time went on, as Brando became ever more famous and gnomic,
this date grew ever more baroque in Elaine's recollection. Brando was soon
taking her not only to the library but a Greek Orthodox church and
a synagogue, to show her the entire range of religions. Was the meal
spaghetti or Chinese food? Was his pet cat prowling the premises in
heat? Did he really demand from her "two things: silence and distance"
when she tried to be friends afterward? One friend said Elaine told
her this was because she had taken out Marlon's visiting mother, an
alcoholic, and encouraged her to drink. George C. Wolfe, who directed
Elaine in *At Liberty*, remembers her describing being fully clothed in bed
with another woman in Brando's apartment, not entirely sure what she
was doing, when her old actor boyfriend from the Pleasant Ridge suburb
of Detroit, James Lee, came up the stairs and banged on the door, and
she ran behind the door to hide and began going over her catechism.

But the underlying substance of the different retellings was the same.
Here was a young woman trying to affect far more sophistication than
she actually possessed. The disparity in sexual experience was underscored
further during the Workshop's forays into summer stock. Marlon seduced
in haylofts and motorcars and was ultimately expelled. One night Piscator "caught me necking with one of the girls in the company but all he

said was 'Ja. So. Brando,'" Anna Kashfi's husband later told her. "The next day it was 'Oudt! You are oudt of zis company!' and I left." In the fall of 1944 the languorously handsome actor would get a break appearing in *I Remember Mama*, a Broadway play produced by Rodgers and Hammerstein. He would be in the first round of creative seekers to haunt the Actors Studio, formed by the producer Cheryl Crawford, the director Elia Kazan, and Robert Lewis, which took a more sensory, primal approach to direction and became known—unfairly, insisted its adherents—for a breed of "mumblers," including Paul Newman, James Dean, and, most famously, Brando.

Elaine continued her direct, energetic, clearly enunciated approach. She paddled wholesomely in rowboats with her Workshop classmates, on Sayville, Long Island, rehearsing on the beach and performing on one occasion for members of the armed forces at nearby Camp Upton. In keeping with Piscator's cooperative ethos, the group of twenty-five also cleaned the theater and attended to scenery and makeup. At age nineteen, her husky voice deepened further by cigarettes, Elaine could already pass for twice that onstage. But she felt more comfortable inhabiting the more ambiguous role of Feste, Olivia's fool in *Twelfth Night*, which Piscator set on a revolving stage.

She got the part because she could cartwheel—"with bells on my fingers and bells on my toes"—better than she could make proper entrances and exits. More significant, "I couldn't play women yet," Elaine said. "I was too scared and too inhibited and if I had a kiss on the stage, that was out of the question. I was very good at it offstage, but I didn't . . . I just couldn't make that transition. I didn't know what I would do with it. I had all the feelings, but I was too afraid to go out there and do it." She believed that Feste was androgynous. "There's no sex to the clown. He is neither female or male. I suppose an analyst would have a lot to say about that, I don't know. But to me, all it meant to me was I did something and they clapped and they accepted me."

Among those applauding with enthusiasm one night were friends of Piscator from the Old World, the distinguished acting couple Albert and Elsa Bassermann. "It was a wonderful compliment to have this famous German actor say that it's finally been done right," Elaine said of her performance as the fool. She was also praised for her singing, which had not yet acquired the bullish quality that would soon have people anointing her the new Ethel Merman. "There were all these quiet songs. They weren't '*Curtain up!*'"

The students worked sometimes up to twenty hours per day, with great seriousness of purpose. "There was no light fare or screwball comedy at the Dramatic Workshop," Harry Belafonte wrote in his memoir (though a course in television was added during Elaine's second semester, in grudging acknowledgment of its increasing importance). "And no stars, at least not in theory. We were all workers of equal standing in Piscator's dramatic collective."

Belafonte noted that Elaine, despite her sexual reserve, "swore more colorfully than any sailor I'd known." Their classmate Beatrice Arthur, the future Maude and Golden Girl of network TV, would "start matching wits with Elaine until the two of them had everyone in uncontrollable laughter. They were a gorgeous, sexy, vibrant pair, Bea the blunt Jewish comic, Elaine the diva."

As the Allied forces progressed through Europe, the mood in New York was increasingly ebullient. The war had only improved the fortunes of the Stritch family and Elaine took little interest in political developments. When Piscator cast her as a Teutonic maidservant in "The Chalk Cross," a playlet in a production of Brecht's *The Private Life of the Master Race*, or *Fear and Misery of the Third Reich*, at City College auditorium at Lexington Avenue and Twenty-Third Street, "I had no idea what I was doing," she said. "But I knew that I loffed the braids and I had the maid's uniform and then I was German and I just loved it. I did it very well. Brecht thought I was a very promising young actress and that thrilled me to death. But he was so unattractive." She thought him "a small, mousy, rather inhibited, round-shouldered little man . . . quiet and precise and very demanding in a sneaky Pete sort of way." Later she discovered "he was quite a big shot."

Back on Long Island in the summer, this time at the Chapel Theater in Great Neck, Stritch stretched further into the Continent, with Russian parts, including a countess named Madame Daruschka in a play called *Claudia*. "The plot was that I had just bought Claudia's house and we were going to have some tea," she told the journalist Alex Witchel. "So I went to get it, on this big tray with cups and saucers, pitchers, silver, napkins, everything, and I slip on the rug and drop the whole thing. The stuff went flying everywhere. And there's this big silence and I said, 'What the hell. I own the joint.'"

Her improvisational irreverence, work ethic, and sociability made a positive impression on Piscator. At the end of the term, he wrote Mother Benziger at the Duchesne to assure that his pupil was granted full credit, praising Elaine's talent and noting particularly her success as Feste: "Her development in art, it is a pleasure to state, has been surprising. She has remarkable ability to adapt herself in her relations to other people, which has made her one of the most valuable members of the school. She is sincere, amiable and has great strength of character."

Such good references notwithstanding, when Elaine announced her wish to continue acting after leaving the Duchesne, George and Mildred insisted she move to the Barbizon, the well-reputed women's residence on Sixty-Third Street later fictionalized as the Amazon in Sylvia Plath's novel *The Bell Jar*. "Within hiking distance of Carnegie Hall, the Stork Club, Twenty-One, Mme. Lilly Daché and the Metropolitan Museum of Art," as the *Detroit Free Press* noted—accompanying photographs showed the winsome residents lounging in an eighteenth-floor solarium with vertiginous views of Manhattan skyscrapers—the Barbizon offered both propriety and fun. Also splashing in the swimming pool and taking afternoon tea in various meeting rooms were a passel of models housed there by a new agent, Eileen Ford, and her husband.

With its strict parietal rules—no men above the mezzanine floor, and none through the ground-level revolving door after 1:00 a.m.—this should have been an ideal roosting place for an attractive former convent girl, but Elaine chafed for more immediate independence. She later portrayed herself as a sought-after belle, telling a reporter how one male suitor who'd been refused admission to the Barbizon because she had a cold "swung like Tarzan" from a lobby chandelier, "shouting my name so loud that the hotel literally shook, rattled and rolled." It was all a very different tempo from the sedate October 1945 wedding of Sally Stritch to Tom Bolton at Gesu Church in Detroit, following the customary battery of parties including crystal and linen showers.

Elaine tried waiting tables at the New School—less for the money than to impress Brando. She sang again for Rodgers, hoping to get a part in the new musical he was writing with Hammerstein, *Allegro* (for which Stephen Sondheim, aged seventeen, would act as a gofer). She did more summer stock.

When she appeared in a play by J. M. Barrie called *What Every Woman Knows*, she was noticed by the then twice-divorced, darkly handsome, brilliant, and notoriously difficult producer Jed Harris, who'd had a run of hits in the 1920s and '30s but had been less lucky since introducing Thornton Wilder's *Our Town* to New York.

Harris was casting a play called *Loco*, and having trouble because of his inability, as he put it, to "find a beautiful girl who can act" to take the role of a model who goes away for a weekend with a married man and gets the measles. An MGM player named Lucille Ball was among those considered, but the producers of the film she was then starring in refused to release her from her contract. Harris began working with Elaine on the part, sitting and talking it over with her in his office for two hours every afternoon—"Jed was a very thorough fellow," she wrote—before giving it to the then known entity Jean Parker. His new, young find got the consolation prize of being cast in another role in the play, as a "very nervous" ingénue named Pamela.

"Now you know a character named 'Pamela' does pretty exciting things in a play—like says 'tennis anyone' or wants to get married and can't and can't get married and wants to and whose most significant line in the whole procedure is 'hi, dad,'" Elaine wrote. "That's how pretty exciting it is."

Twenty-five years her senior, Harris assumed a sort of Professor Higgins role to Elaine's Eliza Doolittle. When she displayed nerves before the dress rehearsal of *Loco*, he took her to the Hotel Edison on West Forty-Seventh Street, where great jazz musicians played. "This was the first time in my life I had ever not ordered my own dinner,"

Elaine recalled. "I was made to order a quart of champagne (a whole quart), followed by a sirloin steak, rare. I was taken back to the Biltmore Theater, went through my dress rehearsal, and I was adorable. Looking back, I can honestly say this was one of the greatest pieces of direction since Lubitsch made Garbo laugh. And even more exciting than all that, I've been drinking champagne ever since, moderately, but consistently."

Many dinners followed with the producer, a committed gourmet. "He scared me to death, but I loved him," Stritch wrote. "I don't know what I learned about the theatre from Jed but I do know this—I sure as hell know where to eat in this town, French, Chinese, Ukrainian, etc." She almost "got the sack" from the play—"every time I see a couple of top-drawer types talking it up in the back of a dimly lit theatre during rehearsal . . . I think I'm on my way out. But Jed Harris fixed that. Jed Harris can fix anything."

Somewhat aghast at the mismatch of her sophisticated appearance with her rudimentary scholarship, the producer also committed himself to furthering Elaine's literary education. *Loco* "laid a bomb," as she put it, and closed after 37 performances (it would be salvaged as source material for the popular movie *How to Marry a Millionaire*), but Harris continued his pursuit. "He was one of the last big spenders in the gift department," Elaine wrote. The Barbizon porter would arrive weekly with parcels containing "goodies" from him, wrapped books like Dostoevsky's *The Idiot* and Stendhal's *The Red and the Black*. "He came on like gangbusters with things I needed like a hole in the head."

Elaine had pulled off embodying Amanda in Noël Coward's *Private Lives* on Long Island. "I was the most disarming, the most sophisticated, the most feminine, elaborate, goofy, polished 'Amanda' ever to hit Great Neck," she wrote. An agent named Jane Broder, presuming Elaine to be in her early thirties, sent her to audition for the producer Kermit Bloomgarden, who cast her in a newspaper caper called *Woman Bites Dog* with a cleft-chinned young actor, Kirk Douglas. Written by the husband-and-wife team Bella and Samuel Spewack, both former reporters, it was about the central political concern of the moment, communism, and thus not particularly interesting to Elaine.

The cast was put up at the Warwick Hotel in Philadelphia, rehearsing at the Walnut Street Theater. "I fooled them all, with a kind of biting, self-confident, 'gangway' scared-to-death security I'd picked up along the way—god knows where," she or her amanuensis typed on pink paper, adding later in pencil, "From Mildred maybe."

But Elaine had no idea how to play a correspondent investigating a Midwestern town supposedly gone red, and she still felt tentative about playing a romantic lead. "There I am, living it up on stage with Kirk Douglas, 'living with' Frank Lovejoy in the play, and I'm coming over like Girl of the Limberlost"—here she was referring to the rural, innocent heroine of a 1909 novel by Gene Stratton-Porter that was made into a 1934 movie.

"Why do they keep saying I'm living with you?" she asked Douglas one night at dinner. Cohabitation without marriage was still a foreign concept to a young Catholic girl.

"Oh my god, we're in big trouble."

"I thought Elaine was superb," Douglas said, praising her "wise-cracking attitude." He also remembered "the imitation she did of me from the stage—she used all her teeth." The Spewacks, though, notorious squabblers, were not impressed. Elaine, they decided, was the problem, and they would replace her with Mercedes McCambridge, a reputable radio actress. Such out-of-town tinkering was far from uncommon at the time—but still, "I was dumbfounded," Douglas said. "She was so talented and I felt they made a mistake."

To console Elaine, he took her for "several belts" of liquor and a steak at a restaurant called Frankie Bradley. "I told Elaine not to worry, she would become a big star someday," Douglas said. "I was right about that, but not about the play. It opened and closed on Broadway within a week."

Another failure was a comedy called *Three Indelicate Ladies*, with the horror star Bela Lugosi ("You'll Die Laughing!") miscast as an Irishman. "I would have welcomed a tennis racket in this one," wrote Elaine, marveling for years how Joey Faye, a comedian who had a small part as a furniture dealer, had packed his suitcase for the out-of-town tryout not with clothes but candy: "Wrigley's spearmint, Clark bars, Milky Ways,

Chiclets, licorice sticks, corn candy, fruit balls, jawbreakers, all-day suckers, Kraft Karamels, heath bars, Juicy Fruit (oh, he had a lot of Juicy Fruit), Dentyne, Beeman's Pepsin." She also told of meeting Lugosi and his wife, Lillian, for consolation drinks after the play closed at the posh Midtown restaurant "21"—so many that a waiter came over and told the table that management was cutting them off. Infuriated, Lugosi stood up and yanked the tablecloth, sending glasses and plates tumbling. "You know, Stritch, if it hadn't been for that goddamned Boris Karloff . . . ," he was said to have growled of his flagging career.

The stage manager of *Three Indelicate Ladies*, Jack Cassidy, who would go on to be a suave comic actor famous for playing roués, took a fancy to Elaine. He persuaded her to leave the Barbizon ("no offense, every red-blooded American girl tries to get out of the Barbizon eventually," she wrote) and helped her find her first apartment alone in New York. It was closer to the theaters, on West Fifty-Eighth Street; a little west of Sixth Avenue, and the building conveniently housed a liquor store on the ground floor.

Cassidy suggested a decorating scheme of dark green and Elaine chose a green-and-white plaid by Wesley Simpson, the husband of the fashion designer Adele Simpson, and covered the walls with it. The lampshade was done in a red-and-green plaid. The small living room was blanketed in "a 14' × 13' lipstick red," Elaine wildly guesstimated, that she dragged down eight flights and through the revolving doors of Macy's into a yellow cab. "I was so anxious to brighten up, jazz up, pick up this Westside outhouse that I thought was the answer to everything," she wrote. Cassidy helped paint one and a half walls, started an argument, and left. Stritch finished the job and papered the bathrooms in an ivy print.

She gave a cocktail party to celebrate. "Elaine, how *Brigadoon* can you get?" a guest asked, referring to the Lerner and Loewe musical about a fantastical Scottish village, and suddenly the patterns that had seemed so snappy seemed shameful.

After a few weeks Georgene Stritch came to inspect the new digs, accompanied by her husband, Frank Moran, who was now out of the army and beginning a career as an accountant. On her little sister's bookshelf, Georgene spotted one of Harris's intellectual literary gifts—*The Basic*

Writings of Sigmund Freud, which include "Three Contributions to the Theory of Sex"—and burst into protective tears. "Thinking I'd read every word and was hardly ready," Elaine explained. "Well, she's right, who the hell is ready for Freud at twenty?" When she went to see Georgene and Frank's train off at Grand Central, they handed her their own present: *The Confessions of St. Augustine.*

Next to arrive, at Christmastime, were George and Mildred; they had visited at that time of year regularly since Mrs. Albert F. Wall had deposited their youngest in New York. "I arrive from year to year with the man of the hour and he gets the one-two-three-all-time going over in the King Cole Bar over a nervous cocktail," was how Elaine described these holiday calls.

Riding up in the apartment elevator after this treatment, Cassidy told George that he had invested $250 into *Angel in the Wings,* a new revue that Elaine was going to appear in. "Your daughter is a fucking winner," he said.

Later, George could not stop pacing his hotel room in dismay.

"Mildred, you don't think Elaine's really serious about that fellow, do you?" he asked.

"Oh, shut up, George. She's only twenty and not very serious about anything as far as I can see. What in god's name are you so upset about?"

"I'll tell you," George said. "That son of a bitch had suede shoes on!"

He was even more disturbed about the location of the apartment building, on whose roof Stritch had sunned herself and met a "buxom redhead" who tried to offer her a gig at a club called the Ha Ha.

George made a few phone calls and found his daughter a place in a more refined area, across town in the Fifties. "East, east, east, east," Elaine said. The new apartment overlooked the water. "Garbo lived next door and the River Club was across the street. Boy, I thought I was swinging." Elaine sold what she could of her garish new furnishings, tipped the new doorman, and bought herself half a dozen pairs of stockings at Saks.

In 1947 Vincent Sardi, Jr., had taken over his father's namesake restaurant on Forty-Fourth Street, with its vichyssoise and veal cutlet sauté "a la Vincent": columnists and press agents huddled daily on red banquettes and caricatures of successful Broadway actors were regularly added to the walls. Struggling actors meanwhile gathered in the Howard Johnson's near Times Square or even Walgreens, "the poor man's Sardi's," where the young Hal Prince and Stephen Sondheim lunched after meeting at the opening of Rodgers and Hammerstein's *South Pacific* (or so Prince remembered) and discussed the future of the theater. Stritch preferred a ritzier atmosphere. "I didn't hang out with the gang. I never went through that drugstore period," she said. "I went to saloons like a crazy person, because boy, that was fun." Mentioned in the Detroit papers since she was in bobby socks and with a thus far unquenchable taste for nightlife, she felt at ease cultivating journalists and needed no press agent to place her in their stories, for "I'd rather talk to someone any day of the week than read a book," as she wrote.

Though Stritch would be covered from time to time by Hedda Hopper or Louella Parsons from the West Coast, her bread and butter were the East Coasters. The king of these was Winchell, of the *Daily Mirror*, who (at least at first) deemed her "tall, blonde, lovely" and a "charmer." The queen was Dorothy Kilgallen of the *Journal-American*, perhaps favorably disposed to Stritch as a fellow Catholic, and wife of Richard Kollmar, a sometime actor with whom she broadcast a radio show, *Breakfast with Dorothy and Dick*, from their five-story town house on Sixty-Eighth Street; with what sounded like a parakeet bleating in the background, the show featured advertisements for chocolate pudding and Tintex fabric dye. Kilgallen was not merely a "personality" whose column, "The Voice of Broadway," rolled across America over the course of several days through syndication, but also a serious reporter who would go on to cover nationally publicized murder trials.

The court jester was at the *Post*: the droll, fast-talking Earl Wilson, nicknamed the Midnight Earl, who prowled the city with his "Beautiful Wife," or B.W., for his column "It Happened One Night," which he liked to sign off "That's Earl, brother." And at the same paper was a squire: Leonard Lyons, né Sucher (he had gotten his start writing for the *Jewish Daily Forward*), who welcomed readers into "The Lyons Den" along with rapidly rising stars like Marilyn Monroe or Frank Sinatra.

In 1947 Kilgallen noted that Jed Harris and Stritch "were swoon-ing." It was the beginning of a long, cordial and mutually advantageous relationship between the two women. "Watch for a girl named Elaine Stritch to be the 'sleeper' of the year," Kilgallen continued. "She's a sort of sophisticated Betty Hutton, and will make her big-time debut as a singer-actress in *Angel in the Wings*, due in December."

The revue was by another husband-and-wife team, Grace and Paul Hartman, who also performed in the show. "I felt, 'Well, I've had a lot of training with Erwin Piscator, and I'm an actress, goddammit, and maybe I can get a little of my Chekhov in the sketches," Stritch said.

The show was light comedy but not untouched by politics. Out of eleven suspected Communists in show business obeying a subpoena from the House Un-American Activities Committee that fall, Bertolt Brecht—concerned about having trouble leaving the country, since he was not a citizen—was the only one not to plead the Fifth. He denied affiliation with the party and answered questions about *The Private Life of the Master Race* and other topics in testimony that was its own kind of theater. The others became known as the Hollywood Ten. The day after the hearings ended, studio heads met at the Waldorf-Astoria in New York and drafted a statement saying they would not work with any in their number. Emissaries from the committee were also sent to interview Elaine and some of her castmates.

"I almost died," she said. "I didn't know what the fuck they were talking about."

Her costumes in the revue bared her midriff and a program showed one actor looming over her leeringly as she fiddles with her brassiere. Mildred was aghast not only at such exposure, but to hear that Elaine had no song of her own. Tremulously, when the show was refining out of town, Elaine asked for one and got "Civilization" ("Bongo, Bongo, Bongo"), a number that had already been made popular by the Andrews Sisters with Danny Kaye and in a separate recording by Louis Prima. It was, as the *Cincinnati Enquirer* called it, "a tongue-in-cheek commentary on atom-age America," depicting a native of the Congo glancing through a missionary wife's magazine, unimpressed by "bright lights, false teeth, doorbells, landlords" and concluding damningly, "They have things like the atom bomb, so I think I'll stay where I am." It is the visitors who are the "savages."

For this performance she changed into a "Me Jane"–type outfit that bared her shoulders as well, topped with a tropical-looking necklace and a headdress. Mildred thought the show cheap and subpar, but a family friend cabled her and George reassuredly: "SHE IS TRULY SPLENDID MAGNIFICENT AND COLOSSAL. YOU AND THE JOBES HAVE NOTHING AT ALL TO WORRY ABOUT. SHE HAS NOT LOST HER HEAD ONE LITTLE BIT. RELAX AND ENJOY HER FUN."

The critics were unexpectedly, universally charmed. Here was welcome relief from the heavier fare of the day, like Brando starring in Tennessee Williams's *A Streetcar Named Desire* at the Ethel Barrymore Theater: a part he'd won after doing repairs on the playwright's summer rental. "The Hartmans are the personification of Mr. and Mrs., which is an American institution, possibly a world one," wrote Lewis Nichols in the *Times*, describing one sketch that was a spoof of the lackadaisical, soothing husband-and-wife radio chats popular at the time. "On the stage, Mr. is a little sleepy, a little vague and given to rambling discourse, and Mrs. is the executive type. This is straight from life, of course, and is general and universal and discouraging to think about." Certainly it echoed George and Mildred's dynamic.

Stritch and Hank Ladd were billed as "the season's newest discoveries." Winchell soon offered an item about her "twosoming at the midnite movies" with a young dancer named Tommy Morton who had appeared in the revue *Make Mine Manhattan* and had a hobby of raising tropical fish. "We did most of our talking up in her apartment," said Morton, now known as Tony Monaco. "She was really serious about getting what she thought she could have in her career, and she wasn't a great singer and I was kind of hoping she wouldn't get her heart broken." When *Angel in the Wings* went out of town, they thought about running away and getting married. "WILL ARRIVE BY CAR SUNDAY MORNING TOMMY COMING WITH ME DON'T WORRY (PUT YOUR ROBES ON)," Elaine cabled her parents from Chicago. But the plan fizzled after a couple of colleagues threatened to play a prank on the pair by telling the police Elaine was underage, though she was merely inexperiencd. "She really had very strong concepts of being in a relationship, that you shouldn't be intimate sexually before you were married," Morton said. "So we weren't."

The famous nightclub chanteuse Hildegarde, whom Stritch impersonated in one of the show's sketches, was among those who came backstage to pay her respects. Another who attended *Angel in the Wings* was Harold Prince, but he didn't think much of the production. "I wasn't anybody who would have loved shows like that," he said.

Later though, his mentor George Abbott was directing "a faltering revue" called *Tickets, Please!*, also by the Hartmans, and hired Prince to be the assistant stage manager. "So Elaine got to be somebody I heard about," Prince said. "She always had a really good, raw singing voice, and she was tall and she was good-looking. And I had no truck with her. I didn't know anything about her really. I just knew that she was famous."

Eager to capitalize on her "it girl" status, Stritch consented to appear in a Piel's beer advertisement. Her picture appeared alongside two chorus girls, Gerri Gale and Gypsy Markoff. "Who can get Piel's Light Beer in the Congo?" was the tagline. "We kinda think Elaine will stay right here—on Broadway, where there's Piel's aplenty!" And at the thirtieth annual convention of the National Knitted Outerwear Association in New York, she would be awarded the dubious honor of 1948 Sweater Girl of the Theater. Her measurements of 34", 24", 35" were reported in newspapers all over the country.

Though validating to one who had fretted about her looks as a little girl, the prize was certainly not one Stritch had aspired to as a student at the Dramatic Workshop. Even being a comedienne, naturally as it came to her, felt like a compromise. "As soon as I hit Broadway it was 'curtain up!' and the pizazz and the musicals," she said. "And I didn't realize it at the time but that's kind of a shakeup. Play Hedda Gabler, and you're suddenly singing 'Bongo, Bongo, Bongo.'"

Notwithstanding any reservations about the quality of the material, she had gotten a taste of being celebrated publicly—of success—and the warmth that followed was as powerful as that from the first slug of whiskey. In fact the two had become inextricable. "I was really living," she wrote. "I was out of the frying pan. I had a doorman, a modern kitchen, a real window with no brick wall in front of it, wall-to-wall carpeting in a soft gray (well, we all have to grow up sometime) and, I almost forgot, I was in a hit show." To an interviewer she emphasized that Catholicism was her religion, not theater. "It's nice to have something lasting about yourself," she said. "There's certainly nothing lasting and definite about the theater. But you know the show at St. Pat's won't close for a long time."

Angel toured and was televised. ("The artistry of the Hartmans was seriously diminished by mechanical reproduction," hmphed one critic.) Stritch hosted Marianna Sterr in New York and was spotted by Winchell "doing the spots" with Kirk Douglas, married but "estranged from the Mrs." Then in the fall of 1949 she was cast as an heiress and the sole American in *Yes M'Lord*, an English play about Parliamentary elections, and invited along with another young actress, Diane Hart, for breakfast in the hotel room of their costar, the veteran A. E. Matthews. "We were in our jammies anyway because it was early morning," she told Hart's daughter Claudia Cragg. "Then he got in bed and said, 'I want you on either side of me.'" A knock came on the door, which Elaine presumed was the room-service waiter. It was Lee Shubert, the eldest of the three brothers who had put their name on half New York's theaters and those in other cities besides. Cragg said her mother and Stritch, who roomed together for a time, were also consorting glancingly and chastely with another set of brothers: the Kennedys, up-and-coming in politics. "They were sincerely backdoor Johnnies," she said. "It was that set, and it was a rarefied set."

Dismissed as "trifling" by the *Times*'s Brooks Atkinson, *Yes M'Lord* was significant to Elaine for at least three other reasons. It marked the beginning of what would become a lifelong affection for the English. It occasioned her triumphant professional return to the Cass stage in Detroit, where she'd watched Bobby Clark as a girl.

It was also the last time she played an ingénue, a type that, like a tight sweater, had never been quite comfortable. Lainey the former convent girl was receding, soon to be replaced by someone more adventuresome and cosmopolitan, always with a highball and a fellow at her elbow, or several of each. Stritch.

3.

"HEAVENS, THAT GIRL AGAIN!"

Sunday, June 24, 1951, dawned warm and bright in Manhattan. Having recently replaced the standby to the formidable first lady of musical comedy, Ethel Merman, in a hit named *Call Me Madam* at the Imperial Theater, Stritch—with time on her hands and restlessness in her long legs—decided to go for a bicycle ride in Central Park.

The sun began to beat down, the temperature passed 85 degrees Fahrenheit. What the hell, the actress thought. She peeled off the T-shirt she was wearing, tossed it in the bicycle's basket, and pedaled around for a while in a halter and shorts. Then she stopped to tan herself on the lawn, removing—"with the lingering, graceful gestures of the theater," one observer noted—her stockings as well.

A patrolman happened to be ambling by. He got out his leather notebook, began to scribble, and then wrote Stritch a summons to appear in mid-Manhattan court the next day. Somehow the papers were alerted. A photographer captured the actress atop a Central Park parapet, bike idling below, waving like Miss America.

"A beautiful girl like you could cause a small riot and cause a large crowd to collect by removing your shirt," the court's magistrate was reported to scold at the brief hearing that followed.

"Well, I was there all day and nothing happened," Stritch replied.

Summarized under amused headlines like "Riot Fails to Materialize" and "Publicity Eager," the episode introduced Stritch's lifelong pattern of tempering exhibitionism with self-deprecatory wit. Mildred may have raised daughters of taste who always preferred the finer department stores, but her rebellious youngest would routinely dispense with garments she deemed unnecessary or uncomfortable, even if—especially if—this startled people around her. She was constantly challenging ideas of what was proper, as if to inspire in perpetuity the narrator of the Cole Porter song "Anything Goes" (which Merman had originated on Broadway and Stritch had played in a summer music-circus production in New Jersey), who marvels at the rapid change of mores since the era when "a glimpse of stocking / Was looked on as something shocking" and rhymes "Mae West" with "me undressed."

Stritch's routine strips seemed not so much to incite desire but to attract attention, as a small child might at a gathering of grown-ups. Like a butterfly in reverse she was shedding the stiff, colorful taffeta frocks of her adolescence, going from Mildred's "more bows than a symphony orchestra" to a simpler, jazzier, more protean form. "I never wore a bra in rehearsal because it constricted me and I never thought about it," she said.

Even if she hadn't displayed her body, it would have been casually and closely scrutinized; this was the order of the day. "Miss Elaine Stritch (heavens, THAT girl again!) manages a split of champagne while toying with a saddle of lamb large enough to be fastened onto Robert E. Lee's horse, Traveler," wrote Whitney Bolton in a protracted column about eating habits of theatrical women that would never pass muster in the twenty-first century. "If most women had a figure like Miss Stritch's there would be fewer divorces in America."

Stritch's prodigious appetite for audience approval, however, would not be so quickly satisfied during the run of *Call Me Madam*. Desiring more dramatic, "serious" work, Merman had at first resisted the part of Sally Adams, a Washington, D.C., hostess and ambassador based winkingly on the real-life Perle Mesta. But having committed to this solid B+

piece of Americana, which spoofed the incumbent president, Harry S. Truman, and his daughter, Margaret, she mastered it with such hyper-typical efficiency and command that the musical was soon nicknamed "Call Me Merman." The star bragged of never missing a performance, and Stritch's thumb-twiddling as she waited in vain to go on became its own second-banana shtick, carefully documented in the columns and beneficial to both performers' images.

As a role model for Stritch, Merman like Brice before her was an appealing alternative to the bombshell women spilling out of strapless gowns on the cover of *Photoplay* magazine. Merman had emerged from secretarial school in Astoria, Queens, lopping a "Zim" from her surname and thus conjuring, aptly, the tidal forces of Neptune. Landing squarely in the upper-tier seats before the era of microphones, her forceful belt had dominated the musical stage since her overnight success in George and Ira Gershwin's 1930 musical *Girl Crazy*. Critics drained their reserves of metaphor to describe her projection, stamina, and consistency; Walter Kerr would compare her voice to a trumpet, penny whistle, and Wurlitzer all in one.

Merman embodied stardom without submission and with unapologetic ambition, which Stritch was beginning to voice as well, encouraged by a confident and sociable new agent, Gloria Safier (pronounced "Sapphire"): a relative of the fabled Selznick show-biz family who'd set up her own shop in 1948, Safier specialized in unknowns—because, as she would later shrug to *Time*, "Anyone can get Marilyn Monroe a job. There's no fun in that."

"I have a terrible desire to be the whole cheese," Stritch told a reporter named Clarissa Start, who wrote a column called "The Little Woman," which more typically covered topics like hairdos and board games than professional goals. "Personally, I don't see any point in being in the theater unless you can be something in it. It's too hard a life. Unless you have a desire to get to the top, there's no use doing it in the first place."

Although Stritch, with her low voice and direct affect, couldn't play the dumb, tittering blonde so then in vogue, she would play up her out-of-towner's naiveté for effect. A passing item by Earl Wilson—"Elaine Stritch reminds me of the time I asked her 'Have you seen Gracie

Mansion' and she replied, 'Is she that new actress?'"—was typical. It was a way of challenging what "smart" people were supposed to know. Like Leonard Bernstein, who refused his mentor Serge Koussevitzky's advice to become Leonard Burns, Stritch was fiercely proud of her background and never sought to obscure it, even when another, stuffier columnist, E. V. Durling, pointed out that Frances Gumm had thrived only after she had taken the more mellifluous moniker Judy Garland. "Now I wish somebody would persuade that brilliant young actress Elaine Stritch to get herself another professional name," he wrote. "Elaine's surname is handicapping her."

But her name also kept her moored to her cherished family, and her father's story of upward mobility. Contained in the dissonance of Stritch—rich, bitch, itch, stitch (which she could do when needed)—was a certain strength. She would consider changing it only if she got hitched, and who knew when that might happen? "Unless the man you marry is very successful himself, it's ruinous to his ego to have you more successful and making more than he does," she said to Clarissa Start, adding that she planned to delay marriage until she had achieved more in her career. "I must say I worry about it occasionally, and I guess eventually I'll do something about it. I'm very independent but I have no intention of spending the rest of my life with only my notices for company."

Meanwhile, Merman was on her second of her four husbands and had two small children. Somewhat oblivious to the demands of family, Stritch later bragged about her superior stamina in the realm of nightlife, how she'd close P. J. Clarke's, the brick-walled wood-paneled saloon on Third Avenue at Fifty-Fifth Street that was featured in the 1945 noir film *The Lost Weekend*, before proceeding to the apartment of the owner, Danny Lavezzo, staying up all night and then heading to whatever matinee she was in after a nap. "Merman couldn't keep up with the dialogue," she scoffed of her elder's social stamina.

Merman counseled discipline. "If you want to do musical comedy and do it right, you've gotta live like a fucking nun," Stritch said she advised. Oft repeated was her injunction, supposedly to Berlin and the book writers of *Madam*, for tinkering overlong with one song: "Boys, as of right now, I am Miss BirdsEye of 1950. I am frozen. Not a comma!"

Her consistency and perfect attendance record left Stritch a shadow, flickering and anxious. "You don't have to stay at the theater if you're a standby," she claimed. "It was a hell of a good job." But cracking wise about the star's endurance to keep her own name in the papers grew tedious. When the producer and composer Jule Styne, remembering Stritch's spirited though unsuccessful audition for Lorelei Lee in his *Gentlemen Prefer Blondes*, asked her to try out for the part of yet another reporter, Melba Snyder, in his revival of the Richard Rodgers and Lorenz Hart musical *Pal Joey*, she accepted eagerly, though winning it would require special dispensation from the Actors' Equity Association brokered by *Madam*'s producer Leland Hayward.

Melba was a small part, but with a big number, and in a show with considerable pedigree. The book, by John O'Hara, was based on stories for *The New Yorker* about a nightclub performer who has an affair with an older, married socialite. When it was first staged in 1940, *Pal Joey* made a star of Gene Kelly, who played the caddish title role. The musical might have lingered longer in the public consciousness but for a ten-month boycott the following year of the American Society of Composers, Authors and Publishers (ASCAP) by radio broadcasters in protest of exorbitant fees, meaning that the musical's best songs, like "Bewitched, Bothered and Bewildered" and "I Could Write a Book," did not become hits right away. After the ban was lifted, the hypnotic "Bewitched" was recorded by Doris Day (going to number 9 on the Billboard chart) and Mel Tormé, among other popular singers, and commercial momentum built to revisit the production.

Some months after Rodgers had passed on Stritch for *Allegro* in 1947, he ran into her outside the Theater Guild offices and mistook her for another actress. Now he was helping to coach her on how to vamp through one of his and Hart's most sophisticated songs. "Zip" was accompanied by a mock striptease imitating one of Melba Snyder's interview subjects, Gypsy Rose Lee. It was a chance for Stritch to show off both the figure that had won her the Sweater Girl title (though no actual clothes were removed) and her developing sense of irony.

She shared a dressing room and a tomboy background with Helen Gallagher, cast as a nightclub singer named Gladys Bumps. "She had great parties," Gallagher said of Stritch. "I remember when she gave a party she'd call up the Stork Club and say 'send over four bottles of champagne.'" The Stork was one of the few nightclubs to be open on Sundays, when the theater crowd could stay out knowing they had the whole next day to relax. It was there that Stritch had been photographed one night in 1948 sitting at a table with a group of people that included a young representative from Massachusetts, John F. Kennedy, his brother Robert, and Robert's girlfriend, Ethel Skakel. Though Elaine did not wait long to broadcast her dates with Brando, she took some forty years to start telling publicly a story that JFK had taken her to dinner, that she'd invited him up for a nightcap and he'd said, "Elaine, if having a nightcap means eating scrambled eggs and listening to Glenn Miller, I'm not going to come up." But there were always plenty of other men to tell stories about, and plenty of people listening to them.

"She was pretty hard to take actually, but we were great friends," Gallagher said. "But I never wanted to get too much in her entourage. I didn't really like being anyone's sycophant. And she had a tendency, because she had such a luminous personality, to collect people that wanted to adore her, and I never wanted to be part of that."

Stritch needed not just adoration but tutelage, as Hart's lyrics again required her to feign a sophistication she didn't quite possess, containing one allusion after another to unfamiliar cultural touchstones like the Jewish cabala and Whistler's painting of his mother.

Soon Louella Parsons was reporting that "the off-again-on-again romance of producer Jed Harris and Broadway actress Elaine Stritch is very much on again." There was a simple explanation: the actress needed her walking Baedeker back. "Take the line 'Walter Lippmann wasn't brilliant today,'" Stritch said a decade afterward, referring to the political commentator and author of *The Cold War*. "Well, I didn't know who he was. 'Heterosexual' came up and that threw me, but I guessed and I was wrong. Then came a line 'I think Schopenhauer was right.' I still don't know about him."

When *Pal Joey* went into rehearsal, *Call Me Madam* was still running, and Elaine didn't want to give up the easy paycheck nor the prestige of being Merman's standby. Her commitment to two shows was complicated logistically, requiring a daily check-in with Merman, twice if there was a matinee. ("On your way, gal. Shoo," Merman would say, or some variation, in the midst of applying her greasepaint.) This was easily accomplished when *Pal Joey* was rehearsing a block away from the Imperial at the Broadhurst, but then Rodgers and Styne decided that they needed a weeklong tryout at the Shubert Theater in New Haven, Connecticut, an hour and a half's drive away.

After Mass on Christmas Day 1951, Stritch put on a Dior suit with boots and joined her old colleague Paul Hartman at Cerutti's, a restaurant on Madison Avenue. After Merman waved her away for the evening, she buttoned up her beaver coat and Hartman drove her in his car, fast, to New Haven. They arrived at the Shubert with seconds to spare. Gallagher was singing the last line of the song preceding "Zip."

"My understudy was in the wings," Stritch said. "Eve Harrington was there! I said, 'Give me the shoes. Just give me the shoes.'" They were two sizes too big; Elaine was referring to the already paradigmatic ruthless young ancillary of *All About Eve*, the tremendously successful 1950 movie starring Bette Davis about, among other matters, rivalry between women—younger ones trying to get to the top and older ones fearing they are over the hill. A pivotal scene has the heroine, Margo Channing, unable to get to her scheduled performance because a friend enchanted by Eve has drained their car of gas, so that the ingénue might get a chance.

According to Dorothy Kilgallen, Stritch and Hartman were then stranded in New Haven because of snow blocking the roads. They "sat up all night going over show changes," and then, unable for some reason to reach Merman on the telephone, drove back to New York to check on her for the matinee. Then back to New Haven for the *Pal Joey* matinee. "And believe it or don't," as Kilgallen put it, back to New York to check in on the evening performance of *Call Me Madam*, "Paul Hartman is stretched out in bed and has left a call with the operator not to waken him until New Year's Eve."

As Stritch told it over the years, as in the narration of the date with Brando, her contortions to meet both obligations grew ever more strenuous. Hartman was cut out of the story entirely and an old Yale boyfriend with an MG was cast in the role of chauffeur. Or Stritch would put herself alone sitting tensely in a delayed train, and then finally the train would start moving, and then she'd arrive at the New Haven station, be unable to find a cab, bust into a private car driven by an Italian man named Giordano with multiple children in the back seat ("it figures"), and then he'd turn out to have a mother and father that wanted to come too, all of whom would be staring up eagerly at our heroine the next night. And the few inches of snow reported in Connecticut turned into "a blizzard."

By making her high-wire dash between the two gigs into a colorful sideshow, Stritch cannily augmented the excitement of her eleven-minute performance, both for herself and for those reading about her in the columns. By the time *Pal Joey* arrived back at the Broadhurst for its opening night, January 3, 1952, "Zip" was making people giddy. "ONE SCENE ONE SONG ONE SMASH NOT ENOUGH YOU," Mickey Rooney would cable after he saw it.

"She doesn't remove so much as a shoelace or a glove," an Associated Press reporter wrote admiringly. "But her pantomime and singing are so suggestive that you would make her exit entirely in the nude."

"Elaine Stritch, a comedienne hitherto vaguely depressing to me, gets, and deserves, possibly the greatest ovation of the evening," proclaimed *The New Yorker*'s Wolcott Gibbs, who had not been kind to *Angel in the Wings*. Walter Kerr bestowed the most lavish praise: "Elaine Stritch winds up for a knockout with her 'Zip' number in the 2nd set and manages her only dialogue scene in a fine jaundiced manner," he wrote. "She gets such magnificent snarl into it that she comes close to running off with the second act."

To reward herself after finishing the song, uttering her few lines, and exiting the stage, she would dash across the street from the Broadhurst to Sardi's and have drinks, before returning for the final curtain call. Richard Rodgers was one of her escorts. "Dick was a little afraid of me," Stritch decided, or blustered, years later. "I couldn't figure out why, so one day after we'd had a couple of martinis, I asked him. He said 'it's just that every time you perform a number I think you're so goddamn good that I'm terrified you won't be able to do it again.'"

She told Leonard Lyons of leaving her parents sitting at Sardi's once they'd seen the show, so they could finish their dinners. "Would you leave HIM to go back to the theater for the final curtain," the columnist asked, meaning a hypothetical boyfriend.

"Of course," Stritch said. "I've never met the fellow who could keep me from a bow." Not even Clark Gable, she insisted. Nor the hotel tycoon Conrad Hilton, divorced from Zsa Zsa Gabor, with whom she'd been spotted in the Plush Room of the Park Avenue supper club Gogi's LaRue, decorated by Kilgallen's husband, Dick Kollmar, in an Empire style with red velvet walls. Old enough to be her father, Hilton "asked me to marry him in front of St. Pat's," Stritch bragged, saying that he'd promised to get an annulment from Rome. "My mother approved the whole match, thought it was a great idea. Mrs. Conrad Hilton, are you kidding?"

On Valentine's Day, though, her sole focus was the stage. She interrupted a conversation between Earl Wilson and the stage manager of *Pal Joey* to tell the columnist, "Ethel Merman's wheezing." Wilson rushed over "to see Ethel collapse," but to no avail. Stritch sat next to him and they watched dolefully as she powered through the play. "Sabotage!" she said. "She's very sick. I should sing that good well."

Merman treated Stritch cordially and with good humor; she was entirely unthreatened by the younger woman's presence in New York. But she refused to leave her small children behind in the city, so Hayward turned his attention to the problem of whether a tour of *Call Me Madam* without her might be viable, and if so, who could carry it. The show was getting healthy grosses, but he worried national audiences would be disappointed without its anchor. "Do you feel that MADAM is really as strong as it could be? Do you feel the play is strong enough to do a second company?" he asked his press representative, Leo Freedman.

Freedman thought so, though with caveats. "Audiences more and more enjoy the musical. I mean aside from Merman," he wrote in a "Dear Boss" letter on the show's official stationery, crested with a caricature of that star's dark-pompadoured visage, with eyelashes as spiky as spider legs. "The corn is becoming better corn every day." The show album, recorded by RCA with Dinah Shore in the lead role because Merman was under exclusive contract to Decca, had been well received (though Merman fans continue to feel deprived). "It is even more melodious," Freedman believed, though he had some concern that none of the songs had yet reached the hit parade, as Billboard's charts were known then. "They are heard on the radio, but are not prominent or popular on the juke boxes." (One, though, "They Like Ike," would be taken up by Dwight D. Eisenhower's presidential campaign.)

Hayward also solicited the advice of his friend Edwin Lester, the founder and director of the Los Angeles Civic Light Opera who would be needed to ensure the success of *Call Me Madam* on the West Coast. The two men mulled a long list of possible replacements for Merman. They were salivating to cast Carol Channing, who had won the part of Lorelei Lee in the stage musical of *Gentlemen Prefer Blondes* and had already been on the cover of *Time* magazine. But Hayward had been impressed by Stritch's appearance in *Pal Joey* and the fat stack of press mentions that followed.

"HAVE BEEN THINKING OVER STRITCH IDEA AND THINK THIS IS ON THE RIGHT TRACK IF CHANNING APPEARS UNSUITABLE OR IS UNAVAILABLE," Lester cabled Hayward. "I HAVE COMPLETE CONFIDENCE IN YOUR JUDGMENT AND IF YOU THINK STRITCH CAN GIVE GREAT PERFORMANCE MY OPINION IS THAT INTRODUCTION OF A NEW PERSONALITY LIKE THIS IS INFINITELY MORE INTRIGUING AND CAN BE SURROUNDED WITH MORE EXCITEMENT THAN PRESENTATION OF A SEMI NAME WHO IS A COMPROMISE PERFORMANCEWISE."

The deal was done by the middle of February 1952, and then the two men began to scheme at how best to announce it, with much mutual male flattery. "WE WILL MAKE YOU THE KEY TO HER STORY AS THE SELECTOR," Lester proposed in a subsequent wire. "I BELIEVE LAUNCHING OF NEW STAR IS MADE IMPORTANT BY THE STATURE OF THE PRODUCER WHO DOES THE LAUNCHING." He suggested pushing a "CINDERELLA ANGLE" with the press and concluded: "P.S. STRITCH BETTER BE GOOD."

There was another person nervous about whether Stritch would be good, and that was Stritch. Though her gyrating turn as Melba in *Pal Joey* had gotten much of the attention, it was Helen Gallagher's performance as Gladys Bumps that got a Tony award for Best Featured Actress in a musical (there were not yet multiple nominees in each category). Whether out of sisterly generosity or wanting some small part of the glory, Stritch offered her help to prepare for the ceremony. There was much dithering over what Gallagher, who'd grown up in the Bronx, would wear to the Waldorf-Astoria. "Elaine tried to get me to buy one of hers. Here *she* was and here *I* was," Gallagher said, indicating her smaller dimensions. "A red satin dress, I remember that. 'Well, you can have it taken in.' Because she was a clotheshorse—she loved clothes."

In later years, masculine dress became Stritch's default; at this stage she cycled through feminine furbelows like the costumes they were: Was she noir? gamine? career woman? "Oh yes, I went through the heavy veils stage, snoods, turbans, ankle straps, chartreuse and fuchsia, the jazzy shoes with the polo coat, the fancy coat with the ballet slippers, the Dior suits with no blouse"—a trick she picked up from Stella Adler. But "whenever I had a date with a big shot I didn't know what to wear suddenly, and I had a closet full of Dior," Stritch said, remembering a strapless black taffeta dress with jacket she wore to a Sunday night meeting at the Toots Shor restaurant with the comic actor Jackie Gleason, after multiple outfit changes.

"Well, how are you tonight, little lady?" asked the restaurant's captain as she came in.

Whoops, Stritch thought. "There was no true sophistication there, see?" she said. "I was like the little girl up in the attic with her mother's fucking clothes on."

She made her way toward Gleason and his entourage.

"Who died, pal?" he asked.

Somehow she hung on to her composure, and was eventually cast as Trixie in the sketches that would become Gleason's *The Honeymooners*, but he fired her before the first episode aired. "The problem is, Stritch, you're as good as me in drag," Gleason told her. "And there ain't room enough for both of us." Stritch shrugged this off; her few forays into television had not impressed her very deeply. It was still a flat, black-and-white medium, easily bypassed, and on set you could not feel the audience's appreciation. Theater was living color; theater held people's attention.

She began concentrating in earnest on the part of Sally Adams in *Call Me Madam*, her first big-time starring role on a national stage.

With Gloria Safier advocating on her behalf, Stritch had become a more confident negotiator. She got her salary up to $1000 per week and insisted on having top or equal billing to whoever would play her romantic lead: Cosmo Constantine, a Lichtenburg general in line for the prime ministry. Edwin Lester fretted over the selection of this male costar, wanting someone who already had name recognition. "IT WILL LEND IMPORTANCE TO STRITCH AND DISTINCTION TO THE SHOW," he wrote Hayward.

They eventually secured Kent Smith, a square-jawed and golden-haired actor who'd appeared in many movies during the 1940s, including *The Fountainhead*, the adaptation of Ayn Rand's novel. A gala performance of *Call Me Madam*, sandwiched by parties, had been booked in Washington, D.C., to celebrate a renovation of the capital's National Theater, after which the new company would take over.

The crème de la crème of Washington society, including Roosevelt-Longworths, Guggenheims, and Tafts, swirled around the event and a local columnist wrote a paean to Merman, heralding her as "the most dynamic, the most electric, the most hilarious, the most superlative, the most terrific, gigantic and miraculous musical comedy star in the world today," adding "Ethel as an ambassador is one of those immortal combinations, like hot dogs and mustard or Bernhardt and 'Camille.'"

Stritch tried to ignore, or at least not to be intimidated by, such homages. Noting that Smith had a personal valet, she secured a maid at a cost of $100 per week to accompany her down to D.C., charging half to the production, and sent her trunk separately.

The replacement players were rehearsed first by the stage manager, and then by the storied director George Abbott. A special matinee had been arranged, with tickets at a cut-rate price for students, to give the newbies a chance to settle in in front of a forgiving audience before the tour began. The original cast was invited to witness the run-through from the second row. Stritch was terrified.

"WE WHO ARE ABOUT TO DIE SALUTE YOU," she cabled Merman beforehand. She got through the matinee, she said, with "rosary beads and a double Courvoisier. I don't know who had top billing: God or the brandy."

Stritch put on a pink negligee for "You're Just in Love," a swinging number that Irving Berlin had added to the show just before its New York debut in October 1950. In this song, perhaps the best-loved of the musical, her character reassured a young, bespectacled male press attaché who is mooning, his heart going "pittter-patter," over a Lichtenburg princess, that it's not "analyzin'" he needs: "I know just what's the matter / Because I've been there once or twice."

Russell Nype, who had costarred with Merman, didn't tour with the production of *Call Me Madam*, but he did get to know Stritch during this transition and performed the song with her in 1954 at the St. Louis Municipal Opera. "I had quite a crush on her in the beginning," he said. "I always liked her, with reservation. She was a selfish performer because she always tried to steal the spotlight." Sally Adams was a mother-hen type but Stritch, he felt, could not help but try to play peacock. "Ethel was more honest in that role, I think," Nype said. "When Ethel and I sang the duet, Ethel meant it. When Elaine and I sang the duet, she was trying to get attention. She was intent only upon having attention on herself."

Abbott saved a letter from one dissatisfied customer, criticizing his new star's timing, calling her "hammy" and saying she'd turned the song into a "contest as to who can outshout whom." The volume obscured that "You're Just in Love" rattled Stritch. Her opening number, "The Hostess with the Mostes' on the Ball," was no problem—as Gallagher had noted, Elaine loved throwing parties. "Can You Use Any Money Today?" was pert and humorous. But with "You're Just in Love" Sally Adams was displaying a soothing worldliness that Stritch, in her late twenties and unsure about love herself, found difficult to mime.

Nype was the one older than Stritch, by five years, and his replacement, David Daniels, only two years younger. Overcome by what she was being asked to convey during one rehearsal, she burst into tears.

Abbott came up onstage. "Stop it! Right now," he ordered.

"He was like a bolt of thunder," Stritch said later.

"You're to get up and finish this run-through immediately," Abbott told her. "And I am not kidding, Elaine."

She looked up at him, she remembered, "like I was five years old, eyes like saucers, sitting on my chair in the pink tulle," and she realized that she "cared more of what George Abbott thinks about me than my father."

Like her father, another steely-eyed long-legged George, Abbott—though no one called him George—took a watchful but essentially benevolent approach toward her drinking. Stritch came down to get notes before opening night with scotch and soda in a mug that she blew on at regular intervals.

"Is that coffee?" Abbott asked her.

"Y-yes," Stritch said, her voice suddenly an octave higher.

"Could I have a taste?" Abbott took the mug from her, blew on it himself, and then took a sip.

"Man, that's good coffee," he said.

Merman, meanwhile, refilled the younger woman's drink at every opportunity, whether it was in a spirit of sabotage or sympathy. "Every glass she poured me I poured in the plant," Stritch said. In her memoir, the older woman admitted she no more wanted to share "her" role—one she'd played for more than six hundred performances, and that she would reprise quite robustly on-screen—than a toothbrush. *Call Me Madam* had been cleared from the Imperial to make way for Hayward's next production, the first musical with an actual swimming pool built into its set: *Wish You Were Here*. It starred Stritch's old boyfriend Jack Cassidy. By now she had a new one: her leading man, Kent Smith.

As a token of good luck and fellowship Smith procured for himself and Stritch matching Marc Cross canvas cases with shoulder straps and buckets for shaved ice, Dom Perignon, two glasses, and ice containers. "Kent was a gourmet—it was like traveling with Alfred Lunt," Stritch said, referring to the eminent actor and director, a devoted amateur chef. Like her earlier beau, Cassidy, Smith was married, though his wife was in Beverly Hills with their young daughter.

Free from such commitments and eighteen years younger than her leading man, Stritch loved the collegiality of being on tour, like a traveling coed boarding school. "We went every place by train—so glorious," she said. Their contracts contained provisions for multiple sleeper cars, close together. "Down would come the walls and we'd all sit there in our jammies after the last performance on Saturday night—talk about swinging from one roof to another."

Safier had emboldened Stritch, but Smith, a man of Hollywood, where perks were commonplace, also nurtured her growing sense of prerogative. "I am supposed to ask you for OUR STAR****LA STRITCH***or maybe she's had the agent ask you—if she can go to Chicago next Sunday via New York Central and on THE CENTURY of course, from New York, AT OUR EXPENSE," wrote one of Hayward's operatives in irritated capital letters from Baltimore. "I told her emphatically NO." The Century was the famous express train, the 20th Century Limited, whose passengers boarded over a red carpet. "I frankly can't think of anyone else I know in the theatre who would ask such a thing," the underling continued. "It's a very unprofessional request and she seems to want to stick the firm any and every time she can for whatever idea or whim she dreams up." Stritch had also gotten fussy about her pink negligee, ordering that the skirt be remade with fabric from France. It had become important to her that the clothing she wore onstage was of the highest quality, partly for verisimilitude, partly because she sought to keep it after the play's run. The costumer deflected the request by pointing out that the show was scheduled to close before the time the material could be shipped and arrive.

Atypically for a woman of the highly domesticated postwar era, Stritch was showing the same drive that had propelled her father from poverty to an executive position at B.F. Goodrich. "This life is no place to sit down and be satisfied with what you're doing," she had said to Clarissa Start.

"You ought to make a few more bucks this year than you did last." She bragged of buying her own clothes and receiving her first dividend check from the stock market and added, "I adore having money. I think it's the greatest thing in the world, especially when it's money you've earned. The independent feeling it gives you is like nothing else imaginable."

After years of hardship, America was suddenly at ease again, the scrubby victory garden now a smooth leisure-lawn; why shouldn't she, too, roll in it? As Adams says to the amused, Continental romantic Constantine in Act I of *Call Me Madam*: "Cabbage! Lettuce! You know, that green stuff! Money, money, money, money, money, money."

During the show's opening night in Los Angeles, Stritch, nervous beyond measure, picked up a call from an unseen "President Truman," one of the show's running gags, before the prop phone had rung. A local reviewer was not favorably impressed: "Miss Stritch, though gifted, is not another Ethel Merman," he wrote.

Meanwhile, back in New York, the air-conditioning in the Imperial Theater broke down during the opening night of *Wish You Were Here*, which had not had an out-of-town tryout due to the impossibility of moving the set, and reviewers there were cranky as well. "Nearly all of them Wished It Were Better," Winchell reported. With the etiquette instilled in her by Mildred, Stritch wrote a polite letter of condolence and thanks to her producer.

Dear Mr. Hayward:

I just had to write you a note to tell you how truly sorry I am about "Wish you were here." I can't say anything else about it except that I so resent the flippant way actors etc. etc. "talk up" an unfortunate situation in their own business. I only wish I could have given you 100% good notices here in L.A. If you've already read them, I think you will read between the lines.

I was of course a little depressed because they were ALL SO GOOD the last four weeks. I want you to know that our opening night was almost our best show. So 2 or 3 of the critics just had a bad attack of "Mermanitis" and the audience reaction is just so exciting I've already forgotten the few bad knocks.

I don't want to oversentimentalize—but I can't thank you enough for this wonderful opportunity. Every performance is a new experience. I feel more at home every night. By the time I get to Philadelphia I won't remember what Merman looks like.

Everyone is so nice to me . . . and the cast is an unusually nice one. Mr. Berlin came last night—gave me quite a thrill by his reaction. Thank you again for what has been and will continue to be a wonderful engagement.

She told a story of practicing her songs one day on the terrace of her hotel when the phone rang and the operator told her there had been a complaint.

"Who complained?" Stritch asked.

"Room 512," the operator said.

Stritch marched over to room 512 and opened the door. Merman, in town for work on the film version, was inside, chuckling.

Conrad Hilton hosted an early buffet supper in Stritch's honor at his 35,000-square-foot mansion in Bel Air, Casa Encantada, with preening cockatoos in the gardens and a thousand-bottle wine cellar. Catching a glimpse of Gleason, Stritch burst into song with Pat Harrington, who played a congressman: "We're a pair of entertaining boys, and we just came out to make a lot of noise."

It was an illustrious send-off for a caravan both stately and jolly. From Los Angeles *Call Me Madam* proceeded to Oakland, Salt Lake City, Des Moines, St. Louis, and Minneapolis. Unlike Merman, Stritch was finding herself a natural nomad. "The open road, the open road," she said. "I always think about it in the movie—the calendar's flipping."

The company stopped next in Chicago, then almost as important for shows as New York, due mostly to the high level of criticism issuing forth from the *Tribune* critic Claudia Cassidy, known as Acidy Cassidy for the tart reviews in her column "On the Aisle." It was there that Stritch got a call from a young woman named Liz Smith, who had been told to look her up by Safier, a mutual friend. Born Mary Elizabeth Smith two years before Stritch, she shared her birth-name initials and her birthday, February 2.

From Fort Worth, Texas, with a slow and toothy smile, Smith was many years from the gossip columnist she would become: working as a sort of minder to the not-quite-stars. She'd traveled to the city at the behest of the comedian Kaye Ballard's manager, who wanted to make sure Ballard wasn't spending too much money. Smith had seen and admired *Pal Joey* and Stritch invited her to *Call Me Madam*.

"She was years too young for the role," Smith said. "But stagestruck, I maybe was." They began going together to burlesque performances after curtain; burlesque was then having its last gasp in Chicago. And there were parties aplenty, one attended by Audrey Hepburn and Henry Fonda. "Everybody knew Elaine," Smith said. "I met a kid named Bobby Short"—a cabaret pianist who would eventually become a fixture at the Carlyle Hotel. "All these things came in very handy afterward." Smith was particularly enchanted by a chorus girl named Conchita del Rivero, just out of high school: "the fucking funniest, cutest kid I had ever met. I just loved her and everybody loved her, and Elaine kept saying 'she's gonna be something.'" She was: Chita Rivera, the musical-theater star.

Chita's mother had been anxious about letting her go on tour. "Elaine picked up that ball," Rivera said. "She was absolutely wonderful for me, and watched out for me, and I lived in the wings and watched a lot and learned an awful lot." Stritch would invite her to the dressing room, and once Smith joined them and Rivera remembered "feeling the urgency to leave," to let them be alone. "Of course in those days you respected your elders," she said.

Assessing her namesake and hearing about Jack Cassidy, Liz Smith detected a pattern in Stritch's romantic life.

"Elaine, don't you see this psychology?" she asked her new friend. "The fact that you fall in love with these men who can't marry you because they've been divorced, or are still married?" Stritch just shrugged. She was longing for companionship, of any sort. She begged Liz to ditch Ballard and accompany her for the rest of the tour, to no avail.

After Chicago came Detroit, her first visit home in two years, where Stritch was welcomed with slobbering enthusiasm by Marchbanks, a sixty-pound boxer acquired in her absence, and proudly introduced her first real movie-star boyfriend to the family. He taught Georgene's oldest son, Frank Moran, Jr., how to play chess. "Handsome guy," his sister Midge said of Kent Smith, though a shadow of judgment hung over the occasion. "You know, we were so Catholic."

Sally by now had also had two children: Sally and Chris. But Tante Elaine, as she asked them to call her in the Continental manner, preferred to stay with Georgene because there was more room. "She was just this wild character that we heard about," Chris said. "Who'd blow into town, raise a lot of hell, and leave town." He remembered his parents having a big party for Kent, and the guest of honor flirting with one of the married women there. Regardless, Stritch encouraged everyone to think that she was on a fast track to marriage with only religious obstacles standing in her way. Mentally she tended to conflate her professional and personal aspirations.

"I think at the base of it, I wanted a guy," she said of those years. "I wanted to be part of a relationship . . . I imagined myself being thrown around, men taking advantage of me, you know. I didn't know a lot about the sex part of it."

By the time the theatrical tour of *Call Me Madam* petered out in 1953 in Louisville and Pittsburgh, Kent Smith had left the show, replaced by Dick Smart. But one columnist was still reporting that a winter wedding was "on tab" for the unofficial couple. "They've got it bad and don't care who knows it." Another was certain that Smith was taking instruction in the Catholic church and that Elaine's "uncle," the cardinal, would perform the ceremony.

It would take almost a year for Kilgallen to proclaim definitively that "the long and serious romance of Elaine Stritch and actor Kent Smith is All Over Now."

Stritch was loath to lose star billing and knew, coming back to New York, that she had to choose her next project carefully. "There are two big fears," she told Leonard Lyons. "The first that you're turning down another *Oklahoma!* The second, that you're turning it down for a flop like *Date with April*," referring to a comedy starring Constance Bennett that had closed after ten days.

Conservatively, she decided on another Rodgers and Hart revival, of the 1936 musical *On Your Toes*, in part because Abbott would again direct her. It was a jazzy piece with choreography by George Balanchine intended originally for Fred Astaire. Despite the rigors of "Civilization," dancing had not proved to be the gawky Stritch's strength, but a song from the trunk, "You Took Advantage of Me," was added specifically to highlight her talents, and it would not require her to posture experience as in "You're Just in Love."

The future talk-show host Dick Cavett, then an undergraduate at Yale, saw this revival of *On Your Toes* as it was trying out at the Shubert Theater in New Haven. "A woman walked out onstage, sort of handsome and steady, and sort of really *planted* herself—one foot a little in front of her, and then she began to sing," he remembered. "And it got better and better, and—I don't think I've ever seen this again—people would clap in the middle of the song, and it drove like a locomotive to the end, and then it was as if a bomb hit the theater. The applause was deafening." Young Cavett got up to go to the bathroom. "Well, kid," said an older man on his way, "you have seen one of the few genuine show stops."

But Liz Smith said, "When I would tell her how great she was at this romantic song, she was just—please." Stritch waved away her friend's compliments. "I wish I had a better part," she said. In New York Elaine saw Merman in the audience one night, expectantly ordered champagne to be chilled in her dressing room, and seethed when the older star didn't show up afterward.

The reviewers were cool on the show—one called it "a flat-footed revival"—but full of admiration for the belting blonde. "Elaine Stritch deserves a paragraph, if not five or six more encores, all to herself," wrote Walter Kerr. "She is very good." The highly esteemed Harold Clurman, a critic as well as director who was married to her old teacher Stella Adler, declared, "Miss Stritch's non-expressive vigor says a lot. All these terrible things happen to me—I am devastated, destroyed by love, etc.—but nothing really happens: I go on being trim, bright, fashionably awry and somehow untouched. The effect is coldly electrifying, the best, almost the only thing, in the show."

Stritch was invited on *The Ed Sullivan Show* to sing the song. She would long complain that the host had on one occasion mispronounced her name as "Eileen Strict," whereupon her mother, watching at home in Detroit, had shut the television off. But this time Sullivan seemed entirely reverent and introduced her properly. Wearing a black suit over a white blouse, Stritch sang with such enthusiasm and expression that the little hat she had pinned to the back of her head popped off, and the host picked it up off the floor, dusted it off, and returned it to her.

Smith marveled at her friend's social as well as professional endurance. "Drinking was a must for people then, and the three-martini lunch was a fact and I just couldn't take it," she said. She had barely drunk until she began to know Gloria Safier. "Gloria would give these cocktail parties on Fridays where nobody would go home and I started drinking in self-defense, but I wasn't a good drinker. Elaine—she was young and strong." Stritch was also refining her hostess skills, from a new apartment at 444 East Fifty-Second Street. Visitors were often surprised to see that her bookshelves, those not stocked with Jed Harris's recommendations, contained a collection of European dolls.

Merman came to one of these parties bringing Judy Garland. "I almost died," Stritch said. Her full-throated singing more ragged these days, Garland was trying with difficulty to emerge from the juvenile roles that had made her famous, through with MGM, which had infantilized her, and embark on a concert tour that would help her find her voice again.

To the same party, the playwright Edward Chodorov, whom Stritch had briefly dated, brought Gig Young, who was building a reputation on Hollywood soundstages as a supporting player to leading men like Errol Flynn and James Cagney. He had in 1952 been nominated for an Oscar as Best Supporting Actor for his performance as a philandering alcoholic in *Come Fill the Cup*.

"Gig, this is Elaine," Chodorov said when she answered the door.

She sized up the actor: taller than most of them at six foot one—tall enough for her to wear high heels—dark-haired, with darting dark eyes that matched her own and a naughty smile.

"How do you do? What would you like to drink?" Stritch said. Privately, *South Pacific*'s major ballad had begun in her head: "Some enchanted evening, you may see a stranger." This was indeed a "crowded room."

Stritch walked into her bathroom to freshen her makeup and found the composer Leonard Bernstein there taking a bubble bath with a "quart" of Dom Perignon by his side. "If I'd have been Bankhead, I'd have gone to the loo as planned, but I didn't go that route," she said later, referring to Tallulah, the notoriously crude star.

The party went on for hours, ending as parties did then: soggily, sootily in cigarette ashes and melted ice, which Stritch was rinsing from glasses when she glanced up and saw Young still there. He helped her finish cleaning up and then spent the night, chastely, in her spare twin bed. The next morning she made him breakfast before he dropped her for a lunch date with Conrad Hilton at "21."

"I'm going to marry that girl," Young told his cabdriver.

The declaration's force was blunted by his two previous marriages. Born Byron Elsworth Barr in St. Cloud, Minnesota, a troubled junior thespian at technical high school and scouted by Warner Brothers after training at the Pasadena Playhouse, he had changed his name upon recommendation of a publicist, after test audiences responded favorably to a mustachioed character named Gig Young he played in a 1942 movie called *The Gay Sisters*. Thus he not only avoided confusion with another actor named Byron Barr, who had appeared in the film noir *Double Indemnity*, but also in one stroke erased a painful origin story that included his father's verbal abuse, and possible sexual molestation by an older female cousin. Young's first marriage had been to a classmate at the Playhouse; his second to Sophie Rosenstein, an older drama coach at Paramount and author of *Modern Acting: A Manual*, who died of cervical cancer. After this loss he began drinking heavily.

Their shared Midwestern backgrounds, their frustration with being perpetually cast as sidekicks, and their reliance on alcohol hastened Elaine and Gig's intimacy. An undated photo shows her seeming to stumble out of a nightclub on his arm, in a low-cut, spangled satin dress, eyes downcast as he arches an eyebrow mischievously toward the photographer.

In the summer of 1954, Elaine brought him to a performance she was doing of *Call Me Madam*, with Russell Nype at the Municipal Opera in St. Louis. At the "Muny," as it was nicknamed, under the dark open sky, in front of thousands of people, she sang with more authority and brio than she had been able to summon for George Abbott: "You're not sick / You're just in love!"

Her parents were among those cheering and applauding. They took her and Young to dinner, where he declared that he cared so much for their daughter that he was going to convert from Baptism; that his previous marriage could be rendered "non-sacramental" once he produced proof that his ex-wife hadn't been baptized.

"Think carefully. This is for life," George said to Elaine afterward.

"God, he's the most attractive man," Mildred whispered, squeezing her daughter's hand urgently. "Marry him in a *cornfield* if they won't allow it in the church."

Stritch said years later, "Mother fell in love with Gig Young—of course: he looked like the cover of *Men's Vogue*—and Daddy didn't. He liked him but not 100 percent sold. Yeah, that was a tough one."

The not-quite-lovers proceeded to Los Angeles, where Young was to begin filming *Young at Heart* with Frank Sinatra and Doris Day, and checked into separate rooms at the peppermint-colored Beverly Hills Hotel on Sunset Boulevard. Unsure of what job she'd take next, Stritch picked Young up from rehearsal one day, at the wheel of his Cadillac convertible. "It was so full of catechisms and *The Life of St. Thomas Aquinas* and oh, please. And he never read any of them," she said. "I'd cue him on the catechism and it was one of the funniest experiences. You know, looking at Gig Young over a martini saying, 'Who made the world?'" He was studying with a priest, a Father Ford, so good-looking that Gig joked to Elaine that he was worried he might "overshoot the runway," a favorite expression: land on a man instead of his planned target (her). "There are few outfits more attractive on men than a cassock," remarked Stritch of the sleek black garment Ford and other clergymen wore. "They're just dynamite. I mean you can be straight as a dime and have that gay, wonderful look about you."

Young moved back into his apartment, where Stritch would visit, keeping her hotel room in Beverly Hills for propriety's sake. Eventually she lost her virginity to him in a Malibu motel. Her relatively advanced age at doing so, which she would later put at thirty, would after the sexual revolution become one of her life's talking points. "I simply can't be bad publicity for the Sacred Heart Convent!" she wrote in 1995 to one journalist who had reported her "first time" occurred at sixteen.

His intensity, though, unnerved her. Young sent flowers and she refused to acknowledge them. He bought her a $3500 diamond engagement ring, and she was careless with it. "She lost it Christmas shopping and hasn't had a trace of it and couldn't be sadder," Louella Parsons reported.

The identity of Hollywood wife fit Stritch poorly, like the little hat she'd worn on Ed Sullivan's show. Despite growing up in Motor City, she disliked being behind the wheel of a car. "I did not know how to drive unless I drank," she said. "Same thing as I couldn't go on the stage without two drinks. I couldn't get in the car without two drinks and I had no talent for it. But when I had two martinis I was a terrific driver. Responsible. Confident. All that shit." Once, zooming back from the house of Dominick Dunne, then angling to be a Hollywood muckety-muck, she passed the former child actor Jackie Cooper changing a tire. Cooper, who had gotten kicked out of a navy training program due to his involvement in a drinking party and then had reformed, knew of her reputation for the high life and advised her to call Alcoholics Anonymous. Stritch demurred, for the time being.

Ambivalent as she was about Young, she invited him home to Detroit for the holidays. Her mother hovered anxiously over her as she unpacked.

"You mean to tell me you spent the whole month in California after those reviews without one offer for television?" Mildred said.

"I had a boil, Mother. Are we going to Mass before breakfast? Do they still have a 12:30 at Gesu?"

"Oh darling, it's Christmas, they have masses every five minutes. What happened about *Silk Stockings*?" (A troubled Cole Porter musical Elaine had passed on, over billing issues.) "Did you have a nice time in California, Elaine? And how about you and the movie? After all those reviews, don't tell me you sublet your apartment. Will you ever learn? Do you think that broadtail is warm enough? And no boots. Honestly! Don't they have any snow in New York? Don't you think you can really settle down and stay here for a while? I've done your room over; I've done the whole *house* over . . ."

Tired of feeling like a canary sprung from a cage for showstopping eleven o'clock numbers, Elaine had brought with her a script for a new play by William Inge, who'd recently won a Pulitzer Prize for *Picnic*. The new work was called *Bus Stop* and was to be directed by Harold Clurman, who'd praised her "non-expressive vigor" in *On Your Toes* ("Who's Harold Clurman?" Mildred asked).

George told Elaine to go to the kitchen and say hi to the maid. "Look, there are two things I don't want to talk about this Christmas," he said. "*Silk Stockings* and *Bus Stop*."

It was all reassuringly cozy and ordinary. But even when nestled in the bosom of her family, Elaine would flout the rules just as she had in Central Park. "I remember her coming down the stairs on Birchcrest in this negligee," said Midge Moran, her niece. "Oh my god: my grandfather told her to go back upstairs and put a robe on and 'do not—' They were like that. And I remember my grandmother chasing her around the house with a folded newspaper. 'Elaine, stop that and don't you talk that way.' But there was no controlling Elaine."

4.

LEADING MEN

Stritch was sitting in the familiar confines of the Detroit Athletic Club with her presumptive fiancé and her parents when she got an excited call from Gloria Safier, her agent, about *Bus Stop*.

She had not won the lead—that was going to Kim Stanley, a quivery dramatic actress who was becoming known as the Female Brando—but it was a substantial supporting role. Grace Hoyland, the owner of a twenty-four-hour diner in semirural Kansas, who is estranged from her husband, serves a group of travelers stranded by a storm in the bleak wee hours of the a.m., taking one to bed.

"I didn't know who Kim Stanley was, but I sure found out in time," Stritch said. Although Stanley was only nine days younger than Elaine, she was playing a "young blonde girl of about twenty," a nightclub singer named Cherie. Grace, meanwhile, was described as "a more seasoned character in her thirties or early forties." By now Stritch was accustomed to such discrepancies and, having accumulated some life experience, even welcomed them. She no longer needed to pour herself into the ingénue mold. And though she may not have taken seriously Jackie Cooper's roadside advice, she felt an immediate affinity for William Inge, whose experience in Alcoholics Anonymous had informed his first hit play, *Come Back, Little Sheba*. The playwright had grown up in Independence, Kansas, concealing his homosexuality; he was as introverted as Stritch was boisterous. But people with a vulnerability to drink have a way of recognizing one another, even in different stages of acknowledging their problem.

Working on this production would also confer upon Stritch a certain prestige, of a different order than singing numbers by Irving Berlin or Rodgers and Hart. Though less remembered today than Tennessee Williams, who had mentored him, Inge is still revived and studied, one of America's most respected playwrights. He had a talent for rendering small-town life, especially the psyches of the women ensconced there, in a manner both reassuring and unsettling to the big-city sophisticates who anointed him. *Come Back, Little Sheba* had been adapted successfully in Hollywood and *Picnic* was to follow.

During the rehearsal period Stritch brought the script to dinner with her family's old friend, Bobby Clark; he grabbed it from her and without reading a word hoisted it in one hand. "Weighs like a hit," he said.

Bus Stop would indeed prove a hit, the most successful play of the season; an "I dreamed I went to see *Bus Stop* in my Maidenform bra" ad ran in its Playbill program. Marilyn Monroe would star in the movie version. Even though Stanley got the most ecstatic notices, critics also singled out Stritch for her portrayal of "a grass widow runnin' a restaurant," as her character describes herself, a woman who neglects to order cheese for the sandwiches because she's not partial to it herself. Stritch responded to Clurman's hands-on style of direction as she had Piscator's, with the satisfaction of feeling seen and cared for, told what to do, parented. "It was glorious to have a warm, knowledgeable, absolutely terrific guy wrap his arms around you and direct you," she said. "It was just thrilling."

Clurman preferred to hold prolonged table readings before blocking out action on the set, for which he'd hired an inventive Ukrainian designer named Boris Aronson, who'd worked in Yiddish theater and then on *The Crucible*. With highly specific stage instructions for the "dingy establishment" from Inge, Clurman suggested that Aronson make it look like an Edward Hopper painting.

"Why not like an Aronson?" countered the designer, who was also a painter himself.

At the Music Box Theater on West Forty-Fifth Street the crew constructed an ominous "sky" with a tree protruding over the roof of the structure and drifts of snow piling at the door. Inside were grim little tables, faded, patterned wallpaper, and doughnuts under glass covers. "I just felt that I lived upstairs in that diner," Stritch said. "And there wasn't even any upstairs. The upstairs was my dressing room." She and another cast member, Anthony Ross, who played a drunken professor with the receding hairline and open face of a "regular guy" character actor, got along so well that they took down the temporary wall between their dressing rooms and put "Lunt" and "Fontanne" on the doors, after the famous married couple of the theater. Absent from the stage for a while with the bus-driver character, Stritch would take off her waitress's uniform and play cards with the stagehands in a slip. "At the first run-through with a small invited audience, I lost track of time—I must have been winning—and when I heard my cue, I just grabbed a chenille robe off the wardrobe rack and put it on," she recalled years later. "Well, the audience thought it was terrific! Because supposedly Grace goes upstairs with Carl to raise hell, but you don't know if they're just smoochin' or sparks really fly. The audience understood what must've gone on when they saw the robe. Harold loved that, and kept it in the play."

In contrast with the cozy collegiality behind the scenes, onstage Stritch was playing for the first time on Broadway the kind of brittle, restless, sociable but essentially lonely character she'd be summoned to realize for much of her career. And "I drank so much beer in *Bus Stop* I was ready to explode," she said, invoking a questionable verisimilitude. "Because that was her drink."

Absent of choreography, Stritch was able to integrate her natural restlessness into the part, leaning on the counter as she made sandwiches, with her backside out. "I have a very expressive body, always have had on the stage," she said proudly. "I act with my feet and legs an awful lot because one does. I remember when you stop smoking and you say, 'How can I smoke on the stage anymore'—I've got no problem. I used to say,

'And that is the way I feel about *that*,' and instead of taking a Bette Davis puff I'd cross my legs—*whappo!*"

But *Bus Stop* was far from the farce this might have suggested. After his romp with Grace, the bus driver, Carl, challenges the bedrock institution of American life at this moment.

CARL: Ya know, sometimes I get to thinkin', what the hell good is marriage, where ya have to put up with the same broad every day, and lookit her in the morning, and try to get along with her when she's got a bad disposition. This way suits me fine.

GRACE: I got no complaints, either.

Planted here was one of those little, hard seeds of skepticism toward the nuclear family that would start to sprout in earnest over the next decade, which Stritch herself was sowing in real life. She had a contract for a new solo record, to be put out by Dolphin, a new division of Doubleday, the publisher, which produced albums "designed for the at-home entertainment of the sophisticated urbanite and the ex-urbanite." The title was going to be *Elaine Alone*, but the producers settled simply on *Stritch*. The thirteen tracks included "You Took Advantage of Me" as well as "Too Many Rings Around Rosie" from *No, No, Nanette*, in which she proffers sweets to four different fellows who won't commit: "I tried to please them all, you know / That's why not one became my beau."

There was not a hint of mooniness or admonition in her rendition of this tune—more gaiety, punctuated by little growls. Promoting the record and consumed by the world of *Bus Stop*, Stritch was also beginning to feel her tall, dark, and handsome real-life leading man, Gig Young, was "becoming a shadow, fainter and fainter and fainter," as she put it. In addition, "his amorous attention was getting a little rough for me. It was a little bit too adult, or wild." Soon Earl Wilson was reporting the "amicable cancellation" of their wedding plans. The reason, she breezily told the columnist, was that "I haven't got enough closet space to get married."

A couple of months into *Bus Stop*'s run, Stritch reached into this over-stuffed closet and pulled out a crisp pink polka-dotted sundress to wear after appearing at the Music Box.

When she emerged into the hot summer air with Kim Stanley, they encountered a young man walking up Forty-Fifth Street whom Stanley knew from the Actors Studio. He was an actor named Ben Gazzara and he had wandered out of the Morosco Theater a few doors away, where he was playing Brick, a hard-drinking former football hero, in Tennessee Williams's new play, *Cat on a Hot Tin Roof*.

Gazzara fixed the two curvaceous, golden-haired women with what Stritch described later as "that kind of surly, sexy, Italiano" gaze. "Girls in their summer dresses," he muttered, alluding to an Irwin Shaw story from *The New Yorker* first published in 1939 but eternal in its portrayal of urban male appreciation for the female form during the warmer months. The three of them strolled along together and decided to stop at Jim Downey's Steak House on Forty-Fourth and Eighth Avenue, where actors tended to pool in the booths between rehearsal, performance, and bedtime.

They sure know how to drink, Gazzara thought of his new friends.

The next day, the house phone rang at the Music Box.

"Is Kim there?"

"No she isn't, but this is Elaine Stritch and I am here," Stritch said enterprisingly. "Who is this?"

"Ben Gazzara."

"As I said, Kim isn't here."

"How are you? What are you doing?"

"Is that because you can't get Kim?" Stritch blurted. (Right away, Negative Nora, she thought crossly to herself.)

"Who knows—maybe so," Gazzara said.

He was five years younger than she was but had a worldly air, having been born in Manhattan to working-class Sicilian immigrants and elbowed his way into the acting business. They had Piscator, whose school he'd attended after trying electrical engineering, in common. And they were both somewhat haphazard Catholics.

They were soon seen breakfasting together in a coffee shop in her neighborhood by Kilgallen, and "hand-holding (and glazed-orb gazing) in the near–8th Avenue side-streets" by Winchell. Since neckties were disdained by the Actors Studio—"hampers the encouraged free expression," Lyons wrote—Stritch took to carrying around a string bow tie in her handbag for their outings to places like Sardi's, which required them.

"There was something very warm and attractive and simple and lovely about Ben Gazzara," Stritch said. "He was that kind of Italian that, as long as he's loved, behaves himself. And as soon as there's anything wrong, he goes nuts, because he's so passionate. And he wasn't a cut-out doll for me at all, but there was something there that was so important between us. I really felt genuinely loved by Ben Gazzara. And I don't think I was old enough to appreciate or wise enough to appreciate what love is. Also, both of us were having several cocktails before, during, and after lunch dates and dinner dates. So that gets in the way of these wonderful, pure, sweet, lovely emotions that human beings have."

Another obstacle was his estranged wife, Louise Erickson, a radio actress. Like Gig Young and many after the war, Gazzara had rushed into marriage early. "What a moron I was!" he said years later. "It's the marriage to feel like a grownup. Of course, she came from another culture—she was what we call a 'white' girl. Swedish. It was that kind of romantic thing, built on nothing."

"With the Ben Gazzaras divorcing, it appears Elaine will find herself in a dilemma she's faced before: loving a man who's free to marry her, but unable to accept him because of religious scruples," Kilgallen tutted. And yet another impediment was Gazzara's mother, who had highfalutin aspirations for her son and, because Stritch was known for appearing in musicals, considered her a somehow lesser class of performer.

"You stay away from my Benny" was the message Stritch got from her.

"Mrs. Gazzara! I'm in straight plays."

"You dance and sing. No, no, no—not for Benny." Despite its transformation by Rodgers and Hammerstein, musical theater in the middle of twentieth-century America for the intellectual striver still carried a whiff of the commonplace—the bawdy chorine.

———

There was resistance to the new couple from the Stritch family as well. For his first visit to Detroit, Gazzara bought a new suit and put on a real tie, a wasted effort. Chris Bolton enjoyed playing catch with him on the porch, but Mildred forcefully did not approve: neither of the fact that he was still married nor of his ethnicity. After they left, Elaine got a phone call from her father, who reported that Mildred "just said to me the other night she wasn't going to get up out of bed until you broke up with Gazzara."

Mildred picked up another extension.

"Mother, what are you so upset about?" Elaine asked.

"If you marry that boy, one morning you're going to wake up in bed and you're going to turn over and he's going to be too dark," Mildred said, as if the new swain were a piece of toast.

"The real reason was that he was not as tall as mother would like my boyfriend or future husband to be and he was kind of rough and he did not look like Robert Redford," Stritch said years later. "And that was it—because that's who she wanted me to bring home."

The movie business was where Stritch might find the sort of refined leading man that would please her mother, but she wasn't making much progress there. Granted leave from *Bus Stop*, she did her first film, a B-picture, as second-rate and often sensationalist filler was known then. It was first titled *Too Late, My Love* and then *The Scarlet Hour*. Her character's most memorable sequence involves pulling up in a car—"Hi, boys"—admonishing a friend for drinking, stripping down to her bathing suit, and joining the friend for a swim. "The part was so terrible it looked like I was visiting the set: I had nothing to say. I just kept running into places saying, 'Hi!' The worst," Stritch said.

Next and somewhat more glamorous was a Western with Charlton Heston, first called *The Maverick*, later changed to *Three Violent People*, in which she played a saloon owner and wore a dress that the costume designer Edith Head plucked off a rack. With some excitement Stritch noticed that it bore a label reading "Barbara Stanwyck," the noir actress known for *Double Indemnity*.

Sometime in this period Stritch claimed she had a tryst with Mike Todd, the producer who would become the third of Elizabeth Taylor's seven husbands in 1957 and subsequently die in a plane crash. "Up we go, up the few steps at the Beverly Hills, down the hall, and I said I just wanted him to put his arms around me because I was really lonely tonight. I got in the bed fully clothed. I had a darling outfit on. I didn't want to take it off. And he was the most adorable man. He ordered cocoa or something real old-fashioned like that from room service and we had hot chocolate and we went to bed. He put his arms around me and we went to sleep," she said.

Burt Lancaster was also a supposed notch on her bedpost, albeit a shallow one. "Both had a nap. It was all about the idea of it," she said.

Mischievously, one afternoon Stritch dialed Mildred from the lushly landscaped patio at the Beverly Hills Hotel.

"Well, Mother, I got a new boyfriend. He's taller than I am, and successful—got money."

"Oh, Elaine, tell me, tell me. You're driving me crazy. Who is it?"

"Harry Belafonte," she said, naming her Jamaican American class-mate from the Dramatic Workshop who'd become the King of Calypso.

There was an aghast silence.

"That was my joke to get back at Mother," Stritch said. At a time when Catholics were considered second-class, to have her daughter dating a man of color, no matter how successful, was unthinkable to Mildred.

Around this time, Stritch decided to begin shaving a year off her age. "I'm twenty-nine, really twenty-nine," she declared to Leonard Lyons at Sardi's not long after her thirtieth birthday. "If I wanted to lie about it, I'd have said twenty-five. No girl who lies about her age picks twenty-nine."

It had become newly chic to enter psychoanalysis, particularly for ac-tors seeking their "motivation," and so she was now also dissembling in twice-weekly fifty-minute sessions with a psychiatrist named Dr. Weber, billed at twenty-five dollars apiece—the first at an hour perennially dif-ficult for her to face: 9:30 a.m. on Monday. "Not only am I late. I lie," Stritch confessed in writing. "Session after session, I lie. But he knows it and he's on the board of the New York Hospital and that's probably why he knows it—and we're off and running at Bay Meadows," the popular horse racing track in California. When she told her analyst the age she'd lost her virginity, "it was the only time I heard him clear his throat," she said. Stritch was sleeping with Gazzara, but guiltily. "The sex when it happened was terrific, but who knew how long it might be till the next time?" he recounted years later. "Here was a woman who loved sex but was afraid of it."

"When am I going to graduate?" she asked Dr. Weber.

"Go on," he said ("as they are wont to do," she noted dryly).

"No, I mean it. If you won't tell me that, what about a report card. Would it be possible for me to get a report card so I know how I'm doing?"

"Maybe when you're nominated," Dr. Weber said.

"For president?"

The sessions were also helping Stritch refine the material of her own life into narrative. Liz Smith was helping her with the would-be memoir, which Stritch told columnists she would call either *Shut Up and Drink Your Champagne* or *Poor Little Stritch Girl*. Both titles suggested a ruefully comic self-assessment, by someone who knew her circumstances were fortunate but had plenty of unsolvable agita.

The Oscars, the movie industry's top award ceremony, had been televised for the first time in 1953, and its pageantry was now nationally anticipated. Wanting to share in some of this stardust, the organizers of the Tonys invited local television cameras to their tenth event at the Plaza and announced nominees well ahead of time. It had been an exceptionally fine season in the theater. "We could have given forty awards, but had to stop somewhere," one voter told the *Times*. *Bus Stop* was nominated for outstanding play, for Clurman's direction, for Aronson's set—and for Stritch's performance, not Stanley's. Gazzara was nominated as well, for a leading role in their friend Michael V. Gazzo's play *A Hatful of Rain*, about a drug addict.

But none of these players won, giving the twenty-dollar-per-plate dinner dance presided over by Meyer Davis and his orchestra a deflated feeling for the little family of *Bus Stop*. (The rising producer Hal Prince was cheerier: the baseball musical *Damn Yankees*, which he'd worked on with Frederick Brisson and Robert E. Griffith, won seven awards.)

With Dr. Weber's help, Stritch was becoming more reflective about how she handled such disappointments. "You find you can't prove your worth either as a person or a performer, because of insecurity, so you spend dough so as to at least *feel* successful or important," she wrote to her parents in a long letter, asking forgiveness for a burst of profligacy. "Just as one drinks to forget his failure and *feel* successful and important."

She praised them as role models. "I find so much more encouragement in doing what is 'right' just from considering the kind of life the two of you have had together than I do from all the harping on what is or is not 'right,' I have tried to do what I think is right, to learn and to develop in every way through association—good and bad—nothing (I think) stays the same except perhaps your own will, if you're lucky." And she assured them that her solitude was merely a phase. Her work was "not so that I will have security 'alone' in the future because I am, first and foremost and let's all remember this, a woman," she wrote. "And I happen to be of the very optimistic opinion that somewhere somebody someone will love me, marry me and look after me. Have no fear for this, I don't." That said, "I would like to be in a position where I do not have to do bad TV scripts, bad movies, 2nd rate plays etc. to pay Saks." Getting down to business, Stritch wrote, "I'm in the hole for $3,594.05. Let's clear it up and in the future, have a lot of less expensive laughs."

Her eldest nephew, Frank Moran, Jr., remembered financial predicaments far more serious than this. "I remember my mom telling me, she got into trouble—twenty-five, thirty-five thousand dollars," he said. "Truth of the matter is, Elaine was a lot of action. Everybody worried about Elaine"—including his own father, Georgene's husband, who had been named partner in a successful certified public-accounting firm.

The extended Stritch family of Detroit had grown ever more prosperous in the 1950s and their neighborhood had been subject to the ugly practice of blockbusting: realtors warning white homeowners that property values were about to diminish because of an influx of black residents, advising them to sell, and then inflating prices to new buyers.

Though it was not in George Stritch's egalitarian character to yield to such pressures, he did want more yard space, and invested in four adjacent lots costing $20,000 apiece on Arlington Street in suburban Birmingham, shaded by pine trees. Eventually the families of both Elaine's older sisters, the Morans and the Boltons, would join them there, building a family compound through which their children could run freely.

Sally Hanley remembered visiting with her cousin Midge as little girls. "Ma Mil would take a bath every day and we would hightail it over there and sit in her luxurious bathroom. She would sit in the bathtub with the bubbles all around her and put her lotions on—that was the highlight of the day. Then we would go downstairs. They had a screened-in porch and Daddy George would be out working in the potting shed and come in all sweaty and dirty, and then she'd say 'George, get us all a cocktail and some corn curls.' He'd bring it all in, then he'd sit down and relax a little bit and we'd sit there with him and it was the best."

One lot had been reserved hopefully for the girls' Tante Elaine, but she would never claim it. To do so would have felt like failure to clear a bar, the height of which only she could gauge.

Stritch's *Bus Stop* dressing-room mate Anthony Ross had died unexpectedly in his sleep one night in October 1955 of a heart attack. Kent Smith, her former beau, replaced him. But she was thoroughly besotted with Gazzara and would not be distracted. "She was crazy about Ben and he was crazy about her," said the biographer and memoirist Patricia Bosworth, who was then an actress and worked with Stritch in her next Broadway play, *The Sin of Pat Muldoon*. "It was sort of a Catholic play, not a very good play, about this guy who was about to die and so on and calling up to his God—sisters constantly trying to comfort him," Bosworth said. Stritch called her "Sis" offstage as well, and both alumnae of the Sacred Heart, they would go to St. Malachy's Church on West Forty-Ninth Street, light candles, and pray that the show would be better. "She talked a lot about drinking and she wanted to teach me how to drink, and it didn't work," Bosworth said. "She wanted me to be a drinking buddy, above and beyond being a friend."

Muldoon closed after a mere five performances without much fanfare, and Stritch didn't mind at all. Thanks again to her agent Gloria Safier's moxie and connections, she had a far more exciting prospect looming. Daniel Selznick, a son of David O. Selznick, who had produced *Gone with the Wind* and *Rebecca*, had been one of the many people impressed by her performance as Grace in *Bus Stop*. He recommended her to his father for the cast of *A Farewell to Arms*, the second film version of the Hemingway novel (the first, from 1932, starred Helen Hayes and Gary Cooper).

The elder Selznick was envisioning this as a vehicle for his second wife, Jennifer Jones, even though she was in her late thirties and the protagonist as written was in her early twenties. This displeased Hemingway, who no longer had claim on the film rights. When Selznick announced a magnanimous promise of $50,000 to Hemingway from any profit, the author sent a telegram in reply suggesting the producer convert that amount to nickels "AND THEN SHOVE THEM UP YOUR ASS UNTIL THEY COME OUT YOUR EARS."

The hero, Frederic Henry, was to be played by Rock Hudson, the director was John Huston, and there were thousands of extras hired in the Italian Alps for the war scenes. Stritch's part was Miss Ferguson, a tough-talking nurse who has to take Frederic's temperature rectally. In one scene, she walks down the corridor with a remarkably protruding bosom, sits down, and then—turning away—unbuttons her blouse and deflates it by removing two liquor bottles for the patient smuggled within.

Ferguson also smokes and offers such knowing asides about men as "They're all alike. I mean they've all got habits. The chief one being they don't want to get married."

Liz Smith had been working for NBC on the forerunner of *The Tonight Show*—well treated, but paid only around $200 per week. Nervous about her assignment abroad, Stritch asked—as she had unsuccessfully during the tour of *Call Me Madam*—whether Smith would accompany her as a paid secretary, along with a new poodle she'd acquired and named Jimmy La Femme. This time her friend eagerly agreed.

Before the two women even arrived on set, Huston walked off the project, aggrieved at Selznick's micromanagement. The more malleable

Charles Vidor soon replaced him. Still excited for their foreign adventure, Smith and Stritch boarded a propeller plane for the eighteen-hour journey from New York City to Rome, stopping in Shannon, Ireland. The renowned Italian director and actor Vittorio De Sica was at the airport to welcome them. He tried to kiss Smith's hand and, as she reported, she shook it hard, "jerking him to his knees on the tarmac. Elaine smiled and swept on, saying over her shoulder, 'Who the hell was that?'"

The two friends were looking forward to staying in a luxurious-sounding hotel in the center of Rome, the Grand Palace. Grand, it wasn't, Smith said. "So we tried not to be disappointed." Their suite had three rooms and a balcony, onto which Stritch ran and began singing loudly from a popular revue showcasing young talent called *New Faces*: "You've never seen us before / We've never seen you before!" At the end of an evening's entertainment, it is proposed that this freshman class and the audience will be old pals.

Tourists came out onto the other terraces and peered up from the garden to listen. Stritch turned around to make her "exit" and the curtain rod fell down onto her foot, and so the two women then had to go find an Italian doctor.

But posters from *Three Violent People*, here called *I Violenti*, were dotted around the city, with Stritch's name on them near Charlton Heston's. "So everywhere we went, people thought she was a big movie star," Smith said. "And she wasn't at all. She was doing okay in the theater."

Smith's "secretary" description was merely for show. "I didn't do anything for Elaine, except field her dumped boyfriends," Smith said. But she did help Stritch keep a diary of daily happenings to be sent home to George and Mildred. She withheld little from them. "Dearest Mother and Daddy. Had a 7:45 call this morning, shooting all of my scenes the week of the curse. But that's the story of my life . . . Little too much party last night but it worked in my favor as I was very relaxed today."

She lunched with Hudson, Vidor, and Mercedes McCambridge, her replacement in *Woman Bites Dog*, who played the stern head nurse. "I think Mr. Selznick is crazy about me. He certainly seems to be anyway—interested in my opinions and me and my possibilities as a successful movie actress."

Giddy about Rome—"I think this is the vacation I've dreamed about ever since Glynn Court," she said, referring to one of the family's earliest and humblest residences in Detroit—Stritch insisted that she was cutting back on drinking, at least hard liquor. "Worked until eight last night, terribly tired. Couldn't even finish one martini, Daddy. I'm not kidding about that. Cocktails are slowly becoming a thing of the past with me. You sit down in a charming Italian restaurant and before you know it you're antipasto-ing it up and then wine is plunked smack in the middle of the table and that's it." She was enchanted with the food, the fiacres, the fountains, and the flirting with Hudson, whose wife conveniently was in California recovering from hepatitis. Stritch wrote home with American pride about the Italian girls flocking around him with giggles to get his autograph.

Lost on her, as well as his adoring female public, was the fact that Hudson was gay. Stritch speculated later that this was precisely why he enjoyed spending time with her, because especially with Gazzara in the background she was somehow "safe." What she had to offer was banter, a relief from his discussions of divorce and his difficult secret.

"Rock Hudson took me to lunch again," Smith typed for her. "Oops— also invited me to dinner next week. Double oops! And to think I can't find an English-speaking confessor."

Still, she couldn't help dressing carefully for their assignations, spending hundreds of lire at the salon of Roberto Capucci, a designer more florid than her accustomed Dior and Norell, to doll herself up. "Dinner tonight with Rock Hudson—he is so cute I can't stand it!" she scribbled to her parents. "Slowly discovering he is a confirmed atheist—and terribly interested in me. I tell you if it isn't one thing it's four others."

Liz Smith was pretty sure Rock Hudson preferred men romantically; they had a mutual friend in the business, and she had heard the rumors. "But I didn't tell Elaine he had a phony marriage," she said, at least not at first. "I thought, Why disillusion her? And she began to talk about him as a real possibility. And so I said, 'Well, I see you've been writing Mrs. Rock Hudson on a pad by your bed, and look, I've been doing the same.' And she thought that was very funny. And she wouldn't believe he was gay. And I'd say, 'Well, nevertheless, he is married, Elaine, if he's interested in you'—which he was, interested in being *entertained* by her."

Smith would come along to their dinners and was in turn being courted by one of Selznick's advisors, who got into a fight with the producer, breaking his glasses, and was in short order fired. "The tension in this movie was incredible," Smith said. But Stritch floated blissfully above the fray. She seemed to be fancying herself some variation of the princess protagonist in *Roman Holiday*, the 1953 movie that had made a star of Audrey Hepburn. "Had a dinner date with Rock in the new dress and I almost blew up with excitement—he is so adorable and I may just die any minute and sweet I can't tell you! We had a divine dinner and danced and drank champagne."

Through Safier's efforts, Stritch already had not only her next show lined up but her first true starring role in a musical called *Goldilocks*. "I guess life is pretty beautiful for me. And I have a lot to thank god for this year," Stritch wrote home, apologizing for skipping Mass on Ascension Thursday but noting that she had scheduled an audience with the Pope.

Moreover, Gazzara, who had borrowed her apartment back in New York, was on his way to Italy, first to visit Sicily and then to spend a week with Stritch. "Imagine the fun of seeing Rome all over again with an Italian who speaks the language of the people," she wrote.

When he arrived, in another fusillade of flashbulbs, Gazzara seemed unthreatened by Hudson's occasional squiring of his girlfriend. He bought Stritch a bathing suit, gave her a hundred dollars for spending money, and took her dancing with David Selznick and Jennifer Jones. "I won't get into some big discussion about Jennifer but she is some complicated girl," Stritch wrote to George and Mildred of Jones, an only child who'd had a ragtag show business upbringing and struggled with depression. "I like her and I guess she just should have grown up in our house with you."

Granted a car and a guide by Columbia Pictures, which had just released Gazzara's own film, *The Strange One*, he took Stritch to Capri and the Amalfi coast. Their drives inspired her to a flight of poesy: "The Mediterranean is a combination of the green in my rug at home and powder blue and all the little villages like Rovetta, Positano, Amalfi . . . all of their houses built up on the mountain are all the colors of the sea and their flowers are mostly powder blue and violet and deep orchid and lots of white—Jimmy's snoot was out the car window the entire trip."

The couple moved on to the island of Ischia in the Gulf of Naples, where the Selznicks had arranged rooms for each of them at the Albergo della Regina Isabella, a brand-new sprawling resort on the water, constructed by the publisher Angelo Rizzoli. "So beautifully elegant and everywhere you go some Neapolitan handsome son-of-a-bee is playing the mandolin and it's almost too much beauty," she exulted.

Liz Smith had returned home, but Stritch traveled up to Florence, marveling at the Arno and splurging on linens; and continued to Paris, where she stayed at the Hotel Raphaël on Avenue Kléber, across the street from where Germans were headquartered during the occupation. "Spooky," she wrote to George and Mildred. She was then summoned back to Rome to see the film's rushes. "Believe me I can take Rome with Selznick footing the bill for as long as possible." She navigated an awkward dinner with both Hudson and Gazzara. "I think Rock likes me but I'm just not going to think about that—anyway, it was fun!"

Hudson was like a supersized version of Gig Young, the Mildred-pleaser: more famous, more of a leading man, and six foot four. And this wasn't helping Stritch's reluctance to commit. "Ben is seeing about an annulment, but I've had a long serious discussion with him," she wrote to her parents. "If he gets it, it will be for him"—this was underlined twice—"not for me"—underlined thrice.

Clapping and cheering, Stritch watched Pope Pius XII, solemn and bespectacled, carried in on a chair the entire length of St. Peter's Basilica by fourteen men, as he reached out to bless children—"with the most beautiful hands incidentally." She was moved to tears. "I'll never get over it."

Using joking, affectionate signatures in her letters like "Elsa Maxwell" after the famous hostess, or "your little roman candle," Liz Smith reassured Stritch that people at home had not forgotten her. Smith reported that, according to a mutual friend, Kilgallen "really digs you, in spite of her bitchy ways." She also wrote, "Your name is still bouncing around New York," and "New York is like a big expensive car with no motor when you are away."

For the moment the motor was idle, and purring. "I'm not promising, but I think Europe has slowed me down a bit," Stritch wrote to her parents. "The nerves seem a bit calmer and life not quite so strained." Gradually she was deducing that Hudson was not a real romantic possibility, and not because of his wife. One male actor on the production had been consumed with heartbreak over him. "It was an interesting way to be introduced to the Land of Oz," Stritch said years later. Still, her affair with Gazzara had suffered from the public flirtation with another actor, and they had not received the expected papal dispensation. Sheilah Graham noted that the couple was "amusing the sippers at the Via Veneto's outdoor cafes—with their lovers' quarrels and every hour kiss and make up."

While together in New York they had attended an Actors Fund benefit showcasing the hit Lerner and Loewe musical *My Fair Lady*. At the exit, Rex Harrison, the star, was getting his coat and hat.

"Hello, Elaine," he said.

"Suddenly I was seven years old—scared to death," Stritch remembered. The older actor was "very English, very vesty, gray gloves, spats and all that junk, terribly terribly terribly. I wanted to disappear with him, forever and ever . . . amen. It was an emotional Niagara Falls for me."

Rattled, she introduced her escort as "Frank Gazzara."

"Jesus Christ," Gazzara thundered at her afterward. "If we'd been out and bumped into Jesus Christ I'd have remembered your name."

The couple had been living together, despite her family's disapproval. Then one night Stritch went out for a drink with Gig Young and didn't return home until eight in the morning. Gazzara lost his temper. "Whappo," she said years later. "I did get slugged, and that was the thing that scared me in the end." She would end their relationship not long after the Italian sojourn, though she was philosophical about his behavior, attributing it to Sicilian passion. "Isn't it interesting how sex can bring out all that masochistic, flagellation thing in a human being?" Stritch mused. "And yet if you hit somebody in life they go, 'oh, you brute.'"

They were maybe more like a pair of Hemingway lovers than those in the new film version of *A Farewell to Arms*, which was bloated at over two and a half hours. Selznick projected confidence, predicting to journalists the release might outgross his *Gone with the Wind* and giving Stritch a copy of the script bound in red leather, inscribed "For Elaine, with thanks for laughs—and with great admiration for her great talent." In December 1957 he cabled her, calling the San Francisco preview of the film a sensational success. "I SINCERELY AND STRONGLY BELIEVE THAT YOUR FINE WORK IN THIS ROLE IS GOING TO SEND YOUR CAREER ZOOMING," he wrote.

At the premiere in Southern California later that month, near the always incongruous sight of Christmas trees in Los Angeles, a bleacher full of fans jumped up and down, clapping. Bedecked with a white fur wrap and dangling diamond earrings, Jones, flanked by Selznick and Hudson, fluttered her right hand regally at them.

But Audrey Hepburn managed to upstage her. Watching Jones's realistic childbirth scene during the movie, she fainted on the stairs walking out of the theater; another audience member made it as far as the lobby before collapsing.

Reviewers, less squeamish, found the movie merely tedious. "A sense of deficiency and inconsequence . . . emerges from the over-long film," wrote Bosley Crowther of *The New York Times*, perceiving a lack of chemistry between the two stars. "The essential excitement of a violent love is strangely missing." He dismissed Stritch's acting as obvious; the *Los Angeles Times*, though, found her "notably clever."

And such was Selznick's power in Hollywood that at least one trade publication suggested that *A Farewell to Arms* was the front-runner in the Academy Awards race, giving Stritch 2–1 odds of being nominated for Best Supporting Actress. But she was not (Vittorio De Sica got the film's sole nomination, as Best Supporting Actor), and on Oscar night David Lean's *The Bridge on the River Kwai* won in seven categories. Thoroughly deflated, Selznick never produced another film, nor delivered on the bright future that he'd predicted for Stritch.

She appeared in two more movies before the decade was finished. One was *The Perfect Furlough* with the married actors Janet Leigh and Tony Curtis, who were associated with the group dubbed the Rat Pack by their friend Lauren Bacall. Frank Sinatra was "pack master," and, Stritch said, they tried to fix her up with him.

"After changing my outfit four or five times at the Beverly Hills Hotel over three or four Gibsons—or was it changing my outfit three or four times over four or five Gibsons?—I don't know. I was a nervous wreck," was the version she settled on with John Lahr for an early draft of her one-woman show. She told of being swept off to Curtis and Leigh's house on Summit Drive and finding "thirty or forty other guests watching 'my blind date' singing on his very own TV special as only he could."

"You can say what you want, but that son of a bitch can sing," Stritch said she joked to the guests.

"Frank, that's your date," Curtis told him.

"You're in the theater, right?" Sinatra asked.

"Yes, I am, Mr. Sinatra, that's right," Stritch replied.

"Yeah, well, people in the theater ain't goin' no place."

Stritch claimed she then faced him down, like an animal in the wild: "Well, you know what, Mr. Sinatra? For years now I've been wondering just where the hell you think you're going."

"Get her outta here!" he supposedly replied, with Leigh timidly complying and Stritch slinking off to Hamburger Hamlet with the chauffeur.

Even if braced by several Gibsons and with her tenuous new status as Rock Hudson's possible homewrecker, this would have been remarkable bravado for an actress of uneven record to summon toward the foremost singer of his day. But Stritch's fierce defense of her favored medium to a dismissive celluloid A-list was unquestionable in spirit. "It's really never-never Land," she would say of Hollywood. "The director and the camera can fool film audiences, but in the theater we can't put one thing over on the customers."

There was no grand premiere of *The Perfect Furlough* and Stritch walked out of a screening. "If I don't get the guy at the end, I can't watch it," she told Earl Wilson, a bon mot she liked so much she used an expanded version of it for her official biography in subsequent *Playbills*: "I prefer the theater to motion pictures and Hollywood doesn't seem a bit upset about it. I discovered that in the theater you don't have to look like Liz Taylor to get the guy at the end of the show."

Her frustration with the movie business was only punctuated by *Kiss Her Goodbye*, a lurid, low-budget psychological drama filmed in Cuba to save money. Stritch stayed at the Hilton and said she "visited all the dives

in Havana," stepping behind the bar at one, the Floridita, to make daiquiris and claiming to spend a long evening with Hemingway, though
any details quickly evaporated. Sharon Farrell, a young unknown from
the Midwest who was also in the movie, remembered her as an entertaining but somewhat dismissive colleague. "I want to try the Actors Studio,"
she told Stritch.

"Well, gee, it's really expensive, honey, why don't you go back to Sioux
City?" the older actress suggested. "You're going to get chewed up and
spit out here; you're too sweet for that."

Farrell felt that the norms of the 1950s would not permit Stritch,
outsize and a little odd, to flourish. "You know, today she would be a
big, huge star like Meryl Streep, but in those days they were looking
for 'pretty pretty,'" Farrell said. "When she had an edge and she was
sarcastic, that's when she was sexy, and they left that out of the movie."
Also, "she really wanted to come off as a leading, leading lady and so she
dumped her personality in the corner."

This would not be necessary on Broadway. There Stritch could continue to pursue her desire to be "the whole cheese" in a way filmdom's
casting directors would never allow. At its core, Hollywood—"that screwy,
ballyhooey Hollywood" as the old song went, "where any barmaid can be a
star maid"—has always been a place for reinvention, and she had no desire
to reinvent herself, only to have her core self affirmed and recognized.
Still she could be seduced by the city's ceaseless, simmering promise.
Landing in Los Angeles and swooshing directly to a palm-tree-ringed
retreat like the Beverly Hills Hotel, the Hotel Bel-Air, or the Chateau
Marmont would forever envelop her in a feeling of grandeur. "There is
this desire to lick this fucking town, to do something," she said. "And to
do something that makes everybody go 'Hey!' In the movies. You bet.
I mean, why not?"

5.

"I NEVER KNOW WHEN TO SAY WHEN"

Some theater actors had long tippled discreetly backstage to steady their nerves, a practice more permissible because of the generally nocturnal nature of their work. There were casualties, of course—most glaringly, John Barrymore, who died in 1942 of among other maladies cirrhosis, a pickled caricature of the idol he'd been. Stritch romanticized the old school regardless of their foibles and liked to quote Barrymore on meeting an audience's expectations: "An actor either is there, or he's dead."

In the mid to late 1950s, her drinking habit was further legitimized by both Lee Strasberg's Method, which held that actors must be relaxed in order to best perform, and thus sent many of them to therapy, booze, or both; and the Rat Pack, for whom cocktails were an essential prop. In his memoir Christopher Plummer describes "the gaggle of fast-living, fun-loving geese" that would gather at P. J. Clarke's or the Palace Grill, though at the latter they were mostly gander. Stritch when there "was representing, all on her own, most of the actresses in Equity," he wrote. "She could drink all of us stalwarts under the table and still be the leitmotif in the room."

In an era when women were still discouraged from drinking publicly (and were still banned from some taverns, like McSorley's Old Ale House in New York City), their inebriation associated with sexual licentiousness, this was bold of her—even as it also was evidence of a growing dependence. She showed no shame on the air either. "Perhaps the tinkling glass is a new trend in interviews," Kilgallen had suggested early in 1957, noting that Dean Martin seemed to be tipsy during an on-air lambasting of his former comedy partner, Jerry Lewis, and that Stritch appeared to be sipping a highball in an interview with the television host Mike Wallace on his new television show, *NightBeat*.

Her dreams of a big movie career dashed and her romance with Gazzara on the rocks, Stritch had decided to return to the dancing and singing that his mother had found so crass, having accepted the role of a silent-film actress trying to leave the business to join high society in *Goldilocks*, a new musical with a book by the critic Walter Kerr and his wife, Jean, to be directed by Walter. Stritch was determined not to be a mere witty sidekick. "I could go to Hollywood tomorrow and make a fortune," she said. "I'd do the young Eve Arden parts—the wisecracking girl who sits on the edge of the table and says, 'martinis, anyone?' But I don't want that for a life."

She had stayed in practice out of town, playing the sophisticated city slicker to Barbara Cook's country mouse in a summer-stock version of the musical *Plain and Fancy*, set in Amish country and composed by Albert Hague, with lyrics by Arnold B. Horwitt. Stritch would mine the song "This is All Very New to Me" years later to describe the experience of her first alcoholic drink, with its chilling similarity to falling in love: "the room is reeling," and the narrator only wants to know how to make the "funny-like, milk-and-honey-like" sensation continue.

But the American musical form had taken two large leaps since *Plain and Fancy* was first performed in 1955. One was the tremendously successful adaptation of a classic English play, George Bernard Shaw's *Pygmalion*, into *My Fair Lady*. Another was *West Side Story*, based loosely on *Romeo and Juliet* but bracingly topical, drawing from the growing problem of gang wars in New York and other American cities. It had been created by what was, in retrospect, a dream team, including the now established figures Leonard Bernstein and Jerome Robbins, the playwright Arthur Laurents, and the producer Hal Prince. And then there were the contributions of a clever young hopeful named Stephen Sondheim, who'd grown up in New York City and been mentored by Oscar Hammerstein, a family friend, after his parents' divorce. Though Sondheim had gone on to study music at Williams College and was eager to compose, Hammerstein convinced him that the experience of writing lyrics for these more seasoned players was worth reserving that ambition for a while.

"The radioactive fallout from *West Side Story* must still be descending on Broadway this morning," wrote Kerr, then critic at the *New York Herald Tribune*, after the opening, praising "the most savage, restless, electrifying dance patterns we've been exposed to in a dozen seasons." But the rest of his review was not so positive, and Laurents fired off a typically touchy letter to Kerr, lodging among other protests that the latter man had a conflict of interest since he was also "a worker in the theatre." Walter and Jean had already collaborated for the stage several times, including a hit revue called *Touch and Go* that appeared two years after *Angel in the Wings*. "It is impossible to look to a critic whose objectivity is open to serious question," Laurents wrote.

Yet the Kerrs would not be deterred from trying a full-scale musical, with its potentially greater financial returns. And to Stritch they had given, she said proudly, "her dream part," one for a "real leading woman."

Jean and Walter must have seemed exceptionally well positioned to offer Stritch this chance. They were *the* New York City media power couple of the mid-twentieth century—though they were technically commuters, living with four small sons (they later added a fifth, plus a daughter) in Larchmont, in what Walter called a "neo-gingerbread" Tudor-Spanish manse at 1 Beach Avenue, looking out over the Long Island Sound: once a stables and carriage house, now with coffered wooden ceilings and beams, sleeping porches, gargoyles, a statue of St. Francis, a twenty-pound door knocker, and a thirty-two-bell carillon that played "Carmen" at noon. In sensibility, if not scale, it recalled 18210 Birchcrest Drive.

Walter and Jean had met when he, eleven years older, was her professor at Catholic University in Washington, D.C.; she—taller, freckled, and apprehensive—often declared that being Catholic was the most important thing about her. Earlier, Walter had courted the future *New Yorker* staffer Maeve Brennan, disappointing her. Perhaps this was why he ever achieved a byline in that magazine; Jean's submissions were repeatedly rejected as too personal or lightweight, though Walter did earn a measure of recognition there when one humorist noted how often his copy, produced on tight deadline and therefore not always with the ballast of dinner, contained allusions to food: "Something was eating him, or, rather he wasn't eating something."

Still, Walter Kerr, who a friend once said resembled "Richard Burton after a night of heavy drinking," had become one of the most respected critics in an era when their ranks were as well-fortified as the gossip columnists: Brooks Atkinson at *The New York Times*, Ward Morehouse at *The New York Sun*, George Jean Nathan at the *New York Journal-American*, and many more. Of these men, and they were nearly all men—with paunches that ballooned in the ceaseless shuttling between theater and typewriter—Kerr had an appealing combination of considerable erudition, lyricism, and a popular touch. He is widely credited with dismissing the 1951 John Van Druten play *I Am a Camera* with the immortal line "Me no Leica" (though his original printed review was quite considered, and favorable).

His wife, in her thirties, was arguably even more successful, certainly in Middle America. Along with being a playwright, she was a coveted writer for the "seven sisters" magazines, like *Ladies' Home Journal* and *McCall's*, that were then a regular and vital part of American housewives' lives (though shortly to be excoriated by Betty Friedan in *The Feminine Mystique*), as well as general-interest publications such as *The Saturday Evening Post*. "Ever since I was first exposed to a kitchen full of pots and pans I've been trying to avoid housework," Jean Kerr said, mildly foreshadowing Friedan's identification of "the problem that has no name." "I honestly think that is the main reason I keep writing these things."

Correspondence on sprightly letterhead flew between her, agents, and editors, arranging lucrative placement of pieces such as a parody of *Lolita* called "Can This Romance Be Saved" and a satire of Françoise Sagan's *Bonjour Tristesse*. Once the editor Clay Felker, then working at *Esquire*, paid Jean a lavish $2500 for a five-hundred-word piece about "station-wagon living" to run in a supplement he was overseeing for *The New York Times*.

Purportedly written from this station wagon parked a few blocks away from her house, the only place where she could get some privacy, her short humorous essays about the Kerrs' suburban life with their children were very popular and had in 1957 been gathered by Doubleday in a book called *Please Don't Eat the Daisies*. It was a Book-of-the-Month Club selection and number one bestseller, and MGM bought the film rights for Doris Day, then the avatar of the all-American housewife.

With her husky voice, lit cigarettes, and affection for last call, Stritch was the very opposite of Day—she was Night. And to *Goldilocks*, an already overcomplicated story that bore little metaphorical relation to its fairy-tale title, she brought, inevitably, additional complication.

First there was the problem of the male lead. When her romance with Gazzara was in full flush she had helped persuade the Kerrs to sign him, to the delight of the columnists. "Ben asks only that the title be changed to *I Love Goldilocks*," Stritch had bragged to one. But Gazzara was not a trained singer and never comfortable in the role, and once the couple broke up he asked the Kerrs to release him from his contract. "You will not need luck with *Goldilocks*," he encouraged. "It will be a great success."

The couple settled upon another non-singer, Barry Sullivan (the approach had worked with Rex Harrison in *My Fair Lady*), with Russell Nype from *Call Me Madam* and a gamine actress named Pat Stanley as the second leads. Leroy Anderson, a composer of light orchestral music, was contracted for the score, and the storied choreographer Agnes de Mille the dances. De Mille had some hesitations, wishing generally for more creative control, as Jerome Robbins had achieved. She wrote to Walter after he reviewed a revival of *Brigadoon*, which she had choreographed: "Composing at the mercy of a star chamber decision is so agonizing that I absolutely dread going to work again with producers and directors and writers who have the privilege of mutilating anything I do to suit either their vanity or their ambition, but that's how it's been and that's why the boys insist on positions of power—and that's why I shall have to try although it will be much more difficult for a woman and much more unpleasant." Her experience directing Rodgers and Hammerstein's *Allegro* in 1947 had not gone well, with Hammerstein eventually seizing control of the scripted portions.

Even when transported to faraway settings, the average Joe and Jane could relate to Rodgers and Hammerstein's work. But *Goldilocks* was a story for show-business insiders about show-business history and convoluted with attempted sophistication. It was a real late-1950s product, a luxuriously appointed, shiny tricked-out Cadillac of a musical—"a very businesslike operation," Nype called it—with scores of singers and dancers, elaborate sets including a scene of "Egypt on the Hudson," costumes by Castillo of Lanvin, and the leading lady (in Jean's words) "borne aloft in a giant slice of silvery moon." And perhaps inevitably for a couple who seemingly had it all—a happy marriage, adorable children, and careers that were both remunerative and prestigious—many were watching eagerly to see if it would crash.

Jean was ready for this schadenfreude. "Think how it would gladden the hearts of millions to have *Goldilocks* a real bomb," she wrote to her sister-in-law, also named Jean Kerr. And Walter, as both cowriter and director, had to endure more than his usual share of hate mail. "We are all waiting with sated breath for the pure marvel of wit, originality and just pure mid-Western shit you and your horsey wife are ramming down our throats next season," wrote one theatergoer.

Girding against more opprobrium, the couple applied themselves with extra discipline. "We are working frantically night and day (I mean that most literally) on *Goldilocks*," Jean wrote her agent in the summer of 1958. She had a secret: she was pregnant again.

Less intimidated by the squaresville Kerrs than by Abbott and Clurman, and older than she had been when working with the last pair of parental surrogates, the Hartmans, Stritch challenged the writers at every opportunity. Nype said that "Walter would tell her to do something and she'd fuss about it—she wouldn't take direction." These creatures of schedule rarely had anything harder than beer—"Jean does not as a rule drink a cocktail," her agent had noted in arranging a lunch with the editor of *Ladies' Home Journal*—and their star's drinking was more troublesome.

"She was a very difficult person," Pat Stanley said of Stritch. "She was very strong, very strong-willed; she had a huge sense of herself in operating terms but I think it was covering a great insecurity." Stanley believed the Kerrs were under their star's thumb. "I feel like Elaine really dragged them around because it was new for them, because they hadn't done any project like this before and it was a big deal for Walter to be directing, and she seemed more experienced. I think she called the shots a lot and they wanted to make it work for her."

With the detachment that allowed her to process the quotidian into wry magazine copy, Jean remained optimistic. "Walter gripes and grouses and stews and frets but my considered opinion is that everything is coming along fine," she wrote to her sister-in-law. "Barry Sullivan is marvelous in the part—and really worth waiting for. We saw Elaine in costume yesterday and she looked dazzling and as we've told you, she is perfect for the part but I had started to worry about how she would look. Well, she is going to look great. The little dancer, Pat Stanley, who plays the lead is so charming that my only worry is that she will get all the notices."

This fear proved well-founded. *Goldilocks* had its tryout at the Erlanger Theater in Philadelphia in September 1958 and the audience reaction was a mixture of confusion, disappointment, and program-fanning impatience. Stritch, who had come down with a cold and was already steamed about winding up billed under the title and after Sullivan, had trouble projecting her hoarse voice to the balcony. The orchestra played too loudly. At one show, prop snow that was supposed to fall during the finale was instead dispensed during an earlier sunny scene in a barn, leaving Stritch to say "It's snowing" when nothing was happening. "The audience went out whistling the sets," Jean Kerr admitted.

The notice in *The Philadelphia Inquirer* was particularly devastating. "This big, expensive musical comedy turned out to be a big, expensive frustration," the reviewer wrote. "With all sorts of potentialities, it was exposed as formless, unintegrated, filled with startling non sequiturs and musical comedy clichés."

"OPENED SLOPPY BUT WE ARE WORKING SAY PRAYERS," Jean and Walter cabled his sister.

In those days dedicated theatergoers often offered detailed written feedback, a more civilized precursor to Yelp, and one audience member from the Erlanger sent a three-page typed letter to Kerr suggesting Stritch's discomfort in the part. "I got the feeling that she wanted to run, but professional that she is, she stuck it out," the Philadelphian wrote. "What did the audience remember? The dancers and Miss Stanley for they made *Goldilocks* the success it was opening night."

Stritch, having already worked with the best that musical theater had to offer, concluded she was now in the hands of amateurs. "She was the only one that knew what she was doing, so the whole thing became a dance concert," the actress said of the choreographer Agnes de Mille. "She kept cutting the book and putting in another dance number and every time I started to get off the ground with a joke somebody would twinkletoes onto the stage."

With her younger female castmate effectively eating her porridge, Stritch could not play benevolent older sister, as she had to Chita Rivera during the tour of *Call Me Madam*. "She just hated me," Stanley believed. "It's because I was doing a part, the kind of cute comic ingénue that always wins the audience over. Her character was not the least bit vulnerable. I think what was intended of course was that she be discovered as this vulnerable person, even though she didn't come on that way. But that just sort of never happened in the script. And therefore she was just very unhappy with my being there. She did everything she could to get any new scenes for me removed."

There was an unexpected visitor to the proceedings in Philadelphia, one who came curious to get an early look at what the famous Kerrs had concocted. He was Noël Coward, the pillar of the English theater who at almost fifty-nine was just beginning to show some cracks. This wasn't the first time he and Stritch had been under the same "high ceiling"; in 1955, when she was starring in *Bus Stop*, they'd both attended a party at the Metropolitan Club on East Sixtieth Street, lustily singing "Happy

Birthday" to the Hollywood journalist Radie Harris. But this was the first time he'd seen her as a leading lady.

A prolific polymath who acted, wrote, directed, composed, sang, pattered, and also painted—he was nicknamed the Master—Coward had become as concentrated, dry, and powerful a distillation of England as the gin he favored (a perfect martini, he once said, was made by filling a glass with the stuff and "waving it in the general direction of Italy"). From a lower-middle-class background, he'd been on the stage since age ten and by his wits had come to embody, if not almost caricature, an idea of refinement complete with silk dressing gown, slippers, and long-handled cigarette holder. He had enjoyed American musicals since visiting the country in the 1920s and borrowed some of their techniques to leaven some of the traditionally stodgy English forms.

Now he was undergoing an intellectual assault of sorts from the Angry Young Men, a loose consortium of writers led by John Osborne, a playwright who had emerged after World War II questioning Great Britain's traditional class structure with "kitchen-sink" dramas that explored raw emotions in mundane settings. Coward, who thought theater should amuse and soothe and permit mental escape, found these plays distinctly off-putting.

A creature of the drawing room who preferred cups of tea (or glasses of sherry), metaphorically speaking, rather than the hurling of crockery, Coward had been bewildered at the mounting hostility to his work. But he proved a resilient and inventive showman, developing a popular cabaret act in Las Vegas that was applauded by the Rat Pack. His general affection for and curiosity about Americana did not extend to the suburban scribblings of Jean Kerr, but he respected her husband's criticism (though was likely still simmering over Walter's indifferent review of a recent revival of his play *Nude with Violin*).

"How does an eminent critic of his caliber have the impertinence to dish out such inept, amateurish nonsense?" Coward wrote of *Goldilocks* in the diary he kept for posterity, calling the musical "idiotic and formless," de Mille's ballets "not really good enough," and marveling at the extravagance of the production's reported $500,000 cost to date. "I must say I couldn't have believed it if I hadn't seen it for myself. It will probably get kindly reviews from his gallant colleagues when it opens on Broadway, but I don't think anything could save it. Serve him and his giggling wife bloody well right."

The one member of the cast he did not find "lamentable," he wrote, was Stritch. Plagued by the problems of *Goldilocks*, she was in her dressing room backstage having what she called "a very, very, very large Scotch" when he arrived and rapped on her door. "Any leading lady who doesn't do a double take when a nine-foot bear asks her to dance is my kind of actress," he said.

To the producer Robert Whitehead, Coward later said, or so he would gallantly convey to Stritch, "I am going to be very, very honest with you. You have no book, no score. And you have a brilliantly talented young actress who is sitting in her dressing room drinking a Dewar's and soda and crying. Something is wrong."

Word of *Goldilocks*'s troubled tryout period had reached Kilgallen in New York. "They say she simply isn't being allowed to be her dynamic self," she wrote sympathetically of Stritch, "and oddly enough, she's behaving with unbelievable docility, on the theory that the show's the thing, not her own triumph as a personality." The show lumbered to Boston, where Julius Novick of *The Harvard Crimson* proclaimed that "*Goldilocks* would be a delight if only somebody in authority would put the entire evening in the hands of Miss de Mille, and send Mama and Papa Kerr back to the woods." He reported that Sullivan was to be jettisoned, replaced by Don Ameche, a veteran of Hollywood, radio, and television. A family man, like Nype, Ameche refused to carouse with Stritch, as Sullivan had. He was also four inches shorter, and she injured herself adjusting to the new clinch angles of their love scenes, dislocating vertebrae and having to wear a neck brace for several days.

In preparation for the Broadway opening she had posed somewhat awkwardly on the November 1958 cover of *American Hairdresser*, her "goldilocks" bleached with Instant Whip Clairol Crème Hair Lightener and swirled into something resembling one of the molded salads popular at the time. Jean Kerr was souring on her star. "Elaine Stritch was quoted in a column tonite to the effect that if *Goldilocks* isn't a hit she'll take in washing," she wrote her sister-in-law, adding dryly: "I'll send her the first load."

With de Mille and the Kerrs hardly speaking, the musical prepared to open at the freshly renovated Lunt-Fontanne Theater on West Forty-Sixth Street in Manhattan. The playwright and director Moss Hart was in the lobby on opening night, and smiled when someone identified him as "Kitty Carlisle's husband."

"I understand they scrapped $70,000 worth of costumes," the Broadway columnist Burt Boyar overheard someone say. He noted that it was strange, since the play was set in 1913, to have Stritch uttering snappy modern lines like (applicably to herself) "Actors don't marry. They sublet."

It couldn't have been easy for Brooks Atkinson, Kerr's rival at the *Times* but also his friend, to file his review that evening, which was read at a party thrown by Gloria Safier at a restaurant she co-owned, Brown's, on East Sixty-First Street.

"*Goldilocks* is a bountiful handsome musical comedy with an uninteresting book," Atkinson began. The plot he found "loose, vague and trifling" and the direction "organized" and "lively" but "not vigorous or versatile." Still, "Miss Stritch can destroy life throughout the country with the twist she gives to the dialogue," he wrote. "She takes a wicked stance, purses her mouth thoughtfully, and waits long enough to devastate the landscape." He declared her a "thoroughbred" in her singing and everything else.

The show was not an outright flop. "It ran for six months but it never took off because the audience never really bought Ameche and Stritch as a romance at all: they didn't care, they didn't feel it," Nype said. Except during her wistful solo:

> The skies are stormy now
> My dreams all bore me now
> No candle lights the lonely nights that lie before me now
> I say it's done, it's done, it's over—Amen!

But then again, and again, and again
I find I never know when, I never know when to say when.

Stritch next ran into Coward at a "sweet party," as he called it in his diary, given by Leonard Lyons and his wife, Sylvia. "It was really great fun, predominantly Jewish, and a glorious mélange of people and talent from David Merrick to Abe Burrows," Coward wrote. "There was music in the air and Arthur Schwartz and Howard Dietz played and sang lovely old songs, and Elaine Stritch, sweet but forgot every lyric."

She tickled a certain kind of fancy for him: a woman brilliant, empathic, and versatile, but underestimated. And with his sun-seeking, nattiness, and dry wit, Coward epitomized her loftiest dreams of the good life.

In early February 1959 Stritch met with Earl Wilson at Dinty Moore's to drum up publicity for *Goldilocks*, gossiping about Merman, pitying her own thumbs-twiddling understudy, and joking that Robert Whitehead had busted her with a bottle of beer on her dressing table and she'd made the excuse that it was what was used to set her hair. Still, she admitted, "There are times when if I didn't have a little brandy in the tea and honey, I don't know what I'd do."

The show would close in three weeks, but its copy-happy star remained a columnist's dream. "I bet Elaine Stritch, like Tallulah Bankhead, talks in her sleep," Wilson wrote, "because there isn't time to say all she wants while she's awake."

In the spring came the Tonys, held again at the Waldorf-Astoria. In a choreographic changing of the guard, de Mille's balletic dances were snubbed, the award going instead to Bob Fosse's jazzy ones for *Redhead*. Nype tied for the Best Supporting Actor honor, his second after *Call Me Madam*, with Leonard Stone of *Redhead*; and bitterly for Stritch, Pat Stanley won for Best Featured Actress in a musical. "Of course she was very put off that she didn't get a Tony award," Nype said of his leading lady. "She was a bit of a spoiled brat."

Themselves denied nominations entirely, the Kerrs felt the musical a fiasco and agreed that they would never speak of it to each other again. Jean went back to writing magazine essays and humorous books, popular as ever on the ladies club circuit; Walter focused anew on reviews. In 1966 the *Herald Tribune* folded, and he was hired to work alongside Atkinson at the *Times*, eventually winning a Pulitzer. Without him, Jean wrote a play, *Mary, Mary*, that was a critical and commercial success. She also made tart lemonade from her *Goldilocks* experience in an essay called "Out of Town with a Show, Or What to Do Until the Psychiatrist Comes," later anthologized in her book *The Snake Has All the Lines*. It contained nothing overtly mean about Stritch. "As I recall, the closest we came to an actual problem was Elaine's wistful complaint that the pressures of kissing both leading men had upped her consumption of Chap-Sticks to two a day," Kerr wrote. But a different passage hinted at deeper regrets. "Some performers that should never, under any circumstances, be cast are: 1. Known alcoholics. You will have trouble enough with the unknown ones."

Thereafter Jean Kerr avoided Stritch when in town, going so far as to change her table when sitting at Sardi's if the actress came in. "Walter would have to go along with it," Stritch remembered years later. "Then he'd come up later and say 'I'm sorry' and I'd say 'never mind, it didn't bother me.' And of course it did bother me."

She maintained resentful feelings toward the couple for a long time. "Walter couldn't direct, and she a pain in the ass," she said. "Every time I got up to do anything on the stage I felt she resented the fact that I could do it. That's a wonderful feeling with the person—it's her show! Wouldn't you think that she'd be encouraging me and making me feel wonderful so that her material would live and work? No way. She couldn't stand me. Godawful."

When Jean appeared in 1961 on the cover of *Time* magazine, Stritch, interviewed for the article as "the lone, whinnying exception" to actors who would not criticize the Kerrs, called Jean and Walter "the classroom mom and dad." Boldly or imprudently for someone who would continue to be receiving his scrutiny, she said, "Once in rehearsal I got into a fight with someone, and Walter walked right down the aisle and shouted up at me: 'Elaine, go to your dressing room!' Dig that. The teacher complex."

And his wife? "She always talks as though she'd memorized her own writing. You want to hear Jean say, 'Gee, you were great, Elaine.' Instead, you get nothing but humor 24 hours a day. They're a clean-cut couple. She drinks beer and he goes in for Cokes and Hershey bars. Jean should swing a bit with a Gibson and find herself."

Stritch's own drinking habit was now so central to her life that she had gone from dating actors to men in the liquor trade. There was Lou Stoecklin, a married whiskey representative; and then there was Joe Allen, an apprentice at P. J. Clarke's who was aspiring to open a place of his own.

Dapper and with bedroom eyes, Allen resembled a young Humphrey Bogart. "The years that I was working there, not because I was there, but they were crazy," he said of Clarke's. "I'd only been working there about maybe a month, I walked into the back room, it was five, five-thirty in the evening, so the lunch crowd was gone, all the tables emptied out, the till was kind of quiet. Sitting at three separate tables, all alone, waiting for someone else, was Marilyn Monroe, Frank Costello, and Hubert Humphrey. And I said, 'I'm in the right place!'"

Allen and Stritch began talking during her own frequent visits, and then spending evening hours together. "From my vantage point anyway, the thing that was most interesting to me about her was, she was chronically drinking, and I'm a kid, struggling, working at a bar—I guess I'm seven years younger than she is—she would never pick up a check," Allen said. "She just wouldn't. She couldn't!"

Still he remembered Stritch as a lot of fun, walking down the street with a martini in a paper coffee cup. And he was impressed by her celebrity connections. Once the two of them went into Goldie's, a joint on Fifty-Third Street, and found Merman.

"Stritch!" she hollered. "How's your uncle, the Pope?"

Low on funds at the time, Allen informally moved in with Stritch. "The age differential would prevent it from going too far," he rationalized. "I remember going home at four in the morning, both of us drunk," he said. "And she'd make an audition the next morning at eleven, she could do that." She was hardly domestic but "now that I think of it, she could cook. Yeah, we didn't stay home that many nights to remember. But yeah, she could cook, at least basics."

One night, he was surprised to find another man there, rattling around the apartment. It was a young actor named Warren Beatty, who was trying to get a foothold in theater; Stritch had invited him to crash on the couch.

Elaine's niece Sally also met Beatty once, when she was thirteen, at a picnic in Central Park with his then girlfriend Joan Collins while he was looking at the script for the Elia Kazan movie *Splendor in the Grass*. Sally's parents, Sally and Tom Bolton, had driven to New York to go on a yacht with rich friends and dropped her with Tante Elaine. They all met at a bar Allen had opened, a predecessor to what would become his bedrock place on Forty-Sixth Street. "And Elaine is flying," Sally remembered. "She's been having the cocktails and stuff."

"We can't leave her here," her mother told her father. But young Sally, "conscious of this little worrisome thing," the designated adult not being quite in command, knew they wanted to proceed with their plans.

Joe Allen went up to Sally's mother. "Everything is going to be fine," he told her.

Stritch and Allen took Sally to a French restaurant and fed her piles of delicious food. The young girl wanted to go for a walk in the fresh air afterward, but Stritch felt too protective. "She would not let me out of her sight." They were sharing Elaine's bed, and in the middle of the night, Sally jolted awake, suddenly ill. Sally was "throwing up like crazy all over the place," and her aunt "was so wonderful, in the bathroom with me: cleaning up, changing the sheets."

With no apparent self-consciousness, Stritch took her niece along to watch as she helped a young actress named Mary Doyle figure out how to audition as a replacement for the Louise/Gypsy Rose Lee role in Merman's new star vehicle, *Gypsy*. "Elaine was trying to teach her how to do it in a cute sexy way." Then for a special treat, as Stritch's uncle Howard had done for little Elaine, to see a musical: Jackie Gleason, squat and mustachioed and jigging in a straw hat with a chorus of amused men in *Take Me Along*, which was playing at the Shubert Theater, and they saw

Merman at Sardi's, along with Natalie Wood and Robert Wagner. "That was just heavenly, heavenly," Sally said.

Next it was to the Stork Club. Here were the menu items to settle agitated Midwestern stomachs: pot roast and baked potato and peach melba for dessert. The waiters brought a doll as a gift to Sally, with a dome over it—"I looked about ten, I was a slow bloomer," she said—and her face fell. "Elaine got the radar and the next thing I knew that was swept away and a thing of perfume appeared."

Sally was used to her aunt's not wearing a bra, but she was surprised on Sunday morning when, after sleeping late, Elaine threw on her mink coat over her nightie, or possibly nothing, à la Elizabeth Taylor in *BUtterfield 8*. Aunt and niece then got into a cab and went to church.

"I was horrified and delighted," Sally said. "So terrified that the coat would come off."

Sitting in the audience of *Goldilocks* one night had been Stephen Sondheim, the young lyricist for *West Side Story* and now *Gypsy*. "I wanted to see Don Ameche," he said. He was working on songs for a TV musical called *The Jet-Propelled Couch*, adapted from Dr. Robert Linder's book *Fifty-Minute Hour*, about psychotherapy.

Sondheim had been raised on Central Park West before he moved to Bucks County, Pennsylvania, with his mother, reentering New York social circles easily after graduating with high honors from Williams College. He believes he met Stritch in person at a party given by George Trescher, a fund-raiser (or "fun-raiser," as the tabloids put it) with many celebrity associations. "I don't know how we hit it off, but I'll give you a 90 percent chance that I sat at that piano, as I did at those parties—because that was my function, was to play songs," he said. "And she came over and started to kibitz with me is my guess, with a glass in her hand, and we became that kind of couple."

Stritch remembered him gallantly walking her home from a party one night. "I had never met him before; he wasn't the big wheel that he is now," she said in 2008. She described them stopping at Donohue's on Lexington Avenue near Sixty-Fourth, just the sort of dark-wood-paneled, green-awninged pub she favored. "I say today that I'd be scared to talk to Steve about anything except A-flat. But that night we got out and had a drink and left that bar at a quarter till five. We were there for three hours. So we have got a lot to say to one another. But I have got to have twenty-five scotches in me in order to do it, and so does he."

Sondheim has no memory of this particular evening, but he does remember running into her at parties—Christmas parties, Oscar parties—given by Charles Hollerith, a college chum of his who, like Elaine, was from Michigan. "Elaine and I would always be there—not together—but we'd meet there, and we'd end up with her on the piano bench and me on the piano and about three people left in the room, there at three in the morning," Sondheim said. He would play "He Was Too Good to Me," a song about a departed sweetheart that they both loved. It had been cut from a 1930 Richard Rodgers and Lorenz Hart musical called *Simple Simon* but became a jazz standard, with a dolorous reference to "sad eyes out in the rain" and wondering "who's gonna make me gay now."

For two people who would come to be called cynics—in different ways, both highly sociable and protective of their solitude—this was a curiously sweet, yearning tune.

Sondheim put *The Jet-Propelled Couch* aside after getting an offer to write the music for *Gypsy*, based on the memoirs of the striptease artist Gypsy Rose Lee, whom Stritch's reporter-character had evocatively recounted interviewing in the 1952 revival of *Pal Joey*. But since Merman hadn't been pleased with her last musical, *Happy Hunting*, which had been composed by an unknown, she instead insisted on Jule Styne, who had a reputation as one of the most dependable and versatile composers around. Sondheim was relegated again to lyrics duty, a position he accepted because Styne was also cheerfully collaborative, and because Laurents and Robbins from *West Side Story* were also attached to the project.

Everything that the Kerrs' *Goldilocks* had done wrong, *Gypsy*, one year later, would do right. It also went back in time, to the vaudeville and burlesque eras. But its plot of two children developing under the control of Rose Hovick, their fierce, frustrated stage mother, was drawn in bold, definitive strokes; its star, Merman, utterly in command; and she chewed the scenery rather than being choked by it. (At the Tonys, however, *Gypsy* would be defeated by a tie between Rodgers and Hammerstein's more uplifting *The Sound of Music*, their last musical together, and *Fiorello!*)

Stritch was at the "gypsy" rehearsal, or final run-through, of *Gypsy*, and found herself coming undone at the point where elder daughter and mother confront each other about the latter's motivations.

"I thought you did it for me, Momma."

"'I thought you did it for me, Momma. I thought you did it for me, Momma,'" Rose repeats sarcastically before beginning one of the most effective eleven o'clock numbers of all time, "Rose's Turn," which Sondheim and Robbins had hammered out together one night, patching it in place with scraps of Styne's music.

"I started bawling right there," Stritch said. "I mean, the nuances in that goddamned thing. To really see that real, real feeling of mother and daughter like that—oh, terrifying, isn't it? Terrifying."

Like the children in *Gypsy*, she feared that if she didn't "let me entertain you, let me make you smile," she would not be seen or loved, like her more conventionally pretty, societally conforming older sisters. Mildred was not exactly a Madame Rose figure, but she had muted her own talent for performance, and was always trying to push her daughter ("Is that a big part? How many numbers?" she'd ask of *Bus Stop*) into procuring more stage time. Well into her thirties, even though Elaine rebelled against Mildred, she continued to slightly fear and want to please her mother. And in her single-minded pursuit of show business at the expense of settled domestic life, she could also see herself in Hovick, that ladylike yet shameless creature who sweeps not only the leftovers from a favorite Chinese restaurant into her purse, but the silverware as well.

Though she was ambivalent about television, Stritch could not resist accepting parts when she wanted to replenish her coffers. It felt somewhat natural to her: "I've been living a situation comedy all my life," she said.

In early 1960, she traveled to L.A. to film a TV series called *My Sister Eileen*, the latest of several creative works to be inspired by a series of short stories in *The New Yorker* by Ruth McKenney. The real Eileen had been married to the novelist Nathanael West, and died with him in a car accident. Show business constantly recycles certain material, and there had already been movies, a play, a radio play, and a musical (*Wonderful Town*, by Leonard Bernstein, Betty Comden, and Adolph Green) based on the stories. Stritch was to play Ruth Sherwood, a writer who moves to Manhattan with her sister, an actress.

The show tried to get a grip on that persistent creature, the "career gal." In one scene, a photographer from a magazine called *Bon Vivant* visits for a profile and the Ruth character quickly realizes it's a girlie magazine and sends him packing. When a sexist boss tries to get her to buy lunch, she asks, "Would you send Edna Ferber for coffee? Pearl Buck for sandwiches? Well then, Ruth Sherwood isn't going either," as a line of younger women poke their heads out from doorways and cheer.

To reporters Stritch was candid about her exasperation with television, which she found generally too hasty. "The pace, the lack of rehearsal time and the constant activity make you feel like a 'victim' instead of an actress," she told one. "You can't put your best foot forward and it's hard to get with it intellectually. Yet I'd be jerky not to get with it. The rewards are so great." CBS had flown her back to New York for a promotional appearance and put her up in the St. Regis Hotel. "For a girl who's usually thought of as the best friend of the maid at a sit-down dinner, this is fun," she said. And the tedium of duties on set could always be ditched for a solo prowl in the "real" world. "When everybody is chasing you around about costumes and things," Stritch told another reporter, "the best thing to do is cut out, head for a saloon, and talk with a bartender."

She was either oblivious or defiant of the different standards for female drinkers shown in *Ocean's 11*, when Dean Martin has to let his lurching fellow Rat Packer Shirley MacLaine down gently in the parking lot. "When a woman drinks it's as if an animal were drinking, or a child," the French novelist Marguerite Duras wrote sagely years later.

Dick Cavett, who had moved to New York and was trying to make his way in stand-up comedy, remembered Stritch bursting with an entourage like the Marx Brothers into a Greenwich Village dinner party hosted by the actress Jane White. "In comic-strip language it would say 'vroom into the room,'" he said. "I thought, God, it's that woman from New Haven."

Stritch was deeply drunk, "soused to the gills," Cavett said. He watched in astonishment as she plopped down into a large easy chair and began picking up objects and commenting on them, somewhat dismissively. An ashtray. A book about the French Revolution. Stritch started to sing, to the tune of "My Favorite Things" from *The Sound of Music*:

> French revolution
> Folks riding in tumbrils
> Tchotchkes and candles and shit in bundles

Then, just as quickly, she and her friends were gone.

6

"SOMETHING VERY STRANGE"

While Stephen Sondheim and his associates were beginning to use Broadway musicals to explore the dark corners of the psyche, Noël Coward was determined to keep his work in the medium fresh, light, and airy.

Eager to set himself up for a comfortable retirement, he had been puttering away on a piece for Broadway called *Sail Away*, hoping to capitalize on the reputation for sophistication and wit he'd imported to a Las Vegas engagement in 1955, and thematizing his love of travel. *Sail Away* had started as a film script—"a brittle, stylized, insignificant comedy with music," titled *Later Than Spring*, which was intended to star him and his friend Marlene Dietrich.

By 1958 Coward was adapting *Later Than Spring* for the stage. He hoped to secure Rosalind Russell for the part of a sassy social director on a cruise ship, Mimi Paragon, a bossy camp-counselor type, "the person whose job it is to herd everyone about and entice them into various idiotic activities," as the weary veteran of many voyages put it. "Frightful occupation!"

But Russell and her husband, the producer Frederick Brisson, were unmoved by the material they were shown and so a mildly miffed Coward mulled Irene Dunne, Judy Holliday, and Shirley MacLaine before realizing he really would like to cast Kay Thompson, a composer and the author of the *Eloise* books for children, about a privileged but neglected little girl wreaking havoc while in residence at the Plaza Hotel. She was also occasionally an actress, having sung "Think Pink" as an imperious magazine editor modeled on Diana Vreeland in the Fred Astaire–Audrey Hepburn movie *Funny Face*.

Thompson had "a complex about appearing on Broadway," though, or so she told Coward. Thus he settled, albeit with a scintilla of compromise, upon the younger and physically similar Stritch, noting her comic abilities. He presented the work to her, wrote their mutual friend, the playwright William Marchant, "like the cavalier with the silver rose in the Strauss opera," taking her for dinner at Café Chambord on Third Avenue, another restaurant popular with theater folk, and leaving pleased but a little dazed.

"I foresee leetle clouds in the azure sky," Coward wrote in his diary. "I must engage an expert understudy." Concerned that she might be called back for a second season of *My Sister Eileen*, Stritch wavered at committing to the musical. Coward reassured her briskly, and quite rightly, that "there would be no second season." Recognizing her talent, he had charged himself with the burnishing of her reputation. Stritch had had "episodic opportunities," he told the columnist Whitney Bolton, the same writer who'd drooled over her figure in the 1950s, but "would have a rich, full chance here," under his personal direction.

However, Stritch's stage was to be shared with the opera singer Jean Fenn, to whom Coward had been recommended by a friend who worked at the Metropolitan Opera, where she was engaged. A captivatingly elegant blonde in the Dietrich mold, Fenn was excited but perplexed by the role of a distressed wife named Verity Craig. "It was a very strange part: she was supposed to commit suicide," Fenn said. "That's not what you think of when you think of Noël Coward."

This was perhaps the one dash of darkness in a piece whose lightness was well illustrated by its poster, designed by Coward himself, featuring Stritch as Paragon holding a bunch of balloons. "A musical of this type should be fun," Coward told another reporter. "It is purely for entertainment, of which there has been too little in the theater in recent years. I don't condemn the modern trend toward a meaningful story in toto, but you know as well as I do that some of them are overloaded with pretentious meaning to the point of boredom." He had drawn ire in London earlier that year with a series of newspaper articles decrying a trend toward grit and realism in the theater, which he asserted should be "a house of strange enchantment, a temple of illusion."

But Coward was not immune to the more rough-hewn charms of *West Side Story*. From its European cast, encouraged by the choreographer Joe Layton, he plucked a lithe twenty-five-year-old dancer named Grover Dale for the "juvenile lead" of a passenger named Barnaby Slade, a beatnik architect, in *Sail Away*. Dale, who played Snowboy, the "intellectual" member of the Jets gang, with dark hair swept to the side and a premature furrow of worry between his eyes, was notified backstage in Paris that the Master would be visiting his dressing room. "Everybody laughed," he said. "After the show Noël Coward showed up then asked me if I would come talk to him over supper. I was speechless. I don't think I said a word at this dinner." Afterward he loped through the streets like Gene Kelly in *An American in Paris*, his blue jacket in one hand and "a cork from a bottle of rosé wine" in the other, telling fellow cast members in the various bars the good news. Born Grover Robert Aitken, Dale had worked inoculating doughnuts with jelly at Nedick's and danced in the chorus of the Pittsburgh Civic Light Opera production of *Call Me Madam*. In the days to follow he would meet Dietrich and others who consorted with Coward at 70 Avenue Marceau, the flat of the Balmain directrice, wartime memoirist, and fabled hostess Ginette Spanier.

Back in New York, Stritch was also practically levitating with excitement. "She wore bouffant skirts and put ribbons in her hair and hummed little tunes to herself as if she were genuinely in love for the first time," Marchant wrote. But she had the presence of mind to insist that her name come first on the program before Fenn; in turn, Fenn did not want to share space with James Hurst, the leading man, because he was a former chorus boy. "Then she shouldn't want co-star billing with me, because I doubled in the chorus line of *Pal Joey*," Stritch told Leonard Lyons, already striking the pose of the warhorse at age thirty-six. She skipped the table reading and "buggered off to Nantucket" for a carefree weekend on the beach with Joe Allen. "Something tells me she may be going to be tiresome," Coward wrote. "She certainly has a reputation for it. I don't think bitchy and vile like some, but complicated and difficult."

Allen enjoyed himself on the holiday, but the relationship was beginning to run out of steam. "It was all antics, there was no substance," he felt of Stritch. "It was anxiety. She was an anxious person. You can't say uninteresting, because she was interesting." He paused. "Maybe she wasn't interesting, except she was entertaining."

When she returned home, Coward took Stritch out again, to the Barbary Room at the Berkshire Hotel, to inspire her for the part, singing along with her until 3:00 a.m. He was already affectionately referring to her as "Stritchie." But she had not yet memorized her lines, and so he ordered her to study them after hours with his secretary, Cole Lesley.

The next day she surprised him by being on time to the first rehearsal at the Broadhurst Theater, and crisp enough to fight over matters such as the pronunciation of "Babel," which she tried to argue should be "babble."

"Stritch, as I suspected, began by being tiresome, over-full of suggestions and not knowing a word, but after a couple of days she saw the light," Coward wrote. "She was never, I hasten to add, beastly in any way, just fluffy and nervous inside."

He devised a strategy for offering feedback. "We're going to play a little game," he told the cast at the next rehearsal. "We're going to put everyone's name in the hat. Whomever's name you draw, this is going to be the 'X' doll."

By luck or design, Coward drew the slip of paper that read "Stritch."

"Why, it's the Elaine Stritch doll," he said in his clipped way. "You wind it up and it makes a suggestion."

Having an idea of how things should be done can be a liability for an actress but is an excellent qualification for a director. In the early 1960s female directors were exceedingly rare and easily discouraged: thus simmered the frustrations of even Agnes de Mille, who'd come into the business with the leg up from her father, William, and uncle, Cecil. Stritch was interested enough in trying to direct herself that she publicly proposed taking on an off-Broadway revival of *A Day by the Sea*, a Chekhovian play about a foreign service employee in midlife crisis by N. C. Hunter: another English writer made unfashionable by the Angry Young Men. "She'll use only Method actors (Bye!)," Walter Winchell reported. Coward also found the young actors who had studied the Method grubby and lacking in basic stage technique. Stritch had briefly enrolled in Lee Strasberg's Method classes when dating Gazzara. "I got nothing but laughs up there," she told Leonard Lyons during the run of *Bus Stop*. Whitney Bolton had told Stritch he was impressed that she wasn't "scarred" by the experience, like most actresses he knew.

"You're not supposed to be scarred," Stritch replied. "You are supposed to absorb and use what is useful. The result is equipment. If you go beyond that and wander hazily in the foggy realms of theory you are almost certain to fall over a bush or stub your toe on a rock. A rock is a theory addict who goes to work with a fat chip dangling dangerously on his shoulder." People like that "make it miserable for everybody from director on down," she went on. The Method "is not supposed to be a way of life. A carpenter finds a hammer useful. It's a tool. He doesn't start a cult with it, he pounds nails with it. The cultists are the ones you mean."

She scoffed at the young actors searching for a "reason" behind their action. "The reason, of course, is that the author put the intent in the script and the director is translating that intent into stage performance." Stritch preferred the pragmatic, collaborative approach of Erwin Piscator and Stella Adler. "Why does there always have to be a 'why'?" she said. "I love the director who snapped at one of these kids when the kid griped 'What is my motivation?' and this darling man snapped back 'Your paycheck is your motivation.' Heaven-sent man!"

Her own paychecks having begun to accumulate nicely again, Stritch had decided to trade up apartments to one in a building at 12 Beekman Place, a small, quiet strip near the East River of Manhattan and the

United Nations. Part of the appeal of the street was that the fictional Mame Dennis, played by Rosalind Russell in both the movie and play of *Auntie Mame*, had lived on it, in a constant state of revelry enabled by not having a husband or children—something considered, at this moment in America, to be rather eccentric and unusual. The plot involves Mame's writing her autobiography, and her oft repeated motto, "Life is a banquet and most poor sons of bitches are starving to death" (changed in the film to "suckers"), might have been a line from Stritch's yet inchoate memoir, *Shut Up and Drink Your Champagne*. Taking her accountant to do her taxes at the Little Club, a restaurant on Fifty-Fifth Street with candy-striped wallpaper, Stritch joked to him: "I've got loads of dependents. People drop in for a drink all the time. Those kinds of dependents."

Mame adores interior decorating and Stritch also sought to give her new place a sweeping makeover. There was a designer popular in her crowd, Howard Perry Rothberg II, a fellow Detroiter whose clients included Dorothy Kilgallen. Stritch liked his style but didn't want to pay his high fee, so Rothberg referred her to his new, young assistant, Maurice Bernstein, an émigré from Cairo.

On a very hot day, Bernstein went nervously to her rental apartment, sweating in a proper suit and tie. It was one of the New York City summers documented so palpably in *The Seven Year Itch*, in which Marilyn Monroe stands over a subway grate letting the breeze caused by the moving train blow up her skirt and exclaiming, "Isn't it delicious."

The door was open and Stritch was inside to greet him. "Isn't this weather godawful? I can't stand it," she said, lifting her skirt and pulling her girdle down in front of the young man she had never met before. "This is killing me," she said.

After Bernstein regained his powers of speech, they began to discuss the apartment. Stritch asked if he could incorporate a few Victorian pieces she owned into the décor, and he came up with the idea of wooden shutters rather than shades and curtains, to affect a cottage-like feeling. She was going out of town with *Sail Away*, she told him, and asked whether he could get it finished during that time. Bernstein said yes. "In those days she liked things that were very frilly and feminine and there was a place that I found in Switzerland that could do all sorts of embroidered organdy," he said.

But Stritch was demonstrably more at ease on the out-of-town circuit than any dwelling, no matter how alluringly appointed. Seasoned from *Madam* and *Goldilocks*, she greeted the audiences on the road like old chums. Fenn was less sure of herself. "Elaine had a lot of style and she was great at selling a number," she said. "Big changes were occurring in musical theater; in order to do well in a show you had to play and dance and look good, when you used to just have to sing."

The show opened in Boston with Kay Thompson, Judy Garland, and the Lunts in the audience, followed by what Coward complained was a "vast and ghastly party given in my honor by the Statler Hilton Hotel." Eleanor Roosevelt came to see the production as well. But the current First Lady, Jackie Kennedy ("to her everlasting credit, an ardent Coward fan," he wrote), caused the most commotion, coming in from her summer vacation in Hyannis Port with her friends Bunny and Paul Mellon. Considering her the equivalent of a royal, Coward was faintly embarrassed by the feverish press coverage that followed, but reminded himself that he was in a country where, unlike Great Britain, "publicity is the breath of life."

Stritch had the lucky break of performing the song "Why Do the Wrong People Travel," about tourists. Depicted as amusing and generous in *Call Me Madam*, the American abroad, with his looming Kodak and garish clothes, had by the early sixties become an embarrassment: "Why do the wrong people travel / When all the right people stay at home (with all those Kennedys) . . ."

Heads swiveled toward the First Lady, neat and demure in bow-trimmed black and white and gloves, which she removed to applaud. Afterward Mrs. Kennedy went backstage.

"I loved the show," she told Coward, of whom she was a devoted fan, and then, to the cast, "you were all marvelous." She shook hands with both Stritch and Fenn and then the crowd parted for her. A few days later the Mellons sent their private plane for Coward and Cole Lesley, and they lunched with Jack and Jackie in Osterville on Cape Cod: the Master and the President, with the Secret Service "festooned from every tree,"

Coward wrote in his diary. Despite the stress of the Russian nuclear tests that were preoccupying the developed world at the time, Kennedy was good, relaxed company, he added.

Then after a convivial train ride south came *Sail Away*'s stop in Philadelphia, absent celebrities and full of the gossipy, inattentive theater parties Coward deeply loathed. Fenn had been annoying him, fretting about her costumes and hair, which he duly had her chop off, but the problems with the show were fundamental. "There's no question about it, Verity and Johnny are a bore and the show sags whenever they came on," he conceded. Meanwhile Stritch was giving her role a sort of Mary Poppins verve—"exalted mummery," Marchant called it—marshaling balloons, children, dogs, and grown-ups around the deck while various love affairs blossomed and wilted onstage.

She "has turned *Sail Away* into a one-woman show," one Philadelphia critic wrote. "As a colleague suggested, let's have the whole thing turned into a revue with Miss Stritch leading the passengers—as she does now—in a wonderland she doesn't care to explore. Let's keep the busy Miss Stritch busier."

It occurred to Joe Layton first that they might not only cut Fenn's hair but her part, an idea he presented to Coward over breakfast and that was eagerly seized upon. However, since Fenn had been in bed with laryngitis, it had to be presented with some delicacy, as well as a guarantee of the Actor's Equity minimum of eight weeks salary. "The great voices should remain forever at La Scala or wherever they are paid best," Coward concluded.

"I felt bad about it but life is not always as they say a bowl of cherries," Fenn said. "I thought my life was over, but it wasn't." As for Stritch, "she was very sad when I left. Somebody said, 'Well, I don't blame her, because now she's going to be stuck with the things that you had to do.'"

It was an unusual circumstance for a sidekick to not only replace a leading lady but have their parts combined: romantic and funny. Underneath her politesse to Fenn, Stritch was delighted. "When you want to do something so badly it's such a joy that they think you can and you're going to be the whole cheese," she said. "Amazing the energy you have."

Coward cut two tunes that were beyond her vocal capabilities and worked feverishly to reconstruct the book. She gave its new incarnation her all, singing the song "Something Very Strange," so sensitively, he wrote, "that I almost cried." Her voice, which had so often been described as brassy, took on rather a cool, shimmering quality, like moonlight on the water, as she sang "All the sounds I hear, the buses changing gear / Suddenly appear to be beguiling." (The cruise ship docks in Tangier, hence the sudden appearance of buses.)

Coward chuckled to himself that when he recorded his own version of the cast album, he'd have to rewrite a line "If only I were younger"; he had been feeling his age and worrying, despite his arguments against the changing times, if he was out of step with them. But now he had an ardent champion almost three decades his junior.

Stritch understood that her new mentor's upper-class facade was a put-on. "He's terribly chic," she babbled excitedly to Earl Wilson after the company returned to New York. "He's always looking like he's going to a cocktail party with Winston Churchill. Strangers invite him out— but he doesn't want to go to the Pavillon with Mrs. Hootenanny. He'd rather go to Coney Island, which he did." Not that Coward was "perfection," of course. "Oh, he has a temper," she said. "He cannot stand irritations and boredom. He can talk to you so tenderly, then suddenly goes into a rage. I love that!"

Being in the audience with him at a disappointing show was like getting on an airplane with a nervous flyer. "If you go to the theater with Noël your arm is black and blue when you get home," Stritch said years later. "You hope it's good, so you won't get hurt. But when it's not good, it's 'Oh god, oh god'—he presses his hand into your arm until it's black and blue. 'Oh Christ, Stritchie, they're going to reprise it.'"

She had come home from Philadelphia on an early train, vibrating with nerves and triumph. Maurice Bernstein had worked tirelessly to finish decorating her apartment, put flowers on the counter and champagne in the icebox, and—as was customary then—had a gold key made.

His phone rang at 6:30 a.m.

"Maurice, I know it's a ghastly hour," came Stritch's voice. "This apartment is so spectacular, I cannot bring my trunks in. I just love it."

She began ticking off the names of potential guests for a housewarming party, including Kilgallen, who had done the actress no favors of late. "Why are you inviting her?" Bernstein asked drowsily.

"Maurice, there are certain people, it's better to be on their good side than their bad side," Stritch said.

Soon thereafter arrived a dozen teasing telegrams, like fortune cookies, sent by Coward to 12 Beekman Place all on the same day to bolster his star for opening night in New York.

"DON'T BE NERVOUS IT ALL DEPENDS ON YOU," read one.

And another: "A SUCCESS WILL IMPROVE YOUR POSITION SOCIALLY."

A schnauzer featured in the show was named after Adlai Stevenson, the American ambassador to the United Nations who had once admiringly told Stritch, "You are one hundred forty-three women wrapped in one." (The schnauzer was later switched for a long-haired female dachshund, Adelaide, given by Coward to Stritch.) On opening night, with Dietrich, Myrna Loy, and Margaret Truman in the audience, one of five or six dogs tangled on a leash onstage answered nature's call. The audience collapsed in laughter, the more so when a line included the phrase "a change in the air." Stritch then decided to improvise a few lines "unwisely," Marchant thought. The love story was received as a comedy.

"Oh no! Twasn't Adlai," Stritch assured the columnist Earl Wilson during the party at Sardi's East afterward, to which Coward had escorted her in a yellow taxi. Marchant observed her making the sign of the cross with spilled champagne on people's foreheads. This amused Coward, who had rejected his Catholic upbringing without qualm.

"Beautifully organized hell," he called the party of 150 guests, which included the Lunts and Lauren Bacall. The reviews that came in later that night did not do much to soothe him.

Howard Taubman of the *Times* had thoroughly enjoyed himself. "A big, handsome, rakish vessel of a musical," he proclaimed *Sail Away*, with "a cargo of shrewdly observed people," with Stritch in particular giving "what must be the performance of her career." But over at the *Herald*

Tribune Walter Kerr was still having food issues. "The new Noël Coward musical looks like vanilla ice cream, slides about as smoothly as though it were melting on the plate, and has no particular flavor," he began. "From this general lazing-about in the holiday sun let us exempt Elaine Stritch." There followed a kind of literary love letter, perhaps even a kind of apologia for the sour taste left by *Goldilocks*: "She is best of all when she is telling us the weary, blistering truth," Kerr wrote, presaging interpretations that would come years later, "the steel in her eyes showing, that 'Oh, Pshaw' smile intervening to say she doesn't mean it, and her long legs tapping beneath a striped canvas chair." The rest of the review was scathing.

"Oh, I guess we missed this time, sweetie," Joe Allen overheard Coward tell Stritch resignedly.

Feeling snubbed and unrecognized at the party, the humorist James Thurber chilled the evening more dramatically with a speech about how he and Coward were "the only ones left who've been writing since 1920. If Coward wrote *Private Lives* today it would be called *Public Loves* and be done out on the street, and *Design for Living* would certainly be called *Design for Dying*." The strange remarks turned out to be the harbinger of a cerebral hemorrhage, and he died a month later.

Stritch had a chance to play Auntie Mame, if only in her own mind, when little Sally's younger brother, Chris, then aged ten, came to New York with his parents for a few days. Enchanted by the show, he came night after night, lurking in the wings.

"Chris, don't you move!" she'd tell her nephew. "Be careful, because those sets are gonna come in and out of there. Stay away!"

During one intermission, rather than go to her dressing room, he went exploring, and went under the stage to get to the other side. "There's this guy down there yelling at this other guy and he's giving him hell about *Sail Away* not having a float in the Thanksgiving Day parade," Chris Bolton remembered.

"You're through," the first man told the second.

Chris crept back up the stairs and found his aunt. "Who was that?" he whispered.

"That was Noël Coward," Stritch said. "Firing his publicist."

The Frank Loesser musical *How to Succeed in Business Without Really Trying* came out later that month. Like *Call Me Madam*, it reflected a moment of American ambition, industry, and good luck rather than the meandering and outdated leisure class depicted in *Sail Away*. "It received the ecstatic raves that I should like to have had," Coward wrote. (And the Tonys, for which only Stritch and his producers were nominated.) But like most successful people, his way was not to linger on disappointments, but to move swiftly on to a new project.

Stritch had befriended a socialite named Sharman Douglas, nicknamed Charmin' for her merry manner (or possibly after the toilet tissue). At the home of the decorator Howard Perry Rothberg II, the two women played a parlor amusement called the Tower Game with Tony Curtis and Janet Leigh, an early version of what came to be known as "Kiss, Marry, Kill" (or more vulgar terms). Players were confronted with two people—say, Mary Martin and Ethel Merman—and pressed to decide whom to throw off a tower and whom to remain with for thirty years. "You must answer instantly and nobody wins," Earl Wilson wrote. "Everyone goes a little crazy."

Stritch's romantic affairs were rarely so dramatic; partners were not tossed over the parapet but faded in and out, drifted away; entered, exited, and returned. By the end of the New York run of *Sail Away*, Joe Allen had been supplanted, sort of, by Grover Dale, the dancer a decade Stritch's junior who had been chosen by Coward to play Barnaby Slade.

"I was a kid from a small town and as green as they come," Dale said. "But with Elaine I had a new kind of comfort level that I had never really experienced."

Dale had grown up in an alcoholic household and there was something primally reassuring about Stritch's habit of showing up at his apartment on West Fifty-Sixth Street with a bottle of champagne in one hand. "I think a big element in being pulled into Elaine's world was the alcohol. That was so familiar to me," he said. "The smell of it. And the fact that someone drank during the performance was so familiar to me. I tried it and it didn't work because I had to dance. One glass of wine threw me off balance."

Sail Away was proceeding to London. The idea of Stritch directing *A Day by the Sea* fell by the wayside. Coward lent the odd new couple his compound in Blue Harbour, Jamaica, for a holiday in between, but Dale did not accompany her on a subsequent visit to Coward's chalet in Les Avants, Switzerland, where she lunched with the novelist W. Somerset Maugham and his lover, Alan Searle, and was treated to a spirited gambling session at the Casino d'Evian on Lake Geneva.

Marveling at his protégée's juxtaposition of devout Catholicism and considerable profanity, Coward rued the effects of analysis on her psyche, and on those of Americans generally: "their egos have grown inwards, like toe-nails," he observed in his diary.

He also dedicated a poem to her, a simple paean to a single, drinking, Catholic life that longs for the moment to be filled "with someone I love" but is resigned that "God didn' will it."

Ere long Coward and Lesley stuffed the actress on a plane to London with a jumble of suitcases and dresses wrapped in plastic dry-cleaning bags: "The hullaballoo was considerable."

The British company of *Sail Away* had a trial run in the city of Bristol, attended on its second night by Coward's old friend Cary Grant, who was visiting his family there—"couldn't have been nicer, sweeter and more enthusiastic," the writer crowed. They then set up in London's elegant Savoy Theater, which had twelve hundred seats in zinnia colors that audience members would sometimes call the box office ahead of time to confirm so that they might coordinate their outfits.

Stritch leased a town house with two apartments from Anne Marie Ponsonby, daughter of the Baron von Slatin, at 9 Anderson Street in the Chelsea neighborhood, in front of a pub. Dale and his female ingénue counterpart, Sheila Forbes, also moved in. "It was crazy," he said of his romantic relationship with Stritch. "We didn't talk—we weren't really honest about what was going on between us, which is that we were sharing a bed together." On one of the few Sundays they had off, the actors took the famous ferry from Dover to the port of Calais and back. "Elaine put on white makeup all over her face," he said. "She was in her transition of wearing pants and hats and men's clothes."

To the London premiere on June 21, 1962, Coward summoned Vivien Leigh, who was still suffering from depression aggravated by her 1960 divorce from Laurence Olivier, as well as the popular British film star Kenneth More.

"I want you to behave yourself," he told Stritch about the opening night party. "I want you to be absolutely perfection."

She proceeded to the department store Harrods, bought a proper, high-necked dress that reminded her of Katharine Hepburn, who had praised her performance in a letter to Coward, and sipped only ginger ale at the party, while the British swells "got fried and flung four-letter words about like confetti," Coward recorded with some rue in his diary. Stritch "behaved impeccably."

"Elaine, I asked you to behave yourself," he scolded her the next day. "I did not ask you to behave like a fucking geography teacher."

Though Coward feigned blasé indifference to critics, he groused about their grudging response to the show: "They do hate me, these little men." But they were thrilled by his American discovery. "When Miss Stritch is absent, the show is deader than the dodo," declared one, calling her "an extraordinarily potent artist" who "saves Mr. Coward's bacon again and again and again."

The Master's associates were also dazzled. "And what about that Stritch girl!" wrote the theatrical manager Henry Sherek, who'd produced the plays of T. S. Eliot. He'd been anticipating a "coon shouter"—a term used for a particular type of female vaudevillian imitating minstrelsy—but found to his relief "not only a splendid singer of songs where not a word is missed . . . but a most sensitive actress with wonderful timing."

At a Royal Gala Performance the following week, Stritch was presented at intermission to Queen Elizabeth and Prince Philip, curtseying low and murmuring niceties as instructed. Afterward, the London show's producer, Harold Fielding, organized a party on yet another boat, chugging up the River Thames, where any lingering concern that Stritch would behave like a geography teacher was hurled to the wind, along with a quantity of champagne glasses.

"By the end of the cruise, in the middle of the night, Elaine was so drunk she could hardly walk," Grover Dale said. "And we went up the ramp to get to a taxi and the door was open and she leaned in and my foot kicked her into the back seat."

Behind them, from another taxi, an agent stuck her head out of the window.

"Oh, Grover, did you *have* to do that?" she said reprovingly.

Through a back window, Stritch held up a middle finger.

Though Dale was also dallying with Forbes, at one point he and Stritch even acquired a marriage license, but it ended in pieces torn by her on the floor as he walked out. "I was a gypsy, I was a bad boy," said Dale, who would go on to date Anthony Perkins, the star of *Psycho*. "I was sleeping around and all I wanted in London was to be with a man and I couldn't find a man, so I slept with women."

There was a steady stream of celebrity visitors to 9 Anderson Street, where Stritch also welcomed the critic and Sardi's regular Ward Morehouse that summer, wearing "a blouse from the Nile, shoes from Switzerland and goldtone slacks" and sipping a gin and tonic. "She has suddenly become a fad and a craze in London's theatertown," Morehouse wrote. During the interview, she called Coward "the best friend I've ever had in the theater. I've worked my backside off for him and we've had some awful arguments, but we really get along famously."

But Coward was already beginning to distance himself, though he had written an avuncular, reassuring cable to Mildred Stritch: "YOUR DEAR LITTLE BLONDE DAUGHTER HAS MADE A TRIUMPHANT SUCCESS AND HAS ALL LONDON AT HER FEET. SHE IS ALSO BEHAVING BEAUTIFULLY SO DON'T BE FRANTIC." His new project was a musical version of Terence Rattigan's play *The Sleeping Prince*, to be called *The Girl Who Came to Supper*. Eager to continue their association, Stritch inquired about playing the lead, and "he told her she was too old, poor darling, for the part," reported Leonard Lyons, after a visit to London in September.

"Of course, dear Noël. Working with you would have aged anyone," she returned snappily.

By January 1963, Fielding had posted notices at the Savoy that *Sail Away* would soon close. Coward wondered privately if among the reasons, including the weakness of the book and the overclever lyrics, might be that "Stritch, with all her talent and vitality, hasn't enough star sex appeal." As the production proceeded to Melbourne, Australia, with Maggie Fitzgibbon in the lead, and as Coward himself retreated to Jamaica, having auditioned and settled upon another leggy and less problematic blonde, Florence Henderson, for *Supper*, Stritch was left in London, tending bar at the Queen's Head pub for a while for free drinks and because she enjoyed surprising customers.

She hired a secretary in one of her regular flurries of organization and wrote letters to Coward, their joviality masking obvious uncertainty about her next move. A possible collaboration was brewing with William Marchant. His best-known play, *Desk Set*, had been made into a film starring Katharine Hepburn, Spencer Tracy, and her old beau Gig Young. Inauspiciously titled *Who? Where? What? Why?*, Marchant's new work, concerning five people summoned to a trial in Europe, had been "more or less" written for her, Stritch bragged in a letter to Coward—"and believe me the 'Stritch doll' is wound up good and proper." But though it was already financed there was not yet a director, and this made her nervous. "It needs a creative giant, with a strong arm and an inventive mind," she believed. Twice she asked a little timorously whether she might send Coward Marchant's script, which she found flawed. She inquired after Coward's servants ("remind Ruby if she's still with you to for God's sake, serve from the left") and promised to send a gift of clothing for his cook Mae's children.

Once again, Stritch was resolving to clean up her act, even more radically than she had in Rome. Teasingly asking what pleasures Coward might be sacrificing for Lent ("is there any rum in your Coca Cola?"), she avowed her own sobriety. "Now, Noël, are you sitting down—ready? I don't drink at all—anything—I mean anything, anymore, and I must say it's an adventure. The results have been world shaking. I look and feel about thirteen years old. I'm up at ten, do my own marketing, walk Adelaide three times a day in the park. I've even been to the Laundromat! One of my biggest decisions in life of late is whether it will be V8 Juice, plain tonic (sugar free) or unsweetened grapefruit juice at cocktail time."

Even with such spartan refreshments she strove to maintain an outsize public persona. An American newspaperman interviewing R. A. Butler, then the deputy prime minister of Britain, observed his subject's eyes light up only when Stritch swanned through Le Caprice in Piccadilly at lunchtime, dripping endearments like loose feathers on familiar customers. "Love you doll . . . mad, adorable fool, you."

When night fell she dined with fellow alumni of *Sail Away* or went to inspect the formidable competition in the West End. Musicals imported there from Broadway that would outlast Coward's included *How to Succeed in Business Without Really Trying* and, at the Strand, *A Funny Thing Happened on the Way to the Forum*, with lyrics and music by Stephen Sondheim, his first fully realized composition to reach the commercial stage. Even though *Forum* had been warmly received, hardly anyone acknowledged the scope of his contribution, or foresaw the astonishing potential of his talent.

7

"WHAT A DUMP!"

After the frothy role of Mimi Paragon, Stritch was once again craving the validation conferred by the legitimate theater. In March 1963, with Grover Dale heading to St. Thomas for a brief vacation and then to film *The Unsinkable Molly Brown* with Debbie Reynolds, she decided abruptly to give up the Chelsea town house and the Marchant project, despite fears that he would be "'bitchy' and god knows what when he hears about this," as she wrote to Coward, having secured passage for herself and Adelaide on an ocean liner to New York.

"I'm still off the booze," she continued, "and believe me six days on the *Elizabeth*, on or off season, is the acid test." This, after all, was a place where you might watch the Royal Shakespeare Company interpreting popular songs, or play Petropolis, "a monopoly type game of kings where you buy whole countries instead of Park Place," according to a brochure, and for dinner eat roulade de veau, canard à l'orange, and chocolate mousse, hoping you wouldn't upchuck it into the churning Atlantic below.

Stritch's landlady Anne Marie Ponsonby had returned to 9 Anderson to find the glass and frame broken over a Philip de László portrait of Ponsonby's father, a specially locked china cupboard open, and the floors unpolished. The actress left it to her own father to resolve the dispute. "The nylon curtains I shouldn't think have been washed since Miss Stritch moved in," Ponsonby wrote George Stritch, requesting three times the security deposit, which he refused. "I must say your demands are actually a work of art. To say they are fantastic is putting it mildly. You people must be out of your minds."

Stritch had given up Beekman Place as well. Riding the high seas back to gravitas and Dale's conveniently empty apartment, she would be replacing the actress Kate Reid as Martha, a professor's embittered wife, in *Who's Afraid of Virginia Woolf?* The play had debuted to thunderous acclaim the previous autumn at the Billy Rose Theater.

Produced by Richard Barr and Clinton Wilder and directed by Alan Schneider, *Woolf* was the Broadway debut of a young playwright named Edward Albee, whose earlier absurdist works like *The Zoo Story* and *The Sandbox* had confounded some audiences and critics. Now, though, he had fashioned a domestic situation particularly relatable to the upper-middle-class readers of the *Times*: a brutally contentious academic marriage. "His new work, flawed though it is, towers over the common run of contemporary plays," Howard Taubman had written in October 1962 after an opening that had taken place after previews in New York rather than an out-of-town tryout, breaking with theatrical convention. "It marks a further gain for a young writer becoming a major figure of our stage."

Martha was a particularly vivid character: "a tormented harridan" with a "brutal bluntness" who provided Stritch with a complete and dramatic volte-face from Coward's trippingly light repartee. The living-room setting would no longer be a cozy backdrop for exchanging witticisms but an emotional cesspool—"what a dump!" Martha proclaims, quoting a Bette Davis movie whose title she can't summon to mind—where the soul's very depths could be plumbed in all their suffocating murk. "The play at its best communicates as a blister does," Walter Kerr wrote in the *Herald Tribune*. "You don't have to ask what's the matter, you feel it."

There was one caveat: Stritch would be performing only the matinees, in the shadow of the prime-time Martha, the revered (and blacklisted) actress Uta Hagen. But it was "very good money and my god, what a part!"

she exulted in a letter to Coward. "I do so want to do a straight play and it *does* seem that this is the best one around. I am really so pleased they asked for *me*, as I understand every actress in New York is after it."

Though Hagen, a fellow disciple of Stella Adler and Harold Clurman, would get almost all of the critical attention, few of those actresses could have been so perfectly cast as Stritch as the abrasive, boozed-up Martha. Likewise Martha was a convent girl "when she was a little twig of a thing," as Albee had her husband, a history professor named George, sneer in the script; she also could be considered "loud and vulgar" by the standards of the day, with a voice that could grate, as in this excerpt from Act I, "Fun and Games":

MARTHA (braying): I DON'T BRAY.
GEORGE (softly): All right . . . you don't bray.
MARTHA (hurt): I do not *bray*.
GEORGE: All right, I said you didn't bray.
MARTHA (pouting): Make me a drink.

There were two more characters, "guests," a younger biologist named Nick and his wife, Honey, and the tongues of this uneasy quartet were all loosened and sharpened by alcohol. Martha preferred a liquid banquet of "Brandy Alexanders, crème de cacao frappes, gimlets, flaming punch-bowls . . . seven-layer liqueur things," according to George's voluptuous recitation. Backstage, Stritch recalled, "the johns did nothing but flush for a full straight fifteen minutes at intermission of every *Virginia Woolf*, because everybody drank a full quart of whatever—tea or water or whatever was going on."

Stritch argued to her parents that the constant tinkle of cocktail refills in the stage directions actually supported moderation after hours. "By acting, I get it out of my system, and so drink less vodka," she told them. The absolute abstinence she'd tried in London, however, now seemed out of the realm of possibility. She was far too nervous about her performance.

Albee's dialogue—the play ran for over three hours, without the respite of song-and-dance numbers—was uncommonly demanding, on occasion exceeding Stritch's powers of memorization.

"Line? What's my goddamned line?" she would on occasion yell during early performances with a snap of the fingers, not breaking character.

Eileen Fulton, who played Honey at matinees, found Stritch, eight years her senior, endearingly girlish in her anxiety. "When she got nervous in rehearsal, she had these beautiful pearls, just a small beautiful bunch of pearls that she wore, and she would put it up on her chin: just 'what is, what is the line,'" she said. "I just thought that was like a child. Eating her pearls."

Waiting in the wings one afternoon to make an entrance toward the end of the second of three acts, "Walpurgisnacht" (a reference to the German holiday when witches dance with the devil), Fulton was startled when an exiting Stritch thrust a prop bottle filled with ersatz liquor in her arms.

"Eileen, you've got to go there and put the fire out," she said.

"What fire?" Fulton gasped.

"I dropped my cigarette in the couch."

On the stage there was indeed a growing smolder emanating from the cushions. "I got that bottle and just kind of dropped it and put out the flames and kept on talking," Fulton said.

Recollecting the incident years later, Stritch had herself and her on-stage husband, Donald Davis, instead niftily improvising some additions to the script.

> GEORGE: The sofa is on fire.
> MARTHA: So?
> GEORGE: Well, you run everything else around here, so put it out.

As Stritch told it, she then brandished Martha's glass of "vodka" (water), quickly reconsidered "wasting" it, and then grabbed George's "bourbon" (iced tea) from the bar to douse the flames, whereupon the audience "fell about" in uproarious laughter.

From time to time, Albee would appear at the theater, a quiet, brooding but gentle presence. Stritch said he told her, "You're not playing the play I wrote, but I couldn't be happier." Albee later told an interviewer, "Stritch, as you know, can be big and bawdy, but the interesting thing was that she played a very, very small performance. It was very good: she didn't go overboard, she was very subtle."

Stritch also took a sisterly, take-charge role with Fulton for the duration of the play: wrapping one of her own skirts around the younger woman to cover up a pantsuit on the way to Gurney's resort in Montauk, which forbade them, and giving her professional encouragement.

"I want to get you with a cracking agent," she told Fulton, who had started what would turn out to be a fifty-year run on the soap opera *As the World Turns*. "You've got to come over and meet Gloria Safier."

"I was so thrilled, but I was so intimidated," Fulton said. "Elaine and Gloria got on my case. They said, 'You're brilliant in the show, honey, but you've got to put on a little makeup. Just because you're homely doesn't mean you have to look homely. You've got to look pretty, so people will care.' I took that to heart."

On April 28, 1963, the Tony Awards were held at the Hotel Americana Imperial Ballroom on Fifty-Second Street and Seventh Avenue. *Who's Afraid of Virginia Woolf?* received five awards and *A Funny Thing Happened on the Way to the Forum* half a dozen, including Best Musical. But Sondheim was not even nominated for the score, and his colleagues forgot to thank him at the ceremony, which sent him into a dark funk. "Steve was so unhappy he wanted to kill himself," Flora Roberts, then Sondheim's agent, told his biographer, Meryle Secrest.

Sondheim had reunited with Arthur Laurents to work on a new musical, alternately called *The Natives Are Restless* and *Side Show*, about an asylum for misfits in a bankrupt American town. They were having considerable trouble raising money for it.

Stritch was one of the many who failed to anticipate what Sondheim would become; she was cavalier, almost dismissive about being solicited for the role of the town's mayoress. "I went to hear Arthur Laurents' and Stevie Sondheim's musical," she wrote to Coward. "I do not like the part they want me to do—a lot of big boff songs, but no real wit in them. The ingénue's part is brilliant and I'm not going to fight them kind anymore." The part they were trying on her would go to Angela Lansbury and that of the ingénue to Lee Remick, and the title was changed again, to *Anyone Can Whistle*.

Safier was urging Stritch instead to do a new play called *The Time of the Barracudas*, whose writer, Peter Barnes, and director, Anthony Page, were both British and very young. Page, who'd had success doing a dark Jacobean drama in London, had seen her in *Sail Away* and "was bowled over by her bittersweet voice, lack of sentimentality, pathos, and true brilliant unique comedy," he said. "I suggested her, supported her as someone absolutely capable of making this part flame. And succeeded in persuading those responsible to cast her in the part. At the beginning of the project, I was exercising a lot of influence as a new wunderkind."

The project had more established names attached: the broodingly handsome movie actor Laurence Harvey (*The Manchurian Candidate*) was to star, and the Hollywood producer Frederick Brisson, an occasional presence at P. J. Clarke's, had marshaled a slate of investors on both coasts, including Alfred Bloomingdale, a department store heir, and Fleur Cowles, the editor of the short-lived, exquisitely designed magazine *Flair*. "You can use more money and also you can be a leading lady and you don't have to sing 'Bongo Bongo Bongo' and 'You Took Advantage of Me'" was Safier's argument.

Stritch would come to regret deeply listening to this advice. "You know, I didn't know choices," she said. "No, Steve wasn't 'Steve' then, but also, it wasn't a bad score and it was a hell of a part for me. The Angela Lansbury part. But what did I want to get up and be Angela Lansbury when I could be—you know, I was going to be dressed by—forget about the costumes, Laurence Harvey was a great fucking movie star."

Stritch was preparing for a performance of *Virginia Woolf* when someone told her Coward was going to be in the audience. Panicked, she bolted two drinks backstage and then threw her raincoat over her bra and girdle and went to the corner bar for another. It was one occasion when this particular iteration (or perversion) of the Method was effective. "She was absolutely magnificent. A truly great performance," Coward wrote in his diary. "If only she could play it in London. She really is an astonishingly fine actress." He wasn't entirely sure the script of *Barracudas*—a black comedy about a man and woman who both kill multiple spouses so that they may collect the insurance money, become romantically involved, and then compete to destroy each other—was worthy of her talents.

"It will work or it won't work," he told Stritch.

But there were other enticements to do Barnes's play, paramount among them that Stritch would be restored to the lead billing she'd been awarded in *Sail Away*. Harvey was dating Joan Cohn, the widow of the Columbia executive Harry Cohn, so out-of-town tryouts would take place in San Francisco and Los Angeles, under the sunshine and away from the exacting gaze of the New York critics. And Miles Davis and Gil Evans were doing the music—an idea proposed by Page, who "seems so bright and creative in his approach," as Stritch wrote to Coward from a brief summer holiday at the cookbook writer Lee Bailey's house in Bridgehampton. "They have made so many changes and so many improvements" to the script, she promised Coward. "All the crap you disapproved of has been cut."

She had received a postcard from him tut-tutting at her failure to deliver the promised clothes for his maid. "I feel like some jazzy phoney actress full of promises for under-privileged children. Believe it or not, I still have Leone's and Jennifer's measurements in my wallet and Mainbocher can't make them out, let alone Macy's." She joked that she'd ask the famed Hollywood costume designer Irene Sharaff instead, and admitted to drinking two beers a day since their brief encounter at the theater—"Well, three today. We all go crazy in the Hamptons."

Stritch cast Coward as confessor. "You have a strange effect on me—every time I see you and talk to you, I somehow immediately go on the wagon. Unless, of course, I'm working *for* you, in which case I double my intake."

But he had moved on, not only to Florence Henderson, the lissome future star of *The Brady Bunch*, but to Tammy Grimes, a star of the Broadway version of *The Unsinkable Molly Brown*, who would, it had just been announced, be starring in *High Spirits*, a forthcoming musical of his 1941 play *Blithe Spirit*. (In his affection for American blondes, only Alfred

Hitchcock equaled Coward at the moment.) "So you see I *must* go to the Coast," Stritch wrote, brightly glazing over even a successful actress's perpetual feeling of replaceability with the hope of her new assignment. "All of this could have been avoided had you offered me the pub owner in *The Girl Who Came to Supper.*"

The ANTA Theater in New York had already been booked for *Barracudas* in February 1964. But the production was troubled from the start. "The problem was Elaine's terrifying, largely uncontrollable addiction to vodka—and her distrust that Larry couldn't bring off the part," Page said. "This led her to emasculate him when she was intoxicated, which was often." Harvey was easily teased for driving a lavender monogrammed Rolls-Royce Cohn had bought him. And he was hardly a model of sobriety as they rehearsed by his girlfriend's pool. "I had a feeling it was out of Kafka time," Stritch said. "He was drinking Pouilly Fuissé all day long. I drank, but I was more serious then. He was just scary. And he was really shooting them back."

She remembered bitterly how, giving her a lift back to the Chateau Marmont, the castle-like hotel in West Hollywood, Harvey refused to drive her up the long winding road to the entrance. "He let me off on Sunset fucking Boulevard with my script in my hand—little girl lost. Sit there and count your fingers. It's a steep hill, too."

In her memoir *Life Itself!*, the novelist and playwright Elaine Dundy described walking through the courtyard of the Chateau with Mike Macdonald, a son of the critic Dwight Macdonald, to hear someone singing "a haunting Cole Porter ballad" out an open window. It was Stritch, who invited Dundy and Macdonald up to her room and complained, of Harvey: "Every bit of stage business I've invented that gets a laugh he copies later on! I've called him on it and he just denies it!"

Macdonald later remembered Stritch trying to bond with Miles Davis by showing him production stills. "Don't show me the pictures 'til the play's right," he told her.

Stritch would come to brag of further involvement (though Davis's name would be dropped from a list of her boyfriends in *At Liberty*). "He thought I was great and I thought he was great," she said, telling of hot nights in the pool at the Chateau Marmont. "But for me, where I came from and my background, strange casting. And it didn't bother me none. And he was married, and that didn't seem to make any difference to me at all because you see, I was in trouble, so the world owed me that. And he was a gift from God."

The *Barracudas* sets and props were elaborate, including a Scottish-style chalet and an exploding toaster, and by mid-October Brisson, writhing from "the throes of completing the rehearsals," requested over-call money from the investors for extra labor. Privately, he was also hoping to replace Stritch with his wife, Rosalind Russell, who thanks in part to his maneuvers played Madame Rose in the movie version of *Gypsy*, much to Merman's ire (she called Brisson the Lizard of Roz). In late-night drinking sessions, Harvey was agreeing that Stritch could take lines from him to speak onstage. "Without prejudice, he was friendly, totally open about himself, eager to experiment and work hard to make the play fly for both Elaine and himself," Page said. "But he was also cowardly and wouldn't put a foot forward to take responsibility when crises began to happen."

At the first dress rehearsal as the company prepared to open in San Francisco, Stritch fell and badly scraped the skin on one arm. "It was the atmosphere of total unworkmanship," she said.

Bay Area reviewers for the most part praised the cosmopolitan leads and heaped their scorn on Page and Barnes. "It is an unsmooth and spotty journey that the author takes us on, jerking us to a suspenseful moment and then letting the joke fall flat before the punch line," wrote Barbara Bladen, the drama critic for the *San Mateo Times*, while praising Stritch as "a lanky sophisticate" and Harvey as a "charmer with a voice to match."

But by the time *Barracudas* reached the Huntington Hartford Theater in Los Angeles, Page had been fired. "I was too young and inexperienced to deal with the alcoholism and Elaine's unbalanced manic ambition," he said.

The stage manager was now in charge. Harvey, having ceded several of his lines to Stritch, was openly hostile, suggesting that her character be blown up with dynamite in the last act.

"Larry, you'll be stoned to death at the stage door—please believe me that that's not the right ending," Stritch said. Still, they were desperate enough to try it one night, to boos from the audience.

And Hollywood gossip columnists were not tucked as firmly in Stritch's pocket as the ones back east. The two stars of *Barracudas* had been feuding "because of Elaine's erratic performances," Sheilah Graham reported in her "Gadabout's Diary" column. "Larry never knows if she's going to be good or not. That can unsettle a chap." Despite all signs pointing to the contrary, Graham's rival Hedda Hopper insisted that the play would make it to New York, but with a different leading lady. Even Stritch's old pal Earl Wilson forwent his usual plug for her, writing instead about mingling with Milton Berle and Esther Williams at the premiere party at Cohn's mansion on Crescent Drive in Beverly Hills.

The dark, beautiful, and contralto-voiced Rosalind Russell was also present.

"You were very good," she told Stritch, who began to tear up in gratitude.

"Would you like to take some advice from an older actress in the same profession as you're in?" Russell asked.

"Oh, yes," Stritch said.

"I don't think you should be in this business. You're far too sensitive, and you'll rue the day that you stayed in it."

Reflecting on this conversation years later, Stritch was magnanimous. "I was thinner, I hasten to say sexier than Rosalind Russell," she said, "but my god, she certainly came over like an intelligent goddamned talent. Maybe not sensitive enough and married to Oaf City who acted so jerky."

That *Barracudas* had been scheduled to run in Los Angeles through November 23, 1963, seemed, in hindsight, its final curse. The day before, many papers syndicated Dorothy Kilgallen's column declaring the play was "a bagel." Stritch's name appears just above President Kennedy's, in an item about Jackie making more public appearances for the sake of the 1964 campaign.

His assassination would be especially devastating to both Catholics and people in show business. "If I were in the picture, he never would have had an open car that day," Stritch's nephew Chris Bolton overheard her remark of Kennedy the next time their family gathered. In public, though, she displayed more ire toward Laurence Harvey than to Lee Harvey Oswald. "If I told you some of the things that son of a bitch has done to me," she said to a *Time* reporter of her costar, "you wouldn't believe it. This play has been the most horrible experience of my life."

At least Harvey had Cohn and her fortune to console him. Stritch and Grover Dale were "no longer close to the altar—if they ever were," Kilgallen wrote, adding cluckingly, "Elaine's always going steady or getting engaged, but she's a whiz at eluding that wedding ring."

The waning days of 1963 were dark, indeed: back home in Birmingham, the Stritches did not even get a holiday greeting from Coward. "WHO DO YOU HAVE TO BE TO GET A CARD THIS CHRISTMAS," Mildred reportedly wired him. "FLORENCE HENDERSON'S MOTHER?"

And her youngest daughter refused to be philosophical or politic about the play that had gone so calamitously wrong. She spoke about it for months and years to anyone who would listen. "Some enterprising record company should cut an LP of Elaine Stritch telling her devastating anecdotes about Laurence Harvey and their tribulations during *Time of the Barracudas*," Kilgallen wrote. "It would sell better than the Beatles."

8

FROM "STAR MAID" TO "BARMAID"

Over the years, many of Stritch's fans have wondered if she had lesbian inclinations. Her low voice; her style of dress and hair, which increasingly tended toward the androgynous or even masculine; her delay of marriage; her many gay friends, both male and female—all provoked certain assumptions. "People used to say that Elaine was gay and that she was a big dyke—I would say, 'Boy, have you got the wrong idea,'" Liz Smith said. "She was like somebody in *Alice in Wonderland*. She was such a softie."

In Hollywood a director told her, "You're coming over a little bit butch, just a little. I don't care what your sexual preference is."

Stritch didn't answer him because, as she remembered, "I'd never had anyone talk to me that way," and they wound up spending the night together.

Later the producer Bill Dozier, for whom she "had a big sneaker," meaning crush, explained to her this was "the oldest gag in the world. The guy out here that accuses the broad of being a dyke and he sleeps with her, because she goes along with it, because she has to prove she isn't." This level of sexual manipulation was baffling to Stritch, who had grown up participating in regulated social rituals and at least the motions of chivalry.

"The fact that I fell for it, I can't tell you the self-loathing that I had for myself a long time after that happened," she said. "I bet it was a good four days." She regretted also a one-night stand with the actor Nicholas Colasanto, a friend of Gazzara's who would go on to play Coach on *Cheers*, who, she said, told her dismissively afterward: "Leave your key under the mat. That was for Benny."

Adrift and bitter following *Barracudas*, she was staying sometimes at the apartment of Sharman Douglas, the socialite, whose intimate friendship with Princess Margaret, the Countess of Snowdon, had become the subject of gossipy scrutiny. "There were a lot of tears in that pullout bed, I can tell you," Stritch said.

After she learned what homosexuality was, purportedly after singing "Zip" in *Pal Joey*, Stritch was generally shrugging about it and without prejudice. "About same-sex marriages, I don't have an opinion," she would say later in life. "Just live and let live, and don't frighten the horses, as Mrs. Patrick Campbell so aptly put it."

Certainly when offstage Stritch flirted, charmed, and maintained deep romantic fantasies about men. Yet Frank Moran, Jr., her oldest nephew, felt there never seemed to be a spark between his Tante Elaine and the many Hollywood actors she brought home, all of whom seemed to be previously married or otherwise unsuitable, as Liz Smith had pointed out during *Madam*. "They were friends or acquaintances or hanging out but I never felt there was anything going on," he said.

"You know what I think is more bullshit than anything?" she told him more than once. "Sex is the most overrated thing there's ever been." Moran supposed that maybe she had sublimated a same-sex orientation into drinking, because of her Catholic upbringing. Or maybe it didn't matter, because Stritch saw show-business personalities as being essentially pan-romantic, before the term entered the lexicon. "She has no sex; she is all sex," Liz Smith wrote.

"I've always had a kind of attraction for someone who is not bisexual but has a feeling, a very strong feeling, for both sexes," Stritch said. "Stella Adler said in order to be a star you have to be equally attractive to men and women in an audience. Which I absolutely think is true. I think there are degrees of that kind of thing in a person's makeup." Stritch called it "some kind of simpatico, some kind of strong feeling for all human beings." Appearing with Smith late in life at the Lesbian, Gay, Bisexual and Transgender Community Center in Manhattan, she told the audience she thought that "there's a little of all of those things in all of us," nodding sagely.

Being attracted to and appreciating others of the same gender was one thing; acting on it physically was another. It was difficult enough for her to be sexual outside of marriage in a heterosexual relationship. "The idea for instance of me making love to a woman is so completely ridiculous," Stritch said. "I'm not going to say repulsive. It's ridiculous! And I heard a word applied to it once that made sense to me: narcissistic. Homosexuality to that degree is very narcissistic. You're looking in the mirror, you know."

"Narcissistic" was also an adjective people would come to attach to Elaine Stritch, but in the mid-1960s, despite the worldliness imparted to her by her European travels, by Hollywood, and by her mentorship from Coward, "naïve" still applied. In the aftermath of the failure of *Barracudas* and the general air of doom and paranoia following Kennedy's assassination, she found herself in the midst of a peculiar adventure.

It began with a Christmas visit to the Malibu home of Shirley Gordon, a onetime sitcom writer who was in a relationship with Patricia McDermott, the publicist for the *My Sister Eileen* series. Stritch maintained some degree of obliviousness to the nature of the ménage. "I was down in the dumps to the point where, I'm sorry, it was scary," she said. "It was real Hollywoodish. It was like Charlie Chaplin in *City Lights*." There had been "a lot of boozing and a lot of loneliness and a lot of terrible stuff."

She soon began to intuit that perhaps Gordon had a "sneaker" for her. "Whatever it was. I didn't even know about that maybe she was gay. I didn't . . . I know she was, it didn't make any difference to me." The first night of the visit, she said, "we had a party and there were no men there at all. I almost fainted. And I had a round bed. Scared me to death."

Stritch emerged from her guest room one evening "in one of those at-home muu muu things" and found Mary McCarty, life partner of the actress Margaret Lindsay, who would later appear in Sondheim's *Follies*.

Surprised, McCarty put her drink down on the coffee table with a click. "What the hell are you doing here?" she asked.

"It was like we were living in some kind of Tennessee Williams play and didn't know it," Stritch said. Despite some significant political actions, much of lesbian culture in America then was still underground, taboo—depicted on the covers of lurid paperbacks. "I mean, stories like this hadn't been written yet. They were going on, and one of them was going on with me in it. You know, I had a big part. It was so strange. You get involved." She got close enough to the situation to be named a correspondent in a custody case after one woman sued her partner over a Korean child they had adopted. But Stritch, though supportive in a sisterly way, found this no Garden of Eden. "I was so sick of looking at broads I nearly exploded."

With no idea what she was going to do next, Stritch got a call from the East. "And it was just a lifesaver. It was—I love the line of Tennessee Williams. 'All of a sudden these gods so quickly.'" (The line, from *A Streetcar Named Desire*, is actually "Sometimes—there's God—so quickly!") "But he took his time this trip, because all I did was just drink and watch television. It was just most horrible."

Richard Rodgers wanted Stritch to replace Eva Gabor for the last week in a run of an old musical he'd written with Lorenz Hart, *I Married an Angel*, at the Royal Poinciana Playhouse in Palm Beach. He was oversee-ing the show personally with the addition of several songs, along with a few wishfully modernizing lines like "let's banish the Beatles and go back to the harp."

Though the assignment would have felt a comedown at an earlier junc-ture, Stritch now accepted it eagerly. "Last billing? Terrific, I'm coming" was how she described her response. "It was a lifesaver because it got me out of the dykes' house in California."

Run-throughs for *Angel* took place in New York. Stritch stayed at the costume designer Theoni Aldredge's apartment on Central Park West, borrowing her clothes to go to the theater and even climbing into bed once with her husband, Tom, another actor. "I had no business doing that," Stritch said, acknowledging that she was "a royal pain in the ass."

Stritch's occasional drinking buddy Judy Garland was flaming out in much more public and spectacular fashion. An eponymous television show, meant to solve Garland's considerable financial problems, was on the brink of being canceled in 1964, and her alcohol problem was severely aggravated by the pills to which she'd been addicted off and on since she was first fed them as an adolescent by MGM executives trying to keep her skinny for the cameras. A few years later Stritch told a reporter of staying up with Garland at a theatrical party, doing improvisations. "I've never said this before in my life, but you win," Garland told her at 7:45 a.m. "I'm going to bed."

The older star's weight had fluctuated dramatically, an alarming prospect to Stritch, who took tremendous pride in her own figure. "I was not a Judy Garland type, but the stuff about my drinking was similar," she said. "I had much more discipline than Judy and much more background. I had much more pride about how I looked. Elaine Stritch would never get fat on booze—the booze would go first. But with my luck every time I went on the wagon I gained weight, because I was the type of person whose metabolism was set up that if I didn't drink I gained weight, but if I did food was secondary to me, so I paid no attention to it."

While promoting *I Married an Angel*, she publicly endorsed an "Upside-Down Diet" that included half a pound of ground beef and steamed broccoli or spinach for breakfast, and shredded-wheat biscuits with artificial sweetener at dinner. Addressing mental health, she said, "A girl's best friend is a sense of humor," adding vaguely, "The higher you can rise above disturbances, the less disturbed you become."

The diet did not account for alcohol consumption, Stritch's preferred method for escaping disturbances. Anxious about returning to the Upper West Side one night after rehearsal, she took a room at the Edison Hotel on West Forty-Seventh Street and went to bed at 9:45 p.m. The house detective had to wake her up the next day. On another occasion she fell asleep with a cigarette by the bed; Adelaide barked her alarm. Late for the run-through, Stritch bolted a couple of Bloody Marys to steel herself.

"Mr. Rodgers, I'm not smoking cigarettes anymore—I'm smoking chairs," she told him. Rodgers did not find this funny. "Of course, everything I did made him so sore because he was drinking but he was doing it on the sly," she said. "And I was out there, living out loud."

Down in Palm Beach, on opening night, Stritch was wearing a ski outfit for her part as a countess, ready to sing a zippy ditty called "I'll Tell the Man in the Street." Adelaide was in the dressing room. Eight chorus boys were in the wings and Taina Elg, who was playing an angel with a harp, finished a chorus: "Have you heard, boom boom boom."

The men made their entrance.

"Ladies and gentlemen, would everyone very quietly leave the theater," came a voice over the loudspeaker. Someone had threatened on the telephone to blow the place up. Stritch ran to get her dog and then outside and the cast wound up in front of the brand-new Schrafft's, a restaurant chain popular with women of leisure, with its colorful sun umbrellas.

"It wouldn't be the first bomb I had," Rodgers said, the easy joke.

The threat proved to be a hoax. Still, quite a few audience members chose not to return to the theater.

A few days later Stritch consented to do a satirical voice-over for a fashion show of local socialites at a fund-raiser for a new hospital, to be named in memory of John F. Kennedy. An assortment of B- and C-list entertainers were flown in for the occasion, including Hildegarde, whom Stritch had impersonated in *Angel in the Wings*. The grounds were decorated with ice sculptures and filled with "toasted tycoons and sun-seared socialites," wrote Yolanda Maurer, a Fort Lauderdale columnist who drove over to cover the party, plus a smattering of minor princesses.

Stritch was barely a blip on Maurer's radar, eclipsed by Eddie Fisher and Jayne Mansfield, but had managed with remarkable tenacity to stay on Dorothy Kilgallen's. A young singer named Tony Mitchell was "madly in love with her, and can be seen ardently smooching with her in Palm Beach," the Voice of Broadway reported. "Romanticists predict a wedding, but New Yorkers who have observed Elaine holding onto her bachelor girl status despite the blandishments of a series of attractive men have to see it to believe it."

Back in New York after the run of the show, she confronted diminished status and a diminutive suitor: Billy Rose, the impresario who stood four foot eleven. He sent a capacious Rolls-Royce to ferry Stritch to a party at Le Bijou in Greenwich Village in New York for Doris Lilly, the author of *How to Marry a Millionaire* and now *How to Make Love in Five Languages*, who along with many other women claimed to be the inspiration for Truman Capote's Holly Golightly. A board member of ASCAP, Rose had been denouncing rock music as "junk" and "obscene." He also took Stritch to Le Caprice and to hear Bobby Short, and out in a speedboat bouncing to his beach house. Not only was the place stocked with cockatoos, like Conrad Hilton's spread in Bel Air, but a violinist sawed away during dinner. "He was getting more attractive all the time," Stritch remembered thinking. "Taller and taller and taller."

As she struggled to find substantive work, it was dawning on her that she was perceived by some as a lush. "I had had, unbeknownst to me, an awful lot of reputation that I had no idea that I had," Stritch said.

She decided to officially take the year off from show business, and declared she would spend it on salubrious activities like riding her bicycle and practicing the piano. But New York's nightlife was alluring, and changing. With Eva Gabor, Stritch watched with wonderment lessons in the frug, a strange new dance step at a temporary club opened by the owner of Gogi's LaRue that Bob Fosse would spotlight in the 1966 musical *Sweet Charity*. And the actors' set had begun to follow the writers' one to a new saloon, with red-checked tablecloths and dark-wooden walls, on the Upper East Side. Named for one of its Manhattan-born proprietors, Elaine Kaufman, it was called Elaine's, and some were already joking, or actually under the misapprehension, that it was named for, or partly owned, by Stritch. The two women were sometimes confused for each other in conversation, though Kaufman was as short, portly, and dark as Stritch was tall, lean, and blonde.

One night, the bartender had called in sick and someone wanted a stinger, a classic cocktail containing brandy and crème de menthe. "Elaine, I can make a great stinger," Stritch told her namesake.

Yeah, sure, Kaufman thought. But Stritch did, taking over bartending duties that night, and volunteered to do so again.

"I didn't think she was going to turn up," Kaufman told the writer James Kaplan. "And then there she was in her little gingham dress and flats, behind the bar, trying to draw a beer." Assuming the legacy of her maternal grandfather, L. S. Job, resurrecting another of his favorite toasts—"here's looking up your old address!"—Stritch could pretend this was her own establishment, or at least enjoy the confusion.

Though she told the papers she was drawing a salary as well as beer, "Elaine didn't pay me anything," Stritch later said. "She couldn't because of the union, and she was thrilled with that. And I wanted to do it for kicks. And then I found out I liked it. I hardly drank at all. That was like the old chocolate-factory syndrome. I stopped eating chocolates."

Among the many people who were amused to be served by Stritch were Jackie Gleason (who would "come up for the gimmick of it," she said), Kenneth Jay Lane, soon to be high society's go-to costume jeweler ("She was funny, she was full of piss and vinegar," he remembered), and the actress Shelley Winters, who according to Leonard Lyons observed Stritch "happily shaking up a stinger-on-the-rocks" and inquired bluntly, "Elaine, who's your analyst?"

"Shelley, if you're deciding whether or not to tip me, that's what I'm here for," Stritch told her, and she wasn't joking. Toots Shor put one hundred dollars in her jar once, and she bragged about taking home between two and three thousand in tips each month. Her sporadic analysis aside, it concentrated the mind in a soothing way, to focus on the various concoctions and interpersonal connections. "Bartending is a lot like the theatre," she realized. "You have your audience and you're the star, but you can speak your own lines the way you want to. You're your own boss."

Kilgallen was soon calling Elaine's "the place to go," noting that "actress Stritch has brought in a whole new clientele—socialites and stage folk, naturally—since she started pouring the Scotch and mixing the Bloody Marys." And Kaufman was nurturing, after a fashion. "She was very nice to me," Stritch said. "She saw I got home every night. It was funny to see her with big sacks of money, go up to the bank, plunk it in at five in the morning. I really felt like Ann Sheridan in some movie, you know?"

Stritch was keeping her name in circulation professionally with the prospect of a new play by Michael V. Gazzo, variously called *All That Jazz*—a title for which Stritch claimed credit, since she used the phrase frequently—or *Warner Brothers Wants to Know*. "There is no doubt in my mind that this is the part for you, also that it would do things for you, that *Gypsy* cannot do for you," he had written a week after Kennedy was shot, having heard the rumor she might go to London to play Rose Hovick. "You can play *Gypsy* blindfolded, and you'll be brilliant in it. But so what—since you know that out-front, what's the challenge?" But he too was having tremendous problems with alcohol. Stritch told a story of running into the playwright's analyst and asking, "How long has Mike Gazzo been going to you? Is it a lot of years?"

"Oh yes, thirteen, fourteen," the doctor said.

"Last night I saw Mike Gazzo in his boxer shorts with a quart of Beefeater's coming out of Downey's," she told him.

"You should have seen what I started with," the doctor said.

A collective unease about the drama business was palpable in New York City. What was better theater than the Beatles, appearing on television? To "tsk" about them was to mark you as part of an earlier, suddenly fusty-seeming era. Only the musical *Bye Bye Birdie*, in 1960, had acknowledged the existence of rock music. That same year Oscar Hammerstein had died, not before suggesting to his protégé Sondheim that he might work with Rodgers. As for Rodgers himself, he had faith enough in the young composer-lyricist, though they didn't get along personally, that he invested in *Anyone Can Whistle*. But that show flopped badly, after twelve previews and nine performances. Though it would become a cult favorite in years to come, it was too experimental, too challenging, too strange for a crowd that was craving escapism after the Kennedy assassination, much as it had during the Great Depression. They flocked instead to dazzling, retro shows like *Funny Girl*, about Fanny Brice, and *Hello, Dolly!*, about a widowed matchmaker at the turn of the century.

Writing for television and later contributing crossword puzzles to *New York* magazine, Sondheim was also among Stritch's patrons at Elaine's. They had mutual friends in Anthony Perkins and Mary Ann Madden, a witty former debutante who'd helped with the decoration of the restrooms and to whom Sondheim handed over the job of puzzles once he returned to musicals. "It seemed to me to fit in perfectly with what I knew about Elaine," he said of Stritch's bartending stint. "It was raffish and free-spirited and she was having a good time. She loved to drink, she loved to talk, and she loved two in the morning. You put those three things together and what's better than to be a bartender? Because you know, if I get bored tending to you and I'm the bartender I say, 'Excuse me, I have to tend the lady over here.' So with Elaine's impatience, she just thought, Oh, he's a bore, I'll go on to this one. Perfect job."

But Liz Smith, who was now the entertainment editor for Helen Gurley Brown's *Cosmopolitan* magazine, was concerned about possible ill effects on her dear friend's career.

"Elaine, why are you doing this?" she said over the phone.

"Oh, Liz, I'm just doing this for fun," Stritch replied.

"She was also doing it drinking and needing guys," Smith thought, standing there like a sort of siren with the bottles and glassware behind her waiting for men to be dashed on the rocks, as it were—"and it was all men, women didn't go up to the bar then."

"Well, I don't approve of you doing this," she told Stritch. "I think it's strange. It's the kind of thing struggling actresses do."

Stritch laughed. "Well, I'm a struggling actress!"

"She wasn't," Smith said. "She always had money and kept it with an iron grip." And after a few months, she added, Kaufman got tired of the stunt and "got rid of her. She couldn't stand the complication. She liked people like me who were in the middle, harmless, and going to do her some good. So that didn't last."

"You just encroached on her," Smith told Stritch, who harbored no bitterness.

"One tough cookie," the actress said later in life of Kaufman, who died in 2010, her bar closing five months later. "I mean, she just went through life like a fucking truck."

Now approaching forty, Stritch would put on a plum velvet smoking jacket, all the rage in mod London, for a night out at Gallagher's, a steak house in the theater district, leopard-printed evening pants for another, making sure Earl Wilson knew about her outing. "Put on your Sunday clothes, there's lots of world out there," she sang to Leonard Lyons in between sips of champagne at the Oak Room at the Plaza Hotel, quoting a song from *Hello, Dolly!* She had just auditioned for its touring company before the choreographer Gower Champion and the fearsome producer David Merrick (aka the Abominable Showman)—"only the rulers of the world," she said, adding plaintively, "I don't want diamond necklaces. I want that job." But it went to Mary Martin.

Another enticing possibility was the new Arthur Laurents musical, *Do I Hear a Waltz?*, based on his play *The Time of the Cuckoo* and the Katharine Hepburn movie *Summertime*, about an American spinster abroad. Rodgers was writing the music, and at the exhortation of his daughter Mary, Sondheim had once again agreed to write lyrics only.

A spinster abroad was an obvious fit for Stritch: *Sail Away*'s Mimi Paragon, this time with middle-aged regrets. But it wasn't a particularly comic role and Rodgers, chary after the experience with *I Married an Angel* and drinking heavily himself (despite regular stints at the Payne Whitney Clinic on the Upper East Side), kiboshed the idea of a leading lady who might join him in his cups. She was consuming no more alcohol than many of her male contemporaries, but she would pay a far higher price in lost professional opportunities.

The new year of 1965 brought a new boyfriend: Gary Pudney, a younger advertising executive working on the General Foods account. Stritch had been playing weekly charades with him in a circle of friends that included Pat Newcomb, who'd been Marilyn Monroe's publicist; Donald Brooks, a popular sportswear designer; and Sharman Douglas. "It was all fun and games and cocktails at five o'clock," Pudney said. "Elaine of course could make a three-act play out of one."

She found a somewhat bottom-feeding movie job, playing a predatory lesbian club owner in *Who Killed Teddy Bear?* Her confusing interlude in California could now count as research. The movie starred Sal Mineo of *Rebel Without a Cause* as a deranged killer and the dancer Juliet Prowse as his target; it would be conveniently filmed in New York. "Come on Thursday—that's when Sal Mineo strangles me," she told one niece planning a visit, according to Earl Wilson: playing Mame to the hilt.

Daniel J. Travanti, who later starred in *Hill Street Blues* and became an outspoken champion of Alcoholics Anonymous, played a bouncer, a deaf-mute who got his throat slit. "I thought, This is a big nothing," he said of the filming, during which the actors carpooled to save money. "The big question I had was 'Why are Sal Mineo and Juliet Prowse and Elaine Stritch doing this movie?' These were big people." Stritch did "the funniest Katharine Hepburn impression of anybody I'd ever heard," he said. He'd heard "that she was difficult. I was told the same thing about Faye Dunaway. And in both cases they were not difficult at all."

In one scene, Stritch and Prowse strip in a sisterly way to lingerie but then Stritch appears to make a pass at her. They "had eighteen thousand brandies before we shot it," Stritch said. "The scene wasn't working, so I rewrote it like when you're on the make for somebody and you're in the wrong pew, if you know what I mean."

Her character, Marian Freeman, indeed speaks in Stritchish cadences when she describes not wearing a bra until she was twenty-eight. "I don't like being fenced in. It's a hang-up of mine." She puts on Prowse's fur coat over a slip. "I dig fur . . . I dig soft things, don't you?"

Mineo was filmed in one scene wearing nothing but Jockey shorts, a likely first in a commercially released American film. Stritch didn't know that he was a closeted homosexual. "No. He was just a little boy to me. And a good actor," she said. After all, "the only gay people in the fifties were chorus boys with sibilant Ss."

With reasonably low expectations for the picture, she invested some savings in a French-Greek restaurant called Soerabaja, run out of a town house between Lexington and Park Avenues, and began pouring drinks there instead. "You know how some women take up needlepoint? Well, I work behind the bar," she said. Kilgallen called it "the new rage saloon," adding, "You can tell because Elaine Stritch has found it."

"At Soerabaja, you feel so much at home that you don't want to go home" was the restaurant's marketing tagline. Pudney had moved into Stritch's apartment but didn't believe they had a future. He felt pressured into a closer relationship than he wanted, with her particular tactic of leaking the news of their supposed betrothal to the columnists. Stritch kept suggesting the wedding would take place that month, that week, before the ink was dry on the next daily edition. She claimed to Earl Wilson that she was turning down the role of Madame Rose in a supposed London production of *Gypsy* "because I don't think a married woman should work."

"Elaine decided that she thought we should get married, which I did not want to do," Pudney said. "I kind of felt I was being railroaded into this thing with her girlfriends after me with all of this stuff." He did take her home to L.A. to meet his parents. "My father was crazy about her. My mother took one look and said, 'Are you out of your mind?' We had a housekeeper named Mrs. Johnson, this very big woman who would come every day and help my mother with her chores. One day we came back from doing errands and the two of them were absolutely bombed on martinis."

Kilgallen continued to monitor the actress's status. "Elaine Stritch keeps telling people she's going to get married, but gee whiz, we've heard that for so many years," she wrote with a touch of weariness. A few weeks later, the columnist followed up: "It looks as though the highly publicized engagement of Elaine Stritch and Gary Pudney has gone the way of all Elaine's other betrothals. She's been in the Ground Floor"—yet another nightclub—"three times since it opened, each evening with a different other squire."

Soon after people read this particular item at breakfast tables in other cities, on November 8, 1965, Kilgallen was discovered dead in the town house she shared with her husband, Dick Kollmar, on East Sixty-First Street, aged fifty-two. The suspected cause was a combination of alcohol and barbiturates, though for years Kennedy conspiracy theorists have insinuated foul play because Kilgallen had refused to accept the Warren Commission's conclusions, had interviewed Jack Ruby at the trial for his murder of Lee Harvey Oswald, and was known to have notes for a book advancing an alternate theory about the assassination.

Kilgallen had put Stritch on the map in New York and never lost track of her, like a watchful surrogate older sister; they had both suffered and stood up to the insults of Frank Sinatra, who cruelly referred to Kilgallen as "the chinless wonder." "Dorothy and Stritch shared some of the same insecurities," wrote Lee Israel in her biography of Kilgallen, "and they apparently had a heady discussion about whether it was better for a woman to be beautiful or funny."

Once at three in the morning, according to Israel, Stritch had called Kilgallen.

> "Dorothy Mae?"
> "Yes?"
> "Funny is better."

The untimely death of her longtime chronicler, commemorated at St. Vincent Ferrer Church in a ceremony attended by more than two thousand people, did not spoil Stritch's appetite for hijinks. Having been sent an invitation to a party for Princess Margaret and her husband, Lord Snowdon, hosted by Sharman Douglas at the Four Seasons, Stritch scribbled her grocery list on the back and then lost it. The invitation was intercepted by Thomas Jackson Cole, described to the papers alternately as a delivery boy and freelance Christmas card designer with a mild case of cerebral palsy. After "fooling around" for a couple of weeks, Cole purportedly read in the papers that Stritch might be denied admittance to the party, so he returned it to her and was invited along.

"That was the most natural thing in the world for me to do," Stritch said. "I hate rank, class and acting the star bit."

The press was not invited to the party, but Earl Wilson, who would be one of Kilgallen's replacements at the *Journal-American*, dressed up as a waiter and snuck in, scribbling down details of the modernist restaurant's signature shallow pool covered with glass to make a dance floor, the midnight buffet of trout and crêpes suzette cooked to order in the kitchen, and the guest list, which included Harry Belafonte and Truman Capote. Posing with Cole, who was wearing a tuxedo with a lopsided tie and a pleased if baffled expression, Stritch made both the cover of the *Daily News* and the society page of the *Times*.

Some months later, Walter Winchell reported that this supposed "grocery boy" was actually a San Francisco socialite, who "squired girls from the Best Families to the snootiest events, etc."

"That was just one of her shenanigans," Pudney said. "I was caught in this whirlwind of this woman who was a former Broadway star who was now a real complicated character, looking for an outlet for her talents." She marked time as a secretary to Peter Falk's lawyer in a CBS dramedy called *The Trials of O'Brien*, a part she secured after walking into P. J. Clarke's and joining Falk's table with the memorable line, as related by the character actor George Furth, "Just get me a bottle of vodka and a floor plan."

"So it isn't *Camille*," she shrugged to a reporter. "No, it isn't *Camille* and I suppose we should all give a small cheer. Camille wasn't exactly my idea of a swinger."

Pudney watched Stritch go to church every Sunday—"there is a great similarity between church and the theater . . . both are highly dramatic," she proclaimed—and rush around town with dry-cleaning bags. "She used to steal my shirt all the time," he said. "It would be the heels and the black stockings and I would get up and tried to get dressed and my shirt would be missing for the office."

"Did you like Gary, Mother?" Elaine asked Mildred Stritch after they met.

"Yeah, I'd like to take a walk with him and get some lollipops," Mildred replied. She had given up on the idea that her daughter was going to marry a Hollywood star. Now she was just hoping Elaine wouldn't tumble into complete disrepute.

Who Killed Teddy Bear? was received coolly, pointed to as an example of declining mores in American society, and even condemned by the Catholic

Church. Panning over the nudie shows that had begun to pop up with increasing regularity in Times Square, the movie was a "grim commentary" on New York, it seemed to the *Los Angeles Times*. "Story hardly needs this touch of perversion," was what the critic there thought of Stritch's sapphic character, "but the trend now is never knowing when to stop."

Mame opened on Broadway in May 1966 and made Angela Lansbury, after the disappointment of *Anyone Can Whistle*, a definitive star of the musical theater. Stritch, meanwhile, had been reduced to summer stock: Irving Berlin's *Annie Get Your Gun* in Toronto (during which a motorcycle she was supposed to ride onstage refused to start); Rodgers and Hammerstein's *The King and I* at the Lawrenceville Music Circus in New Jersey; and Clare Boothe Luce's *The Women* in Dayton, Ohio. The cast of this last production included Gloria Swanson and Marge Champion, the dancer and choreographer then married to Gower Champion.

"Welcome, Women," read the marquee of the motel in Dayton, where the cast stayed. Stritch, playing a former chorus girl called Miriam, bunked with the company's hairdresser. Swanson had a trailer nearby, Stritch remembered, where she "cooked her own seaweed, guru beads, nuts, and god knows what."

On opening night, Stritch brought a half-gallon jug of wine backstage, pouring glasses for every member of the cast, which they ignored as she partook. She was naughty onstage, stretching out lines for laughs, mocking Swanson's use of "olé," a prearranged cue for a line reminder, and mugging exhaustion and boredom during Champion's monologue.

The curtain descended just before midnight, forty-five minutes late or more. "I mean, she milked every line, every gesture," said the director, John Kenley. "And the audience adored her!"

"Even when you're drunk, you're a better actress than the rest of them," he told Stritch.

But the next day someone in the cast called Actors' Equity. The rest of the cast had conferred and was threatening not to go on unless Stritch was replaced. "I had to let her go," Kenley said. "But—god!—she really put on a show, if only for a night!"

The Women was a relic. Theater in America was changing rapidly, reflecting the incursion of rock 'n' roll and hippies. Stritch veered sharply to a freakish character in a musical version of *The Grass Harp*, based on the Capote novel and subsequent play, in Providence, Rhode Island: Baby Love, "a revivalist who had all these babies," in Stritch's words. "*Me.* I traveled around the country in my truck with all these babies," she recalled with incredulity, adding of the number "Babylove Miracle Show," "I don't know what the hell it was about, but it was a great big rousing good song. It was the first time I ever found a reason to use a mike." And the musical was "a big gay time in the theater," she said. "I mean we were all having a ball."

Done with Pudney, she began an affair with the conductor of the production, who was married to a decorator in New York. "I fell madly in love with him and vice versa," she said. "It was all carried out like a French movie." Back in the city, he invited her to lunch, by which time Stritch had gotten tired of the whole idea. "I had a white Courrèges coat and hat on, and I met him and then I started acting—see, it wasn't real anymore—I started acting the part of a woman in love with a married man in New York City," she said. "And then it was La Cote de Boop-puh-dup-puh-doo on the real West Side. Saddest lunch." Jonathan Tunick, who orchestrated the production, as he would go on to do for many of Sondheim's seminal works, was ignorant of this affair, but enjoyed Stritch's blast of personality, while feeling her miscast. "Though by nature I'm rather reticent, for some reason she didn't cow me," he said.

They developed an easy bantering rapport, despite their different backgrounds. He had attended Juilliard, the top music school in the country. "I don't know that she ever studied," he said. "I don't think she knew how to count a rest. She was all street smarts." But "we seemed to more or less get along. I liked her. She was funny and she was smart, even then exhibiting the zany qualities that have always been associated with her." He came to think of Stritch as a thoroughbred, skittish, or like a temperamental Italian race car, which won't start some days but, if it does, performs like no other model.

Many were perplexed at her stalled, or at least slowed, career. "Why Miss Stritch is not the number one musical comedy queen of Broadway is something I shall never understand," wrote one critic after she appeared, again as Ruth Sherwood, in a City Center revival of Leonard Bernstein's

Wonderful Town. "Instead of being the performer's performer which she is, she should be as well-known to the public as Miss Russell, Miss Martin, Miss Verdon, Miss Lansbury et al." But despite the reviewer's use of the word "Miss," all of these women had the support—emotional, financial, professional, or all three—of a spouse: Russell had Brisson; Martin, Richard Halliday; Gwen Verdon, Bob Fosse; Lansbury, Peter Shaw. Stritch continued to go it alone. Drink was her only constant companion, her steady escort, her abusive husband.

In July 1967, George and Mildred Stritch celebrated their fiftieth wedding anniversary with a party on Arlington Street. "THAT'S WHAT YOU GET MARRYING FOR LOVE," cabled Elaine's old swain Kent Smith and his new wife, Edith, using a phrase from *Call Me Madam.*

Had *everyone* paired off? Ben Gazzara was now with Janice Rule. Gig Young had fathered a daughter with his fourth wife, Elaine Williams, a real estate agent, after divorcing Elizabeth Montgomery, who would become known for the television show *Bewitched.* Even Sharman Douglas, Stritch's boon companion in the freewheeling life, would soon be hitched to an English food importer. Helen Gurley Brown, who'd parlayed the best-sellerdom of her book *Sex and the Single Girl* into the editorship of *Cosmopolitan* and was married to the movie producer David Brown, also sent a congratulatory telegram to George and Mildred. Stritch flew home for the occasion, posing for newspaper photos with her sisters, who now had between them seven children. She did not bring an escort, and who could blame her? After the Sidney Poitier movie released that year, Mildred would take to saying of dates she disdained, "Guess who's *not* coming to dinner?"

Stritch had taken over the torch of the "single girl" from Brown and hoisted it even more proudly. She went to Daly's Dandelion, the conductor Skitch Henderson's nightspot in Manhattan, wearing a minidress twinkling with tiny lights, the battery hidden in her bra. She appeared on a television show called *Girl Talk* with a young Nora Ephron. She greeted the first widely known trans woman, Christine Jorgensen—"Ooooo, I've heard so much about you"—at a party for Rex Reed's book of collected interviews, *Do You Sleep in the Nude?* She entertained at a rally for Eugene McCarthy, though she was not paying much mind to the highly charged political environment. "I was about as aware of that as I am what the weather is like right now in Tokyo," she said. "I don't give a rat's ass. And I don't mean to be smart-assed and say I didn't care; I just had enough on my plate and I didn't know that there were flower children, and I didn't know about the Beatles worth a dime and I didn't know, I didn't know, *I didn't know*, what was going on except my work and that I had the best deal at the hotel and was I running around with people that I had a good time with and had I written my family—you know just personal, personal, personal. I didn't really care about anything else."

One positive new association was with Judith Ann Abrams, a gamine young blonde woman who had been doing theater for children, using the name Pixie Judy, and was planning a show to benefit another Kennedy-family foundation. "I was thinking that we could maybe do more business if I got a name to do the show," she said. Someone suggested Stritch.

"I had a list of other people to call, but she was the only one listed in the phone book," Abrams said. Stritch was still living with Sharman Douglas at the time. "And to meet Sharman and Elaine at the same time was so scary, I can't even tell you."

But Stritch was more than game. "I'd like to do one of your shows," she said.

"Really? I would love that," Abrams said, beaming.

"No, I mean I'd like to *direct* one."

"Have you directed before?" Abrams asked. (Some big shot, she thought.)

Stritch hadn't, but when cast in a revival of Coward's *Private Lives* at the Theater de Lys in Greenwich Village, she took it upon herself to find a leading man after the first one quit. "I don't know, I hate to think that men don't like strong women because I've had a lot of men like me, and I'm strong," she said. "But I guess I'm not, and that's why they like me. I guess there's a vulnerable side to a woman that a man gets to and likes and admires. But when it's applied to work, I'm saying it's hard when a strong woman in the theater is out looking for a lead." She managed to persuade Russell Nype, her costar in *Call Me Madam* and *Goldilocks*, to take the job. A family man now, he was taken aback by how much Stritch drank. "She was still having her brandy," he said. And yet she monopolized the notices.

"As a Noël Coward evening," the play was "not all it should be," led the *Times* reviewer. "But as an Elaine Stritch evening it's a smash."

Noël Coward at this moment was decidedly passé; the "it" musical of spring 1968 was *Hair*. In limbo between the hippies and the settling-down of her peers, Stritch was living with Judy Abrams in a terraced apartment at the Sutton East, a white-brick building on East Fifty-Sixth Street, near the Mr. Caruso salon where her favorite hairdresser, Vincent Roppatte, worked. She tried to persuade Eileen Fulton, who had been her costar in *Who's Afraid of Virginia Woolf?*, to move in across the hall, getting the key and bringing Fulton up to show it.

"Now, you stay here," she said. There was a backdrop of wallpaper patterned with blue stars. "We'll have such fun—party after party, and you can come to my apartment and sunbathe on the terrace."

Fulton demurred, but she remained fiercely loyal to her former costar. She was at Sardi's when she overheard someone disparage Stritch as a has-been and an alcoholic. She slammed her own drink on the table. "I heard that," she said sternly, protectively. "Don't you ever say that about Elaine Stritch. She is the greatest, the most wonderful—she is a true actor."

In one's life, as in theater, sometimes a walk-on part changes the entire course of the action. For Stritch this came in the person of Lee Israel, a devoted fan since she had visited *Bus Stop* to interview the actress for a column called "From the Acropolis" in her junior high school newspaper. "Met her backstage; she took me to the corner watering-hole and bed me ***(I cannot RESIST leaving in the previous typo. Freud just did handstands in his urn) . . . FED ME*** three dry martinis" was how Israel, not the most reliable narrator, recalled the meeting in an email to a friend.

Once again whether unwittingly, tolerantly, or manipulatively, Stritch drew close to a woman who happened to be gay. She had tried to enlist Israel to help with her memoirs when Liz Smith got too busy. (Perhaps it was for the best she failed, because Israel later admitted committing widespread literary forgery, including of Coward's letters, in a memoir called *Can You Ever Forgive Me?*, made into a 2018 movie.) Staying close to Stritch when she was "virtually unemployable," as Israel put it to a friend years later, the two women traveled to Birmingham to borrow rent money from George and Mildred. "They picked us up at the airport and Elaine's scatty mother pointed out all the hot spots, including the locus of Jew-hating Father Coughlin's activities," she recalled. On Arlington Street that night, after Israel removed her stockings, Stritch took them to the bathroom to rinse; Israel wondered whether this was a gesture of seduction, but it resulted in nothing.

One Sunday afternoon back in New York, the two were working on the book in Stritch's apartment when the phone rang. "That was Liz Smith," Stritch said. "Yelling. Jealous that you were here. She must be knockin' back the gin again."

"This was not a sexual thing, of course," Israel believed. "Just about jealousy."

The material they gathered resulted not in a book, but a feature story Israel placed in *The New York Times*. It depicted an actress of universally acknowledged talent who was now believed to be a bad risk. "They all love Elaine," Israel wrote of the producers and directors she'd called. "But along the way lots of people have ceased to trust her, or can understand why people have ceased to trust her. She drinks, they say."

Stritch's response to this charge was, in essence, "heck yes, but so what." Regally she wore a white turban, last fashionable in the 1940s, to Sardi's, where, *Private Lives* having closed, she was once again "at liberty," as the article grandly put it. "I'm not a bit opposed to your mentioning in this article that Frieda Fun here has had a reputation in the theater, for the past five or six years, for drinking," she told Israel, sawing into a steak. "I drink and I love to drink, and it's part of my life. And it will always be a part of my life, because it's a wonderful thing for social communication."

Israel also included a scene in the piece at the terraced apartment, which was decorated in "tasty, toasty orange and beige," with a pack of matches from Andy Warhol's Factory at the ready on the coffee table. Stritch quoted an old Scottish ballad, "As we journey through life, let us live by the way" (omitting the line "then bring us a tankard o' nappy brown ale").

"I have done just about everything, really, except have a baby," she said. "And I've got to hurry if I want to do that." She was forty-three, and though she wanted to direct, she also wanted again to be directed: "All I'm looking for is somebody who knows more than I do. If they're interested, they can call."

Not long after the article was published, Stritch accepted the role of Vera Charles, the drunken friend who had been played by Bea Arthur on Broadway, in a tour of *Mame*; Janet Blair would play the title character. The traveling show was choreographed by Diana Baffa-Brill, who'd been the dance captain of the Broadway production. "She was a character from day one," Baffa-Brill said of Stritch. "Very gruff and funny, but there was also a very dear side." A number called "Bosom Buddies" had a vaudeville flavor with real steps. "And one of them, she just could not get it. And Janet Blair was perfect. She got it first try. Elaine called it 'the motherfucker step' and from then on it was 'the motherfucker step.'"

When Adelaide, the dog, died in Boston, this seemed the absolute nadir for Stritch—a definitive reminder that her old genteel way of life was gone forever. (However, the cast got her another dog, a long-haired dachshund that she named Bridget.) Then on June 22, 1969, Judy Garland's fifth husband found Judy dead, at forty-seven, sitting on the toilet in their London home. What was the joy in finally getting to play Mame, in summer stock at the Cape Cod Melody Tent in Hyannis? "The biggest mistake of my life," Stritch said. "Vera is better than Mame."

Not long thereafter the phone in her hotel room rang and the voice of Hal Prince, Broadway hit maker, came booming through the receiver. "I know more than you," he said, referring to Israel's article. "How would you feel about doing a musical for me?"

With special resonance for anyone in the theater, the project was to be called *Company*.

9.

"EVERYBODY RISE"

E ven when confronting serious issues, the American musical had long been befrilled like a valentine, with performers descending staircases in feather boas, cavorting alongside exuberant sailors, taking measure of the corn in Plasticine Technicolor, or singing sweetly in the rain. Even the cast of *Hair*, the 1968 rock musical, handed out flowers to the audience.

Company by contrast was bare, spare, and sour: "the acid inside the sponge cake," as one of Stritch's soon-to-be colleagues, Larry Kert, the original Tony of *West Side Story*, put it. Essentially plotless, it featured five wedded couples and three single women hovering over an impassive Manhattan bachelor on his thirty-fifth birthday, urging him to commit in one breath and decrying the institution of marriage with the next. "It's an absolute total departure from the run-of-the-mill musical, which I think is going out of style, anyway," Stritch said in a radio interview with Lee Jordan to promote the show.

Company had evolved after an intensive series of letters and meetings between George Furth, who was writing the book; Sondheim, writing both lyrics and music for the first time since *Anyone Can Whistle*, and

Prince, who'd agreed to direct and produce. "It's *Oh! What a Lovely War*, about marriage," Sondheim said during one discussion, referring to the 1963 World War I satire directed by Joan Littlewood. *Company*—with sleek chrome-and-Plexiglas sets suggested by a Francis Bacon painting of a blurry man in what looks like a cage and rendered by Boris Aronson of *Bus Stop*; strenuous choreography by Michael Bennett, who would go on to glittering glory with *A Chorus Line*; and a cast of mostly unknowns— was, per its title, the consummate ensemble piece. But for Stritch it was the most important part she'd had since *Sail Away*.

Unbeknownst to her, she had figured in the material since its inception. Furth, who'd recently appeared in *The Boston Strangler* and *Butch Cassidy and the Sundance Kid*, had been for some time writing a series of one-act plays (named variously *My Married Friends* and *A Husband, a Wife, a Friend*) as a psychoanalytic exercise. One of the plays was about a leading lady drinking heavily with two men in her dressing room after a performance in New Haven, Connecticut. Her name was Laraine Birch, and Furth's unpublished draft shows she was based unsparingly on the woman he'd encountered for a decade or so in the backstages and bars of their shared trade.

"Her voice comes from the absolute bottom of the vocal register," he wrote. "Her tone has an almost monotony of sarcasm. She is very quick with 'one-liners' the basis of her humor being an almost ceaseless reversal of things as they are."

Demanding chilled champagne, stashing vodka under her dressing table, Birch calls herself "Sarah Souse," echoing Stritch's reference to herself as "Frieda Fun" in the 1968 *Times* interview conducted by Lee Israel. Birch bemoans her inability to enjoy sexual intercourse—"the act of love pains, brother . . . Gentlemen, do you know the honest and truthful reason I've never enjoyed it is because I'm a nice girl"—and find a partner who can equal the sanctified image of her father. "I have been like Diogenes looking for that man, but they don't make him like that anymore," she declares, going on to describe plaintively the ambivalence about commitment that would form the thematic core of *Company*. "And I am forty-two and I don't mind alone. I mean I want someone. I do. But I can survive alone—I don't know if I can survive together. That's crap.

Forget I said that. I want together, that's what every woman wants. Can you believe that I've been shrunk. Honest injun."

Furth's notion had been that this tortured soul, and the other female characters in his plays, about various couples, would all be played by one woman: Stritch's costar in *Bus Stop*, Kim Stanley, the foremost disciple of Lee Strasberg and his Actors Studio, who had been nominated for an Academy Award, but retreated from acting and descended into drinking after being booed by Londoners for a disastrous performance as Masha in Chekhov's *Three Sisters*.

Sondheim, a friend of Furth's, had shown the material to Prince, who thought it would be a good basis for a musical. The three made the protagonist a man whom they named Robert, with the lyrically fertile nicknames Bobby, Robby, Rob, Bubby—whatever the other characters want him to be. The Birch character, though or as a consequence of being married "three or four times," was the most vocally skeptical about the institution.

Prince had not particularly kept track of Stritch since *Angel in the Wings*. In the previous decade, as she had been floundering, he had become a theatrical colossus with offices in Rockefeller Center and Munich, producing (*Fiddler on the Roof*) and producing-directing (*Cabaret*, *Zorba*, *She Loves Me*). When he called her, Stritch reported that she "practically jumped through the phone." Acknowledging to Jordan that she was "an old repertory theater girl at heart," she did her best to sound with it about *Company*, calling it "a more sophisticated version of *Hair* . . . a sophisticated collection or collage at what the kids are doing today, almost like a Noël Coward version of rock 'n' roll." She was especially proud to serve as Furth's muse, repeating to the *New York Post* a line he'd said to Sondheim: "Every time you run into Elaine Stritch, you know you're in New York." Stritch elaborated liltingly, "I guess it's a kind of madness that follows me around, I don't know. Hair nets on Park Avenue." She was frank about feeling psychologically unmoored: "I have a feeling that there's something very unreal about life . . . I have a feeling of unreality. The older that I get."

A script merely containing Laraine Birch's anguished monologues would have surely hit too close to home. But the character had evolved, first into Alice, a widowed mother of two daughters idling at the park; then JoAnne and finally just Joanne, no longer an actress but just "the richest of them all," a hard-boiled serial divorcée married to a pin-striped three-piece suit named Larry (played by Charles Braswell, who had had a small role in *Sail Away*). All the couples berate Robert to settle down, first annoyingly, later movingly. One scene takes place in a "swank bar," Furth wrote, "and Robert is sitting with this couple. SHE is Elaine Stritch, or better, SHE is Mrs. Robinson to his Dustin Hoffman." The draft was sent in January to Prince, who queried in the margin: "Steve: Is this all a song?"

Was it ever. It was Furth's sketch of the jaded, vaguely predatory Joanne, along with Sondheim's own long-term if affectionately arm's-length knowledge of Stritch, that would inspire him to write "The Ladies Who Lunch." Performers including Alan Cumming, baring his biceps; a young Anna Kendrick clutching a martini glass in the movie *Camp*; and countless drag queens have made the song a cabaret staple, requiring someone of obvious middle age for maximum effect. Its lines are regularly cited as book titles (*I'll Drink to That*; *Everybody Rise*) and for comic effect (Sondheim was amused, he once told *The Guardian*, to spot a muscled man in Greenwich Village wearing a tight T-shirt reading "off to the gym / then to a fitting"). Another line is perhaps the most perfectly succinct expression of nostalgia for the pre-Camelot era: "Does anyone still wear a hat?"

Sondheim's first sketch of the number also suggested a longing for rapidly fraying midcentury mores. It was called "Crinoline," after the outdated underskirt that stiffened party frocks (Sondheim's mother, Janet, known as Foxy, had been a fashion designer). In an early incarnation, Joanne was supposed to hail from the Midwest. "I thought, That's sort of interesting, because most upper-class broads are New England debutante-type characters, but an upper-class broad from Chicago—that's a good idea," Sondheim said. "And I couldn't make the song work so I just stopped."

Furth was gradually converting Joanne into a dyed-in-the-wool Manhattanite, specifying that she was that type of "self-satisfied New Yorker who never leaves" and going so far in script notes as to switch the college she attended from Bennington to Vassar. Sondheim put on the record Stritch had made for Dolphin and mulled the sort of high-society Upper East Side women Foxy had associated with at places like "21," and the number, at first called just "Drinking Song," came easily after that, he said. And Stritch understood it intuitively from the start, though she dined out for years on being confused by the lyric "Perhaps a piece of Mahler's." "She came into rehearsal and said, 'Listen, you've got to explain this to me. What is this, a schnecken?'" Sondheim said. "She was street-smart; it's not necessarily that she was ill read. She knew who Molière was, she just didn't read the plays. She knew who Beethoven was, but she'd never heard of Mahler so, you know, she was not a concertgoer. She was the man on the street from that point of view."

It was becoming one of Sondheim's artistic hallmarks to give the audience invigorating shocks. So, like "Rose's Turn" in *Gypsy* with its "m-m-m-mommas," intimating Hovick's breakdown, "Drinking Song" would interrupt Joanne's blasé recitation with a sudden shriek, as if from the primal-scream therapy that was just becoming modish ("Aaaaaaaaaaaaaaaaaaaaaaaaahhhhhhh!").

"The one thing I had to coach her on was the scream, which is the whole point of the surprise and the song, so to speak," Sondheim said. "I remember when I played the song for Hal and Michael Bennett and I got to suddenly screaming, they both leaped out of their chairs and I thought, Yeah, that's what I want. That'll make everybody's hair stand on end. Elaine didn't understand what I wanted. And she would always go 'Ohhhhh!' And I said, 'No, no, the idea is to make it go'"—and here the composer made a soaring-down noise—"like an airplane." (Playing the role in London in 2018, Patti LuPone said that Sondheim advised her to just think of how she felt after reading the newspaper.)

But the success of the song is that it not only disturbs but rouses. Fueled by vodka stingers of the variety Elaine whipped up at Elaine's circa 1964, Joanne arrives at a climactic finish, addressing the bar's phantom patrons as well as the paying customers of the theater: "Everybody rise! Rise!" And then again the exhortation to "rise," half a dozen more times—an idea inspired, Prince said, by the end of the somewhat sunnier

"A Wonderful Guy" from *South Pacific*, whose lyrics had been written by Sondheim's mentor, Oscar Hammerstein.

"I said, 'Look right at the women in the audience,'" Prince said of his direction to Stritch. "Tell them to get the hell up out of those chairs and assert themselves. It's kind of feminist." Sondheim said he came up with the idea to try to secure Stritch a standing ovation (much less common in those days). "I said, 'If this number works, the audience will rise.' Now that never happened but that still was the idea. It's about breaking the fourth wall." Stritch would insist it was hers. "Rise, you bastard, rise," she said, reminiscing years later. "I was the one. I mean, I said to Steve and he took it very well. I wanted more rises. I didn't do that so the song would really be a 'Whoa.' I did it because I felt an emotional need to do it. And I had a feeling that he knew that. And he said, 'Okay, we'll try it.' So I did it and of course they"—the audience—"flipped but they never showed too much." Archly assessing the upper-middle-class wife's situation—"keeping house but clutching / a copy of *Life* / just to keep in touch," the song reached beyond the stage. "I almost think of Joanne as a member of the audience," Stritch told Lee Jordan. "She's a dame who's very ahead of her time. She knows too much to be happy."

Stritch made clear that she was not in fact interchangeable with this jaded creature. "I'm not married in real life, which I want put on the air, constantly." To one reporter she sounded like a walking personal ad: "Everybody thinks I'm brassy. Maybe I look like a Vegas type—but I ain't. I'm a New England–cottage type—fireplace, books and martinis. And yes, I want to be married."

Among friends, though, Stritch was more ambivalent about the institution; indeed she was as much Bobby as Joanne (presciently, as the former character would, in the 2018 London production, be played by a woman, Rosalie Craig). "I told the Elaine Stritch wish of just moving in with people and having no place of her own," Furth reported of another meeting. "Giving them money, just to use their things, wear their clothes, have no responsibilities. This can be incorporated into our hero's wish." (Critical analysis of *Company* focused less on that hero's renunciation of bourgeois capitalist values, though, than what some saw as his ambiguous sexuality. But though the creators had mulled making him gay, they deliberately had decided against it. "Should the man be a homosexual?" Prince said in early discussion, according to Furth's notes. "No, we say. If he is trapped and cannot do something positive, then that is one play. But here, if he can but doesn't, that is another play.")

Anthony Perkins had considered playing the affable, inscrutable Robert, but he dropped out to direct and star in *Steambath*, an off-Broadway play by Bruce Jay Friedman. Perkins was replaced by the Hollywood actor Dean Jones, a friendly face to audiences after the Disney movies *That Darn Cat!* and *The Love Bug*, who therefore commanded a high salary and perks negotiated by the William Morris Agency.

Auditions for the rest of *Company* commenced at the Imperial Theater on West Forty-Fifth Street in May 1969. Some actors were called back multiple times to read for Joanne, including Sada Thompson, Millie Slavin, and Jessica James, who would be booked as Stritch's standby. But the part was never really anyone else's. Not having quite forgiven Gloria Safier for the disappointment of *Time of the Barracudas*, Stritch had moved on to a new, young agent, Michael Hartig. Prince's general manager, Carl Fisher, was already midhaggle with Hartig, facing a demand of $1250 per week, more than twice what Fisher was offering (and about a third of what Jones was promised). Hartig also requested billing equivalent to another early hire, the younger, doe-eyed Barbara Barrie, who'd won a Best Actress award at the Cannes Film Festival for *One Potato, Two Potato* and would play Sarah, a wife with eating issues using karate to work out her sublimated marital hostility. "As a matter of fact, it was a mistake because she never had a solo," Barrie said of accepting this particular role over another, "and I didn't realize that, and that was really one of the things that made me crazy."

Pressed by Hartig, Fisher came up to $1000 per week for Stritch. "I told him the billing problem would have to be worked out, but we would certainly not keep her position in the show a secret," he wrote to Prince. Barrie was signed at $650 but contractually assured billing "equivalent to the Actress playing Joanne," winding up just under Jones, with Stritch singled out at the bottom, like a punch line.

"She certainly was a bigger star than I was, except I was featured above the title, but that was because I had a great agent," Barrie said.

Now in her midforties and conscious of being the oldest woman in the ensemble, Stritch also wanted her own hairdresser, and though Fisher thought she should be content with the one from Elizabeth Arden provided for the rest of the cast, she got Vincent Roppatte.

Rehearsals took place downtown, at the American Theater Laboratory on Nineteenth Street. "We were all kind of edgy, and we stayed that way," said Steve Elmore, who had auditioned for Larry, but was deemed too young and secured instead the part of Paul, the zealous groom to Beth Howland's frantically reluctant bride, Amy. (Amy's patter song, "Getting Married Today," is performed less often than "The Ladies Who Lunch"; it's spectacularly difficult, a tumble of words in a frantic tempo that recalls Rimsky-Korsakov's "Flight of the Bumblebee.")

Wanting to focus closely on what was unquestionably the most exciting professional opportunity she'd had in years, Stritch would occasionally stay with Bridget the dachshund in the Hotel Chelsea on Twenty-Third Street, also then home to Patti Smith and Robert Mapplethorpe. The residence of the Welsh poet Dylan Thomas in his dying days two decades earlier, this was perhaps not the most felicitous location for a high-functioning alcoholic.

Stritch had become an obvious employment risk. "She said Hal Prince had to pick her out of the gutter to see if she could even stand up," said Merle Louise, who played Susan, another one of the wives, a Southern belle. "Hal Prince took a big chance with her," said Donna McKechnie, who had been cast as one of Bobby's former girlfriends, Kathy.

But there was nothing abashed about Stritch at the table readings. "Elaine did that thing great actors do," said Elmore, who was from Niangua, Missouri, and had seen her during the tour of *Call Me Madam*. "If you ask them to read, they read it almost deadpan—like they don't want to show any of their shtick."

The two of them developed a routine of gossiping and doing bits from *The Honeymooners*, and after rehearsal they would sometimes repair to Peter McManus, a wood-paneled Irish pub around the corner from the studio. "She would have a glass of wine or something, but everyone was watching her," Elmore said. One night, though, while several other members of the cast scooted home to tend to their small children, the two of them went on a real bender. "We went out, hit several places. At that time I discovered that when Elaine drinks she likes to sing," Elmore said.

Together they belted out lyrics discarded from the husbands' hey-buddy number "Have I Got a Girl for You":

> Perf! You never saw so much perf in one broad
> You've gotta curb yourself not to applaud
> And all she wants is a man who's a man
> Tall, blond and rich, and her name is Joanne

Self-insulated though she was from the political roiling of the moment, Stritch had to confront, at least, that her version of Manhattan was changing. Walking into another pub, a bunch of young men were hanging around the jukebox.

"Play Tony Bennett," Stritch suggested.

"Fuck Tony Bennett," one of the men said.

At evening's end, Elmore took her through the lobby of the Chelsea and up to her room, where he chastely put her to bed.

"That's the first time I've gone to sleep without removing my makeup first," Stritch told him the next day.

Finally, she had occasion to incorporate the intimacy and warmth and despair of these many late nights, the sawdust-floor ambiance, into her acting. John Cunningham, cast as one of the husbands, Peter, remembered the first time he heard "Drinking Song," with just the piano as accompaniment. Stritch was wearing her now customary rehearsal costume of an oversized white oxford-cloth shirt over black tights. "A picture of it burns in my brain," Cunningham said. "It was like the barroom—echoing, emptyish. It wasn't this kind of Broadway thing."

After she showed up late to one 11:00 a.m. call, Fritz Holt, the stage manager, was given the responsibility of making sure Stritch got to and from practices and then performances in a timely manner. "When she got really soused she would stand outside of the theater before the curtain went up and entertain the audience on the sidewalk, and the stage manager would have to bring her into the theater," Barrie said. Holt was dark, tall, and younger, and though (or partly because) he was gay his charge quickly developed "a sneaker" for him. "I was just mad about Fritz," she said. "We got along so well."

Stritch was voluble in rehearsal. "It was well deserved, the reputation coming ahead of her: that she could be a gigantic pain in the ass," Cunningham said. "It was, somehow, 'Wait a minute; it's all about me and my problem.' But the other way that I look at it is that she was fixed on trying to get it right. She didn't say, 'No, I'm going to shoulder everyone else out of the way.' It was because she felt that she had to get it right or she couldn't do it."

"She and Steve and Hal would have a lot of very heated discussions," Barrie said. "She knew exactly what she had to bring to the show, which we didn't, because we were all less experienced than she."

Though Stritch confronted the creators as an equal, she seemed to prefer socializing with the greenest small-town actors, with whom she could assume the role of rollicking auntie or seasoned advisor. Pamela Myers played the young, modern girlfriend Marta and was given a sparkling solo of her own, "Another Hundred People," which described the classic excitement of arriving "off of the train / and the plane / and the bus" to Manhattan. She was a true ingénue—fresh from the Methodist church choir in Cleves, Ohio, excited to secure a Listerine commercial—and Stritch made "a huge impression," she said. "Everything she did left me with my mouth hanging open. She also wore Norell perfume, and so of course I started wearing Norell. I wore it for years."

Teri Ralston, a golden-haired and open-faced soprano from Holyoke, Colorado, who played the wife, Jenny, said, "People were so afraid of Elaine—I didn't know to be afraid of her. She would come across very gruff." She remembered reproaching the older actress for being rude to Hal Hastings, the bespectacled conductor of *Company*'s orchestra. "And consequently she totally respected that, and we became great friends."

Then there was McKechnie, who like Stritch had fled the suburbs outside Detroit for the performing life. Michael Bennett had given her a supercharged erotic dance that served as a commentary on Robert's sex scene with a wifty stewardess, April, played by Susan Browning, to the instrumental "Tick Tock." Though grateful for this sliver of limelight, McKechnie was continually anxious about being dismissed as just a dancer, a lightweight. "I wanted to be a dramatic actress, like she was," she said of Stritch. "I listened to her stories. I took it right in." A few years later, McKechnie would star as Cassie in *A Chorus Line*, marrying Bennett briefly during its record-breaking run. She said he admired Stritch ("talent loves talent") but was frustrated by her resistance to some of the choreography. "We'd have to do these clumps—'Bobby, Bobby,'" she said, referring to the opening number, during which the married members of the ensemble fawn imploringly upon the protagonist. Stritch, though, displayed a mysterious aversion to joining the love parade. "Don't touch me," she instructed other cast members.

"I never understood that," McKechnie said. "We'd reach out, and Michael had us all touch, but—'don't touch me!' And I went, 'why is she so . . . ?' It was very hard for her, touching. And it was along with not being vulnerable in an intimate connection. 'Don't touch me physically, don't touch me emotionally.' I thought there was some trauma there, some fear misplaced."

Commanding and cool, newly excited by the increasingly assertive talent of his old friend Sondheim, Prince had another interpretation of Stritch's trouble in the chorus line. "She was not precisely an ensemble player," he said dryly. During the number "Side by Side by Side," another homage to Robert, and the longest number in the show, Stritch was "the loudest," Prince maintained. "Michael Bennett staged it brilliantly, with everyone coming out with musical instruments and all that stuff—she would always be a little out of step with everybody else, and that was deliberate. She was having a great time, but she was also getting the audience."

Such onstage grandstanding frustrated Furth, who did not want his words, so painstakingly refined over years, overshadowed during their first high-stakes public airing. He thought that Stritch was working too hard, as he wrote in the production notes:

"She's playing too many things. It's all written down, she doesn't have to do all that acting or filling up with meaning. She should have a good time doing the scene not a bad one."

"Stritch must be told that the audience will supply the drama if she supplies the laughs . . . the reverse will not be so."

"Stritch makes too much of her lines."

"I think Joanne is too, too much in the swearing section."

And then, bearing down on his pencil:

"Stritch walks over and *throws* the hat and cane off stage while everyone else takes theirs off stage. Could she be persuaded to do what the others do . . . Unable to enter with the hat and cane with the other couples."

These last difficulties might have had to do with a lack of physical stamina; other than McKechnie, no one in the *Company* cast was a trained dancer. While still rangy and possessing a striding energy once she got out of bed, Stritch was not in peak physical condition. "Hal and Michael Bennett were slave drivers," Barrie felt. "There was no letting up. If you fell down during a dance rehearsal and started to bleed you had to go on. It was like being in boot camp."

Long hours were spent perfecting the contrapuntal opening title number, which involved a great mass unraveling of sheet music, piling up toward the back of the rehearsal room.

"Wait till they try to do this shit in stock," Stritch barked one day, to howls of laughter.

When the production moved to the Shubert Theater in Boston for its tryout, "Side by Side by Side" ran ten-odd minutes. "We would go on the stage and off the stage and on the stage," Barrie said. "One day she said, 'I'm not going back on.' She just sat down. We all said, 'Elaine, you have another entrance.' She said, 'I'm not going to do it.' She was right! By that time we were all panting and exhausted. And she didn't do it, and they restructured—not for her, but because it was too long." The number was cut down. ("Not by much," Sondheim said.)

One day she was late to rehearsal, Prince was grumpy, and Stritch lost it. "You know, it's easy for you and a lot of other people in this company. You've got Judy, you've got Daisy, you've got Charlie"—his wife and children—"and you've got a maid and you've got a home and how would you like it if your only contact with the outside world was Maude?"

There was a pause.

"Who's Maude?" Prince asked. Maude was Stritch's answering service, a now outdated human precursor to automated voice mail. (Furth had suggested Bobby carry an early cell phone–like recording device called a Codaphone.) In the contemporized 2018 production of *Company*, Sondheim changed the end of the lyric "Look I'll call you in the morning or my service'll explain" to "or I'll text you to explain."

Stritch also asserted herself over the matter of *Company*'s costumes. Wanting a chic, mod look consistent with Aronson's sets, Prince contracted Sondheim's friend D. D. Ryan, an Upper East Side style setter with a severe chignon and rigorously plucked eyebrows. "She was the first person to marry in a babushka, and you can't know how radical that was," Liz Smith said. Ryan had mingled with Cole Porter, worked as a photo editor for Diana Vreeland at *Harper's Bazaar*, and helped broker the relationship between Kay Thompson and the illustrator Hilary Knight that resulted in the beloved *Eloise* books. She was icily glamorous but inexperienced in the theater. Barrie remembers Aronson rolling his eyes at the tunic produced to do her karate chops in, which lacked gussets for ease of movement, and the heavy woolen suits manufactured for *Company*'s male characters. "She was just a dilettante," Barrie said. "We all rebelled. Elaine barred her from the dressing room."

Disliking in particular a heavy Cossack-style dress, white with red piping, made for Joanne by Barbara Matera at a cost of $600, Stritch proceeded to Bonwit Teller and brought back a large assortment of off-the-rack black frocks to choose from instead. "This is what I'm going to wear," she told Prince.

"Okay, okay."

And the white dress disappeared from the production. An even more expensive black panne velvet coat with silver appliqué was also eliminated from the rotation after Furth wondered, "Why does only Stritch wear a coat in the play? It's so odd."

The torrent of Furth's feedback continued. While he had notes for almost every character, Joanne, perhaps because she was the most fully realized, got the brunt of them.

"Playing too drunk from the beginning. I meant for her to have more fun commenting, showing, jabbing."

"At the song now she is not enjoying and is making us share the discomfort. Can she be helped in any way to enjoy. It's an ugly scene now."

Along with "Drinking Song," situated in Act II, Stritch was serving as the anchor of an Act I number, "The Little Things You Do Together," in which she leads a small Greek chorus describing how the minutiae of everyday life support "perfect relationships." Though most of the song is cynical, at least one quatrain could have described the view from the back seat of George and Mildred's automobile:

> It's not so hard to be married
> When two maneuver as one
> It's not so hard to be married
> And Jesus Christ, is it fun

Prince had staged "Drinking Song" carefully, after seeing the Austrian opera director Walter Felsenstein's production of *La Traviata* in East Berlin, with numerous waiters shuttling back and forth. For *Company* "they would run on cue by me from one place to another onstage—disappearing always with trays, as if they were busy serving people and never paying attention to her, and it rattled her, which was good," he said.

On opening night in Boston, however, Stritch's nerves overcame her. Unable to remember more than the first few lines of the song, she put her hands in her mouth and began gumming them. McKechnie had just finished her dance and ran to her mark on the second level of the set, where all the women were sitting in black hats with their backs to the audience, sweating and catching her breath. She looked at a panel of Plexiglas and saw Hastings, the conductor, reflected in it, "kind of throwing the words" at Stritch. Oh my gosh, she thought, horrified and fascinated.

The musical progressed without further incident. After the curtain fell, the audience cleared and the cast dispersed backstage, the director issued an announcement over the loudspeaker: "Mr. Prince would like to see Miss Stritch in her dressing room tomorrow morning . . ."

McKechnie, unable to wait until after that, rushed there at once to find Stritch taking comfort in Bridget, her dog, and a flask of Hennessy. "What happened to you?" she asked.

Marion Elaine "Lainey" (also spelled "Lainie") Stritch was fond of giving this baby picture to friends, including the gossip columnist Liz Smith and the actor Nathan Lane. (Courtesy of Liz Smith)

George Stritch had hoped for sons but adored his three daughters: (from left) Georgene, Elaine, and Sally. (Elaine Stritch Bay Trust / The New York Public Library)

Stritch (second row from bottom, far left) at the Academy of the Sacred Heart Convent school. "She was a thorn in the nuns' side, I'll tell you," a classmate said. (Elaine Stritch Bay Trust / The New York Public Library)

Trained at Erwin Piscator's Dramatic Workshop, Stritch's breakout performance was in the revue *Angel in the Wings*. Her mother, Mildred, was concerned about the risqué costumes but also pushed for her to get a solo song, "Civilization (Bongo, Bongo, Bongo)." (Associated Press)

Visiting the Stork Club in the late 1940s, sandwiched between a young John F. Kennedy and his brother Robert's girlfriend, Ethel Skakel. (Elaine Stritch Bay Trust)

For company in an early New York apartment, Stritch maintained a large collection of European dolls. (The New York Public Library)

In rehearsal for the overwrought musical *Goldilocks* with the critic Walter Kerr, who directed from a book written with his wife, the humorist Jean Kerr, and Barry Sullivan, who would be replaced by Don Ameche. (The New York Public Library)

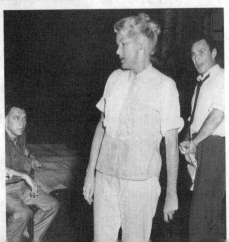

TOP: Pretending to be shorter than her boyfriend Ben Gazzara in Rome, where she was filming *A Farewell to Arms* and flirting with her costar, Rock Hudson. (The New York Public Library)

ABOVE: Seeming to stumble out of a nightclub with Gig Young, who, like Stritch, also suffered from alcoholism. He would later kill himself and his fifth wife. (Globe Photos)

RIGHT: With Kent Smith in *Call Me Madam*. Before joining the show's national tour, Stritch was the standby for Ethel Merman in the lead role of Sally Adams, while also playing Melba Snyder in *Pal Joey*. (The Museum of the City of New York)

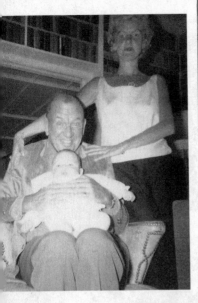

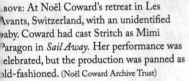

ABOVE: At Noël Coward's retreat in Les
Avants, Switzerland, with an unidentified
baby. Coward had cast Stritch as Mimi
Paragon in *Sail Away*. Her performance was
celebrated, but the production was panned as
old-fashioned. (Noël Coward Archive Trust)

ABOVE RIGHT: On the avenue with Liz Smith,
the most loyal of a coterie of amanuenses and
columnists helping Stritch chronicle her life
in print. (Courtesy of Liz Smith)

RIGHT: After appearing in the flop *The Time
of the Barracudas*, which closed a day after
Kennedy's assassination, Stritch bartended at
establishments including Elaine's on Second
Avenue, which many mistakenly thought was
named for her. (Getty Images)

George and Mildred Stritch celebrating their fiftieth anniversary in 1967 with (from left) Sally and Georgene—both now married with children—and Elaine, who was at a low point in both her career and her personal life. (Elaine Stritch Bay Trust / The New York Public Library)

ABOVE: In rehearsal for *Company,* an electric cattle prod in the flan of musical theater. At the piano: Stephen Sondheim. Standing, from left: George Furth, librettis Dean Jones, actor; Stritch; Hal Prince, director and producer; Barbara Barrie, actor; and Michael Bennett, choreographer (Leo Friedman / The Museum of the City of New York)

LEFT: Posing for photographers a the Savoy on the day of Stritch's wedding to John Bay, whom she met on the set of Tennessee Williams's *Small Craft Warnings.* The couple would live there for almost a decade. (Harry Myers for Pic Photos / Shutterstock)

ABOVE: In between playing significant roles and drinking heavily, in 1979 Stritch worked on an elaborate fashion show for the Liberty Silk Cut collection with the choreographer Larry Fuller, who worked on *Sweeney Todd* and *Evita*. (PA Images via Getty Images)

LEFT: With Donna McKechnie, a fellow cast member from *Company* with whom Stritch stayed close. Stritch had hoped to star with her in a London version of *Gypsy*, but the producers cast Angela Lansbury instead. (Courtesy of Donna McKechnie)

ABOVE: After Bay's death in Nyack, New York, in 1982, Stritch found solace in renewed friendships, like those with the producer Judith Ann Abrams, Liz Smith, and (standing) the entertaining expert Lee Bailey. (Courtesy of Frank Bowling)

LEFT: Sharing a bow with (from left) Phyllis Newman, George Hearn, Lee Remick, Stephen Sondheim, Barbara Cook, and Mandy Patinkin at one of two concert performances of Sondheim's *Follies* at Lincoln Center in 1985. Stritch got a standing ovation for her rubato rendition of "Broadway Baby." (Photofest)

ABOVE LEFT: As Claire in the 1996 revival of Edward Albee's *A Delicate Balance*, Stritch played drunk, though she was freshly committed to sobriety. She was disappointed to not win a Tony for this r nor for her performance in Hal Prince's 1994 revival of *Show Boat*. (Joan Marcus)

ABOVE RIGHT: In Stritch's last Broadway appearance, she replaced Angela Lansbu as Madame Armfeldt, mother to Bernade Peters's Desirée, in Sondheim's *A Little Night Music* at a theater named for Walter Kerr. (Courtesy of Liz Smith)

With the director George C. Wolfe (left) and the drama writer John Lahr, collaborators on Stritch's resoundingly successful one-woman show, *At Liberty*. Lahr later sued her for unpaid royalties; the matter was settled out of court. (Scott Gries, Getty Images)

In front of a celebrity crowd, Stritch's longtime accompanist Rob Bowman backed the performer during her final cabaret series at the Carlyle in New York, before she returned to Michigan. (Todd Heisler / *The New York Times* / Redux Pictures)

Stritch shrugged. "I couldn't find the words!" she said. "The same thing happened during *Sail Away*. But it only happens on opening night."

McKechnie proceeded to the Tiki Hut, a nearby bar, where Prince, his production supervisor, Ruth Mitchell, and Sondheim were gathered. "Don't worry, it only happens on opening night," the young actress told them cheerfully. ("I was totally clueless," she said.)

"They were worried about her, and the more worried they got about her, the more she gave them things to worry about," John Cunningham said. He and the other "husbands" discussed their fears that Stritch could get so tipsy that she might topple off the vertiginous upper level of the set.

The next morning, when Stritch breezed back into her dressing room, Prince was waiting for her as promised.

"I thought it went really wonderfully last night," she said, in his telling.

"Did you really?" Prince said. There was a long, awkward pause.

"Are you trying to be Judy Garland?" he asked.

"What's that mean?"

"'Cause you're not. You're Cardinal Stritch's niece. You're fancy-fally from outside Detroit somewhere. None of that applies to you at all. And stop it."

"What else?" she said defiantly.

"That's all. I'm going."

He left and, whether it was because opening night had passed or this bit of stern surrogate parenting was effective, Stritch learned the song cold. Indeed, she developed such a confident delivery that Furth began to express a specific worry that "Drinking Song" was dominating the show, to its detriment.

"All the venom, ugliness, insecurity and audience terror comes to the front," he jotted glumly on April 2, 1970. "It becomes an entire evening about Elaine Stritch and *nothing* can follow it. The rest of the scene is a lie because we have seen just how demented this woman is. She used to have wit, comment, joy and a good time with it. Now it is horrifying and unpleasant and negates everything in her we have worked for. It does a great dis-service." Furthermore: "I would rather rewrite the scene than endure this moment of *tilt* in the evening. Her problem so exceeds Robert's that we've been telling the wrong story it appears."

But Robert's story and Joanne's were in fact intertwined, like Carl Jung's anima and animus. Those who were dazzled by *Company* were so in spite of, not because of the dialogue; years before *Seinfeld*, it was a "show about nothing" and yet . . . everything: love, sex, community, mortality. Finally Sondheim's songs—gymnastically amusing in *A Funny Thing Happened on the Way to the Forum*, perplexingly allegorical in *Anyone Can Whistle*—had drawn from topics that were universal, at least in Manhattan. The theatergoer looked at Aronson's sets and the actors' strenuous but untrained dancing in chic clothes and saw reflected back . . . himself. Herself.

Many recognized Joanne as the strongest, truest portrait of the lot. "Acid would melt in her mouth," wrote Kevin Kelly admiringly in *The Boston Globe*, adding that the "Drinking Song" "says more about contemporary suburban society than most of our playwrights put together." Filing to the *Harvard Crimson*'s "Theatergoer," the undergraduate critic Frank Rich wrote that "unfortunately—and this is the show's major flaw at this point—the book is short on structure," but called Stritch "wonderfully bitchy."

Sondheim was still fiddling with songs. He replaced Robert's final number, "Happily Ever After," with the more optimistic, expansive "Being Alive." But Stritch's role was, if not quite BirdsEye frozen à la Merman, set like a Jell-O shot. And once she was surer of herself, she relished being part of an ensemble, as she had since the Piscator days, to Furth's relief. "Everybody is a star" in the production, she said in the radio interview. "That's exciting to me." The best part of being in the show, she added, was 8:30 to 11:00 p.m. (the period when she was onstage), when she could get the director out of her life.

Yet by the time they were back in New York, she and Prince were becoming friends. After one show at the Alvin Theater, he took her to Forno's, a popular Mexican-Spanish restaurant next door where Stritch was partial to the banana daiquiris. "She practically dropped her face in the plate, she was so drunk," he said. "And I got her a cab, got him to see her home and so on. Somehow or other we got her home. Well, that was the only time I saw Elaine really stinking drunk. Not on the stage"—

though the rumor among cast members was that even a cigarette lighter on set was filled with a little hooch, just in case.

"I think Elaine was frightened of everything," Prince said. "I think the convent girl was always scared. She trembled. And quivering outside, not just inside. I mean, when she was in the dressing room saying 'I thought it went very well last night,' she didn't think it went well at all. She was terrified."

This fear could manifest in spiky cruelty. McKechnie recalled going to Forno's after the show with an ex-boyfriend, married, visiting from Venezuela. "He's doing very well, in pharmaceuticals, and I'm sitting there and Elaine comes in and sits on our table and goes, 'You finally got a date, huh?' and it was mortifying. And that's the only time I really saw her in a bad way."

Barbara Barrie was subjected to less of this behavior, rushing home to her young family after curtain each night. Per the contracts, she had been given a large dressing room at the Alvin on the same floor as Stritch's. "They were considered the star dressing rooms, ho ho, I don't know why I got them, but I did," she said. Her two toddlers, Jane and Aaron, were frequently brought to the theater and Elaine would play cards with them. "She was very sweet to my children. People say that she was not interested in kids. I think she was." The producer Judy Abrams, for whom Stritch directed a youngsters' production, *Tom Sawyer*, remembered that when her friend had downtime, she would go and read to children at the Alice in Wonderland statue in Central Park.

And Pamela Myers noticed Stritch's romanticism, in contrast to the hardened Joanne. "She wanted to be married so badly," she said.

The opening of *Company* at the Alvin on April 26, 1970, cemented Sondheim's status as a composer overnight. But even those who shrugged at the musical's innovations found Joanne fascinatingly discomfiting.

Clive Barnes, the drama critic of the *Times*, was among those generally unmoved by the show, but wrote that "Elaine Stritch, with her denmother arrogance, is superb. She gives bland lines a bite, and sharp lines the kind of blinding accuracy line-writers dream of." Walter Kerr, who was now the *Times*'s Sunday theater critic, observed that "Miss Stritch has what funny lines George Furth has chosen to write," adding that "The Ladies Who Lunch" (as "Drinking Song" had been retitled) was "a great number, perfectly done."

If the song was faintly disturbing to Mildred Stritch and her two other daughters, Georgene Moran and Sally Bolton—ladies who lunched, albeit in the country clubs of Birmingham rather than "21," their days filled with bridge, children, charities, churchgoing, dancing, drinking, driving, gardening, shopping—they never would have shown it. "Her sisters treated her like she was not important," said Charlotte Moore, a theater director who met Stritch during the *Company* run. "Certainly they were not afraid of her." And they lacked her feeling "that if I didn't express myself I'd explode," as she told her nephew Chris Bolton, though they shared so much else.

Pamela Myers said, "George Furth said the reason nobody is as good as Elaine in this part is that she has breeding. And that's not the most attractive word—you think of horses. However, I knew what he meant. She came from that background. That's the life she knew."

On opening night, flowers from the family Stritch and others filled her dressing room at the Alvin. Roppatte sat there, waiting, until the last curtain. She wanted him to escort her to the party afterward, where early word of the notices would be received.

Before they went, though, she made him join her in filling up their arms with bouquets, and the two of them walked from the theater to St. Malachy, the Roman Catholic church three blocks south known for its Actors' Chapel, and laid the flowers on the altar.

On May 3, the Sunday after opening night, the cast arrived at Columbia Records' Big Church recording studio on Thirtieth Street and Third Avenue to record the production's official album. Stritch came at two in the afternoon, a peace-sign necklace dangling around the placket of her white blouse, a white sailor hat clapped on her head, the sort she used to fling into the audience from the stage of *Sail Away*. "My cab driver thought I was Phyllis Diller," she told *The New York Times* later. "I either look like a Ziegfeld girl or a fisherman from Maine."

By this time, Dean Jones had given his notice, privately citing difficulties in his marriage, which *Company* surely threw into too sharp relief, but publicly blaming hepatitis. Larry Kert would take over as Robert. However, Prince had released Jones only on the condition that he sing for the recording, which was to be filmed by three of the documentary filmmaker D. A. Pennebaker's handheld cameras as a pilot for a TV series.

Jones's throat was a little raw, and he wanted to record the demanding ballad "Being Alive" as soon as possible. Stritch offered to trade the times of their solos. "She didn't want a whole lot of people around when she did what she felt was really one of the biggest numbers of her career," said Thomas Z. Shepard, who produced the recording. There was a case of white wine on ice in the studio, Prince said. As the session wore on, "there was a bottle that had been killed, and maybe another bottle opened. And I knew she was off and running."

Sondheim said, "She had all afternoon to nip. That is to say, she had a nip before lunch, and then a nip at teatime. It was just enough so that— she didn't get drunk but alcohol, you know, is not good for the vocal cords."

Stritch's problems doing take after take of "The Ladies Who Lunch" in the wee hours of Monday morning were condensed to fifteen minutes in Pennebaker's film. The cap came off, the hair was raked upward into stiff brush, visible sweat stains formed under the arms of the blue striped shirt she had changed into, and she slurred piteously at Sondheim, clearly desperate to please. Their main concern was that she was "speaking" the lines rather than singing them. "It's just flaccid," Shepard told her.

She was sent home despondent, holding a pack of cigarettes, and slept all day.

Before returning to the studio, Stritch had been made up and coifed by Roppatte for the matinee, and this time delivered the song with confidence. "She triumphed," said Steve Elmore. "Elaine has a way of doing that."

Prince said, "I always thought that the recording session might have been subconsciously, and I do mean subconsciously, planned. I don't think she knew exactly she was doing that. But why didn't she have any makeup on in the first session? Why did she look so terrible? She didn't have the best skin in the world—she had a great face, great presence, and she looks very happy with all the other people while they're singing. But she couldn't nail the big number and then she came back for a session only on her own and she was fully made up and she looked terrific. So I'll never answer that question."

Shepard believes that Stritch was always more of an orchestrator of such moments than she let on. "You got the impression that she was uncensored but I don't know if that's the truth," he said. "She gave you the impression that you were in the middle of a free association, like you're tuning in on a stream of consciousness. But I don't know. I mean, she was a very smart, very clever woman, and the chances are she controlled her spontaneity to an extraordinary degree."

Funding hiccups notwithstanding (Eastern Airlines had withdrawn sponsorship because of the wayward stewardess character), the TV pilot aired on WNEW and was added as a documentary to the New York Film Festival slate that fall. It was also screened downtown, where Shepard saw it with his wife and daughter, cringing at how his taut feedback during hours of recording, compressed on film, read like cruelty to a Stritch-besotted audience. "When I said to her, 'It's flaccid,' or 'Sing it,' they booed me and hissed me," he said.

Stritch was back in business. Freed of being a romantic lead, she could now be a heroine; having exposed her process and vulnerability, she could now be sympathetic. And as much as anyone on the production, she informed the emerging idea of the modern individual as fundamentally alone, walled off by the technology that purports to connect. Indeed, she wished for more fellowship from the cast, even realizing the transcendent success of the production they were a part of. "It was a cold show and a cold company," she said years later, "because the show was about people going in their own direction anyway. But wasn't that good for the show? That's what the show was about"—to invert the *Babes on Broadway* song famously covered by Frank Sinatra—"'I like New York in June, how about me?'"

10.

STOMPIN' AT THE SAVOY

The Tony Awards had been awash in nostalgia practically since their inception; one of the first musicals to be cited, in 1948, was *High Button Shoes*, set in 1913. But on the night of March 28, 1971, with *Company* nominated in twelve categories, they were drowning in the sentiment—one Prince, Bennett, and Sondheim were scrutinizing more pointedly (and fractiously) in their ambitious next project, *Follies*.

It was the twenty-fifth anniversary of the awards, and the evening's entertainment, held at the Palace Theater, was a two-hour canter through musical-theater history. At regular intervals actors would burst through a tinsel curtain to present the Tony organization's nickel-plated medallions, the size of a medium pancake.

Angela Lansbury was one of four hosts. To introduce a number from *Damn Yankees*, she was rhapsodizing about the lost era when "men were smiling over Marilyn Monroe" and "it seemed as if the entire country were moving to the suburbs and you just weren't with it if you didn't have an outside barbecue grill," when a power cable shorted onstage, sending dramatic plumes of smoke around the podium. "Wow. That's Marilyn!" Lansbury ad-libbed gamely. But in hindsight the moment seemed less like disruption from a blithe spirit than yet another symbol of post–World War II America losing its juice.

Outside the gilded confines of the Palace, stagflation loomed, drug use was spreading, and crime was surging on the streets of New York. Stritch experienced this writ small and furry when Bridget, her dachshund, was snatched off the top of the bar at J. G. Melon. "They were kidnapping dogs then—they used to sell them to hospitals for medical experiments," said Judy Abrams, who dispatched a six-foot-five stagehand with $200 ransom while her friend spent a sleepless night praying to St. Anthony, patron saint of the missing, swearing she'd never touch booze again.

Like those made before it, that resolution did not last long. "I gotta have a drink," Stritch said once Bridget was returned safely.

"What about St. Anthony?" Abrams asked.

"Fuck St. Anthony! Do you know what I've just been through?"

The Tonys were a different sort of ordeal. With her third nomination, again for Best Actress in a Musical, Stritch was competing improbably against her young fellow cast member Susan Browning, who'd played April, the stewardess who sings the languorous postcoital duet "Barcelona" with Bobby. (Myers and Barrie were each nominated for Best Featured Actress, but Beth Howland was neglected.) The other challengers in Stritch's category were the stars of two revivals: Sandy Duncan in *The Boy Friend* and Helen Gallagher in *No, No, Nanette*. Walter Kerr, now the chief nostalgia apologist of the critics' circle, was energetically plumping *Nanette* in the *Times*, mourning a vanishing genre of "Musicals That Were Playful, Responsible and Blissfully Irreverent," contra the Prince–Sondheim collaboration, which he perceived as dark and cold.

Favored to win by Jack O'Brian, Dorothy Kilgallen's successor as the Voice of Broadway, Stritch tried to defuse the tension. "If one of those other two broads wins, let's have a drink at Joe Allen's," she had whispered conspiratorially beforehand to Gallagher, her old dressing-room mate from *Pal Joey*.

But Stritch's posture in the auditorium betrayed her nerves. She sat bolt upright, her ash-blonde coif crisp, drop earrings glinting against a high-necked black dress, and face impassive as Lauren Bacall, who had won the previous year for *Applause*, ticked off the nominees and opened the telltale envelope. Prince had already won for Best Director, giving *Company* a seeming momentum, and the movie star's bellowed "Helen . . ." sounded enough like "Elaine" that for a fraction of a second it seemed Stritch might have finally received the prize she craved so powerfully.

But it was the lithe dancer Gallagher, in a shoulder-baring gown with large purple paillettes, who would return to the stage, nineteen years after she had won her first Tony for playing Gladys Bumps. Walking toward the stage, Gallagher gave Stritch a friendly punch on the shoulder, and her improvised speech seemed to acknowledge not just her contemporary but every theatrical veteran in the audience. "To all of us that have stuck in a business maybe long after anybody wanted us," Gallagher said. "Stuck because we didn't know what else to do, no imagination. Stuck because we had to stick! It's for us that stick. Thank you."

Soon afterward, Furth and Sondheim would collect their first Tonys, the former thanking his "married friends," the latter Hastings and Tunick. The central male triumvirate of the project had triumphed, and Aronson was honored for his sets, even as Bennett lost to *Nanette*'s choreographer, Donald Saddler; and Myers and Barrie to *Nanette*'s Patsy Kelly. "Long story short, all of us canceled each other out," said Myers, who nonetheless sat entranced, the kid from small-town Ohio in front of Sirs John Gielgud and Ralph Richardson. With tonsil surgery scheduled for early the next morning, Stritch did not linger at the party after the ceremony. But even knowing Stritch's tendency toward epic benders, Abrams was worried when her roommate did not return to the apartment that night. A few days later she would turn up in the Winter Garden Theater, where *Follies* was finishing an exhilarating but problematic preview period.

When Stritch arrived at the new show's rehearsal to get a glimpse of the action, Fritz Holt, who was stage-managing again, asked a young gofer to welcome her by the stage door. The gofer happened to be a scion of the New York Steinway–Chapin cultural dynasty, and he also happened to be taking detailed notes on his experience.

"I'm Ted Chapin," he said, extending his hand.

"I don't give a fuck who you are," Stritch replied.

Such churlishness toward an underling covered up feelings of disappointment and abandonment. As the elaborate *Follies*, examining the curdled hopes of aging showgirls and men in midlife crisis, opened to great fanfare and fascination in Manhattan, with its star Alexis Smith high-kicking in a red dress on the cover of *Time*, Stritch would be going on the road with *Company*. Sondheim said his late nights with Stritch at the piano singing songs like "He Was Too Good to Me" helped inspire a number for the *Follies* character Carlotta Campion. "It was based on my experience with Elaine. Because she'd be drunk at two o'clock in the morning, and she'd forget some of the lyric. I might have been drunk too, but I'd remember the lyrics. I thought, That's a theatrical moment." He first wrote a song called "Can That Boy Foxtrot!" which by utter coincidence mentioned a grocery clerk (Sondheim has no memory of the Thomas Cole incident). Built around the joke of "foxtrot" suggesting a cruder f-word, the song would be discarded and replaced with the panoramic "I'm Still Here."

But he never considered casting her; Yvonne De Carlo, a former film star now known for her role on *The Munsters*, was playing Carlotta, and Sondheim and Prince were preoccupied with their new project and no longer in Stritch's orbit with any consistency. "They were the daddy figures of the show, and Daddy left home," said Barry Brown, who had recently become Fritz Holt's partner in work and love.

With the worries about increasing crime in New York, Stritch had lived for a time in the maid's room of the two men's West End Avenue apartment, often having to be carried to bed, Brown said, after too much Courvoisier, and had given Holt a puppy, an Irish setter, as a birthday present. She insisted it be named Patsy, after Kelly.

Stritch's spirits were bolstered by the arrival of a new Bobby to the *Company* tour: George Chakiris, the cleft-chinned dancer who'd won an Oscar for his performance as Bernardo, the leader of the Sharks, in *West Side Story*. "Somebody in the cast, while we were in rehearsal, said about Elaine, 'Don't invite her to your house because she'll never go home,'" Chakiris recalled. "That was my inkling that there was a reputation of some kind there."

But he liked his new costar instantly. One rainy day he sat, shy and awestruck, at a round table at Forno's with Stritch, her sometime understudy Marti Stevens, and Noël Coward, as coats and umbrellas accumulated around an openmouthed employee. Stritch said, "Noël, will you just turn around and say hi to the hatcheck girl? She's beside herself."

"She's hardly got room," Coward joked.

A year and a half after a celebration of his seventieth birthday that he had called Holy Week, or Dad's Renaissance, Coward was himself fully inhabiting the age of homage, a knighthood and an unexpected uptick of interest in the interwar years giving sudden starch to his once sagging reputation. Every week a new revival or revue of the Master's work seemed to surface somewhere in the English-speaking world.

Nostalgia also permeated the *Company* tour's first stop, at the Ahmanson Theater in downtown Los Angeles. Stritch checked in to not the Chateau Marmont, with its bad vibes from *Barracudas*, but the more convenient if equally haunted Ambassador Hotel on Wilshire Boulevard, where Robert F. Kennedy had been shot fatally three years earlier, and where Walter Winchell, a recluse since his son committed suicide, lived out his final years. The hotel's fabled ballroom, the Cocoanut Grove, had recently gotten a thorough renovation under the direction of Sammy Davis, Jr. Out were the palm trees and balcony for gazing at actual stars in the sky; in were black, purple, orange, pink, and silver décor, a new name (the Now Grove), and a younger clientele congregating in a glass-enclosed "cocktail court." Stritch dined frequently there before performing at the modernist Ahmanson, or at Scandia, a popular restaurant on Sunset Boulevard, with its menu declaring *"Velkommen Tilbords!"* and Aquavit served ice cold with beer. She gossiped with Chakiris about the English actor George Sanders, who'd starred with Merman in the film version of *Call Me Madam* and written a deliciously dry autobiography called *Memoirs of a Professional Cad*. "Can you imagine introducing that guy to your sister?" she said, marveling at Sanders's marriages to first Zsa Zsa and then Magda Gabor.

That June, when Chakiris had to lend his dressing room to the former

Grace Kelly, Princess of Monaco, who was hosting a fund-raiser for the Motion Picture Relief Fund at the Ahmanson, Stritch made him leave a note propped up against the rotary phone. It read cheekily, "Just in case you need to call home, I have the key."

At the benefit, Kelly's onetime costar and consort Frank Sinatra was introduced by a teary Rosalind Russell and gave the valedictory performance of what would prove, at fifty-five, a short-lived, self-imposed retirement. Army Archerd of *Variety*, the most enduring of the midcentury gaggle of alliteratively named columnists, observed Ryan O'Neal and Barbra Streisand in the front row, holding hands: "spellbound, watching Frank's last, dramatic appearance": a set of eleven standards ending in "Angel Eyes," from 1946. The party afterward was at the Brissons' home. This time, Stritch was not on the guest list.

Though Sinatra's slight about "people in the theater ain't goin' no place" might have been reverberating in Stritch's consciousness, she would have the consolation of working with another member of the graying Rat Pack: Dean Martin.

While in L.A., Stritch, in between her duties as Joanne, taped several appearances on Martin's variety show. In them she generally reprised her new character of hardened matron who could take or leave love. One sketch featured her wearing a ruffled pink frock, dropping a handkerchief and sitting on a park bench and singing "Someday My Prince Will Come" with dogged stridence as Ernest Borgnine—Merman's fourth husband, if only for thirty-two days—flitted around her, clad in powder-blue velvet cape and quill, proffering box after box of glass slippers. Eventually Martin arrives on the set, and is beginning to draw Stritch into a seductive clinch when Borgnine fits a shoe onto him instead, and the two men run away with each other, wrists flapping, leaving our heroine alone. Forty years before Neil Patrick Harris gleefully decreed Broadway as "not just for gays anymore" at the Tonys, overt if mincing caricatures of homosexuality had managed to seep into white-bread network television (a different segment in 1971 featured Liberace in hot pants), even as the long-idolized Martin was beginning to draw the ire of women's libbers with his scantily clad backup troupe, the Dingaling Sisters.

"In every marriage there's always chores that a wife doesn't like to do," Borgnine said, introducing another sketch. "Sometimes it's cooking, sometimes it's cleaning, and in some marriages the wives are just not affectionate. Ah, but *here's* an enterprising wife who hired someone to perform this little chore for her." The wife was Stritch, in a caftan right out of "The Ladies Who Lunch." The someone was a blonde Dingaling Sister in a French maid outfit, there to kiss, fondle, and be carried off by Martin for a clearly imminent bout of lovemaking.

"And they say you can't get good help these days," Stritch declared, left alone again and looking triumphantly straight into the camera.

Rip Taylor, the confetti-tossing comic who appeared regularly on the program, found Stritch armored and remote. "People thought she was rude—she wasn't friendly," he said. "She never ever ever ever got out of character, ever. She was caustic: 'How are you?' 'How do you *think* I should be?'"

Still, it was reported that Stritch wanted to do more work on the program, but Prince would not release her from her contractual tour obligations; she was too vital to the show's success. So it was on to San Francisco, where she and Chakiris dined at Trader Vic's with Marlene Dietrich, whom Stritch waggishly introduced to the *Company* audience as the theater's cleaning woman during a curtain call. And to Denver, where she met the local newspaper's drama critic at cocktail hour in the Gondola Room of the New Palace Hotel. Wearing a new mink coat over a "snappy black Cardin suit," Stritch ordered a martini and insisted that she'd "like to play every city in the country." She told the entranced critic, "You—the audience—you shouldn't have to get on a plane or a train to see a show and see it well done. We should bring it to you." And to Toronto, where she performed at a local socialite's dinner party with Liza Minnelli. And to New Haven, where the idea of Laraine Birch had originated, and from where Stritch wrote to Prince's business manager, officially terminating her previous contract.

A new agreement was drawn up for the impending British production. Always grand, her signature now swooped over a full third of the page. For the London run, she had secured a 50 percent raise, $500 more per week than Larry Kert would be making. More important, her name in the program would be as big as his.

Kert was concerned that an English audience wouldn't "get" *Company*. "I mean, it's so American," he fretted to a reporter during preparations. "It's middle class New York marriage at its harshest."

But the production was received with tremendous enthusiasm. "*Company* was loved there because it was edgy, and after World War II there was a cynicism and a darkness in London," McKechnie said. "They're not put off by that." Kenneth Hurren, the *Spectator*'s theater critic, singled out "most particularly, the irresistibly acidulous Elaine Stritch . . . magnetic in her two solo songs and giving her every line that astringent edge that transmutes mere drollery into quartz-hard wit." Writing for *The Times* of London, John Higgins lamented how "Miss Stritch's whiskey sour voice, her legs of a length and style which only seem to grow in New York, and her eyebrows which can devastate at a twitch have all been absent from London too long," urging readers to "take advantage of them while they are here."

In fact Stritch was in no rush to leave. To bypass the country's strict six-month quarantine law, she had sedated Bridget and shoved her into a piece of carry-on luggage from the T. Anthony store on Park Avenue, into which Holt and Brown helped put a false bottom. They used boxes of Kotex and Cashmere Bouquet soap for insulation and stuffed scripts in the side pockets.

The journey went uneventfully, the actress told Brown later, except for one stage whisper from a flight attendant: "Miss Stritch, your bag is jumping around on the floor."

At Heathrow Airport, the English production's lighting designer, Richard Pilbrow, was waiting to greet her with an assistant and a press representative. Stritch tore past them, wearing fur and clutching what he perceived to be a large handbag. "Get me out of here!" she stage-whispered.

"Elaine, where's your luggage?"

"Get me out of here! I can't wait for my fucking luggage."

"But Elaine, customs will only let it through if the owner is there in person."

She opened her bag and a small, soft head craned upward. Warily Pilbrow noticed a nearby constable and squashed it back down.

"Elaine, dear, this is really serious. I told you. You cannot bring a dog into the country. It's against the law. You'll be arrested. You'll go to jail. The show won't be able to open!"

"Get me out of here!"

Pilbrow resigned himself. The assistant, American and unfamiliar with driving on the right side of the road, took the wheel of his car and careened off to London with Stritch and Bridget, and he and the press representative remained to wrangle the rest of the luggage and follow in a cab.

Later, they concocted a story that the *Company* company had given Stritch a new dog as a present, like Coward had during *Sail Away*, which the newspapers eagerly published.

At the venerable oak-paneled Connaught hotel Stritch befriended Frank Bowling, the night manager, who would go on to help her with many hotel arrangements over the years. "She would come in after the show usually with a group of young people, laughing raucously and then before she went to bed, would tell a rude story that she knew would make me blush," Bowling said. "I told her at one point to fuck off, and I think that was the beginning of our friendship."

Joking that she "Connaught" face the bill there, Stritch soon moved to the Savoy in the Strand, a shorter walk to Her Majesty's Theater, where *Company* was playing. The hotel gave Stritch a heroine's welcome. During the *Sail Away* days, she had requested nine pillows to read in bed. When she returned, there were nine pillows already arrayed in her suite.

"The Savoy doesn't take dogs, and Elaine didn't give a shit," Prince said. "She'd walk around with Bridget's head sticking out of a bag. And everybody worshipped her. She was the pet of the hotel."

Savoy brass had ample motivation to indulge the star's eccentricities; her presence there was superb publicity for them. "Right from the start . . . the Hotel has surpassed all rivals in that most delicate of all enterprises—the art of avoiding obscurity," Israel Shenker wrote in a monograph commissioned for its 1989 centennial. And Stritch was perhaps the most committed spokeswoman in this long history. Far from seeking privacy and seclusion, she made certain to drop the name of the hotel in each of her frequent interviews. Her second living room was the American Bar, with its dedicated stewards offering cocktails like the Moonwalk, commemorating Neil Armstrong and made with grapefruit juice and orange liqueur and rosewater. Stritch preferred the Black Velvet—champagne topped with Guinness—often sending the chief barkeep, Victor Gower, running across the street to restock the stout.

Kurt Peterson, who had originated the role of Young Ben in *Follies* but left to star in a revival of *On the Town*, became one of the many devoted hangers-on of the London company of *Company*, which played for 344 performances. "We would party and party and party," he said. "They were the toast of the town and I was following the toast of the town." (He was also dating Donna McKechnie.) One night the crowd wound up at Stritch's suite, where on the mantelpiece she had items displayed that people had given her, things that she would wrap up and regift for opening night presents.

After smoking a joint in the bathroom, Peterson became mesmerized by one of the hotel's famously oversized chrome shower heads: almost ten inches in diameter, with some three hundred water holes. "I just stood there and stared at it," he said.

"Elaine, I have just seen the most beautiful shower head. In your bathroom," he told his hostess.

"Oh, you did? Wiiild."

As he was leaving the party, Peterson was beckoned over by Stritch, who had screwed off the shower head and slipped it under his tuxedo as a goodbye present—not an uncommon practice, according to Shenker, but a daring one for a long-term resident.

Stritch was just as cavalier with the personnel, one day propping up the pillows on her bed, placing Bridget there under the bedclothes, with paws on the coverlet, and hiding with Fritz Holt and Barry Brown in the bathroom as she summoned room service in a fake voice. "The three of us watch as the waiter wheels his thing in," Brown said. "And the dog stayed put the entire time. Bridget did—as most people did—whatever Elaine told her to do."

But this didn't mean she could order up any role she chose. Holt and Brown were moving into the production business and had optioned the rights to put on *Gypsy* in London at last. "Right from the get-go, we wanted to do it with Angela Lansbury," Brown said, but Lansbury had been busy with the movie *Bedknobs and Broomsticks*. So they offered the starring role of the strident stage mother Rose to Stritch, who'd been angling to play her abroad since at least 1963, when she had floated the possibility in a Kilgallen column. Now she had the excited idea that they should throw into the deal McKechnie as Louise, the awkward older daughter who morphs into the satiny burlesque star Gypsy Rose Lee. Arthur Laurents, who had written the show's book, seemed enthused. "Elaine is a performer. She loves audiences," he told an American reporter in May 1972, comparing her favorably with Merman, whom he accused of arrogantly walking through shows. Stritch could identify closely with Rose, who so longs to bust out of her constrained circumstances.

> Some people can be content
> Playing bingo and paying rent.
> That's peachy for some people,
> For some hum-drum people to be,
> But some people ain't me!

She longed to play this part, taking on a character whose thick fumes of ambition, frustration, and restlessness matched her own. But "she wasn't a big enough name, financing was difficult to come by, and it didn't happen," Brown said. "The truth is, she was not our first choice. Doing it with Elaine would have been wonderful, a swell idea, but it's not who we really wanted."

This was a hard blow, especially considering how close she'd been to both men in New York. Then again, after the marionette rigors of *Company*, the endless burbling of "Bobby" and its variations, *Gypsy* would have been the very opposite of reprieve, with its choreography after the exacting Jerome Robbins original and multiple over-the-top numbers. Maybe it was a relief to have the music stop for a while.

"This is the Savoy—what a hotel," Stritch wrote Mildred on a postcard in early 1972. "Staying by myself all day today. By choice. Good for me."

After finishing the run, she repaired with Abrams for a brief holiday to Cornwall, where waves splash against the rocky coast and where—at least for the first few nights—she drank only soda. "And I went down to the dining room at night like a lady, like a prop-a lay-dy, and I had my dinner ran down the beach," she recalled. "I just went—yay! It was like World War II had just ended. It was like somebody went and walked on the moon."

One of the many visitors backstage at Her Majesty's Theater had been Vivian Matalon, a dark and raffish young director who'd taken on the William Marchant play that Stritch had ditched a decade before to do *Who's Afraid of Virginia Woolf?* The Marchant play had closed quietly out of town, but Matalon had thrived in the intervening years. He was the new artistic director of the Hampstead Theater in London's Camden district and was reading a play by Tennessee Williams that had played off-Broadway near the Bowery and then moved to the New Theater on East Fifty-Fourth Street. It had been pushed out by, of all things, a revue called *Oh, Coward!*, which Walter Kerr enthused predictably was "an island of entertainment in the sea of our troubles."

Small Craft Warnings, by contrast, was set where the sea of troubles crashed, "on a bar along the Southern Californian Coast," where had gathered a crew of oddballs, including an attractive, dissolute ingénue named Violet, played in New York by the transgender Andy Warhol acolyte Candy Darling, and an unlicensed alcoholic doctor, Doc—played, in the production's last weeks, by Williams himself.

The part for Stritch was Leona, a middle-aged beautician with a penchant for sailor's caps who was mourning her homosexual younger brother, who'd died of pernicious anemia, and obsessively listening to a recording of the violinist Jascha Heifetz playing Tchaikovsky's *Sérénade Mélancolique*.

Though the role was not physically demanding, it had several long monologues. Matalon spent many nights at the Savoy with Stritch going over them, "drinking like a fish with her," he said, "because there was no other way to deal with her."

One of Leona's speeches seemed to presage eerily the coming AIDS crisis ("I know the gay scene and I know the language of it and I know how full it is of sickness and sadness; it's so full of sadness and sickness . . ."). Another gave voice to that peculiarly Stritchish itinerancy:

> When I come to a new place, it takes me two or three weeks, that's all it takes me, to find somebody to live with in my home on wheels and to find a night spot to hang out in. Those first two or three weeks are rough, sometimes I wish I'd stayed where I was before, but I know from experience that I'll find somebody and locate a night spot to booze in, and get acquainted with . . . friends.

Among Stritch's many new friends in London was a young actor named Eric Deacon, who had the small part of a young gay cyclist in *Small Craft Warnings* and whom Stritch adopted like Steve Elmore before him, getting his hair dyed beach-boy California blond by the Savoy's campy hairdresser-in-residence.

"She treated you exactly the same whether you were famous or not," Deacon said. "She was irascible, but the other side was this extraordinary warmth."

Frances de la Tour, who played Violet, maintained more of a distance. Newly pregnant, she was put off by Stritch's drinking, though admiring of her talent. "She told me about her life, about being a Catholic, that it was hard—that she wasn't going to sleep with everyone," de la Tour said. "She'd do her Hail Marys and go to the confessional box." Stritch fretted about the not-quite-star status that had failed to secure her *Gypsy*. "All my life, I've been 'and' billing," she complained to de la Tour. The smallest part in *Warnings* was that of a policeman who breaks up a fight between two of the misfits. It had been given to an American actor named John Bay, sometimes known as J. M. (for Marshall) Bay, whom Matalon had seen in Shelagh Delaney's kitchen-sink play *A Taste of Honey* in 1958.

Bay was forty-four, hardly a neophyte, and yet often he would linger at rehearsals as if soaking up the atmosphere.

"I used to say to him, 'John, I won't be needing you today, you can go home,'" Matalon recalled, "and three or four times he'd say, 'Can I just stay behind and watch?' And I'd say 'sure'—I was very flattered. I thought, Oh, he's so impressed with my directing."

One Saturday after work ended the two men accompanied Stritch to the pub, where Stritch had a drink and gave Bridget a saucer of beer. After a while Bay left.

"Boy, he's a hell of a nice guy," she said to Matalon.

"Yes he is," Matalon said. "It's a pity he's so goddamned boring."

She drew herself up. "I don't think he's boring at all!"

Whoops, that's why he wanted to stay at rehearsal, Matalon thought to himself.

Bay had perhaps more in common with Stritch than many of her previous suitors. Born three years after her, on November 30, 1928, he was from Kenilworth, Illinois, a small planned community on Lake Michigan, north of Chicago. With his thick brown hair just beginning to go gray, full lips, and six feet of height, to her he recalled another John: Kennedy. Bay had a knack for impressions, particularly Groucho Marx and Vincent Price, and a seen-it-all air that reminded Eric Deacon of Humphrey Bogart or even Sinatra. "John was a really, really funny man," Deacon said. "You looked at him and thought, Man, this guy has been in some places with some people."

John was a scion of Bays, a company that was to Thomas' English muffins what Pepsi was to Coca-Cola: less successful than the dominant brand, but believed by some to be superior. As Elaine was the youngest of three sisters, so he was the youngest of three brothers. The eldest, George W. Bay, Jr., known as Bill, had flown in World War II and was a longtime pilot for United Airlines. The middle brother, James N. Bay, Sr., had in 1968 taken over the muffin business, started in 1933 by their father, George W. Bay, Sr. Recently, Bays had been contracted by Ray Kroc of McDonald's for a new breakfast sandwich, the Egg McMuffin, its product being sturdier and better-suited to a blanket of cheese than Thomas', with its yielding nooks and crannies. After McDonald's arrived in the Woolwich neighborhood of London in 1974, Stritch proudly snapped a photograph of an advertisement for the McMuffin sailing past on a double-decker red bus.

If not exactly a black sheep, John had wandered onto a different path than his siblings. He had attended the School of the Art Institute in Chicago and enjoyed doing comics and calligraphy; it was he who had created the majuscule white-on-red Bays logo that continues to adorn the muffins package. After serving in the army infantry in the Korean War, he'd moved to London, finding small and often comic parts in plays and on black-and-white television shows. He had met Stritch fleetingly at Harold's Show Spot, a pocket-size bar across from the John Golden Theater, when she was in *Bus Stop*.

"How do you do—can I have a Heineken please?" she'd said to him indifferently. Bay was captivated, but "didn't want to mess with Ben Gazzara."

Now, though, Bay "was just what she needed," de la Tour said. "A man that loved her that wasn't starry, that wasn't famous. He was just a good man who clearly adored her."

Years before, Stritch had told Leonard Lyons that she'd never met a beau who could keep her from a bow; Bay would never dream of doing so—indeed, he'd be watching in the wings. "An unbelievably talented guy without any jealousy," Stritch said. "He didn't give a flying fuck if I did Hamlet in drag and made the cover of *Time*." Nor, it turned out, did a woman wooed by Conrad Hilton care about riches, for he had but minimal funds from his family, if any. "Who do you think you want to marry, they'd say when I was a kid," she would say. "'I want to marry somebody who will buy me a house that takes a half hour to get from the road to the front door.'"

If it took Bay and Stritch a half hour to get from road to front door, it would be because of mutual intoxication. "He was warm and wonderful," Prince said of Bay. "And he drank. They had a drinking companionship, the whole time."

Paul Gemignani, who would succeed Harold Hastings as Sondheim's go-to conductor after Hastings died suddenly, remembered sitting with Prince and the couple once in London. He said, "I know that is the most

I've ever seen two people drink in my life. I've never seen anybody drink like that in my life. And I've been in places where people drink like crazy."

Tennessee Williams brought to this behavior the keen and judgmental eye of an advanced alcoholic. He had flown into London for a few days to see rehearsals of *Small Craft Warnings* and took each of the female actresses to lunch individually to buck them up for their parts. At Pinewood Studios, he told de la Tour that she reminded him of Kim Stanley. "He was worried about Elaine, but he admired her so much," de la Tour said. "You have to be goddamned sober, to act a drunk." Williams's lunch with Stritch is lost to the mists of time and Angostura bitters. "May we have 'Rob Roys' together forever—I adore you," he wrote to her afterward on an ivory note card, signing it "Tennessee Will-y-ams."

Matalon felt Williams was being hypocritical. "He was absolutely horrible about her drinking," the director said. "This from a man who when I met him, we went to lunch, and he told me that he no longer drank, and I watched him drink one liter of red wine at that lunch. So wine did not count as liquor! Well, here's the man who wrote the line 'I have always depended on the kindness of strangers'! He had very little kindness for people who shared some of his problems."

On the opening night of *Small Craft Warnings*, Stritch repeatedly forgot her lines, needing prompts from the director, adding half an hour to the show's total running time. "Elaine was all over the shop that night," remembered Deacon, who got a lift home from Matalon. "I've never seen a man so depressed." Williams had refused to go backstage.

"I think we've blown it," Matalon told him.

But the reviews, though all acknowledging that this was not one of the playwright's better efforts, overlooked the well-lubricated American's flubs. Irving Wardle, the critic for *The Times* of London, thought it Stritch's best part so far in his city. "Her movement, spasms of energy exploding from total relaxation, continually suggest a baseball player unaware that there is no one else on the field," he wrote.

"Elaine Stritch dominates," read a subsequent listing. "Vivian Matalon directs."

———

In the middle of the Hampstead run, Stritch had another birthday. Though she would continually, casually, shave a year, two, or more off her age to the newspapers, she was now forty-eight and, although past childbearing age, longed for more consistent male companionship. Once, when Michael Bennett was visiting London, they took a cab together and as he was getting out, Stritch threw her arms around him and kissed him goodbye. "Because I loved him, I wanted to be associated with him, I wanted to work with him on a stage—god, I could eat him with a spoon," she told the journalist Kevin Kelly.

"Michael, let's a year from tonight go by and if you're not married and I'm not married, we'll get married."

"It's a deal," he replied.

Here was a far more suitable candidate, frame to her canvas. And she was no longer a coed in rustling crinoline who would have to wait for her boyfriend to get down on bended knee and flip the lid on a velvet box. She decided to herself suggest marriage to Bay, staging the proposal artfully in front of the bust of Arthur Sullivan, the operetta composer, in the Embankment Gardens at the back of the Savoy, overlooking the Thames.

"Why not?" was his answer.

"We pooled our rehearsal pay, crossed the Strand to a little jewelry store, and bought two gold wedding bands," as Stritch told it later on. She also telephoned home to see whether her parents wanted to meet her fiancé before the ceremony.

"No, just marry him," George Stritch said. "Don't let him get away."

On the morning of February 27, 1973, a prenotified photographer for the *Evening Standard* captured the couple walking out of the Savoy. Bay wore a raincoat, like someone in a spy movie, and aviator glasses. Stritch's bridal ensemble was a skirt, cashmere turtleneck sweater, and ski cap, with Bridget nestled compliantly in her arms. They were headed to a Roman Catholic church on Maiden Lane in Covent Garden.

There they were met by a smattering of friends, including Abrams, in London working on a fashion documentary; Barry Brown; Fritz Holt; and George Pravda, a castmate from *Small Craft Warnings* who had witnessed the license, on which Stritch was identified as a "spinster" and

Bay disclosed a previous marriage dissolved. It fell to Matalon to walk Stritch down the aisle.

"Isn't this fucking ridiculous?" she whispered to him as they proceeded.

"Elaine, be quiet. You're in church!"

"What, you think they've never heard the word 'fuck' before?"

On the way down the aisle she paused and put a hand on Holt's shoulder. "So long, kiddo."

After the ceremony, the small wedding party returned to the Savoy, where the priest was among those availing themselves of an enormous bottle of champagne. "It was as big as I was," said Deacon, who got so drunk that he couldn't get his key in the lock when he returned home.

"Everything everybody said, we toasted," Stritch said. "It was just goofy, goofy, goofy."

She invited the guests to join the wedding couple upstairs in their suite.

"Elaine, you're on your own," Abrams said.

"Did I do the right thing?" Stritch asked her in an aside.

"She was nervous," Abrams recalled years later. "It was one of the great performances of her life."

In lieu of a honeymoon, the newlyweds attended a showing of *The Mousetrap*, the Agatha Christie mystery that had been playing at the Ambassadors Theater since 1952, hoping for a good omen. Stritch's jitters dissipated quickly. "The real deep-down security that I felt about being married: that is inexplicable. I can't explain it," she said. "It was some hole in the donut filled up. It suddenly turned into a bran muffin."

On March 13 *Small Craft Warnings* moved from Hampstead to the Comedy Theater in the West End. Two weeks into the run there, while en route to the playhouse, Stritch decided to stop at Rules, the oldest restaurant in London, for a glass of red wine. A waiter came over with tears in his eyes. Word had arrived that Coward had died, aged seventy-three, at his estate in Jamaica.

"All these bartenders stopped making drinks and everybody stopped moving," Stritch said. "It's interesting because whenever anything sad happened like that I never went to alcohol. I went to alcohol more to quiet the joy—just keep it down, don't get too excited. But my god, what a shock. I remember I burst out crying. It's like somebody turned a faucet on."

Drafting her one-woman show, Stritch said that she encouraged the waiters and "a few afternoon boozers at the bar" to begin singing one of Coward's best-known (and most complicated) songs, "I Went to a Marvellous Party," inspired by his visit in the late 1930s to the renowned hostess Elsa Maxwell in the South of France, during which they observed a harlequin tableau of "society / Scampering past."

Entertainment had become considerably more licentious, the single nude scene in *Hair* mild compared to those in the English critic Kenneth Tynan's revue *Oh! Calcutta*. Earl Wilson's son, Earl Wilson, Jr., was working on an erotic musical called *Let My People Come*. Stritch's fondness for profanity notwithstanding, she found most of this repugnant. One of Bay's qualities that she most appreciated was his talent for mimicking the more genteel stars of bygone years, which he'd picked up going to the movies on Saturday afternoon as a child. Prince's children enjoyed his imitations of Daffy Duck, splashing in the pool at the family's vacation home in Majorca, Spain. "I married Marlon Brando, James Cagney, Jack Benny, Edward G. Robinson," Stritch said. "He was the greatest mimic I've ever known in my life. He did Mel Blanc like—there was no difference. It was wonderful."

Together they built a cocoon at the grand hotel: a simulacrum of domesticity and fabulousness that sheltered them from the ugliness of Vietnam, Watergate, and every other way the America they had known went wrong. "I just felt like 'staying put' with him because I loved him," Stritch wrote. "The Savoy was not hard to take either. Coming home every night to ice in the bucket on the bar, clean sheets, fluffed-up pillows on the chair and sofa, curtains drawn, phone messages in longhand slipped under the door, a view of the Thames, a fireplace and John Bay into the bargain, not a bad deal. Not bad at all."

11.

TWO'S COMPANY

By all accounts, including Stritch's, her marriage was built not on eros but agape (and the grape). "Sex was not the big thing in my relationship with John," she said. "When I saw him I went 'whoa,' at rehearsals, but it segued. And it could be because we married a little late in life. But at the same time John was the kind of guy who was not sexually driven."

Liz Smith and others suspected that Bay was gay, that Stritch was appealing to him partly, as she had appealed to Rock Hudson, because she was a lively conversationalist who would not make sexual demands. To Jeffrey Bernard, a notoriously dissolute habitué of London's Soho neighborhood who had performed with him in a 1964 play called *A Kayf Up West*, there was something childlike about Bay's fondness for monsters and old-time movie stars. Rather cruelly, Bernard wrote of a woman who had woken up one morning with a bad hangover, opened her eyes, and seen on the ceiling a large poster of Groucho Marx. "'Christ,' she said, 'I'm in bed with John Bay.'"

Stritch saw in him neither homosexuality nor childishness but a version of the generosity about gender, the openheartedness, that Stella

Adler had suggested was endemic to good acting. "He loved people," she said. "Men, women—that he loved. I don't think he ever did anything about it. And that doesn't necessarily—in the opinion of this reviewer— have to be a problem that he didn't do anything about it. Do you know what I'm saying? So there were two selfish people in dawn's early light."

She might casually mention to him that it had been a few months since their last physical encounter.

"Go to the movies," he'd respond in a laid-back way.

Their personalities were echoed poetically in their surnames. Stritch (anxious, wiry, dissonant) found that Bay (calm, quiet, placid) soothed her and smoothed her rough edges. "I didn't want to disagree or didn't want to fight," she said. "I think it was kind of a thing of 'don't let anything happen to this.' I don't know why that was. I was relaxed, totally relaxed. But also as we were married longer and longer, I got more self-assurance to say 'no I don't agree with you, John'—because that's hard for me. My authority and strength as a woman—'oh, I wouldn't want to mess with her'—is only on the stage."

After *Small Craft Warnings* closed she accepted an invitation to star in the first English production of Neil Simon's *The Gingerbread Lady*, familiar territory about a cabaret singer named Evy Meara who comes out of rehab and slides inexorably back into drinking. When Stritch first read the play, she was convinced Simon must have had her in mind, but the word was he had written it for Maureen Stapleton, whose subsequent performance had won her a Best Actress Tony at the same 1971 ceremony where Stritch had painfully been snubbed.

The author of dependable jollities like *The Odd Couple* and *Barefoot in the Park*, Simon was with this project courting some of the gravitas and critical respect routinely accorded Williams and Edward Albee. "Is it a comedy? No," he told the *New York Times* reporter Mel Gussow. "It's not funny? It is funny. It's drama? No, it's too funny to be drama, too dramatic to be comedy." He called Evy "a self-defeating woman" and said that in creating her he'd been subliminally aware of Judy Garland.

Although Stapleton had done well in the role, reviews for the play had been subdued—American audiences didn't really want Neil Simon to be dark—and rights for the first run in England, at the Royal Windsor

Theater, had been secured by a novice American director named Jerry Harte, recently married to the actress Julia McKenzie, who had played April in *Company* there. McKenzie had lived in a small flat in Kensington owned by the father of the playwright Peter Shaffer, along with an assortment of young show-business folk including the actor Stephen Greif, who had secured the part of Evy's guitar-playing ex.

Rehearsals took place at the producer Howard Burnett's well-appointed quarters in Regent's Park. "Almost immediately, things began to get uncomfortable," Greif said. Harte was having a tough time with his leading lady, who was frustrated with the director's lack of experience. And another actress, Vivien Merchant, was distracted by troubles in her marriage to the playwright Harold Pinter.

One Sunday afternoon, Stritch convened a meeting of the producer and cast. She wanted Harte fired and replaced with Matalon from *Small Craft Warnings*.

Greif was affronted on Harte's behalf, "even though I knew in my heart she had good reasons," he said. "I pleaded with Elaine that none of us would be here without him. He was the architect of the entire production and everything it entailed, even going so far as to arrange that Neil Simon himself would be flown over from the States and with us for a few days in Windsor. It was, I contended, grossly ungrateful, unfair, and just plain wrong to deal him this humiliating knockout blow and I implored her to give him another chance."

This she did but not without adding plenty of pauses and bits of stage business of her own, causing the running time of the play to be routinely over by thirty to forty-five minutes. "Which almost drove Vivien insane," Greif said. Merchant was scurrying home to London each night from Windsor to try to salvage what was left of her marriage.

Greif asked Stritch respectfully if she might close the gap in one of the speeches.

"I'll think about it," she said.

The next day, before the matinee, she called up from her ground floor dressing room, wearing her stockings, stiletto heels, and white shirt, to negotiate his request.

"My god, Elaine," Greif gasped. "Those legs go up to heaven."

"Well, honey, the good Lord gives each of us something," Stritch said.

An Australian actor named Kevin Lindsay played Jimmy, a gay friend of Evy. One day in rehearsal he somehow got on Stritch's wrong side and became convinced he was going to be fired. The next day, he presented Stritch with a small gift-wrapped box and a card reading "Sorry." Inside the box was a pair of solid sterling-silver cuff links from the House of Garrard, the royal jewelers, to go with the white shirts that she loved to wear at rehearsals.

"Oh, Kevin, you shouldn't have, but thanks, honey," Stritch said.

She no longer collected dolls from around the world and indeed was entering a phase of renouncing attachment to material things, though when in character, said another cast member, Luie Caballero, "she wouldn't wear the false fur coat. It had to be a real one." The phrase "at home on the stage" rang true to her. "All those kinds of expressions come from a very deep feeling that . . . it's safe, you know?" Stritch said. "I feel very safe on the stage and I always put things of my own out there." Around the set of *The Gingerbread Lady*, she had placed pictures of Hal Prince and his wife, Judy, and Sondheim. (Also comforting, if hardly stabilizing, was the bottle of brandy she'd asked Caballero to bring her before performances.)

At the end of the show on opening night, Simon came backstage escorted by Bay, who "looked and moved, it seemed to me, as if he had just stepped out of a Bogart movie," a cigarette dangling from his lips, Greif said.

Stritch wasn't particularly impressed with the playwright. "Boy, was he El Square-O," she said. "But I convinced Neil Simon, I don't know how, to cut the nymphomania of the play. I reasoned with him. I said, 'Neil, I just think being an alcoholic is enough in this piece, I don't think she should sleep with the delivery boy, you know, who comes from the liquor store.' That was enough. It was really enough. And he agreed."

The besotted London critics stretched their metaphorical limit describing Stritch's stage presence: "a wisecracking female Pierrot clanging out her agony like a town-crier" . . . "she paces her Manhattan apartment like a blonde tigress" . . . "her angular body looks as if it had been welded together out of elastic and a Meccano set."

This may have also marked the first reference to her as "Stritchnine," used by Robert Cushman in his review when the show was transferred to the Phoenix Theater, "directed of course by Vivian Matalon," Greif said.

Though he was even more frustrated with her drinking than he had been during *Small Craft Warnings*, Matalon found Stritch's ability to manipulate the audience remarkable. "There's a whole birthday cake in the play, and she's getting drunk in the play and they keep saying 'try to get her to eat the cake,' and she said, 'I'm not ready for the cake.' A laugh. 'I tell you when I'm ready for the cake.' That was a second laugh. 'I didn't rent it.' A third laugh. 'I bought it outright.' A fourth laugh. And it was amazing. The only other person that I ever worked with that had that ability was Coward himself."

Validated so completely as the star of a "serious" play, albeit Neil Simon's version of serious, Stritch saw little reason to return to New York, where the Sondheim–Prince collaboration was blooming with *A Little Night Music*, not just a critical sensation but a commercial success, with more than six hundred performances on Broadway and half a dozen Tony Awards, including Best Musical. Sondheim appeared on the cover of *Newsweek*, looking beatific and slightly medieval in a red turtleneck, as "Broadway's Music Man." The song "Send in the Clowns"—written as specifically for the voice of the actress Glynis Johns as "The Ladies Who Lunch" had been tailored for Stritch—became particularly, unexpectedly popular. Frank Sinatra, having emerged from his short-lived retirement, recorded it on an album that went gold, and when Judy Collins did too, in 1975, it reached Number 36 on the pop chart (two years later, after she sang it on *The Muppet Show*, it went up to Number 19).

"Congratulations, I just heard about Judy Collins," Joe Allen said to Sondheim, who'd walked into his restaurant.

"I don't write hits!" he said Sondheim replied. Nor did hits come from musicals much anymore, other than rock musicals, and often not even then.

In a bar near Regent's Park, far from all this excitement, Stritch played "Send in the Clowns" on the jukebox for a starstruck local reporter and did an imitation of Johns singing it in her delicate, husky, faintly gasping way.

The British capital felt much safer than New York still, but one night a large explosion outside sent a piece of the *Gingerbread Lady* set falling. Stritch dropped her prop drink in shock.

"What was that?" she said.

"Oh, keep going," begged an English voice from the audience.

"No, I don't think I *will* keep going. I think these people here would like to know what's going on." Lindsay was known to have a heart problem and she put her hand on his chest. "Are you okay, honey?"

He was. After a few minutes Stritch continued the performance, reminding everyone (soberly) that she had been drunk in the scene. Eventually the stage manager came on and evacuated the theater. The noise had been a car bomb a block away, set off by a member of the Irish Republican Army.

Other than having a general knowledge of who was in power, Stritch generally declined to engage with politics. "I don't think Elaine knew where Vietnam was," said John Lahr, the theater critic and journalist, who had moved to London at around the same time. Like his father, Bert Lahr, a seasoned actor of the stage dogged to the end of his days by having played the Cowardly Lion in MGM's *The Wizard of Oz*, Stritch was "old-school," John Lahr thought, with that "succeed or die mentality. All the old-school people, and this includes Elaine, were fairly poorly educated."

Matalon was struck by Stritch's willful obliviousness not only to political problems but to technological developments. He remembered rehearsing a scene in *The Gingerbread Lady* during which Evy had to turn the television on. "So she turned the television on and then went and busied herself with something else. I said, 'What are you doing, what is this silence for?' She said, 'I'm giving the television time to warm up.' This was *years* after the television came on instantly."

Despite her indifference to the medium, it was with a television series that Stritch would consolidate her celebrity in England, and steady her roller-coaster finances. The executives at London Weekend Television had noticed the copious publicity she had attracted for her residency at the Savoy, which was near its headquarters. Bill MacIlwraith had written an acerbic play called *The Anniversary* (made into a movie starring Bette Davis), but found steadier work in television. Familiar with Stritch from years in the West End, he wrote with her in mind the script of what would become *Two's Company*—no relation to the popular U.S. sitcom that would follow it, *Three's Company*, itself based on a different British sitcom. (Even more confusing, *Two's Company* would inspire a short-lived American version called *The Two of Us*.)

It was about an American expatriate named Dorothy McNab, a writer of thrillers living in Chelsea, Stritch's old neighborhood from her *Sail Away* days, who hires a butler played by Donald Sinden. Stritch wrangled Sammy Cahn, who had contributed lyrics to an unrelated 1952 Broadway revue starring Bette Davis, also called *Two's Company*, to write the opening theme for her to sing and Sinden to speak. Thereby she injected a slightly drab sitcom with some of the romance and class of the old-fashioned musical theater, with echoes of both what was still thus far her biggest success ("Whenever I choose company / I gotta say two's company") and one of Cole Porter's biggest hits ("Night and day with you / there's no way with you").

"He's marvelous, but it's too long," the show's producer, Stuart Allen, told her of Cahn's work. The show was allotted twenty-five minutes. "I would prefer the opening to be half as long."

"Oh no—I can't possibly cut his song," Stritch said.

Naturally, she prevailed, and the duet was set to animation of an eagle in a sexy white peignoir and a British lion marching alongside. "She wanted things, she got them," Allen said.

Stritch wangled more favorable terms at the Savoy—$1000 per month for a suite on the Thames, some expenses included—in exchange for her on-air plugs. "Anytime my butler and I went to lunch, it mentioned the Hotel Savoy. The Savoy, Savoy, Savoy," she said.

"The show was well written and I was very hopeful," Allen said. "I didn't realize she was such a difficult person to work with until I got to know her." His stage manager would walk through the set, picking up glasses from which Stritch had quaffed, and then would joke bitterly that when she took her dog in a bag around in the Savoy, it was "to stop the gin bottles from rattling around."

Allen decided to try reverse psychology. "I dealt with her by telling her to do the opposite of what I wanted her to do. If I wanted her to smoke, I told her not to smoke. If I told her to sit, she stood up."

Exhausted, he handed off the project after the first season—much of which was improvised, he said, because Stritch could not remember the right lines.

The friction between the costars was unpleasant. "My father had a serious problem with drunks," said Donald Sinden's son, Marc. "He couldn't bear them—he was almost religious about it, as most actors are once you've been on the stage. She was drinking a bottle of brandy a day, and it was pretty frightening."

In August 1975, Stritch received a long, heartfelt letter from her brother-in-law Thomas Bolton, an especial favorite of hers in the extended family. He remarked on how alike they were, wanting to be "noticed and admired," enjoying an audience. The owner of an insurance agency, Bolton loved to sing. "He was a party guy and all that—a fun guy," his daughter Sally Hanley said. But for him the party had ceased to be marvelous, and he had just returned from his second stay in the Brighton Hospital, a well-regarded rehabilitation facility near Detroit. The first time, he thought, they had the wrong fellow. This time he'd remained seventeen days. "Finally it dawned on me that this wasn't pride at all . . . it was arrogance," he wrote. "I'm not bangin' the drum against booze, but from my life and from watching some others, it's a damn dangerous run and can louse you up so badly you can't always get back, believe me."

Bolton stopped short of confronting his simpatico sister-in-law's own drinking problem, but his long letter arguing the merits of sobriety for himself, concluding "Merman couldn't carry your night case," had a powerful effect on her. Stritch saved the letter and shortly thereafter attended her first Alcoholics Anonymous meeting in London.

The organization had become mainstream, with the millionth copy of its de facto bible, the Big Book, presented to President Richard Nixon in a 1973 ceremony at the White House. The counterculture was more interested in illegal drugs, but bourgeois America and to a lesser extent Britain was sharing in a collective hangover following the ebullient cocktail culture of the 1950s and '60s. Stritch felt perfectly at home in meetings, with their resemblance to church—four of the twelve steps refer overtly to God—and the confessor-like role of the "sponsor" who is available to hear about a member's temptations and slipups. In fact, meetings were better than church, because the congregation did not have to remain silent. It was highly sociable, and occasionally theatrical.

She liked to tell of the proper English sponsor who reassured a new member: "I'll be right over. Do you have any alcohol in the house?"

"Yes—I have a very lovely bottle of scotch."

"Put it right down the toilet. I'll be on the way."

"I poured it into the toilet," the member confessed, "but I didn't flush."

Stritch was one of several celebrities who made Alcoholics Anonymous, whose members are supposed to keep their identities private, less anonymous. Appearing on Dick Cavett's talk show in 1979, she called it the "most glorious organization that I've ever come into contact with." "People in AA are the kind of people I've been looking for all my life," she said. "They're selfless! They're just so unselfish and so caring. It made it all dramatic and interesting to stop drinking." But she continued to hold herself apart. "I'm not sure if I'm an alcoholic or not," she said. "I stopped drinking from my head because I was mad at myself."

By the second season of *Two's Company*, Stritch had gone "paranoically dry," Marc Sinden said, though this wouldn't last. "The wit and timing was back." Then in his twenties, he became a walker of sorts for her when Bay, who hadn't found steady acting work, didn't feel like going out. They got along very well. But "I don't ever think I ever knew 'Elaine,'" he said. "I knew 'Stritch.' She hid a lot. There was a lot of pain in her life, but she wouldn't talk about it."

Indeed, when Tennessee Williams urged her to appear in an outré autobiographical play he had begun years before and to which he had now returned, *Vieux Carré*, Stritch said, "I just can't. Because I'm just too happy."

"That's impossible. It's not impossible to be happy, but it certainly is impossible to be too happy. This will sustain you. *That's* not going to last."

But Stritch wasn't confident she could handle the subject matter, which included drugs and starvation in New Orleans. "I mean, this was heavy-duty stuff," she said.

Her ongoing bad luck in Hollywood continued to rankle. Neil Simon had liked her work in *The Gingerbread Lady* enough to offer her a part as Robert De Niro's agent in a movie called *Bogart Slept Here*, about an off-Broadway actor who finds himself a worldwide celebrity after the blockbuster success of his first film, based on the experience of Dustin Hoffman and directed by Mike Nichols. With great fanfare Stritch flew to Los Angeles—irking the producers of *Two's Company* by bringing along her wardrobe from the show for personal use—only to find De Niro fired by the studio and the project falling apart. Nichols went back east, and Simon wound up casting Richard Dreyfuss and reworking the material into *The Goodbye Girl*, a big hit directed by Herbert Ross.

Stritch signed instead to do *Providence*, a movie about an aging novelist played by John Gielgud, directed by Alain Resnais (*Hiroshima Mon Amour*). Filming was intended to take place in New England. "It should be noisier and more fun with Stritch back," Liz Smith wrote hopefully in her column. But due to budget concerns the production soon rather shot scenes in Brussels, Antwerp, and Louvain; then at a château in Limoges; and then at the Lancaster Hotel on the Champs-Élysées, where Stritch set up with her customary popping of champagne corks and Bay in tow.

"I remember them in the lobby of the hotel after a day's shooting, just carrying on at the top of their lungs and me creeping away," said Ellen Burstyn, who was also in the movie. "They were a very rowdy couple."

Resnais and Stephen Sondheim had collaborated on a previous film, *Stavisky*, and Sondheim had mulled doing music for this one as well, but he was too busy adapting the score for the movie version of *A Little Night Music* to fulfill the commitment, disappointingly for Stritch. *Providence* was intended as a Schubertian string quintet, with her as a double bass, Resnais said, Gielgud a cello, Ellen Burstyn a violin, and the onetime matinee idol Dirk Bogarde a piano (David Warner was the oft disrespected viola). The script by the playwright David Mercer was challengingly abstract: "strange torrents of words," Bogarde called them.

Assigned an article about the movie, the colorful feature writer Rex Reed took a dismayed taxi ride through graffiti-covered Paris and tripped over a rumpled carpet—"Ah! Even the Lancaster goofs in this careless age"—on his way to meet Burstyn, who crowed about how she and Stritch were both from Detroit and the psychological complexities of the script. Then came Bogarde, recently of *Death in Venice*, a handsome veteran of the British army who had helped liberate the Bergen-Belsen concentration camp and would write unflinchingly of the terrible atrocities he'd witnessed. He was one of Stritch's staunchest fans.

"Come now, I'm going to take you to the truly talented member of the cast," the actor told Reed, and the two men found Stritch out in the courtyard, wearing white satin pajamas and pearls.

"Dirk has a face like an angel and he has done everyzing naughty and Elaine has the face of someone—boom, boom, boom—who has done everyzing, but has really done NOZZZING!" she said, adding, "I have a rapport with Resnais like Christmas morning."

She again called herself Frieda Fun, referred to Resnais as "Andy Artist," and bragged that he'd kept a scrapbook on her for years. (He kept a scrapbook on many actresses, he clarified.)

"This is all very emotional to me," Stritch said. "For a really artistic director to see beyond casting me as Robert De Niro's agent with my elbows on the desk barking jokes is wonderful. He saw beyond all the creeps I've played and saw me as a woman—all feminine."

But the movie had its own intrinsic creepiness. She was playing Helen, the mistress of Bogarde's character, Claude, but with the facial features of his suicidal mother, and Helen herself is afflicted with an incurable disease. And Stritch was still embodying the so-called spinster.

"How glad I am, I chose to live alone, right from the beginning," Helen says when Claude complains about his marriage.

"Are you?" he asks, massaging her shoulders.

"When you love someone, you're sensitive to their tastes," she goes on. "It's rarely mutual. And that's because one is rarely loved."

After filming wrapped Bogarde wrote to Stritch from his retreat in the South of France, near Grasse, to which she had sent him a copy of her 1955 Dolphin record. His favorite track was "Too Many Rings Around Rosie," which reminded him of her sitting at the hot studio with a steaming mug of Pernod.

"I am still haunted by your performance in 'P,'" he wrote, comparing her with Garland in *A Star Is Born* and fondly remembering "telephones and ice tinkling and rooms swaying."

He was shuddering at the thought of the coming press junket, and his fears were justified. The French appreciated *Providence*, the Americans thought it head-scratching and pretentious. The *New Yorker* critic Pauline Kael was particularly brutal. "As Elaine Stritch's lover, he looks small and bewildered—if this is the point, nothing is made of it," she wrote of Bogarde. "And Stritch acts like a soap-opera tired wife; her baritone could be from cleaning fatigue."

The ever perspicacious Kael was onto something. On one episode of *Two's Company*—which had been nominated for multiple awards but won "nozzzing"—John Bay appeared as Dorothy McNab's cousin Clarence, in a red plaid blazer, munching on a sandwich and looking hearty. But his wife, who'd conveyed an unusual fragility in *Providence*, was downright drawn, thinner than she had been in years. During one drive to the country she noticed that she was having trouble whistling, and was exhausted and oddly thirsty.

At first Stritch attributed her weight loss to mere overwork. She would appear in the annual Royal Variety Performance in the presence of Queen Elizabeth and Prince Philip (along with the pop group Boney M.; her first time performing sober, she later said), been cast as a nonsmoking teetotaler in a revival of George Kelly's play *The Fatal Weakness* at the Theater Royal, and studied hard for a Radio 3 version of Albee's *A Delicate Balance*. A colleague noticed her boniness, and that she was chugging Coca-Cola after Coca-Cola; she advised her to be checked out by a nurse.

And before long Stritch, down to under one hundred pounds—"I looked like a Vogue model"—was in the hospital. She was unperturbed by this. "I'm a good patient," she wrote later. "I have always had a child-like faith in hospitals and doctors, so much that I often make the Freud-ian slip of saying 'when I was in the *hotel*,' when I mean 'the hospital.'" She enjoyed ticking off choices on the meal card and the bland food that arrived thereafter. "I think that after all the glamour of restaurants with rich delicacies, a good simple meal can be very exciting."

The diagnosis handed down was most unexpected: diabetes, so-called juvenile (now called type 1). Heavy drinking was not the cause, but couldn't have helped, and the disease could not be cured.

"Why me?" Stritch thought somewhat wretchedly in her hospital bed. "Then again, why not me? I lay mulling over the situation, trying to feel like Bette Davis in *Dark Victory* but, just between you and me, sorry for myself."

A visit from Quentin Crisp, the dandified author of *The Naked Civil Servant*, brightened her spirits.

"You're just slowing down for a bit, but you'll pick up again," he told her.

"Quentin, when you were a little boy, what did you want to be when you grew up?" she asked.

"An invalid," Crisp said.

"I got the idea that this man had had very little love in his early years and he must have felt that if he became an invalid he'd get love and at-tention," Stritch wrote. "What better way . . . oh, Quentin, what sadder way? But what an honest guy to admit that about himself."

A strict regime was prescribed, involving daily multiple insulin injec-tions and a carefully controlled diet. Food would from now on be meted out at regular intervals and have to be carried around with medical equipment, which Stritch would often choose to do in rustling shopping bags from stores like Chanel or Bergdorf. "It's an extra makeup case," she would shrug to Cavett of the burden.

Stritch would do nothing to conceal her affliction—quite the contrary. Her friends all learned what to do if she were in the throes of a hypo-glycemic attack, which can cause a range of symptoms from trembling to losing consciousness. Once Stritch figured out how to administer insulin shots, she would do so with gusto, recounting several times with amusement how people who saw her injecting herself in public bathrooms would suspect that she was a recreational drug abuser. Diabetes also imposed upon her a new and salutary discipline—forcing her to rest. "Almost like an imaginary Mommy and Big Daddy backing me up," she wrote.

Having removed her clothes in public for years, Stritch was not about to be discreet about her treatment; indeed, her exhibitionism was a natural complement to the new program, with an expanse of leg or stomach always available for the roving needle. "If they hijack your plane and you've got diabetes, tell the hijackers and ask them if they can get a little insulin on board," she wrote brightly. "Be honest. Who knows, you may be the first one off the plane." (The actor Theodore Bikel, late of *Fiddler on the Roof*, and the Hollywood agent Sue Mengers had been among those on a hijacked 747, in a decade filled with them.)

Stritch had reason to feel gratitude for her second chance. Two former swains came to gruesome ends in the late 1970s. Jack Cassidy had burned to death after falling asleep with a lit cigarette on a Naugahyde couch in his penthouse apartment.

Then, coming over with Bay for a visit to America on the ocean liner *Queen Elizabeth II*, she answered a telephone call in their cabin and learned that Gig Young had shot himself, along with his fifth and much younger wife, Kim Schmidt, in a murder-suicide.

Her mother was particularly shocked by this development; Young still loomed in Mildred's mind as the one who had gotten away. "She disliked all the boyfriends except Gig," Stritch said, "and he ended up nuttier than a fruitcake." When she complained about her mother's needling, though, Bay chided her. "I love your mother and I don't think you should talk about her that way and I don't want to hear it," he said.

"And I got a new respect for my mother," Stritch said. "Not to mention John."

In the summer of 1979, a year after Liz Smith reported that the disco movie *Saturday Night Fever* had driven five thousand music executives "berserk" with joy at a conference in Cannes, the Savoy celebrated its ninetieth anniversary with a pianist tinkling Rodgers and Hart's "There's a

Small Hotel." By Christmas, the hotel disbanded its famed cabaret, its small orchestra and eight dancing girls let go. Jackets were no longer required for dinner. "Today the fashion is to dress in such a shabby way you won't be anything but a liberated tramp," the chairman of the hotel's holding company said.

Even Ethel Merman had recorded a disco album, singing "Alexander's Ragtime Band" against synthesizers on *The Tonight Show*. And Hal Prince's new production with Tim Rice and Andrew Lloyd Webber, *Evita*, about the Argentine first lady Eva Peron, had a rock beat. It opened in New York half a year after the apex of his collaboration with Sondheim: *Sweeney Todd: The Demon Barber of Fleet Street*, a Grand Guignol–influenced tour de force starring Angela Lansbury as Mrs. Lovett, a diabolically dotty cannibalistic baker in nineteenth-century London.

To Stritch this was further proof of how gravely she'd erred choosing to do the play *Time of the Barracudas* over Sondheim's *Anyone Can Whistle*. In her imagination Lovett, like Madame Rose, could and should have been her role. (Gemignani, the conductor, thought she would have been wonderful as Rose, but that she was too elegant to play a working-class shop owner.)

"I have a resentment about Angela Lansbury. I think she gets away with murder," she would grouse years later. "And she's too fuckin' nice." Lansbury, one of the most respected and beloved actors in the business, was ignorant of this bad feeling. "Truthfully, I really knew her only briefly, and I didn't know her that well," she said. "I didn't even know there was a question of her doing *Anyone Can Whistle*."

Deprived of both the plum new parts and a bread-and-butter role like Carol Channing in *Hello, Dolly!*, Stritch brought complete creative commitment to even commercial assignments. In December 1979 she was asked to emcee a two-day fashion show extravaganza at the renowned department store Liberty of London sponsored by Silk Cut cigarettes. An elaborate simulacrum of a theatrical event featuring clothes by Yves Saint Laurent, Calvin Klein, and other top designers of the moment, it was produced by the store's head of publicity and marketing, Peter Tear, whom she'd met at a *Company* party, on a budget of about two hundred thousand pounds. Larry Fuller, who'd worked on *Evita* and *Sweeney*

Todd, choreographed, up to a point. Stritch ended up commanding the models while in fluffy slippers, smock, curlers, and shower cap. "Eventually she took over because she knew exactly how to make things work," Tear said, and she announced each designer with pomp. "She relished every second of it. All those ladies with their shopping bags—she just gave them what they came for."

There were three daily performances at five pounds apiece and they all sold out before the first day. "It has more punch and pulchritude packed into its 51 minutes than most West End musicals twice as long," commented one newspaper.

"I have one thing to say to you," Stritch told Tear afterward. "Get the fuck out of fashion, and into theater where you belong." And so he did, becoming a successful producer.

Two's Company having run its course, Stritch had begun helping rewrite scripts of Hollywood's *Maude*, a U.S. success for her old schoolmate Bea Arthur, into an English series called *Nobody's Perfect.*

More ambitiously, she had tried and failed to produce Lillian Hellman's *The Little Foxes* in London, wanting to play the scheming Southern heiress Regina as Tallulah Bankhead had in 1939. "Miss Hellmanned her right up the wazoo," Stritch said. But the writer would not give up the rights. "This has nothing to do with your talent," Hellman told Stritch on the phone from Martha's Vineyard. "I've seen you perform and you're very good. But this is my baby and I really don't want it done for a while and I have to be very circumspect about who . . ." She chose instead Elizabeth Taylor, who'd starred in the unsuccessful movie version of *A Little Night Music* and who would open in the play in 1981.

"Oh, my heart sank," Stritch said. (She would later get a kind of revenge, playing a harridan-like Hellman in Peter Feibleman's 1993 drama *Cakewalk*.)

However, John Bay had amplified his ongoing Groucho Marx impression into a one-man show called *An Elephant in My Pajamas*, which was beginning to get bookings in America. A writer named Dick Vosburgh cast him as Groucho for a revue in a converted mortuary called *A Day in Hollywood/A Night in the Ukraine*. It moved to downtown London, running for nine months, and a UPI reporter called Bay an "uncanny copy" of the star, who had died in 1977.

He and Stritch had bought a Rolls-Royce with a copper bottom and a taupe top. "I remember riding in their Rolls-Royce to Lady Camoys' house, which is absolutely storybook English village, with the little dotted sheep," said George Bay, one of John's nephews, who had attended the Cordon Bleu cooking school and helped introduce the Egg McMuffin in Paris.

Ever comfortable as a brand ambassador, Stritch accepted an offer from the British Tourist Authority to travel to America and talk up "bargains, breakfasts, buttons, bumbershoots and the Bard."

"I feel living in London is becoming to me," she said to a reporter in Detroit as a limousine and driver idled outside. "My life is less harassed, less hysterical. I paid my dues. I was in New York 22 years and I beat it, I made it. My name was up in lights." She was drinking Sanka. "The theater didn't take me over, I took it over. The thing that thrills me is that I can handle it now. I feel so grown-up. I didn't want to know all that when I was young, and yes, I loved that period of not giving a damn."

But there was an element of doth protest too much to all this English boosterism. The taxes were high there; the pound was weak. In addition, there was a new manager at the Savoy, and the Bays were worried he might not honor their favorable rate.

In New York, where the twin towers of the World Trade Center now loomed muscularly, if not majestically, over downtown, Stritch walked around wearing a badge that read "London Is . . . Theater with a Capital T." Truthfully, it sounded rather limp next to the soaring "I Love New York" campaign that was all over the television, with Lansbury and the *Chorus Line* dancers and Sandy Duncan as Peter Pan soaring into the night. The Yankees had resumed winning World Series, as they had when she had first arrived on the Detroiter in 1943. The air was still filthy, but it was once again fertile with possibility.

"I'm not saying goodbye," Stritch told Victor Gower, her favorite bartender at the Savoy, when she announced her decision with Bay to move out. "I'm saying au revoir."

12.

WHO'S THAT WOMAN?

MY FAVORITE RECIPE
Take an hour's nap
Shower
Cologne-up
Apply makeup
Put on a pretty dress
Get into a very rich man's Mercedes
Cruise drive to my favorite restaurant
—*Stritch's contribution to the Paper Mill Playhouse's* Cookbook of
the Stars *(1985), to which other actors offered instructions for home-
made zucchini appetizers, chocolate cake, and the like*

Like the agenda of the Irish Republican Army, women's lib was not a
cause that particularly moved Stritch. She had been raised in a household of forceful females, and respected—even sometimes coveted—
their choice to lead lives as traditional wives and mothers, despite herself
having chafed against the limitations of such roles. Joe Allen's grudging acknowledgment of her cooking notwithstanding, she had adroitly

avoided domestic labor, and neither marched against the tools of oppression nor (heaven forfend) examined her nether regions with a flashlight in consciousness-raising circles. She was unaffected by protests against Dean Martin's Dingaling Sisters. She went so far as to attend a luncheon meeting of the Feminine Touch, a British anti-libbers society led by Bettine Le Beau, a concentration-camp survivor who had appeared as Professor Dent's secretary in *Dr. No* and on *The Benny Hill Show* and had taken a Frenchified version of her husband's name, Lebow.

Paying a visit, *The Guardian* dryly reported that the group had been "formed by women who want to wear hats again, and frills and ringlets, and let men stand erect again in serene possession of the territory they stake out with their mighty thews and superior business sense."

Stritch had voiced vague support for the founder of *Ms.* who'd gone undercover as a Playboy Bunny. "I think you should stand up for Steinem," she said. But her idols were not radicals but rather tough, independent "broads" of the old school, be they famous (Merman), fictional (Mame), or familial (Mildred). "You don't have to knock men, you just have to show what women are capable of" was her general feeling.

This attitude jibed with that of a new neighbor in her new town, Nyack, New York: Terry Martin Hekker, a mother of five who'd inflamed feminists with a 1977 article in *The New York Times* called "The Satisfactions of Housewifery and Motherhood in an Age of Do-Your-Own-Thing." "The rate it's going I calculate I am less than eight years away from being the last housewife in the country," Hekker had written. "Anthropologists will study my feeding and nesting habits through field glasses and keep notebooks detailing my every move." The essay had led to a deal with the publisher William Morrow and a book, *Ever Since Adam and Eve*, which became a bestseller, its straight-talking comic suburban voice squarely in the tradition of Jean Kerr's *Please Don't Eat the Daisies*.

But Stritch was far from a homemaker with concerns about a good school district. So why did she choose to settle in Nyack, a quaint village on the Hudson River about forty-five minutes north of New York City? Maybe because Helen Hayes, the First Lady of the American Theater, lived there—"I thought I'd move there and give her a run for her money," Stritch would joke to Johnny Carson. Maybe because her occasional so-

journs with Bay into the English countryside had enhanced her appreciation of the pastoral life. Or perhaps it was simply because, as her friend
the actress Arlene Dahl put it, "she found a bargain on a house."

Built in 1910 and more than three thousand square feet, 10 Voorhis
Point was on a hilly cul-de-sac overlooking the water, with multiple fire-
places and sun dappling the carpet through stained-glass windows recalling those at Gesu Church back in Detroit.

"We became friendly very quickly," Hekker said. "A, she didn't know
anyone here; and B, she didn't drive; neither she nor John drove." (Someone else had usually been at the wheel of the Rolls.) "So to go to the super-
market or anything, I was the designated driver." Babes in the wood in
their fifties, the couple didn't have any furniture—though Stritch had
managed to pack up and bring back a full set of the Savoy's china—and
so Hekker took them shopping at Ethan Allen. "And they just wanted
to live in one of the furnished rooms there because it was cozy," she said.

Among Stritch's old retinue of faithful columnists documenting
her every move, only the devoted Liz Smith and Earl Wilson were still
around to herald her return to New York. Wilson informed her of a new
custom of doggie bags in restaurants.

"I'm ahead of you," Stritch said. "I'm taking not only the steak but
the bottle of wine too." It was temporarily ta-ta to AA: her diabetes now
managed, her eating and insulin injections routinized, she had returned
freely to her old alcohol-proud persona, authorized by her doctor to drink
in moderation.

She had developed a line about Ronald Reagan. "I got homesick when
I learned they'd elected an actor to the White House," she said. "I didn't
want to miss any of the entrances or the exits. Or the laughs. I felt I
should check out the President. See how well he was following that advice Noël Coward always gave to actors: Say the lines and don't bump into
the furniture."

Reagan's election had further calcified nostalgia for the lost world
of the 1950s and even as punk supplanted disco, homages to aging or
departed figures of old-time show business were everywhere. Johnny
Carson dug up a clip of him and Stritch on the old show *Pantomime Quiz*.
Stritch participated in a program commemorating the underrecognized

lyricist Dorothy Fields, who had written words for "The Way You Look Tonight" and "A Fine Romance." At a Cole Porter tribute that she plugged on *The Dick Cavett Show* (Cavett himself sang "Don't Fence Me In" wearing red cowboy boots), she ran into her old castmate Helen Gallagher, of *Pal Joey* and *No, No, Nanette*. Elaine described her renovation troubles to the audience. "I thought, Boy, I wish I had that chutzpah," Gallagher recalled. "To think that people would be interested in whether she did her kitchen or not. But they were. Because she made it interesting."

Yet Stritch was having considerable trouble finding her place in an irrevocably changed musical-theater landscape. She was considered but not booked as a replacement to play the embittered lush Miss Hannigan, the director of the orphanage, in *Annie*, and the past-her-prime actress Dorothy Brock in *42nd Street*. And these were shows whose argot she understood. What was rising on the horizon of Broadway, following the success of *Evita*, was rather the megamusical, with its fog machines and often circuslike special effects.

Sondheim had gone in another direction. Shortly after *Sweeney* opened, he had, like Stritch, landed in the hospital. He'd had a heart attack, at forty-nine. His next project was a musical update of an old George S. Kaufman–Moss Hart play, *Merrily We Roll Along*, whose plot runs in reverse: about three old friends, two men and a woman with a drinking problem, who go from disillusioned middle age to youthful idealism.

After the elegance of *A Little Night Music* and the operatic complexity of *Sweeney Todd*, audiences felt cheated by the minimalist *Merrily*. They were baffled by the director Hal Prince's decision to cast young people (including his daughter, Daisy), costume them in T-shirts and jeans, and position them on simple risers. Many people walked out before the curtain fell, and *Merrily* flopped more loudly than *Anyone Can Whistle*, closing after 52 previews and 16 performances and scorned by critics and columnists, including Liz Smith. Sondheim found the reaction so painful, particularly the inexperienced cast's letdown, that for a time he considered abandoning the musical theater, and he and Prince took a break from their partnership.

An architect of the new spectacles, Andrew Lloyd Webber of *Evita* had also left the lyricist Tim Rice and begun writing a new musical based on T. S. Eliot's *Old Possum's Book of Practical Cats*. He spoke to Stritch about a narration role.

"If I'm involved in it the way you're explaining it to me, Andrew, I would want to be a cat," she said.

"And the last I heard of it was that," she recalled later, "and then you hear *Cats* and everybody's a cat."

Prepared to be regretful, Stritch went to see a preview of the show at the New London Theater in the West End. "I just hated every minute of it," she said. "The first act, I was all dressed up and the cats came out through the audience. They were mussing people's hair and—you, now touching me! One of them came near me—I remember looking at it and saying 'don't touch me.' That's how much I hated that show. I didn't want anything to do with it."

She walked out at intermission. *Cats* would run for almost eighteen years and 7485 performances on Broadway, with Eliot winning posthumous Tony Awards for the book and score.

Despite a degree of underemployment, Stritch and Bay enjoyed themselves for a time in Nyack. They had a group of regular visitors. Abrams was one. Donna McKechnie, who had been diagnosed with arthritis and told she would never dance again after a shining turn in *A Chorus Line*, then even more successful than *Cats*, was another. Stritch had told her a story about traveling back to Ohio in a navy suit, white gloves, and pearls and getting Bay restored to his parents' will. "Like a movie from the 1940s," McKechnie said. Ellen Burstyn, Stritch's costar in *Providence*, was impressed to see there not filched hotel china but a collection of crystal vases. "Very elegant and tasteful. She was somebody who set a beautiful table, beautiful linen, and silver and glasses—elegantly formal, but not stiff." Frank Bowling, the hotel manager Stritch had befriended at the Connaught, had moved to New York to work for the Ritz-Carlton Hotel and also trekked out to see them, joining Liz Smith with her longtime partner, Iris Love, and Lee Bailey. "We all drank and smoked like Turks and had these wonderful evenings," Bowling said. One Christmas Eve, they went to midnight Mass at a picturesque chapel on Snedens Landing along the line of steep cliffs known as the Palisades and were surprised by a visit from Arlene Dahl's handsome son Lorenzo Lamas, then starring in *Falcon Crest*.

Dahl was living with her soon-to-be sixth husband, Marc Rosen, in nearby Sparkill, in a house they called Treetops, where they frequently entertained. For a while she and Stritch worked on a female version of *The Odd Couple*, but the small regional theater where it was supposed to be shown closed before the play could be staged. This aborted collaboration was, Dahl said, "the thing that saved our friendship. So I'm grateful." They began a tradition of throwing a Christmas party and for many years Stritch and Russell Nype would sing "You're Just in Love," the duet from *Call Me Madam*, during the festivities.

Bay planned to do a performance of *An Elephant in My Pajamas* to benefit the local playhouse in Nyack. A reporter visiting Voorhis Point noticed he was resting a sore leg, which Stritch attributed to an overenthusiastic show during a tour stop in Arizona. "Instead of Groucho, you may see Lionel Barrymore come out," she joked. (Barrymore had used a wheelchair for much of his career.)

Bay said he'd like to take the act to nightclubs, maybe even open for Tony Bennett. If that didn't work out, he shrugged, there would be voiceover work. "Or if Jerry Orbach ever decides to leave the cast of *42nd Street*," he added, referring to the leading man of the hit musical.

On the Friday night after the journalist's visit, at a local restaurant, Bay began leaning precipitously into the lap of Hekker's husband. "What are you doing?" Stritch yelled. He hadn't been drinking any more than usual. And he didn't straighten up in the car ride home.

Saturday morning, she turned up in Hekker's kitchen. "Something's terribly wrong," she told her. "John can't get his shoes on."

The two women took Bay to the hospital, where he was given a CAT scan and diagnosed with a brain tumor.

While small incidents like missing eyeglasses or an improperly cut lemon might agitate her, in a true crisis Stritch tended to become calm and generous, and this was the case now, though she didn't think highly of her own motivation. "You feel invulnerable when someone else is sick—'I'm fine, you're not.' Now you do everything," she said. "And kindness comes easy. Kindness comes pouring out of you, not because you loved the person, were in love with the person, but because you're so glad it's not you. Sickness changes everybody. They belong to another tribe, another group." She found a surgeon at the Maryland Medical Center in Baltimore who would take Bay's seemingly hopeless case.

The couple had been used to socialized medicine in England. With mounting doctors' bills, Stritch would get a two-day job on the long-running soap opera *One Life to Live*, joining her old *Company* costar Larry Kert, to qualify for health insurance. Hekker drove her down the West Side Highway to ABC's studios, with Stritch scribbling on a copy of the script in her lap. They were greeted pleasantly at the facility by the production team, including one of the writers.

"I made a few changes," Stritch told him.

The writer looked at her with a mixture of confusion and offense.

"What?" she barked. "It's not fucking Voltaire!"

Hekker drove the couple to Baltimore, and got Bay set up in the hospital and prepared for surgery. During his recovery, Stritch returned to New York and auditioned for a part in the film version of Peter Shaffer's *Amadeus*, which she didn't get.

Upon returning to the hospital, the two women found Bay in a wheelchair in the hallway.

"Do you love me?" he asked them.

"Of course."

"Then help me jump out this window, because I just can't take this anymore."

"How are you dealing with this so well?" Hekker asked Stritch quietly afterward.

It seems that it was *A Farewell to Arms* all so many years ago that had prepared her. "I'm playing the part of a nurse," she said.

Stritch had long been a mild kleptomaniac, but the tendency was growing more brazen. When they visited a market on the way home from the hospital, a store detective busted her walking out with a wrapped piece of Brie cheese in her pocket.

"Let me tell you this," she said imperiously. "I'm having guests in about an hour. That Brie was on ice. I couldn't have served that to anybody. What kind of people do you have working here? If that wasn't in my pocket I couldn't have served it. Had to warm it up."

On November 7, 1982, Bay suffered a pulmonary embolism after taking exercise with a real nurse in the hallway. Shortly thereafter he died.

"John is gone," Stritch told her relatives.

Her husband was buried a few days later in Chicago, under a tombstone that read "Hello, I Must Be Going," after the Groucho Marx song in the movie *Animal Crackers*.

For the rest of her life, in his memory, Stritch would send packages of Bays English muffins to a long list of friends and colleagues as Christmas presents. "John never came to full bloom about the artist that he was, which breaks my heart," she said.

"A bad day at Black Rock," she called his death to a reporter. The phrase obscured how thickly the months that followed were fogged by grief. "Now that I have lost John—now I know how I really feel about a human being and sometimes they have to disappear to have you realize," she said. "Because of your lack of maturity, your lack of who the fuck you are and also because of drinking—hello, Dolly!" But she was not drinking any less; in fact, she was drinking more.

Stritch busied herself by working on a book about her diabetes called *Am I Blue? Living with Diabetes, and, Dammit, Having Fun!* She went on *The Tonight Show* to plug it, slurring her words in a sequined pantsuit. "How does it feel to be an authoress?" Johnny Carson asked her. "Well, I thought that I'd buy some butch hats, because intelligent people are very plain," she replied.

In 1984 Stephen Sondheim rebounded resoundingly after the disappointment of *Merrily We Roll Along* with *Sunday in the Park with George*, written with James Lapine and starring Mandy Patinkin as both the nineteenth-century painter Georges Seurat and his twentieth-century descendant. The characters' twinned ecstatic and despairing devotion to the act of creation, their wish to make something that lasts, seemed the most straightforward expression yet of the composer's own soul. While the show lost six Tonys, including Best Musical and Best Score, to *La Cage aux Folles*—suggesting that the "simple hummable show tune . . . is alive and well at the Palace," Jerry Herman, the winning composer, exulted at the podium—it won the Pulitzer Prize for Drama. Sondheim's place in the canon was now not only assured but bronzed.

Stritch, meanwhile, was reduced to doing voice-overs for the commercial for *La Cage aux Folles*, which had been produced by Barry Brown and Fritz Holt. She was a guest speaker at a reception for Planned Parenthood. And she continued with a kind of listless compulsion to decorate the house on Voorhis Point. For upstairs she had found eyelet curtains in a luxurious triple width. "Once they got up and the whole place was"—clap!—"then she could move," Hekker said. The man who bought the house discarded the curtains, and died before he moved in. The next buyer divorced her husband soon after assuming possession. Stritch began calling the cul-de-sac "Voo Doo Point."

Loss, both personal and public, was suddenly looming everywhere. Bridget, her beloved pet, had to be put down. Tennessee Williams had choked fatally, according to a medical examiner, on a plastic bottle cap in his suite at Manhattan's Hotel Elysée in February 1983 while trying to ingest secobarbital. Ethel Merman died, following a brain tumor, the next February. Gloria Safier, the glamorous agent Merman and Stritch had shared, followed a year and a half later, at only sixty-three. And AIDS had begun to decimate the show-business industry utterly.

Stritch had no inkling her Rock Hudson was ill until they taped a TV special together, *Musical Comedy Tonight*, with Danny Kaye's wife, Sylvia Fine Kaye. "I don't think I've ever done that good an acting job because I was so thrown I couldn't believe it," she told Hudson's biographers Jerry Oppenheimer and Jack Vitek. "You could hardly recognize him. He looked so terrible." Hudson, whose scenes were later cut for this reason, told her he had been struggling with anorexia, and she didn't question him, no matter her suspicions—but still the announcement that he had what was then sometimes referred to as "the gay cancer" was deeply shocking, the darkest of codas to their carefree Roman holiday.

In Los Angeles Stritch had also auditioned for a new NBC series, about four older women sharing a house in Miami, created by the respected soap opera parodist Susan Harris. "Hairspray City," Stritch said derisively of Harris, having informed her and the casting agent that she liked to change lines sometimes. "I hope it's just the punctuation," was the reply.

Stritch called Teri Ralston, her *Company* costar who was living in L.A., to help go over the script and drive with her to the studio.

As they pulled into the parking lot, one of the city's rare pedestrians walked in front of the car. Stritch rolled down the window. "Get out of the way!" she hollered.

Then to her friend: "Isn't it awful how I treat people?"

Ralston sat in the lobby as Stritch entered a room of black suits. "I hope you all don't mind that I've rewritten some of these lines to fit me," she told them. "I'm Catholic, so I don't want to say 'oh God.' I can't stand that. How about 'what the fuck.'"

The script had the line "Where's the butler?" Stritch rendered it as "Where's the fucking butler?" The executives stared back at her, aghast.

Her old classmate Bea Arthur would get the part on a series called *The Golden Girls* that would win all of its stars Emmys and national affection for forefronting postmenopausal female friendship. "I'm just glad I got out of there alive," Stritch said years later. "I hate that show. Who'd be crazy enough to live in Florida with two other women and their mother?"

Besides, a very different set of "golden girls" was being assembled in New York City, and they wouldn't be mall walking or playing bingo on rattan couches. The belated consecration of Sondheim's reputation was occasioning a new look at *Follies*, the haunting, elaborate, and money-losing 1971 musical he had written with James Goldman, in the leaner form of a staged concert with the New York Philharmonic.

This would be the cultural event of the season but was also a practical matter: the original recording had been mercilessly condensed to fit on one disc and a faithful one was needed for the historical record. Not needing to worry as much about the ages of characters as he would in a conventional production, Sondheim, with Thomas Z. Shepard, hired top-flight singers, including Barbara Cook and Patinkin. They also added some old favorites, like Lee Remick as Phyllis (though she had not sung on Broadway since the poorly received *Anyone Can Whistle*), and Adolph Green and Betty Comden to do the pastiche number "Rain on the Roof." And Stritch, after some angling. "I got the job because I'd called Steve and I'd never done that before," she said. "That was my one and only 'I can do this.' A little premature self-assurance."

She was initially offered "I'm Still Here," the defiant catalog of personal and historical moments that Sondheim has said was informed by the long career of Joan Crawford, the echt-show-biz survivor.

But Stritch, now sixty but seeking a new start, wasn't ready to take the stance of weathered old-timer. "I think you should be either Yvonne De Carlo or eighty," she said. (Carol Burnett took the assignment.) She persuaded Sondheim instead to let her play Hattie Walker, the tireless trouper whose number "Broadway Baby" encapsulated her own original ambitions ("learning how to sing and dance / waiting for that one big chance"); her hunger for renaissance ("heck I'd even play the maid / to be in a show"); her tendency to prowl the entirety of Manhattan ("a spark to pierce the dark / from Battery Park / to Washington Heights"); and her swing back to austerity ("I don't need a lot / only what I've got / plus a tube of greasepaint and a follow spot!").

She was back to a pared-down gypsy mode, showing up to the hastily put together run-throughs at Avery Fisher Hall, the Philharmonic's home in Lincoln Center, in fisherman hat, white shirt, and shorts. "I went to rehearsal every day and I was so happy," she said. "I had a song that I loved and I was with all the folks and back in the swing of things."

"Someday, maybe . . . ," she warbled as Herbert Ross, the director, looked on. "Geez, I sound like Lionel Stander," she said, referring to an actor who'd been in *Pal Joey*.

"It's a very Jolson-esque, Swanee kind of a song and it's all about a gal hoping to see her name in lights someday and I find a little choke in the throat when I sing it," she told an interviewer from the PBS show *Great Performances*. "I don't think it should be sad, sad, sad, but I certainly think it tells a tall tale of a struggling young performer in New York."

The row of actors sitting against the wall watched with a combination of affection, admiration, and perhaps a little horror as she rehearsed. And in the corner Sondheim sat in a familiar pose: a half-smile on his face, but his pained-seeming forehead buried in his hand.

Patinkin could see that Stritch, whom he'd just met, was a nervous wreck. "She couldn't remember the words," he said. "She was flustered. I thought it was an age thing. She was just clearly the polar opposite of being relaxed. She couldn't hear the sound. It wasn't loud enough. It was too loud. It was too soft. Everything was wrong. She couldn't get comfortable. And she was undone. And I tried to just comfort her and she shooed me away."

Stritch had not faced a real New York audience since *Company*; Avery Fisher Hall had twice the capacity of the Alvin; and this was not a pit orchestra but "the fucking New York Philharmonic." Just before she walked out for "Beautiful Girls," the show's first, heart-swelling number, during which the attenuated showgirls descend a staircase, she crossed herself.

"Hats off, here they come, these beautiful girls," Arthur Rubin sang.

After two songs and two-thirds of a montage came Stritch's solo, for which she was given what one attendee called "a primal howl of welcome from the audience."

"I'm just . . . a Broad . . . way . . . baby." She stretched out every word like a wad of bubble gum.

Standing at the podium, Gemignani, the conductor, was surprised. "That was not the tempo we rehearsed it at," he said. "But in my job that's something you have to be aware of: at the moment is where it counts. That you didn't rehearse it doesn't mean diddly-squat. So that didn't throw me, except that I was very surprised that it was that slow. But I know her and I know she can pull it off. And I wouldn't have done anything anyway. We're on television, for crying out loud."

As Stritch was most exquisitely aware. "To be in a show . . . ohhh."

There was a huge, amused round of applause from the crowd, as she built to "Still / I'll stick it till / I'm on a bill . . . all over Times Square."

Stritch looked around, her eyes slightly wild. And then Comden and Green and Liliane Montevecchi came to join her onstage as the song combined with two others for its climax. "Working for a nice man . . . like a Ziegfeld, or a Weismann. In a great! big! Broad! Way! show!" She reached her arms, and her eyes, audience-ward and heaven-ward. The clapping and the cheers pelted down.

"Standing ovation. Applause. Fabulous," said Dahl, who was in the audience.

"Here's our friend Elaine—all she is to me is my friend," Dahl's husband, Marc Rosen, said. "And she comes out and stops the show."

Backstage, the *Great Performances* team made their way to the ladies' dressing room. "You want to come in here and get a few nude shots?" Stritch asked.

"She looks great in her girdle!" someone cracked.

"Is this dialogue?" Stritch asked. "We were all saying, 'Never, ever has there been a night like this.'"

"I liked everybody but you, Elaine," Adolph Green's wife, Phyllis Newman, said mischievously. "I have some notes for you."

"I've never liked you, and I've never known you that well." It wasn't clear if she was joking or not. (Newman, who as Stella Deems led a female ensemble with hand mirrors singing "Who's That Woman?," had been astounded when Stritch instructed her, "You gotta take the stage more," after dress rehearsal.)

At dinner, Rosen asked her what she was thinking during the ovation, expecting her to say "I was fucking terrible," her usual refrain. But on this night Stritch was calm. "I stayed in character," she told him. "I thought I was the character who had never gotten applause in her life, who was imagining she was getting applause."

Years later, she remembered it as one of the best nights of her life. "It's almost, like—ascension time. It's almost like we all died and went to heaven. The thrill of coming down those stairs is, that is when I really knew: My god, I belong to almost every era! I belong to every era.

"I felt the way you do after a terrible bumpy flight landing. I felt like

I had low heels on, Easy Spirits on the stage. Everything was grounded. I knew exactly what I was doing. I went home, I couldn't go near the saloons where everybody was drinking. I had to go home. And I went home with one of my flowers. To church, and I walked to the Ritz-Carlton. Broadway baby, indeed."

A week after the triumph of the *Follies* concert, *The Golden Girls* debuted on NBC. Its title would prove apt; it would air for seven and a half more years, earning hundreds of millions in syndication. This gnawed at Stritch for years, try though she might to rationalize her self-sabotage.

"For me to work with Betty White every day would be like taking cyanide," she told a *Newsweek* reporter, later apologizing to White.

Despite Stritch's reluctance to sing "I'm Still Here," she had now entered the "someone's mother" phase of her career, of the title character on ABC's *The Ellen Burstyn Show*, though in real life she was only seven years older. In fact, since Burstyn's character had an adult daughter, played by Megan Mullally, and a five-year-old grandson, Stritch was not just a mother but grandmother and great-grandmother all at once. "*That* put her in touch with the fact that she was aging," Judy Abrams said. It lasted thirteen episodes.

Her own mother and father were now in their nineties. George's eyesight was worsening, though he refused to admit it. When Georgene, who oversaw their care from a couple of doors down on Arlington Street, took away his car, he called the police. "'Listen, I'm ninety-three years old and I have a driver's license and my daughter stole my car,' he said. 'I want it back.'"

The police went to Georgene's, got the car, and returned it to him. "What else were they going to do?" Elaine's niece Midge Moran said.

Mildred Stritch was cause for greater worry, her once sharp mind dulled by progressive dementia. "It was hard to watch," Midge recalled.

"She'd walk through the house crying for her mother, that kind of stuff." George took care of her as best he could. In time Mildred forgot everyone in her family but her husband. She began disappearing on occasion.

After a nurse forgot to restrain Mildred and she fell out of bed and had to be hospitalized, Georgene took her mother to Georgian East, a nursing home in nearby Bloomfield Hills. Upon hearing of this development, Tante Elaine flew in from New York, promptly checked Mildred out again, and drove her to Georgene's house.

"My mother is not living in a nursing home," she said, ordering, "Do something about it." And then she was gone.

Georgene hired live-in help for Arlington Street.

Despite Elaine's concern, her fundamental feeling of obligation—of family—lay elsewhere. After *The Ellen Burstyn Show* was canceled, she ran into Shirley Eder, a gossip columnist, at Mortimer's, an Upper East Side restaurant, and told her of plans to spend Thanksgiving Day not in Detroit but on the Concorde to do the flashy revue *The Night of 100 Stars* at the London Palladium. "Having my turkey on that plane will be divine," Stritch said. "They have a much better cook than I have. I know that for a fact, because my cook is me!" With some irony, the event was a benefit for the charity Help the Aged.

She was back to the old reflex of making a punch line of her solitude. "Promise me one thing: get married again," Bay had said to her before he died.

"After you, who?" she asked, or so she told Carson on *The Tonight Show*.

"Well, think about it for a minute," the host said.

Stritch's ideas were Jack Lemmon, Walter Matthau, and Cliff Robertson. "All married to terrific girls, so now I'm looking for a fisherman with a long beard who will fish all day and then bring the fish home and rock me at night," she said.

"Isn't that a big jump from Cliff Robertson?" Carson asked. He then suggested naughtily, "We could go down to Redondo Beach and hang around the pier and see what comes in on the skiff."

———

In early 1987, after years of shout-singing, Stritch had two operations on her throat to mend worn vocal cords, joking that she was relieved to not "end up sounding like Julie Andrews," as she feared she might.

"Mr. Allen is calling," her agent told her one day.

"Joe?" Stritch asked him in confusion, thinking he meant the restaurateur.

It was another "piece of Mahler" moment. At that moment, Woody Allen was perhaps the most prestigious movie director in America, having proved he could do daffy comedies (*Bananas, Sleeper, Everything You Always Wanted to Know About Sex but Were Afraid to Ask*), period pieces (*Broadway Danny Rose, The Purple Rose of Cairo, Radio Days*), and family dramas (*Hannah and Her Sisters*). Along with the Yankees and Ed Koch, he had helped rehabilitate New York City's dismal image with the love letters to the city *Annie Hall* and *Manhattan*, which featured a famous scene in her old haunt, Elaine's. And he had admired Stritch's work for a long time, he wrote to her in a letter that was both flattering and cautionary, offering her the part of a formerly well-known actress who comes to the summer home of her depressive daughter, played by Allen's then girlfriend Mia Farrow, in a film called *September*. She would be replacing Farrow's own mother, Maureen O'Sullivan; Allen, dissatisfied with his early rushes, had recast several other roles as well. Having heard that Stritch was "brilliant but difficult to work with," he advised compliance with his direction "so that things will not come to a sudden awkward premature end." He added that she should "keep the questioning to a rock-bottom minimum."

Stritch would celebrate her casting by buying a co-op apartment on East Seventy-Second Street, in a sedate doorman building between First and Second Avenues. While it was being decorated by Maurice Bernstein with French furniture and a fake wall that looked like a library full of books, swinging open to reveal her bedroom, she moved at the production's expense to the Carlyle Hotel, where she and Bay had spent some of their last days together.

She was quickly besotted by Allen. Putting on shoes one day on the set, she said, "Oh boy, Woody, I don't care what you say. There's something sexy about high heels. And listen . . ." She kept going. "If we ever dated, I don't think I could stand it, because I'd have to go shopping and

I'd have to get a lot of low heels, good-looking matching low heels, just so I could go out with you, so I wouldn't have heels on. But then I'd lose all my sex appeal, because I *love* the high heels."

"Well, I'll wear them," the diminutive, nebbishy Allen told her.

He had less good humor about her costumes, which she couldn't help herself from offering ideas about.

"You do as you're told," he said to her in the makeup room. "You wear what I tell you."

Stritch instantly regressed to the childlike state she'd assumed when rebuked so many years earlier by George Abbott.

"I don't want to lose this movie and I don't want to lose an opportunity of working with you over an argument," she said. "I want to do as I'm told."

Allen softened. "Well, you think about it and then you come in," he said.

Stritch was starting to tear up. "But listen to you, let me tell you what happens to me. The reason I was so upset about the costumes and the—"

"Don't cry!" Allen warned her sternly. "It only makes me madder."

"Okay," Stritch said. "Then I want to tell you this. The reason that I caused so much trouble about the costumes and everything is because—" She was getting angry. "Let me tell you this. It is very difficult."

"Oh god, get to the point," Allen said.

"Wait a minute, I'll get to it. I'm sure you've heard this a million times before, but let me tell you something. It is very hard to be funny if you don't feel pretty."

There was a thoughtful pause.

"No," Allen said. "I've never heard that before."

Thereafter they got along beautifully.

Even though this wasn't Broadway theater, Stritch would come to work without pants, just silk stockings, inciting an eye roll from a cameraman.

"Jesus, it's just musical comedy," Stritch said. "I've been running around with no clothes on for so many years with faggots, and nobody gets excited." Her use of the derogatory word belied her complicated attitude toward gay men throughout adulthood: by turns familiar, imperious, delusional, and dependent.

Allen, though, paid her a compliment. "Nice pins," he said.

"I thought that was terrific," Stritch told Liz Smith. "What woman wouldn't? What red-blooded, Catholic woman wouldn't?"

She was "so smitten by her movie director that she can hardly bring herself to say his name," Smith reported in her column. But when asked about the plot of the movie, Stritch got quiet. "Baby, I haven't got a clue," she said.

In her one-woman show she claimed to have hit bottom, to use addiction parlance, the night *September* finished filming. Stritch had been allotting herself two vodkas per day, saving them for just before the cameras rolled, but on the last day there was a retake. Then came the wrap party; the vodka kept flowing. The next thing she knew she was on the floor of the hallway of the Carlyle outside her room after a hypoglycemic attack, being revived with a Pepsi by a minibar waiter. (She told an almost identical story to Christopher Kennedy Lawford for his book about sobriety, but set it at a dinner celebrating Jackie Gleason.) Yet another "sometimes—there's God—so quickly" moment, she said, alluding again to Tennessee Williams. "So, I decided to pay Him back. I quit, I quit, I quit . . ." But her most constant companion would not be relinquished so easily.

The week after *September* finished filming, Stritch traveled to Birmingham to celebrate her parents' seventieth wedding anniversary. It was there that she found out that Michael Bennett, the choreographer of *Company* who'd gone on to direct *A Chorus Line*, had died of AIDS. "I guess it would be impossible to be Michael Bennett in this age of AIDS and not get it one way or another because I think Michael was full of love—crazy love," she would tell Kevin Kelly, who became Bennett's biographer. "A lot of people would say Michael was selfish. I don't think Michael was selfish. I think he got to a point where he was like Momma Rose: 'When is it my turn? What about me?'" He had answered that question with *A Chorus Line*; Stritch had not. "I think everybody with that kind of talent suffers that problem," she said.

She felt the death of Fritz Holt from the same disease, just twelve days later, even more keenly; unlike Bennett's career, which had lit quickly and burst like a firework, Holt's was kindling slowly. "He didn't go out like a champion because he was so . . . Imagine how angry he was?" Stritch said. "I can't blame him. Boy, do I understand. He'd just done *Cage aux Folles* and was on his way to being . . . boy, was he angry." Both men had been in their midforties.

It was difficult in an entirely different way to see her once formidable parents diminished in tandem by old age. Elaine was twitchy on Arlington Street, sparring with her sisters. She left as soon as she could. But when she got back to New York, she got word that Mildred had died, as if the final gathering of her daughters in her presence had given her some kind of permission or release.

"I'm not going back there," Stritch told Hekker.

"Elaine, you have to go to your mother's funeral," Hekker said. "You *have* to." She drove her friend back to the airport.

Midge Moran, George's granddaughter, had been charged with getting him ready for the ceremony. "Does anybody have a cigarette?" he asked, and then: "Did I see everybody last night at the wake?"

"Yeah, George, you did," Midge told him.

"So you don't think anybody's coming to the funeral that I didn't meet and talk to yesterday?"

"No," Midge said.

"Well then, what the hell am I going to the funeral for?" George asked. "I want to be with Mother." He took the cigarette out, smoked it, removed his tie, lay down on the couch, and went gray. Taken to William Beaumont Hospital in Royal Oak, he too was declared dead.

"The ebullient, energetic Stritch clan experienced both a stunned sense of loss and yet a certain inner jubilation," Liz Smith wrote of this remarkable end to a storybook marriage. "They felt Mildred and George had somehow transcended the pains of earth and rejoined, in the same romantic manner in which they'd conducted their lives."

Hekker's phone rang two days later. Stritch, having self-medicated heavily at an airport bar in Detroit, told her she was flying back into La Guardia. "If you could meet me that's fine, and if not I'll kill myself."

"No, I'll meet you," Hekker said.

She located her friend in the baggage department, distraught and yet still capable of a one-liner. "I've lost my mother, I've lost my father, and I've lost my luggage!" Stritch yelled. The almost simultaneous deaths of her parents, she would tell a reporter not long thereafter, "was the most dramatic thing that's happened in my life. And that's saying a lot."

She had switched her two-drink allotment from vodka back to old familiar Beaujolais. One day Hekker's phone rang again. "I have to go back to AA," Stritch said.

"Okay, what happened?"

"You know how I'm always shopping for bigger wineglasses? When I bought two new ones today, the girl rung them up—they were vases."

Not long after Stritch strode into an AA meeting at Jan Hus Presbyterian Church, a brownstone building on East Seventy-Fourth Street. Two women sitting there recognized her instantly. "I'm not touching *this* one," whispered Mary Doyle, the same theater actress whom Stritch had helped coach for *Gypsy* years before; Stritch was godmother to her daughter. The other was June I., a divorcée and real estate broker at a top firm in Manhattan. She had first met Stritch when she was in *Pal Joey*, and would become her sponsor for almost a decade. "Lainey chose me and we had a very close relationship," she said.

Hekker would soon start accompanying her to meetings—this was against the rules of the organization, because she was not an alcoholic herself, but Stritch's diabetes meant that she had to be watched.

The actress who had once sat in Sardi's and told Leonard Lyons that she scorned "ladies' room gab" and "when you're in trouble, it's always better to call a feller" was depending on other women like never before.

13.

ROLLING ALONG

The Hollywood Bowl resembles an egg or spaceship, with scrubby hills behind it and eighteen thousand seats before it. Here in 1988 stood Stritch: newly hatched into the strange new land of committed sobriety in front of the largest live audience she had ever faced. Also performing were Carol Channing, Mary Martin, and Bea Arthur. "The ladies who last," Dan Sullivan of the *Los Angeles Times* called them.

Backstage Stritch had met a young man named Michael Feinstein, a passionate revivalist of the Great American Songbook, who once assisted Ira Gershwin—a bridge between her childhood and her current rebirth.

"I'm afraid I'm not going to be good," she worried.

"Just be adequate. Get through it," he told her.

"The thing that I found fascinating was she'd go onstage and she'd come off and say, 'You know it doesn't get any easier,'" Feinstein said. "And I'd say, 'Elaine, I don't understand that. When you're onstage, you know what you're gonna do. You have a microphone. You have lighting.' That's when I feel safe. That's when I'm in control. But she didn't. She always felt like something could happen, or like the rug was gonna be pulled out from under her."

Hollywood had disappointed Stritch yet again. *September* had bored and baffled critics and fans, and a strenuous campaign to get her nominated for an Oscar had been unsuccessful. Her performance had, however, won her another movie part: in *Cocoon: The Return*, alongside Don Ameche, her old costar from *Goldilocks*. Their characters had to decide between living on a dull planet offering eternal life or returning to the excitements of Earth and accepting mortality. "If you could go to such a planet leaving Earth behind forever, would you go?" Shirley Eder asked her.

Stritch replied, "I guess I'd go . . . especially if they were making movies up there. I'd like to conquer that medium somewhere." The material was far from the high literary standards she had known, but of course the film industry offered other seductions. "Now, all of a sudden, hot-and-cold-running limousines," she said dryly.

Money was ever more on Stritch's mind since the annus horribilis of 1987, during which she'd not only lost both her parents, a bulwark of financial sense if not bottomless riches (their savings had not quite financed their old age), but watched the stock market crash. She was not personally affected, having invested primarily in Treasury bills since she moved to London, but she witnessed the deflation in the fortunes of many wealthy acquaintances as she mingled at Mortimer's Sunday night buffet with the socialites Betsy Bloomingdale, Nan Kempner, and Pat Buckley—the most dedicated "ladies who lunch."

Fierce about negotiating salary and perks since her days in *Call Me Madam*, Stritch was now becoming downright fearsome. "She got taxed mightily on her income because she had no deductions," Hekker said. "So anything she could get on the side which wasn't taxed, if she could get them to throw in a limousine or a dress, anything, then she felt she won."

Ben Gazzara, now married to Elke Stuckmann, a German model and actress, felt Stritch's parsimony was entwined with her sobriety. "When she drank, she was the most generous woman in the world," he told his wife. "When she stopped, she counted."

Though many of her friends enabled this quirk of her personality, it did sour some precious old relationships. Barry Brown, Fritz Holt's surviving partner and Stritch's onetime roommate, chafed at being stuck with the bill for a $2500 dress from Saks that she wanted to wear to perform in charity reunion performances of *Company* at the Long Beach Civic Center and Lincoln Center in 1993. "Everybody else was taking cabs to the thing—Elaine insisted on a car and driver," he said. Also hair and makeup. "It cost $1200. For an AIDS benefit." (By then, Larry Kert was yet another member of the original production who had died from the disease, in 1991.)

Even as her moneygrubbing intensified, though, Stritch was also learning to practice emotional generosity, in part because of her new devotion to twelve-step recovery, with its final commandment that one should help others similarly afflicted. The program felt, again, like a combination of church—with a theology simpler and more practical than the Catholicism that had brought her so much guilt—and group therapy, with an added element of performance in the "qualification," a monologue describing how one came to arrive there, and the timed "shares" that form the substance of the meeting. "It was a little bit of a show if she qualified and if she shared it was also a little bit of a show," June said. Another member remembered Stritch's qualification ending with "'And I always thought life would be just a bowl of cherries, and it's raisins.' She did the Hermione Gingold thing!" (Gingold had originated the role of Madame Armfeldt in *A Little Night Music*, singing the Sondheim composition in which the "sumptuous feasts of old" are now "not even figs" but raisins.)

Old intimates of Frieda Fun now had to contend with a just as outspoken Betty Buzzkill. "Over the years, she got almost hostile with me," Joe Allen said. "No, she *did* get hostile with me, in a subdued way. Because she had stopped drinking, and therefore the whole world was supposed to stop drinking."

"I hope it's not the year of the liver," she'd tell him when he said he was going in for his yearly physical.

"Once again, flying colors," he'd reply.

"She got almost religious about it," Allen said. "If she was doing it, it was therefore the only thing to do."

But *was* she doing it? "I tried my best," June said. "I stayed with her as much as I could—we had a lot of fun." But though she had bragged of 103 days of sobriety to a *People* reporter in 1988, Stritch soon stopped tallying as strictly. Special dispensations were made for flying on a plane and other stressful situations. "My sponsor said to me, 'She's not taken a sober breath in two years, what are you doing?'" June said. "She did try . . ."

Liz Smith also noticed her friend's evasions. Toward the end of her life, Stritch started speaking publicly of allowing herself one drink per day. "I think she had been having one drink all along," Smith said. "And she was a control freak, so she could control it pretty good, but she was too sweet and accommodating, and the last few times I had the one drink with her, taking her to dinner or something, she would be so accommodating and nice and unlike herself—and I noticed that the one drink—she would say, just give me a little more."

Tricia Walsh-Smith, an English actress and playwright Stritch sponsored, said flatly, "Elaine was never sober. Typical bloody Catholic. She confessed, it was okay. Twelve step, same thing. She was such a rogue." Still, Walsh-Smith felt nurtured by her, calling her "my New York mom" and later appointing her matron of honor at her wedding to the powerful Philip J. Smith of the Shubert Organization (a marriage that would end rather spectacularly amid intimate revelations posted on YouTube).

Stritch also significantly helped the Polish actress Elzbieta Czyzewska. Once known as the Marilyn Monroe of her country, Czyzewska had left to marry the *New York Times* journalist David Halberstam, frequenting with him Elaine Kaufman's bar in its heyday, but floundered after their own divorce. Czyzewska's beauty was exquisite, and her talent was undisputed; however, her accent was thick (the model for Meryl Streep's in *Sophie's Choice*), her name hard for Americans to spell, and her native country had rejected her as a deserter. Stritch took her up. "She was one of Elaine's handmaidens, and a peculiar one," said Andre Bishop, the producer and director. A mutual friend, Scott Griffin, who has also produced theater, thought their relationship was more one of equals— "Elaine viewed Elzbieta as a peer. And she was," he said—and the playwright John Guare mentioned it in *Elzbieta Erased*, a one-act play he wrote about Czyzewska's life.

b: Elaine Stritch had become fascinated by this tortured soul and helped her.

a: Elaine Stritch? *That* Elaine Stritch?

b: Yes, Elaine Stritch had rescued her. Elzbieta was sober.

Stritch decided abruptly to sell the co-op on East Seventy-Second Street, and with June's help she made a handsome profit. Bob and Joan Tisch, owners of the Regency Hotel on Park Avenue at Sixty-First Street, were clients of Maurice Bernstein, and the decorator helped arrange a special rate for her there. He moved in her furniture, including a bed of which she'd become fond, so high she needed a small set of stairs to ascend to it. "I couldn't stand the bed," he said.

More modest than the Savoy, the Regency was nonetheless elegant and private. It also gave Stritch a sense of continuity with her past; it was just three blocks from the Barbizon. This was precious to her now as she navigated a world without a constant scrim of booze. Playing Rose, a tipsy socialite claiming a past affair with John F. Kennedy, in her friend Dominick Dunne's 1991 miniseries *An Inconvenient Woman*, was not a heavy lift, and for this Stritch got her first Emmy nomination; she lost to Ruby Dee. Two years later she won for a guest role on *Law & Order*, but the honor meant little to her; once again she could not help but compare herself with Angela Lansbury, who hosted the ceremony in 1993, and who not only had gotten several of the Broadway roles she coveted—like Mame, Madame Rose, and Mrs. Lovett—but made a killing with the long-running series *Murder, She Wrote*, for which she was nominated a dozen times. Meanwhile Stritch was making rather a piecemeal living with small parts on *The Cosby Show* and *Head of the Class* and *3rd Rock from the Sun*, with John Lithgow: more extraterrestrials.

"Here was the thing—there were always benefits," said the columnist Michael Riedel, of the early 1990s, when he started covering theater. "They weren't the big glamorous things they were now. And the people always trotted out at benefits were Elaine Stritch and Dorothy Loudon. I got to know Dorothy first and she said, 'Elaine and I are queens of the benefits; they only want us for benefits.' They weren't working."

Once again, Hal Prince would come to her rescue.

Prince had not recovered quite so quickly from *Merrily We Roll Along* as Sondheim had, and put out a few more flops, but they were obliterated by the spectacular success of *The Phantom of the Opera* (1988), which remains the longest-running show on Broadway, and the more modest but still successful *Kiss of the Spider Woman*, starring Chita Rivera. Now he'd been persuaded by Garth Drabinsky, a swashbuckling Canadian entertainment mogul who'd produced those two shows in Toronto, that the time was right to collaborate on a revival of Jerome Kern and Oscar Hammerstein's 1927 musical *Show Boat*. Drabinsky wanted it as the inaugural production in a splashy new arts complex he was opening in the North York neighborhood of Toronto.

Prince was not generally fond of reviving other people's shows. But *Show Boat*, best known for the sonorous ballad "Ol' Man River," was a special case. Based on the bestselling novel by Edna Ferber, about a floating theater that travels to towns on the Mississippi River, it had been the first major Broadway show to have a racially integrated cast, and one of the first in which the songs and dancing advanced the plot—a sweeping, multigenerational story of miscegenation and racial prejudice—rather than interrupting it with unmoored entertainment. *Show Boat*'s original producer, Florenz Ziegfeld, had been nervous about its commercial prospects, however, and cut some of its best and most complex music—notably the black chorus's lament "Mis'ry's Comin' Aroun'," much to Kern's ire. Three movie versions had sanitized the story further. Drabinsky envisioned a historically faithful restoration—"with a realistic, 'gritty' documentary feel, not one full of the usual make-believe Hollywood nonsense, a pretty, pastel empty thing," he wrote in his autobiography.

But the civil rights movement had cast *Show Boat* in a new and critical light, especially Hammerstein's use of the word "niggers" in the opening chorus, sung by black characters who seemed resigned to their lot. Subsequent versions substituted "darkies" or eliminated that portion of the song entirely; Prince would go with the less incendiary but historically accurate "colored folk." This would not mollify a group that formed in Toronto calling itself the Coalition to Stop Show Boat, which stated,

"The entire play, its plot and characterizations demean black life and culture." Members began picketing the arts center, protesting the use of taxpayer dollars on the production; then one activist, Stephanie Payne, said on television that "always usually a Jewish person is doing plays to denigrate us." (She later apologized.)

The ensuing conflict was, in hindsight, unbeatable free publicity. Critics wrote thoughtful essays defending *Show Boat* and Hammerstein's reputation; Drabinsky enlisted the prominent African American scholar Henry Louis Gates, Jr., to argue for the work; and Prince pressed on.

He hoped Stritch would take the role of Parthy, the wife of the ship's Cap'n Andy (Robert Morse). "Because that's always been played in a kind of conventional old-fashioned crotchety maternal thing, and I thought Elaine could bring some fire and ice to it," he said. But his partner needing convincing.

"Hal, she's very *urban*," Drabinsky said. He thought uneasily of *Company*, which, though in his estimation contained perhaps the best music of Sondheim's career, hadn't turned much of a profit.

"Where is the energy gonna come from?" he wondered.

"She can do it," Prince said.

Drabinsky agreed to meet the actress.

Stritch had a new agent, Alan Willig. But as was beginning to be her custom, she decided to conduct her own negotiation. She and Drabinsky agreed to meet at five thirty at Joe Allen's, where they basked in the glow of their shared charisma. Childhood polio had left Drabinsky with an awkward gait, his left leg lagging behind his right—but he was handsome, with a full head of dark, glossy hair and an indomitable air (some colleagues referred to him as Garth Vader Drabinsky).

"I got an hour—let's see if we can make a deal," he told Stritch.

"What do you wanna offer me?"

"$7500 a week."

"What, are you kidding? $7500? Forget it."

"What do you mean?" Drabinsky said, stunned. "It's a lot of money. You're not making $7500 per week, what are you talking about?"

"I will not accept any payment less than $15,000," Stritch said.

Drabinsky leaned back and thought hard. He did not want to disappoint

Prince, a role model and mentor. He wanted to return to the older man and be able to say "I did it."

But still . . . "If I do $15,000, you're gonna be the highest-paid actor onstage," he told her.

"I'm worth it. I'm worth every cent of it. And you know I am."

"How the hell do I know that?" Drabinsky said in exasperation. "We're opening in Toronto, we're not opening on Broadway. And yes, you have a history, but it's *Toronto*. Toronto doesn't run to the theater for Elaine Stritch."

By the end of the meal, he had consented to pay her $15,000 per week. Stritch, of course, also left him with the check. And a compliment. "You know, Garth, the sexiest, most attractive thing about you is your limp."

Designed by the architect Eberhard Zeidler, Drabinksy's new performing arts center looked a bit like an enormous Cuisinart—which was apropos, as the rehearsal experience was tumultuous enough that cast members (often running a gauntlet of protesters to get to rehearsal) would eventually print up T-shirts reading: "I Was in *Show Boat* and I've Got the Stritch Marks to Prove It."

Prince had decided to bestow Parthy with the tender "Why Do I Love You?," formerly given to lovers at the beginning of Act II. He made it a lullaby that she sings to her baby granddaughter. "Not logical, and I knew it, but I thought, You cannot have her in this show not singing a note. She's got to sing a note. It's the only thing I could think of," he said. Some critics grumbled at the change, but audiences loved it.

"What happened was she took this crusty, powerful, ballsy, surveying woman and turned her into a sap," Drabinsky said. "And you never even thought that she could hold the kid properly." Many in the ensemble cried after Stritch rehearsed it for the first time.

Susan Stroman, the clever choreographer who'd just won a Tony for *Crazy for You*, came up with the idea of ending the song's reprise with a change of tempo and a Rockettes-inflected dance line. Stritch did not like this at all. From *Company* to the "motherfucking step" in *Mame*, dancing onstage had long been a challenge for her. And now she was sixty-eight years old. "I'm not doing this. I'm not doing this," she said in rehearsal. "I'm not doing any fucking line, standing there with all those gorgeous women with their legs and everything else. I'm not doing that. It's not who I am." She won this battle as well.

Another problem: since the rise of *Cats*, and since Stritch was last in a proper musical, singers had begun wearing body microphones, to ensure projection in larger, more "wired" theaters such as the North York, to be heard among heavily amplified orchestras and, sometimes, to compete with elaborate digital sound effects. Stritch hadn't minded wearing a mike pinned to her lapel like a corsage in the concert performances of *Follies* and *Company*. But the idea of one while in costume for *Show Boat* appalled her. In the era of Martin, Merman, and Garland, there were no such crutches to help singers reach the back seats; Stritch had worked for years with a vocal coach, Bert Knapp, on enunciation and projection. And then there was the fact that, aside from regular massages with a trusted therapist, she was generally averse to being touched.

The frustrated stagehands implored Marjorie McDonald, a freelance sound technician from Nova Scotia with a notably calm personality, to intervene. McDonald had no idea of Stritch's theatrical legacy, just that everyone was treating her like "a Tasmanian devil in a box," as she put it. She approached cautiously with the mike.

"They want you to wear this in your hair," McDonald told the actress.

"I don't understand—every other time I've worn it in my jacket," Stritch said.

"Look, the thing is that *everybody* is wearing it in their hair, and if you wear it elsewhere you are going to sound different from everybody else," McDonald said. Sticking out slightly had served her well in *Company*, but this was not a role tailored to her specific talents. It was a period piece in which a special and possibly precarious place had been carved. "She understood that if everybody's got a tin ukulele and one person's is wooden, the whole ensemble will be thrown off," McDonald said.

Stritch grudgingly agreed to the mike in dress rehearsal, tucked into a small hairpiece to make her coif seem fuller.

"Nobody's putting it on me but you," she told McDonald.

And so Stritch added to a circle of trust whose contours would shift continually but that would guard and protect her into old age. McDonald, who had suffered family tragedy, was staying in the Cabbagetown neighborhood of Toronto and she would come retrieve the actress at the Four Seasons downtown and walk her to North York, a distance of over five miles, and they'd talk and talk.

Aside from this friendship, Stritch held herself generally aloof from the ensemble, though Michel Bell, the bass-baritone who played the stevedore Joe, remembered her inviting him to her dressing room for feedback. He'd been instructed to stand off center while singing "Ol' Man River," but she told him to defy Prince and seize the stage for the climax: "It just keeps rolling along . . ."

"You give it up, Louise!" Stritch said, invoking the *Gypsy* character. "You just take center, and you open up wide!"

Then she asked for advice in return.

"You hold the baby in your arms and your eyes are straight up to the third tier," Bell told her. "Look at the baby."

There were police on horseback at the opening previews of *Show Boat* in October 1993, sent to contain about a hundred demonstrators yelling "Shame, shame!" and "Go home!" at audience members. But the general cultural current continued to turn in the musical's favor, thanks in part to a long article by John Lahr, now *The New Yorker*'s theater critic, explaining the play's history. It stated unequivocally that "the show chronicles slavery not to condone it but deplore it" and praised Prince and each of his directing choices. "Stritch's chin juts out at the world like a fist," Lahr wrote, calling her "sour and very funny." Another review called her "tart as a fall apple."

The cast celebrated a largely triumphant opening with Thanksgiving dinner at a restaurant, during which Stritch banged her glass with a spoon.

"All right, kids—I just wanted to give you all an insight," she said. "I've been in this business for quite some time and I want you to know that any project or musical being mounted of this magnitude, which I would say is the golden years of Broadway musicals, will never happen again, so I want you to take note and enjoy the ride and hold on to your hats."

Morse, though, was soon thrown overboard, reportedly because he had "driven Stritch to distraction" with onstage ad-libbing and had questioned Prince's stage direction. "He was a problem in the show—the most wonderful human being, but going up on his lines all the time," Drabinsky said.

And so when the show rolled on to New York the following autumn, it was with John McMartin, who'd originated the role of Benjamin Stone in *Follies*, as Cap'n Andy. Stritch took the change of venue as an opportunity to try for a raise. "My darling, angel, turkey, sweetie, poopie, precious, adorable, divine, attractive, gifted, Ziegfeld of the 90s," she wrote Drabinsky. "What do you say to a flat $25,000 a week starting now, with no increases until my contract ends in New York? In the event that I win a TONY, any or no increase will be entirely up to you. Unless I'm offered a movie with Robert Redford. Then, of course, Garth, you'll just have to fuck off."

Stritch did not get her raise, nor a movie offer, nor did she win a Tony in 1995. To her tremendous disappointment, she was not even nominated, though McMartin was. The cast was asked to perform the "Why Do I Love You?" reprise during the ceremony, and Stritch dragged her feet at rehearsing it, "because Garth, my darling, after 2 shows today and no day off for the past 4 weeks, I would probably wind up at Lenox Hill, or possibly a 'hat factory' somewhere in upstate New York," she wrote, and added a doleful P.S. "I guess I'm just a little lonely, a little sad and overlooked, and a lot tired." During the intricate number, during which the company comes together like an interlocking puzzle, she stood conspicuously to the side, gesturing upstage.

"That beats a nomination, doesn't it?" she said pointedly while presenting the costume, lighting, and scenic-design awards alongside Gloria Foster, who was appearing as a slave's daughter in the oral history adaptation *Having Our Say*. But when Prince won for Best Direction of a Musical, after thanking Drabinsky and the rest of the production team, he singled out his old friend over everyone else. "To Elaine Stritch, whose interpretation is one of the backbones of this production, and who's never missed a performance on Broadway."

Physically and emotionally exhausted, Stritch exited *Show Boat* three months later. "I am Welsh and I have heard a little bit about the coal miners in Wales, but believe me, eight shows a week in a musical comes very close to the pits," she said. She bided time recording audiobooks of seven Dorothy Parker short stories for Penguin, including the devastating "Big Blonde"; was inducted into the Theater Hall of Fame; and prepared to play Lillian Hellman again.

At a Rainbow Room luncheon she reunited with the playwright Edward Albee, who had recently won his third Pulitzer Prize for *Three Tall Women*, a complicated depiction of motherhood and mortality that explored his own issues being the gay son of a cruel parent. He liked the idea of Stritch playing A, the crotchety ninety-two-year-old aristocrat at the play's center, and his producer suggested that she might replace Maggie Smith in the London production. Stritch wasn't sure. "She sent me the script and my advice—which she took, which was unusual—was that there were too many lines at a time she was having trouble remembering lyrics," Terry Hekker said.

More manageable (and also giving her another chance at a Tony) would be a supporting role as Claire, a witty alcoholic, in a new production of Albee's play *A Delicate Balance*, for which he'd won his first Pulitzer in 1967. Claire lives with her older sister Agnes and brother-in-law Tobias, an upper-middle-class couple in late middle age whose uneasy peace is tested when their best friends, beset by a nameless existential terror, show up expecting to be sheltered and soothed.

Andre Bishop, the artistic director of the Lincoln Center Theater and a native of Manhattan, had admired Stritch since, as a teenager, he'd seen her on the closing night of *Sail Away* and she had interpolated jokes about *My Fair Lady*, which would be replacing it in the Broadhurst Theater, into the songs. "The greatest musical-theater performance I had ever seen," he said. "That combination of wryness, sophistication—that kind of Middle-American gal-ness."

An appointment was arranged at the Regency. Stritch stood Bishop up. On the second try, she was late. They set off "at a ferocious clip," he said, on Madison Avenue toward the tiny and bustling Viand coffee shop, a favorite of hers, but it was too crowded, and so they wound up at the Carlyle.

"You know, Andre, it's so *obvious*, that I play Claire," she told him. "If you were smart you'd want me to play the other role. I really wanna play the other role." She meant Agnes, the star, the "fulcrum" of the play, the one who gets dramatic speeches like

> Time. Time happens, I suppose. To people. Everything becomes . . . too late, finally. You know it's going on . . . up on the hill; you can see the dust, and hear the cries, and the steel . . . but you wait, and time happens. When you *do* go, sword, shield . . . finally . . . there's nothing there . . . save rust, bones and the wind.

Yes, Stritch was back to wanting unapologetically the "whole cheese." But though intimidated at meeting an idol of his youth, "somehow I stuck to my guns," Bishop said. Anyway, the role of Agnes had already been promised to the English-born actress Rosemary Harris.

This time Alan Willig handled the salary issue; Harris and George Grizzard, who was playing Tobias, were each getting $5000 per week plus 2.5 percent of the gross, and Bishop insisted on a "favored nations agreement"—meaning not one of the stars was going to make more than anyone else. Lincoln Center Theater is a not-for-profit.

"Elaine, I know this is very far from what we have been asking for, but it is more than twice the original offer, and I have been able to wrest from them a very important concession—and that is an out for a film," Willig faxed. "What can be said, Elaine? Lincoln Center is standing firm."

Stritch took the pay cut, but it seemed to aggravate the kleptomania Hekker had witnessed outside the grocery store. "You know, she'd go through twenty-five panty hoses a week, and fifty lipsticks, and the toilet paper would disappear from the theater," Bishop said. Hekker also noticed during a trip to Florida for an event honoring Prince that Stritch brought way more luggage than needed. It contained all her winter things to be dry-cleaned at the hotel, at the production's expense.

Directing *A Delicate Balance* was Gerald Gutierrez, an unusual character who carried his Yorkshire terrier, Phyllis, everywhere. "They were a couple of similar characters—a little over the top and a little addictive," Bishop said. "No one was funnier than Gerald," Wendy Wasserstein believed, "but the humor was cloaking a real seriousness about the theater." And this he had in common with his new friend.

A Delicate Balance had gone over rather seriously in its initial production, but now its comedic notes sounded louder, with Stritch delivering lines like "I apologize that my nature is such to bring out in you the full force of your brutality" with the air of a schoolgirl in detention.

Standing in the back of the Plymouth Theater with his longtime partner, the sculptor Jonathan Thomas, during a preview performance, Albee heard something he hadn't before from an audience at *A Delicate Balance*: laughter. "He couldn't believe it," Bishop said.

Stritch had demanded a stage-level dressing area at the Plymouth Theater, and she would wander around in her bra and panties, even venturing into the lobby to check on house seats. Grizzard felt that she was milking her lines onstage and that Gutierrez was being too permissive. One night, she tried to hit her costar with a curling iron, and he slugged her. "You know, actors are so sensitive—she might have been getting in the way," Harris said, insisting they were all "great friends" who shared a hired car home after the show.

But Elizabeth Wilson, who played Agnes and Tobias's friend Edna, remembered Stritch's bad behavior with their various drivers, cursing when they didn't make a light. "I don't ever remember one person in a play causing such problems for the other actors," she told the biographer Brian Kellow. "Stritch needs to dominate. When the rest of us were working, having our scenes, she would be on the floor, moving around, tearing papers, coughing, or doing something to divert attention (away from the rest of us). And there was nothing Gerry Gutierrez could do."

Still, Bishop felt all the Sturm und Drang was worth it; whatever was happening behind the scenes, he, like Drabinsky, had utter confidence in the performance Stritch would deliver every night. "To give her the credit

she was never given: she had to play a character who indulges in two habits that she had had a hideous time stopping her whole life: smoking and
drinking," he said. "And that was an act of incredible bravery, I thought."

On opening night, April 21, 1996, Gutierrez gave Stritch a pendant that
had belonged to his mother and a postcard he made of Noël Coward
painting at an easel "Gutierrez Loves Strit . . ." He quoted *Gypsy*:

> Thru thick or thru thin
> all out or all in
> and whether it's win place or show.
> With yes love, Gerry.

Bishop and his executive producer, Bernard Gersten, also cited *Gypsy*;
he recalled that Walter Kerr had written of Merman during her triumph
in that show "that she had piled up all her past successes and seemed to
be standing on top of them. The same could be said of you in *A Delicate
Balance*."

Theater has been referred to as "the fabulous invalid" since the 1938
play of that name by George S. Kaufman and Moss Hart; 1996 was
the year journalism joined it in the permanent recovery ward. On January 22, *The New York Times* had tiptoed online, introducing what it variously called "a Web site" and an "electronic newspaper." Walter Kerr's
intellectual heir apparent at the *Times*, Frank Rich, had been nicknamed
the Butcher of Broadway for his supposed power to kill shows during
his tenure from 1980 to 1993. However, by the time Rich himself was
succeeded, by Ben Brantley, the democratizing force of the internet was
already looming. The ranks of not just newspaper critics but their jollier
colleagues, the night-crawling columnists who had helped Stritch con-
struct her career, would become significantly diminished with the arrival
of blogs and chat boards, and later Facebook and Twitter.

Michael Riedel, who would become known for his unsparing chronicles of the theater industry in the *Daily News* and then the *New York Post*,
was a rare upholder of the old ways, styling himself consciously after

Walter Winchell. He took Stritch and Liz Smith to Swifty's, the successor to Mortimer's. "If you were twenty years older and I were twenty years younger, we'd be putting up the jam together," Stritch told him.

"There was no one better at stealing the scene out from someone," Riedel believes, remembering watching Stritch in *A Delicate Balance* when she was leaning on an ottoman and then slipped "tipsily" to the floor. "It's like, the end of Rosemary Harris," he said. "The audience goes nuts. And you think that's the end of anything that comes before or after because they're going to remember Elaine on the ottoman, slipping on it."

But Stritch's arresting presence on the stage, her demands for equal time and attention, ended up working against her in the Tony race. The producers lobbied doggedly to get Stritch nominated in the Featured Actress category, which had included the character of Claire during the play's first run, but they were unsuccessful. She and Harris were both nominated for Best Actress, which would split the vote. Sondheim consoled and confused her by dismissively comparing the awards to a bridge competition—easy for him to do, as by now he had a whole collection of them.

The prize went to Zoe Caldwell, who played the soprano Maria Callas in Terrence McNally's *Master Class*. Grizzard won Best Actor. "For all of their difficulties and all of the crap that went on," said Bishop, who was sitting near Stritch, "she was the first on her feet cheering."

The play's run was extended, but it closed on September 29. Ten days later Stritch's longtime advocate and onetime colleague, Walter Kerr, would die in a Dobbs Ferry, New York, nursing home. In 1990 the Ritz Theater on Forty-Eighth Street had been renamed after him, but the idea that a theater would ever again be named for a critic seemed increasingly remote.

14.

HER TURN

Even with all the homey accoutrements installed by Maurice Bernstein, Stritch was getting antsy at the Regency, and the feeling was mutual; management wanted to cut down on longtime residents.

"I'm gonna buy a house in Sag Harbor," she told her sister Georgene one day on the phone.

"Uh-huh," Georgene said skeptically. "What are you thinking? A hundred and fifty servants at the Regency can't make you happy. Why the hell you think you'd be happy by yourself in Sag Harbor is completely beyond me."

Click. Elaine had hung up.

She had been sober for a decade, more or less, and she was now past seventy, but bristling with the energy and ambition of someone half her age. She might have been through "touring in stock," per the Sondheim song "I'm Still Here" that she still was iffy about singing, but "top billing" was hardly assured, and despite her bravado to the commentator Charles Osgood on CBS—"If I think I should win, I don't have to"—not having won the Tony for *A Delicate Balance*, twenty-five years after *Company*, infuriated her. It was a moment to retreat, but not too far. (Months after she moved, she still was conscripting wake-up calls from the telephone operators at the Regency.)

The Hamptons contained many happy memories for Stritch—it was where she had recuperated from *Who's Afraid of Virginia Woolf?* with Liz Smith and Lee Bailey—and in the fizzily affluent late 1990s the village of Sag Harbor had become enough of a mecca that *The New York Times* assigned the reporter Judith Miller to do an article on a "third wave" of creative people moving there. (This was several years before her widely condemned coverage of the search for Iraq's weapons of mass destruction.) Miller interviewed among others the monologist Spalding Gray, the novelist A. M. Homes, and Stritch, who had just secured her new house, a white four-bedroom colonial at 214 Main Street costing around $700,000. There was a large linden tree in the front yard that came from one of a dozen saplings on a ship from Europe that had run aground long ago in Mecox Bay. "It's just what I wanted," she told Miller, "an up-market Andy Hardy house where I can swing out a gate and walk into a grocery store in town or get a cappuccino. I want to be part of the scene, not out in Greta Garbo land."

This time she wanted from Bernstein not just a decoration job but a complete overhaul, though it was not long before she was complaining about the expense, to the point where the actor Dan Aykroyd, who appeared with her in the 1997 movie *Out to Sea*, instructed his business manager to send her a check to cover the cost of a new refrigerator.

Another lure was the Bay Street Theater, a ten-minute walk away: a local, year-round playhouse with considerable provenance. It had been cofounded by Sybil Christopher, the first wife of Richard Burton. She'd run a discotheque called Arthur in the late 1960s, on the site of the old El Morocco club on Fifty-Fourth Street in Manhattan.

Like a ship being christened, the stage at the Bay Street was about to be named ceremoniously for another Elaine, Steinbeck—John's widow—whom Stritch had gotten to know through Albee. Slim and elegant, Mrs. Steinbeck had been the stage manager of, among other productions, the original *Oklahoma!*; in recent decades, she had turned her attention to managing her late husband's estate. In her honor an audience of three hundred people were paying a few hundred dollars apiece and would be treated to the unlikely juxtaposition of Bruce Springsteen sing-ing an acoustic version of "Oh, What a Beautiful Mornin'" and Betty Comden and Adolph Green doing an impression of Nelson Eddy and Jeannette MacDonald. Introduced by Albee, Stritch performed a scene about a topless bathing suit from *A Delicate Balance*. It was an odd mix of swells.

Stritch herself had a project brewing at the Bay Street called *Elsa Edgar*, written by an Englishman named Bob Kingdom, about the curious commonalities of two midcentury power players, Elsa Maxwell and the FBI director J. Edgar Hoover, both to be played by one person. Prince had deemed it an excellent choice, though her decision to move to the area baffled him. "What the hell was she doing in Sag Harbor?" he said. "She was a hotel girl." (Even Bernstein was forced to concur: "She basically was better off living in a hotel, because she loved picking up the telephone: 'Oh, I need a lemon.'")

Kingdom, a skilled impersonator who'd devised the piece for himself, had resisted Stritch's casting before being persuaded by an English pro-ducer that to have his work performed by an American theatrical legend would lend it cachet. But he was still skeptical. "She's tall and thin. Elsa was short and fat, more like my dimensions," Kingdom said. "I knew from the start it was doomed."

Maxwell, the famous hostess and Coward's onetime intimate, was a known quantity who had called Stritch, with Lucille Ball, one of "my two favorite comediennes" after running into them at a Sherry-Netherland party in 1961. But Hoover was infinitely less approachable as a character; Stritch was hardly a buff of government intrigue and couldn't remember playing a man since she was Feste in *Twelfth Night* at the New School's Dramatic Workshop.

The stage manager of the production, which was to be directed by Gene Saks, was a young man named Rick Borutta, who had previously worked for the tall Texan Tommy Tune. Stritch asked him to run lines with her at night. "After a week, it became clear that Elaine was extremely frustrated with the material," Borutta said.

There was a line about the actress Dorothy Lamour, between whose names the Maxwell character was supposed to pause meaningfully and sip from a martini. Stritch wondered about the reason for the pause, and Saks didn't have an answer.

"'A friend of Dorothy' for gays is what 'a friend of Bill' is for alcoholics," Borutta told Stritch, trying to be helpful.

"What I didn't know was that Gene Saks was trying to legitimize the material by not making it gay," he said. "And yet that was the writer's whole shtick as a solo performer! So there was this thing in the room that didn't get talked about."

Stritch knew her lines cold at night but was having trouble remembering them during the day. Eventually Saks quit and the producer, Murphy Davis, stepped in to direct. The atmosphere got more charged as Stritch felt what was supposed to be her star vehicle, her own even-more-impressive *Master Class*, careening out of control. "Elaine was screaming, Elaine was angry at everybody and very demanding," Borutta said. "It was emotionally abusive and exhausting for everyone involved." At the dress rehearsal, Stritch called for cues from him so much that the hundred-odd people invited to watch, ushers and friends, wanted to know why "the Rick character" didn't take a bow at the end of the show.

Kingdom, meanwhile, had by this time flown over and sat in the audience during one rehearsal with Sybil Christopher, openmouthed. Afterward, a meeting was hastily called in Stritch's dressing room and it was agreed backstage that Kingdom would take over the part, with a day's rehearsal and his costumes hastily couriered from London by a friend.

The opening night was well attended by famous local residents, including the *Sound of Music* star Julie Andrews, whose daughter was a partner in the Bay Street. Stritch castigated herself, considering the botched chance to triumph before them. And yet "all the reviews were about the thing with Elaine rather than about the play and me," Kingdom noted.

By closing night, which came swiftly, she had calmed down and, playing the good sport, came to watch him with Maurice Bernstein, her decorator, as her date. "If I don't show up, they are going to say awful things about me," she told him.

"As if they weren't already!" Bernstein said with a cackle.

———

A week after this disappointment, Stritch called Borutta and asked him to pick her up to help with some errands. Not wanting to get behind the wheel was another reason she'd chosen a house in town.

"What would it take for you to be my assistant?" she asked him.

"I told her no," Borutta remembered. "I told her more or less that she was too much of a bitch to work with."

In a matter of months Stritch had gone from "and" billing to top billing and now abruptly she was back to being Queen of the Benefits. At Phyllis Newman's gala concert for breast cancer, a regular stop of hers, she would sing a duet from *Woman of the Year*, "The Grass Is Always Greener," with Glenn Close.

Stritch and Close met to rehearse in the Upper East Side apartment of Larry Grossman, a composer and skilled accompanist. "Elaine was not known to do duets," Grossman said. "Of course, she wanted all the laughs." Nonetheless it went well.

Soon after, he got a call of his own. "This guy's putting another salute to fucking Judy Garland," at Carnegie Hall, Stritch told him. "They want me to sing 'If Love Were All,' and I want to do 'But Not for Me.'" Grossman thought about it, realized the songs convey basically the same message, and devised a way to knit them together.

"This guy" was John Schreiber, a producer who had fallen in love with musical theater as a little boy, growing up in Queens and taking the subway into Manhattan by himself to see shows. One of them, at age fifteen, had been *Company*, and like Andre Bishop watching *Sail Away*, he'd been instantly smitten by Stritch in particular. "I was just gobsmacked by her in that role," Schreiber said. He had also seen her in a 1989 performance of *Love Letters*, with Jason Robards, on the Upper West Side. "And the thing about her that I noticed was how totally authentic she appeared to be. How she was just telling you the truth all the time. There was no artifice at all in the way that she acted."

The day of the Garland tribute, Schreiber agreed to pay for Grossman and Stritch's car and driver and was then told by her agent that he also had to pick up Vincent Roppatte's hairdressing bill. Jesus Christ, he thought. Then the actress arrived, "and did this singular piece that was basically like a three-act play in ten minutes," he said—interspersing her memories of Coward with the songs. Standing at the back of Carnegie Hall, Schreiber got a rare sensation: goose bumps.

What if she could do this for an hour and a half? he thought.

Backstage, Schreiber asked Stritch if she would have a conversation about doing a longer piece, more stories, more songs.

"Sure," she said. After all, she'd been taking notes for an autobiography for almost half a century.

Grossman was engaged to sit with Stritch and take down her memories; this was convenient because he had a place in Water Mill, fifteen minutes from Sag Harbor. He knew her world, having worked frequently with Hal Prince, and not just professionally but culturally: at the time of Dorothy Kilgallen's death, he had been her son-in-law. "There's a population that you share," he said.

When he and Stritch tired of her "studio," a sunroom at 214 Main that contained a piano bearing her Emmy for *Law & Order*, they moved to the Golden Pear, a local café, where, Grossman noted with astonishment, "we'd go through the line and she'd get through the checkout person saying 'I don't have to pay, do you know who I am?'" He was aghast again when she brought half a dozen friends to an East Hampton movie theater to see *Autumn in New York*, in which she'd had a minor part as Winona Ryder's grandmother, and refused to pay for the tickets.

"She felt this sense of privilege, entitlement," Grossman observed, "that was not commensurate with who she was."

She didn't mind being cut down to size by Woody Allen, who'd left Mia Farrow for her adopted daughter Soon-Yi Previn, but was not yet persona non grata among the cultural elite. He was making a movie called *Small Time Crooks* and had a part for Stritch. "Originally I had in mind a young Hepburn but then someone suggested Ernest Borgnine and that led me to you," he wrote. "I know it's not big and meaty but it will give you a chance to keep your hand in craft rather than where you always seem to put it. It's a lark and if you hate the idea, don't give it a moment's thought, I'll still send you any part I think you'd be right for like if I decide to do a remake of *Bride of Frankenstein*."

Stritch chose to be amused rather than insulted by this and, of course, took the job. Miscreants were rarely deprived of her ferocious loyalty. Garth Drabinsky was also facing scandal; his company, Livent, had sought bankruptcy protection and was undergoing a regulatory investigation. He and his partner, Myron Gottlieb, would eventually be found guilty of forgery and fraud, incarcerated and shunned by a wide swath of Toronto society. Nonetheless Stritch continued to telephone Drabinsky every New Year's Eve at 12:20 a.m. "Always her. Every year," he said. "She knew the pain that I was going through, though was never quite sure how to talk about it. She was always in my corner."

In her own corner Stritch now had Grossman and Schreiber, but it wasn't enough. She called Rick Borutta once more. "I want you to do for me what you have done for Tommy," she said. And like Liz Smith before him he agreed, with the condition that he get a credit on whatever she came up with.

After negotiating salary, Borutta moved to the third floor of 214 Main, where he had his own bedroom, sitting room, and bathroom. Stritch kept a regular schedule of going to bed around two to three in the morning and sleeping until noon, having left Post-it notes around the kitchen for him. "That would be my to-do list," he said. There was a housekeeper shared with her friend from Treetops, Arlene Dahl, so devoted that she drove three hours from Manhattan every other week.

Stritch was again faithfully going to AA meetings, and there she befriended an art consultant, Julie Keyes, who came through the house to paint the pattern of an oriental carpet on the floor.

"Every time I got close to finishing it, she would tell me that she wanted me to change the color," Keyes said. But the job gave her a front-row seat as Grossman and Stritch accumulated over twenty audiotapes of Stritch discussing her life, mostly in the form of a free-association monologue encouraged by Grossman's gentle prompts. Their breaks for food she mostly took standing up, no longer entertaining graciously as she had in Nyack. "The people who put place mats down and light a candle and sit down with a knife and fork and spoon and a teaspoon and a salad fork?" she said. "Hello, Dolly—I can't do it."

Borutta was charged with sorting through her copious television and film clips, as well as grocery shopping, fruit chopping, and ensuring an endless fount of cappuccino.

With Grossman she wondered repeatedly if Sondheim might write a song for what was amorphously but forcefully becoming a memoiristic one-woman show in her imagination.

"Would you do that for me, Steve, you son of a bitch? I called him, I always think of him around, you know, emotional times like Christmas and New Year's. My god, Larry, he's tough," she said, and went into an impression. "'Well, oh, yeah, Elaine, yes, um-hmm, yes, thanks. Uh-huh. Right.' That's it. 'Everything's all right with you, Steve?' 'Yeah, everything's all right with you? Right. Fine.' He's just . . ."

"Doesn't give you anything," Grossman said sympathetically.

"Fake it. Do anything! And I know he likes me," Stritch said. "That's a given. I mean, nobody argued that point with me. I mean, he gets mad as hell at me, but he likes me and he admires me and I got notes to prove it. But, boy . . ." She didn't have much hope that he would contribute. "But I'm going to hit him with it anyway. And it would be wonderful for him when he knows the spirit of this and the way we're doing it. He might get an inspiration." (According to Sondheim, she never asked him.)

Stritch was still nursing regret and jealousy about her perceived missed chances to appear in *Anyone Can Whistle*, *Gypsy*, and *Sweeney Todd*. "If you go for the truth, if you go for the goddamned truth, I am doing this because I'm sick of Angela Lansbury," who'd appeared in all of those, Stritch told Grossman. "That's why I'm doing this show and I'm sick of people doing parts that I should be doing. I've gotten a lot of them. I mean it's not like I'm a failure coming up for *air* here with this show. That isn't true at all . . . but the idea being it's a Momma Rose line: 'what I've got in me and I ain't done yet?' Holy shit."

The sessions stretched on for over a year, like psychotherapy with musical interludes. Grossman was beginning to tire of their intensity. "I was not looking forward to meeting with her—I started to make excuses," he said. He forced a confrontation. "Elaine, you need someone who is more available to you," he told her.

Schreiber took stock of what had been produced and decided they had enough material. He and Stritch, with Borutta's help, began considering writers. One possibility was Mark Hampton, who'd worked on *Full Gallop*, a one-woman show about the legendary fashion editor Diana Vreeland that had tried out at the Bay Street Theater. But Schreiber also had coproduced a new festival staged by *The New Yorker*, where the magazine's John Lahr, who'd so passionately defended *Show Boat*, was making an appearance. For Schreiber, Lahr's biography of his father, Bert, *Notes on a Cowardly Lion*, had been a formative text.

Lahr agreed at once to take on the project. He had reviewed Stritch in many shows over the years, including in London, where he had lived for some time, commuting to Broadway. "She was exceptionally good; she was true onstage; she was angry and open and feisty and memorable," he said. He was dexterous in several forms, including biography and scripts, of which this would be an exciting amalgam. But, perhaps most important, he could map commonalities between her and his problematic forebear.

"My father famously was panic-struck his whole life," Lahr said. "Why I did so well with Elaine was I recognized that in her. And she was actually the most panic-struck person I ever knew—more so than my father—and the truth of Elaine was her real great acting was convincing the world that she was loosey-goosey—that was a complete act. And the world bought it! But actually in private she was reading her AA book, she was trying to calm herself down, she was a hysteric, and completely terrified." What he recognized was someone of the old guard, who knew how to stop a show. Someone with no "Plan B," as he put it; someone whose very survival, psychological and economic, depended on her performance, and the audience liking her performance.

While convinced Stritch should "put the pedal to the metal" on the project, Hal Prince was not sure Lahr was the right choice—"it's a chic name and he has talent, but he lives in London and that will slow things down," he cautioned in a letter to her. But for once her friend and perennial white knight was overruled. Stritch saw that Lahr was tapped into the source of both her successes and her failures. "It was particularly my pedigree," Lahr said. "I think it meant a lot to her that I was the son of

Bert Lahr, because I understood her." Here was another quavering lion: "completely terrified, which is why she was such a bully, because if she roared and you didn't run away, she had no backup."

This odd but simpatico couple commenced winnowing down the transcripts in Stritch's open-plan kitchen. Lahr made a storyline of her sprawling, rambling narrative and suggested songs to intersperse, and then Stritch would change the rhythm of the writing to suit her speech patterns, making it seem improvised or casual, even though it was anything but. "Part of the gravitational pull of taking a role onstage is that you've got a script and for someone like Elaine, having the words, knowing where you were going, was essential to her sense of well-being," Lahr said.

Once he had real drafts done, they began what Lahr called the "Orso polish," sitting in the slightly nicer of Joe Allen's neighboring restaurants, where Stritch liked being seen, back in action.

Meanwhile, Schreiber, who had never before put on a show of this kind, went to theatrical veterans for advice and possible investment. Though he'd been so encouraging and would offer notes later, Prince wasn't interested. (The involvement of Lahr, like Kerr before him a critic who was also a "worker in the theater," might have been a deterrent.)

"I don't think it will work," he told Schreiber.

Next was the longtime producer Roger Berlind. "Too much drinking" was his verdict.

"I thought, Broadway is not a good place for this, because she's old—Broadway's old. There's nothing cool about it," Schreiber came to believe. He called a friend of his at Joe's Pub, the cabaret of the Public Theater. "Let me talk to George," the friend said. George C. Wolfe was the artistic director of the Public. He had won Tonys for directing the first portion of Tony Kushner's landmark play about AIDS, *Angels in America*, and the tapping and rapping sensation *Bring in 'da Noise, Bring in 'da Funk*. And the Public was where Michael Bennett had developed *A Chorus Line*.

Wolfe had loved Stritch in *Company*. But with some unease he remembered meeting her at a Drama League luncheon and overhearing her say that she had seen "a real Hattie McDaniel type," referring to the African American actress who played Mammy in *Gone with the Wind*, in the restroom. (Wolfe is African American.) "I remember finding that sort of startling and disturbing and completely inappropriate," he said. Still, he was intrigued enough by the idea of Stritch doing a one-woman show to go meet her and Lahr at the Regency.

"No, John, *no*," he heard as he approached the room.

Stritch opened her door wearing a T-shirt and stockings over a leg brace; she had broken her knee falling down her Sag Harbor stoop. She and Lahr had been refining something he'd written. "I was sort of astonished by how meticulous she was and how completely and totally brilliant she was at dissecting the language," Wolfe said. "It was as if she were a writer, because she had an understanding of language like writers have an understanding of language." Stritch had never been shy about offering input on scripts. Moreover, she was supremely skilled at the particular kind of theatrical conversation that takes place not between actors but a player and the audience. Even when Stritch had been in a large cast, she found a way to reach around them and across the footlights; now this "dialogue" would be formalized.

"It's a play, it's really a play," she would tell a reporter. "Not loose, cabaret bullshit." Still, but for her musical accompaniment, she would be alone, and this was daunting. "She was terrified because she didn't know if this was going to work," Julie Keyes said. "If this didn't work, she didn't know what else she was going to have."

But Stritch had also been offered a part in a new musical, *The Royal Family of Broadway*, by William Finn and James Lapine, as the matriarch of a theatrical family based on the Barrymores. It too would allow her to explore the history of show business, but she'd be sheltered in a role surrounded by the familiar comfort of the ensemble.

When she hedged to Wolfe, he drove to Sag Harbor to persuade her that she would be both protected and showcased. "The character of Elaine is amazing. I can think of no one more perfect for the role," he wrote to her in a long letter afterward. "In the other show, your name will be above the title. In our show, your life will be above the title." To assuage her fear of censure, he added a line she took to repeating often: "If they run you out of town, get in front of them and pretend it's a parade."

Stritch needed no more convincing. And this time negotiation went smoothly. Through a new A-list agent, Sam Cohn at ICM, she finagled accommodations at the Regency, a per diem of $150 per day, hair and makeup by Saks, costumes—her white shirts would be silk; her black tights Wolford, her shoes handmade in Italy—massage therapy twice per week, dressing-room expenses of $150 per week, a car and driver, and Marjorie McDonald's paid assistance as well as Borutta's. Rob Bowman, whom she'd met at a workshop of *The Royal Family*, would be brought in to arrange and accompany.

Wolfe had praised the "healing" and "humor" of the show. "God knows the world desperately needs both," he wrote. "Will it need those qualities next year?"

It would, more than he could have known. Their first day of rehearsal was scheduled for September 11, 2001.

15.

STRITCH, INC.

After terrorists pointed two jumbo jets into the World Trade Center, felling the Twin Towers and killing almost three thousand people, Manhattan was cleaved within minutes into two cities. There was downtown, filled with wreckage and death and smoke billowing over the river, and uptown, emotionally shocked but physically untouched. Sequestered at the Regency, Stritch fell into the latter camp, but the Public, where her show was going to debut, was below police lines on Lafayette Street.

Along with the chorus of worried messages in George Wolfe's voice-mail box on what quickly became known as 9/11 was one from Stritch. "Well, I guess we're not going to rehearse today," she said.

On September 12, the creative team went to the Shubert Theater in Midtown, because Bowman had worked on *Chicago* there. On September 13—in a demonstration of the "show must go on" ethos that had kept Stritch performing through a threatened explosion in Palm Beach or a nearby car bomb in London or a splattering of beef stroganoff during a collapsed dinner theater in Virginia or a group of protesters in Toronto—they snuck past the barricades erected downtown. "She was in one of her all-white outfits with the cane, and there were all these young guys and women all dressed in black with earrings coming out of them, everything pierced, and she was staring at them like they were the oddest set of creatures," Wolfe said. "And they were staring right back at her."

The title Lahr had presented, *Elaine Stritch: At Liberty*, was informed by C. L. Barber's book *Shakespeare's Festive Comedy*, which states a "basic antithesis between control and liberty, decorous prudence and impudent recklessness." (Mildred would have been pleased at this.) The notion that Stritch would be permitted to be at liberty, Lahr said, helped relieve her from the worry that she might lose her way, and gave her more leeway in her stories. "They're based on some truth," he said. "Of course she'd embroidered them."

"At liberty" were the sailors of *On the Town* when she arrived in New York; "at liberty" was what she was in Lee Israel's article in 1968 (mentioned in the show, to Israel's delight); "at liberty" even recalled her fashion show at the London department store (omitted, to Peter Tear's disappointment). It now also fortuitously suggested freedom, independence, and democracy, as represented by a female statue, at the precise moment when these qualities and even that statue seemed under siege.

But even with her own name in the title, Stritch was concerned about getting sufficient credit. One late night at *The New Yorker*'s offices on Forty-Second Street Lahr was applying final touches to their creation when the phone rang.

"John, I want to change the billing," came the now familiar rasp.

"Elaine, look, dear, I just want to get the script in," Lahr said.

"You're the writer," she said. "No one's going to believe that I had anything to do with this!"

"Elaine, we're coauthors—it's okay."

"No. I've thought about it, John, I want to say 'Constructed by Elaine Stritch and Reconstructed by John Lahr.'"

Those words went on the poster and promotional materials, but then Stritch realized that the joke was in "reconstructed," so she reversed the billing again.

"The reconstruction means I had the last say," she explained to *Newsweek*. "Damn right I did."

"We're off to see the wizard," Stritch mumbled to no one in particular as she prepared for the show's opening at the Public Theater on November 7, 2001. She was being trailed by Rick McKay, a cabaret singer turned documentarian who had a special interest in the golden age of Broadway. "I felt like the day before I got married," she told him. "I couldn't sleep." She calmed herself with an old piece of theatrical advice: "What the audience thinks of me is none of my business. That doesn't mean you don't care—you care *wildly*—but it is none of your business while you're up there. Then I rush and get the papers—what did they think about me? I love notices; I love critics."

So she made a practice of reading her reviews? McKay asked.

"Oh puh-leeze! I don't believe any actor that says he doesn't," Stritch said. "What is that bullshit?"

The show began with an announcement: it was perfectly fine for the audience to crackle candy wrappers and take copious photographs, so long as negatives were left at the stage door. With orchestrations by Jonathan Tunick and an eight-piece band led by Bowman, what followed was carefully scripted to have an improvisational, jazzy feel. Like a perfume that refused to leave the room, it was the essence of Stritch: avaricious, profane, confessional, chaotic—chronologically scrambled, factually massaged—but with a consistent feeling of complete directness. She would begin the second act, at last, with "I'm Still Here" and a joke about her age—now seventy-six—and would end it, in part, by declaring "Fuck fear," a message that now seemed relevant not only to her personally but to the entire population of New York.

At Liberty was like nothing else on offer that shattered season, and its elemental candor was balm. Some people told Wolfe this was the first time they had laughed since the attacks. Scores of others who had struggled with addiction or merely frustrated ambition saw in Stritch someone who'd refused to give up, had endured and triumphed. And more than any Tony anniversary program, this romp through musical-theater history was also a valentine to New York, the center of the industry. We have seen worse, conveyed Stritch's face—life's furrows decking her brow, unsmoothed by the suddenly de rigueur Botox—and we will get through this.

Schreiber was sitting in front of Roger Berlind on opening night. At the end of the performance, the veteran producer turned to the fledgling one. "I was wrong," he said.

At Liberty went on to break box-office records at the Public. Stritch struck a deal for an audio recording and asked D. A. Pennebaker, the documentarian who had so memorably captured the *Company* cast album recording session in 1970, to gather footage for a movie version, this time *officially* starring her. And George Hodgman, an editor at Henry Holt, was one of the many people, including Tina Brown and Michael Korda, who could envision *At Liberty* as a book.

Hodgman made headway with Stritch because he was also in recovery. "Of course you know you have the makings of not only a rich theatrical memoir, but a lasting, moving and above all non-sermonic (Please God!) testimony for all of us who share and battle every day with our disease(s)," he wrote to her, adding, "Anyone who tries to saddle you with a ghost writer should be shot in the public square!"

Holt offered a $450,000 advance. Stritch sat on the offer for a few weeks and made a few notes, but she wouldn't commit. She was too restless to sit down and write it by herself, as the experiment of *Shut Up and Drink Your Champagne*, her unfinished memoir from decades earlier, had proved. "She needed a spine, or someone to create structure and discipline," Hodgman said. Lahr was invited to a meeting in her dressing room. Peggy Lee was playing. "How do you see the book?" someone asked Stritch. "Well . . . ," she said, looking blankly at her cowriter. But she was not prepared to pay him again, not sure she had more to say than she'd put on the stage, and the deal would fall apart in subsequent weeks.

Lahr meanwhile was dismayed by Stritch's thank-you speech at the end of the second act to the Regency, her hairdresser, and everyplace else that she was getting freebies from, and wished she would cut it from *At Liberty*. "Because Elaine was doing business," he said. "Once she was a hit she strip-mined everything. It was a form of greed."

The show from the Public, "this darling doll's house," as Stritch called it, moved to the former Alvin Theater, where *Company* had played—now rechristened the Neil Simon Theater—on February 6, 2002, for a limited run that would end days before the Tonys. It would be replaced by *Hairspray*, a candy-pink example of the movie-inspired musicals that would become increasingly popular at the beginning of the twenty-first century; while often well-rendered, they appealed most to tourists visiting a Disneyfied Times Square.

This time Stritch was nominated in the category of Special Theatrical Event, which had been created a year earlier after Susan Stroman's *Contact*, with no orchestra or singing, won Best Musical. (The Special Theatrical Event contest would be eliminated in 2009, after not enough shows qualified.) She would be competing against Bea Arthur's own one-woman show, *Bea Arthur on Broadway: Just Between Friends*, and Barbara Cook's *Mostly Sondheim* as well as John Leguizamo's *Sexaholix: A Love Story*.

All nominees were told to keep their speeches to one minute. But Stritch had waited too long to be succinct. When her old *Call Me Madam* castmate Chita Rivera read her name, the expected result to most in the industry, Stritch marched up determinedly wearing a creamy skirt suit with turtleneck recalling her wedding costume, her collaborators trailing her.

"Don't take up my time," she told the applauding audience, to laughter. She told about a presentation she'd given earlier at which a young girl came up, asked her for her autograph, and said she wanted to follow in her footsteps.

"Wear comfortable shoes," Stritch advised the would-be Eve Harrington. Another laugh.

She praised her fellow nominees for "having a go at it up here alone. I applaud all four of us. But judging from the Greek chorus behind me, there's no such thing as a one-man or one-woman show." (Indeed, Lahr also won a writing award, the first critic to do so in the ceremony's history.)

The Radio City Music Hall orchestra started playing as Stritch began her thanks, to Schreiber, "who made me do it"; Wolfe, "who told me how to do it"; and Lahr: "Oh boy, how he helped me do it." The Tony executive producer, Gary Smith, asked CBS if he could have thirty more seconds, but they said no. The orchestra got louder and more insistent.

"Rob Bowman . . ." Stritch tried to continue. "Please don't do that to me!"

But she was left under the cold blue lights as the network cut to a commercial. Her speech had run three minutes and twenty seconds.

Backstage, Stritch, in tears, clutching her Tony, told the assembled press: "I am very, very upset. I know CBS can't let people do the Gettysburg Address at the Tonys"—the Gettysburg Address was only two minutes, but who's counting?—"but they should have given me my time." She wanted to tell the audience what this had meant to her, she said, after fifty years in the business. And to misquote a Sondheim lyric from *Anyone Can Whistle*: "What's hard comes easy, what's natural comes hard." "They can go fuck themselves," she said of the network as reporters, by now used to actors anesthetized by corporate publicity teams, scribbled excitedly.

One told her Federico Fellini had once been cut off at the Oscars.

"So what," she said. "Fellini can take it, he's more grown-up than I am."

She apologized the next day in Michael Riedel's column.

Proud of the piece but exhausted by his star's antics, Schreiber sold touring rights for *At Liberty* to the producer Scott Sanders, who'd helped him move it to Broadway and now was planning a transfer to London and then visits to cities across America, "the open road" Stritch had savored since the 1950s.

"I was well out of it—I declared victory," Schreiber said. "I think she was entirely dependent on so many people to enable her life but at the end of the day I think she felt herself to be alone. So I don't think she could really have genuine intimate relationships with people."

Alone with her newfound acclaim in Sag Harbor, Stritch found a lone rose among dead blooms growing on the trellis on the side of her house. She cut the excess leaves off, put it in a small Steuben vase, and set it on a bureau in her bedroom. For a moment, she felt suffused with warmth and contentment. Then she started to cry. Jesus, where am I going? she thought. Maybe no place for very long.

"I wish I could forget about the god damned show but I can't," she wrote, though she was glad about returning to London. She acknowledged her emotions of exhilaration and gratitude. But there was something else as well, less pleasant, and mysterious, given the rewards for all her hard work, the receipt of everything she'd ever wanted. "I have got—so deep inside of me, the most profound feeling—in my whole life I have never felt before—of being alone. Totally!"

Never fond of flying, Stritch, spooked anew by 9/11, would return to the Savoy on the *Queen Elizabeth II* with Pennebaker's crew in tow. Playing in London, at the Old Vic, was bittersweet. *The Telegraph* liked the show, *The Guardian* found it mawkish and sentimental. The British people had always appreciated Stritch for being acerbic; now, at least for some stretches of her monologue, she was as vulnerable and "connected" as a guest on *Oprah*. "In the last few years of her career, she lost a little of her irony, spikiness," Prince said. "I missed it."

But irony, as he and Sondheim knew, doesn't tend to go over well with the masses. Irony is a privilege of the elite: an unmuddied story of recovery and redemption tends to do far bigger business. And so the fact that Stritch had not renounced drinking completely became subsumed by the higher "truth" and the better narrative arc that she was going on almost fifteen years of sobriety.

Many actresses, as they age, fade out of public view. Stritch had never before been in such sharp focus. And she was discovering to her surprise that celebrity, the outpouring of strangers thinking they knew her intimately, could be tedious and isolating. "I never saw her at ease yet," Pennebaker told *Playbill*, having gathered thirty to forty hours of footage. His crew followed Stritch back to Sag Harbor, where she held a 1:00 p.m. yard sale after putting the Main Street house on the market, tagging the baby grand piano at $12,000 and selling individual dishes from a set autographed piece by piece. "What the heck?" Ben Gazzara asked, visiting with Elke.

"No, this makes me money," Stritch said. "Such a restful shade of green," she sighed of cash, to Terry Hekker.

At Liberty moved on, to Dallas, to the good old Ahmanson in Los Angeles, to San Francisco, to Chicago (where it was compared to Anatole Broyard's memoir *Kafka Was the Rage*), to Minneapolis, to Philadelphia, to Boston, and to Toronto, en route to which Stritch insisted on a car and driver, claiming she was afraid of getting the SARS virus at the airport. She was America's sweetheart, senior edition, and she was increasingly exhausted.

When Stritch was ordered to have a hysterectomy after a tumor was found on one of her ovaries, Hekker spent the night at the hospital with her, against intensive-care rules. "I think she told them I was her sister," Hekker said. "In the morning, Liz Smith was there, and Liz and I walked her up and down the hall. Liz was always there." Stritch recovered at the Carlyle.

Sheila Nevins, the executive at HBO who would acquire Pennebaker's film, heard about the procedure, which she'd also had. She had loved Stritch since *Company*. And she wanted Stritch to love her.

Nevins decided to set the tone for their relationship by buying a toilet-seat riser at Caligor, a pharmacy specializing in medical supplies, and getting it gift-wrapped and messengered to the hotel.

Three hours later, Nevins's phone rang.

"Get that fucking thing out of there!" came the voice on the other end of the line.

"Oh, Ms. Stritch . . ."

"Because *it's* not as hard—as having *that* in this room!"

Was *At Liberty*, contra its name, actually a form of imprisonment: long-term solitary confinement? Or was it a retirement plan?

After another Emmy for Pennebaker's documentary, Stritch had accepted a small part in the Jennifer Lopez movie *Monster-in-Law*, playing Jane Fonda's mother-in-law, though she was only a dozen years older, an echo of her experience with Burstyn in the 1980s. From TV, Marc Cherry, a former *Golden Girls* writer who'd created a hit ABC dramedy called *Des-*

perate Housewives, wanted Stritch to play the nettlesome mother of Felicity Huffman's character, Lynette Scavo. Talks progressed, but Stritch couldn't stop herself from offering script changes and negotiating for perks. After she requested a suite in the Peninsula Hotel for the entire six weeks of filming, Cherry lost patience and pulled out.

"I think I really fucked up," Stritch told Michael Feinstein. And to her namesake niece, Elaine Kelly, she said, "I'm an out-of-work, broke actress!"

But Stritch had also become too much part of New York's firmament to wrench herself with any commitment to Los Angeles, especially with the advance of years. "She hated going out there," Larry Grossman said. "She referred to it as an ATM machine."

Instead, with the death of the Carlyle's longtime habitué Bobby Short in March 2005, she decided at age eighty to make her most favored Madison Avenue hotel her base of operations and with Bowman's help produce a looser, shorter, singing show, the kind she'd been wanting to do since the 1950s. She would call it *At Home at the Carlyle*.

Greg Dinella, the hotel's director of finance, who had previously been at the Pierre, worked out the terms. During the two-month period Stritch was rehearsing or performing, she would pay no rent for room 309. Included were at least two massages per week and unlimited decaf coffee, water, soft drinks, and soup. "But she didn't need steaks and chops; she didn't need red wine and bottles of scotch," Dinella said. "Everything was simple."

The ten months of the year she would have to pay rent to live at the Carlyle would be eased considerably by an offer from Tina Fey, who was creating an alter ego, Liz Lemon, and a show based on her experience as the first female head writer of *Saturday Night Live*. The single "career girl" was, remarkably, just as fascinating a creature as she'd been in the era of *My Sister Eileen*.

Lemon's boss, an Irish Catholic named Jack Donaghy, would be played by Alec Baldwin, and the boss's dominating mother, Colleen, would be played by Stritch, for $30,000 per episode. She would be one in a panoply of guest stars including Al Gore, Oprah Winfrey, and Jerry Seinfeld, appearing in only nine episodes (one with her original *Company* castmate John Cunningham). But Stritch's role was vitally important: Colleen

Donaghy was the only character capable of cutting down the imperious Jack (or Jacky, as she called him), instantly causing him to regress with a single "brilliant zinger."

30 Rock premiered in 2006, a year after the introduction of a website called YouTube, on which television clips and other performances could be instantly uploaded and relived into infinity. With its quick cuts and one-liners, Fey's show was a natural fit for the new platform. And so too was the long quotable Elaine Stritch, a woman who had generated sound bites since they were just penciled by gossip columnists between bites of hamburger at Sardi's. Before long, pieces of Pennebaker's 1970 film of *Company*, of *At Liberty*, and of her most obscure films would find a new home and an audience on YouTube. And as social media grew in popularity she would come to be frequently quoted, sampled, and vaunted.

The internet would prove much less judgmental and more appreciative of nonconformity than the Hollywood studio system had been, as well as a stay against the ephemerality of the theater. Everything was coming up roses, this time for meme.

Stritch would get a third Emmy for her performance as Donaghy. The show was widely lauded and beloved, though Liz Smith didn't approve of its more cartoonish aspects. "*30 Rock* is not funny and some of the characters are really creepy," she wrote to Stritch. "How can this kind of shit win awards?" Nor was she happy when the Metropolitan Opera conductor James Levine began coming to see Stritch's set at the Carlyle, by his account more than ten times.

"She talked about him and meeting him and how she had this big sneaker for him," said Smith, who'd heard rumors about Levine. "And I got ahold of her and said, 'Elaine, not only is this guy, he may be a genius, he may be the nicest thing in the world, but you gotta drop this. It reflects badly on you to say that you were attracted to him.' She was just shocked." (Accused by multiple men, some alleging sexual abuse by Levine when they were underage, he was fired by the Metropolitan Opera in the spring of 2018.)

"She was the most naïve person I ever met," Smith said of her friend, not unkindly.

Hundreds of less problematic characters were also flocking to the Carlyle, where Stritch would continue to reprise her cabaret under various titles and reintroduce a more intimate variation of the show she'd done on Broadway. Joshing around with her became a rite of passage for some visitors and she treated the staff as her extended family. "There's an elevator operator over here—a gentle older operator," Dinella said. "He would say to me, 'You know, she punches me, Mr. Dinella.' I said, 'Yeah, Frank, but she's in her eighties.'"

"It *hurts*, Mr. Dinella."

When Barack Obama was elected president in the fall of 2008, Stritch ran through the lobby in her bathrobe and slippers, trailing sparklers. Maybe it wasn't so bad to be alone after all.

> Marriage may be where it's been
> But it's not where it's at

Sondheim had written these lines presciently in 1970, when people living alone were only 17 percent of households in America. Now they constituted almost a third.

Terry Hekker's husband had served her with divorce papers after forty years of marriage, leaving her for another, younger woman. Hekker ran for and took the office of mayor of Nyack, and Stritch provided the title for her new memoir, *Disregard First Book*, self-published in April 2009.

The following month Georgene Moran, Elaine's older sister, the consummate homemaker, family loyalist, country-club woman, and lover of nature and poetry, died at ninety. This unleashed something in Stritch: grief and anger and terror and what-the-hellness.

And the month after that John Lahr filed suit in New York State Supreme Court, contending that Stritch had breached the agreement they'd signed to coauthor *At Liberty* and was depriving him of income she was making doing versions of the show. "Stritch has profited at the expense of Lahr," it read in part. "Lahr is entitled to restitution from Stritch based on unjust enrichment."

The dispute was quickly settled out of court, "to mutual satisfaction," said Lahr's lawyer, Carl Koerner. But Stritch would never speak again to the man who had given her some modicum of order, design, tension, composition, balance, light, and harmony, to quote the T-shirts inspired by *Sunday in the Park with George*. "I gave her to a certain degree a format that made her a legend, but she could not be grateful," Lahr said.

Not long after this series of events, it was announced that Stritch was altering the Carlyle program to honor her favorite composer, with the name *Singin' Sondheim . . . One Song at a Time*. Now she would have a chance to perform every role she hadn't gotten.

"What next?" she asked one audience after opening with "I Feel Pretty" from *West Side Story*.

"Man, that's a good question. What next? What next? What follows what? What would be right next? I thought about this a lot. And it crossed my mind. What about if I—oh no, I *couldn't*, could I? Well, I said, wait a minute. Wait a minute? Why not? Why not? Why the *hell* not? Here she is, boys!"

Bowman and his musicians began the underscoring of "Rose's Turn," the eleven o'clock number from *Gypsy*, and Stritch, in between the lines, interspersed some bitter patter.

"I never got a chance to do that show. *Gypsy*, the musical. *Gypsy*. Nope! No, I *never* got a shot at Momma Rose for one reason or another, some reason or another. Never mind. I can do it here. For you, here tonight, in the Café Carlyle."

"Yea!" yelled a few people, thumping the tables in encouragement.

"Let's go! Cabaret style if you will. No runway, so what. I can handle that. Let's see what we can do."

I could have been better than any of you. What I've got in me, what I've been holding down inside of me. If I ever let it out . . . there wouldn't be signs big enough. There wouldn't be lights bright enough.

In her gonzo fierceness one could sense echoes of Mildred Stritch, educated but constrained, and of her youngest daughter who "got out," no matter the cost, but still felt she had unfathomable depths within. "Theater is an escape, cabaret I'm right here with you," she said. "I like the fact that I can do anything I want. I think I've always wanted to do anything that I wanted." And the number was whispered, snarled, shrugged off, and howled.

Sondheim believed performances such as this were where Stritch came into her element. "Elaine had jazz inflection and that smoky speak-song singing voice, which she did even when she was a young woman. It's not a singer's voice. It's a performer's voice. Which is why she could do good nightclub work," he said. He would occasionally coach her. "She always said how she was afraid of me. I mean, she made a joke of it. And there was no need, but I know exactly what it was, it was somebody who's not educated facing someone who's educated and using his education as a writer. And I'm educated musically too, which she wasn't. She was instinctive as a musician. What she knew was songs."

He and Prince attended the last performance of this show, arranged for the evening of her eighty-fifth birthday. A month and a half later, Sondheim's eightieth was celebrated at Avery Fisher Hall. Stepping from a circle of his leading women, all wearing red and sitting in chairs, Patti LuPone sang "The Ladies Who Lunch," turning to Stritch with the line "Does anyone still wear a hat?" and giving her a long appreciative look. Surprised, Stritch, who was indeed in a hat (as well as the only one wearing a pantsuit), improvised looking abashedly into her lap.

When it was time to rise, she sang, of course, "I'm Still Here," substituting one line: "I lived through Barbara Walters, and I'm here . . . ," unbuttoning her jacket, and ending jumping up and down. And the standing ovation was a foregone conclusion.

In 2010 Stritch would get a final gift from Sondheim: replacing Lansbury in a revival of *A Little Night Music*, to perform alongside one of his favorite stars, Bernadette Peters, replacing Catherine Zeta-Jones. The Stritch who had once stood in an English bar and imitated Glynis Johns's voice singing "Send in the Clowns" as Desirée was now ready for the role of that character's snobbish mother, Madame Armfeldt. "She was entirely wrong for the part," Sondheim admitted later. "You can't believe for two seconds that she's an Old World courtesan."

But giving Stritch the role would be a hard elbow to the box office. And Peters, remembering years before when Stritch had called to wish her luck playing Rose Hovick, found her brimming with a new charm. "She was trying to give back to actors," she said. "She softened. It wasn't just about her." Peters noticed that on her dressing-room table Stritch kept photographs of her husband, and herself with her sisters, wearing bathing suits, when they were children. There were brightly multicolored throw pillows on a white sofa, an old decorating trick from Noël Coward's house in Jamaica, and Stritch had special handkerchiefs embroidered in case she needed to dab at her nose onstage. Lansbury lent her a portable piano to practice songs.

Stritch bestowed her own special name upon several cast members. The young buck Hunter Ryan Herdlicka, who played the student Henrik, was called "Later," after his main song. His understudy, Kevin David Thomas, was called "the Gay One" (much to the amusement of the two Henriks since Kevin was straight, and Hunter was gay). Keaton Whittaker, a teenager playing Fredrika, Armfeldt's granddaughter, was "young Bacall over there."

This wasn't just to be amusing: Stritch's memory was beginning to fade, as a performance for Obama at the White House painfully showed. "You don't know how bad I feel right now," she said in the middle of singing "I'm Still Here" as Bowman patiently kept playing, waiting to get her back on track. But she rallied, with enough presence of mind to whisper to the president afterward, "What are you doing for New Year's Eve?"

In *A Little Night Music*, Stritch would blame her lapses on the props. "Why is this flower here?" she complained. "No, we don't put a flower on the tray at this point. You know, I can't work if everything is going to be different every time I do the scene. Let's get the flower moved!" Backstage, a closely guarded list of her entrances and exits included instructions for filling lowball glasses with Fernet-Branca, the bitter liquid Coward drank, and checking blood sugar.

The director, Trevor Nunn, approached her about wearing an earpiece and she refused as strongly as she had the microphone in *Show Boat*. "She couldn't remember her lines and they were all printed out. And she would seek cues—radio calls from the police," Sondheim said. When she did have her lines cold, she took her time saying them. The musicians loved this, because they got overtime every night.

Seeking to ground her, Nunn sent a three-page instructive fax. "You break all the rules and we love you for it," he wrote, but asked her to affect a more English pronunciation, hoping that she would get up from her wheelchair to sing "Liaisons," though Armfeldt "commands her world (like you said your mother did) from a seated position."

One night, she called Herdlicka into her dressing room and asked him to sit on the couch. Did I mess up a line? he wondered.

"You are in on the joke," she told him.

"Yeah—it was a great joke!" Herdlicka said, thinking she was referring to some earlier punch line.

"No, you are in on the joke. The joke being life. You get it. You see it for what it is."

She added him to the roster of late-night phone calls she would make: to Tunick, to her doctor, Jeffrey Glick; to her lawyer, Joseph Rosenthal; to Feinstein; to Baldwin; to Nathan Lane; to Michael Riedel . . .

Six months after *Night Music* closed in January 2011, Sally Stritch Bolton, her second-oldest sister, died at ninety. Elaine grew increasingly morose and physically weaker. Walking with her after dinner alongside Pamela Myers, Donna McKechnie was struck that this time, instead of saying "Don't touch me!," she leaned, afraid of falling, on her old colleagues.

Borutta having moved on to pursue study of alchemical healing (he later created his own one-man show, *Nobody's Bitch*, based on his captivity to *At Liberty*), Stritch wore out several other faithful assistants before hiring Herdlicka at $400 per week. She was also navigating a new phalanx of cameras from yet another documentary that was being made about her, called *Shoot Me*, by Chiemi Karasawa, an erstwhile script supervisor whom she'd met first on the set of *Romance & Cigarettes*, directed by John

Turturro and starring James Gandolfini, and then at Vartali, an elegant hair salon in the Galleria building on East Fifty-Seventh Street that Stritch had begun to favor because it was closer to the Carlyle than Saks.

Karasawa filmed as Stritch continued to perform, but the actress increasingly became dependent on Bowman for prompts, which he managed so skillfully that some audience members thought it was part of the act. Michael Riedel suspected that Stritch made a routine of forgetting lyrics, a sort of "wait, wait, don't tell me" that kept the crowd engaged and on her side. "You have to understand, she knew better than many actors how to manipulate an audience," he said.

But Feinstein was concerned. "Elaine, just use a music stand," he told her. "Rosemary Clooney used it. Barbara Cook uses it. Just use it. Nobody cares."

"Well, maybe . . ."

"But ultimately she could not do it," Feinstein said. "She would not do it. She would never do it. Because for her to lose her memory represented a lot of bad things to her."

Stritch had continued to accept work almost compulsively, and she rehearsed the cabaret act with Bowman in sessions of marathon concentration. For *River of Fundament*, his film that would run well over five hours, the avant-garde artist Matthew Barney hired her and Dick Cavett, among others, for a scene simulating the late author Norman Mailer's wake, in what was supposed to be the parlor of his Brooklyn Heights brownstone (there were also several scenes in Detroit). Stritch was delivering the eulogy, lines from Mailer's novel *Ancient Evenings*.

"We were looking for people who in some way or another could belong in that parlor, either from the social circle of Norman Mailer, or people that you could imagine being in that circle," Barney said.

Stritch, he admitted, didn't completely understand what was going on. "But I also think she was energized by that," he said. "There was a kind of animal quality to Elaine, the rawness to her that is superexciting and supervolatile; she kind of occupied the room in a way that nobody else did."

She had walked down a long road, from the dawn of the talkies to the rise and fall of matinee idols to an inscrutable filmed conceptual art opera. Now, finally, Stritch was starting to slow down. Her perambulations from the Carlyle to the Battery, or around Central Park, were no longer possible. And her professional and social circles, always inextricable, got smaller. "There were just people who stopped calling," Herdlicka said. "She became too demanding, she became too old." Stritch had developed a phobia about taxis, and without a production paying for a car and driver, she would often choose to walk instead. One day, coming out of the Carlyle, she fell, hurting her eye and needing surgery. Then she fell again, breaking a hip. "She couldn't see, she couldn't walk, and that's when she got serious," he said. Stritch wanted to move back to Birmingham.

"I need to go where my relatives are," she told Liz Smith, who thought it was a bad idea. "I begged her not to go," Smith said.

Scott Griffin, the producer who'd also known Elzbieta Czyzewska, was one of those she called from the hospital to decant Fernet-Branca into Coke bottles. "With me, Elaine would get very drunk and we would be sitting talking about getting drunk and what it means," Griffin said. Not losing control, she suggested, but defining a certain relationship between self and environment. "And every time it ended on the same punch line. She'd say, 'Scott, there is nothing more dangerous in the world than talent.' Over and over and over again."

What was Stritch's talent exactly, with that word's suggestion of unrealized, unrecognized possibility? It wasn't beautiful singing, though she became an expert at cadence and modulation. It wasn't really acting per se, since most of the characters she played were variations of herself. It wasn't dancing, obviously.

It really was entertaining, the root of which means "to hold together." In a drawing room or from a stage, Stritch could command the entire space. In solitude, she gathered people around. And if she could no longer entertain in this manner, then she would have to retreat. "I don't want to be one of these old actresses who dies in a hotel," she told Hekker, who also tried to dissuade her from moving.

"Look, you have everything here. People waiting on you. You're taken care of. You're around your friends. You could go out or not go out."

Stritch insisted. With Herdlicka's help, she began packing her possessions. "She didn't give things away," he said. "She took them back."

Greg Dinella, of the Carlyle, suggested a final show. "I can't prepare—I don't have the time," Stritch worried. But she couldn't resist a proper farewell to her fans. She would call it *Movin' Over and Out*.

Using a cane, wearing tights, a white shirt, and a long black vest, Stritch wrote key words of various stories, her greatest hits, and put them in a silver bowl, and guests picked them out, as for a game of charades. She bantered and posed for pictures with Tom Hanks, Martin Short, and Liza Minnelli. And she sang a ribald parody of Cole Porter's "You're the Top" called "You're the Pop" ("My mistake / was in getting plastered / What a break / for the little bastard"), one hand unfolding and slashing definitively in front of her as the audience whooped in delirium in front of their twenty-dollar martinis and the colorful murals depicting ethereal ballerinas and strumming minstrels.

"They captured a moment," Dinella said. "Like Janis Joplin in Monterey."

Stritch had long smuggled out china and linens when leaving hotels; now she went further, instructing Herdlicka to toss in packets of Sweet'N Low, flatware, lamps. And also the silver bowl. She was breaking down the set of her life.

Stritch's niece Midge Moran, who was now a real estate broker, found her a condo that was clean and spacious, across from Birmingham's Booth Park. It was even in a building called the Dakota, like the famous Upper West Side building.

But "this is not New York," said her new neighbor Kim Hagood. "It's beautiful and we have Park Avenue–level apartments, but this is not New York. It's slow."

Stritch's caretakers, found by her nephew Chris Bolton, had little experience with her personality type. Most of them had never seen a Broadway show, much less a Broadway actress. "I'm dying here," Stritch joked to the actress Holland Taylor when she called to check in. Stritch told Hekker she'd made a big mistake by moving, but she had become too frail to pack up again. Hal Prince, who was considering moving with his wife into the Carlyle, and Sondheim wrote notes of reassurance.

Meanwhile, Stritch and Hagood were becoming good friends. Her new neighbor's daughter was about to move to New York to work in the fashion industry. Also, Hagood was Catholic. She had been trained in mortuary science and felt comfortable with life's final stages.

Stritch had sounded brave when interviewed by a *New York Times* video producer about the End. "I look at death as—my god, what an experience, what an adventure it's going to be," she said. "And if it's nothing, are you kidding? There will be no more interviews about nothing! It's a line in Richard Rodgers's song! 'Nothing comes from nothing / nothing ever could . . .' That's the greatest explanation of an afterlife that I ever heard. Because if it's nothing, it's *nothing*. But I don't think so . . ."

Privately, she was having panic attacks. "I've left my life in New York," she told Hagood. "This place is no New York. This is not what I'm used to. I've left the people who love and adore me." When they went out for walks, at least one person would recognize her, but it was nothing like being constantly hailed in her promenades down Madison Avenue.

Bernadette Peters visited, as did Bowman, and Keyes, and Karasawa. Stritch was also reaching out to those from her deep past, like Kirk Douglas, by now in his late nineties.

"I hope to see you before I turn one hundred," he wrote.

Stritch sent him a poster advertising the documentary, in which her long legs were planted firmly past shoulder width as she gazed into a hand mirror.

Douglas wrote back approvingly that he planned to hang it over his TV. "I remember that girl!" "That" was underlined several times.

She followed up with a screener of *Shoot Me*, which Douglas enjoyed. "Tell me, what are you doing now?" he wondered. "Raising pigs or chickens?"

Charmed by their correspondence, Hagood had printed Stritch stationery with her married name on it. "You are a true romanticist and you are letting me know about it. How good can that be? I truly love you and you do not know how often I think about you," wrote Mrs. Elaine Bay.

As she weakened, Stritch continued to give advice. "When I put my daughter on the plane to go to New York, I was like, 'She's gone, I don't know what I'm going to do,'" Hagood said. "She said, 'What do you mean you don't know what you're going to do? Get a life! Let her go!'"

She found Stritch a rescue dog, a dachshund named Marshall. Now more than ever, the actress needed company; she was terrified of dying alone. "Audiences are not strangers to me. They're the best friends I have in my life," she had said to someone, somewhere, a quote that would be amplified by Lin-Manuel Miranda, the creator of the 2015 blockbuster musical *Hamilton*, and printed on laminated inspirational posters. But now the audiences were dissipating, though she managed one more concert with Bowman in Detroit. "Send In the Clowns" was the final song she performed for paying customers.

After that, Stritch's drinking, which she'd called "such a warm embrace" in Karasawa's documentary, increased. Fiji water bottles were filled with cosmopolitans.

On New Year's Eve of 2014, Stritch looked pale and off. Hagood summoned her doctor for a home visit and test results turned up an extremely low red blood cell count requiring, they said, an immediate transfusion.

Stritch, once so willing to hand herself over to medical authorities, panicked. "I'm not going to the hospital!" The ambulance came.

Hagood stayed with her for the procedure. "And at midnight these beautiful fireworks go off. And so she and I sit in the bed and we're holding hands and the fireworks, and so everything's good." But the next morning, an endoscopy found internal bleeding and advanced stomach cancer. It fell to Hagood to deliver this news. Stritch's blue eyes "got as big as saucers," she said.

A caretaker, Diana, ran from the room screaming.

"Honey, come back, come back—no, it's okay," Stritch called.

She sat there accepting Hagood's arms around her.

"I guess I'm gonna die," she said.

"Maybe eventually you are going to die, but there's probably some things we can do and we'll figure it out," Hagood said. "I'll be there. I'm going to be here with you. I will not leave you. Whatever you go through I'm here."

"Honey, you promise?"

"I promise."

Somehow Stritch and Hagood managed to travel to New York City one more time, for the premiere of *Shoot Me*, staying at the Lotos Club. She appeared on *Today with Kathie Lee & Hoda* and casually, cheerfully, somewhat nonsensically said the word "fuck."

"Oh dear! Oh dear!" Kathie Lee Gifford said.

The incident was received with titters, as further evidence of Stritch's now legendary audacity, but she was probably addled by pain medication of one kind or another; unbeknownst to everyone, including herself, she had a hairline fracture in one rib. Liz Smith went early to the *Shoot Me* screening to get a seat. "It was a mess, and I didn't see her," she said. "Finally, after a lot of people getting up and speaking alfresco, Elaine's voice rang out and she got up from wherever she was and made a kind of pitiful speech that I wish she hadn't made, where she talked about falling, and it was sad." Smith decided to leave quietly and call her friend on the morrow.

After Stritch returned to Birmingham, she had successful surgery on her stomach, but alcohol withdrawal necessitated over a week in the hospital's intensive care unit. Her nieces and nephews, and their children, began to visit more frequently once she returned to the condo, and two more caretakers were hired, so that she would have round-the-clock medical attention. Karasawa was particularly attentive.

Stritch watched the Turner Classic Movies channel often—"She had opinions about all the movies," Hagood said—and slept a lot, with Marshall beside her. She had never eaten much, but soon she couldn't be tempted into anything but a few bites of soup.

Hospice was called, though Stritch was still rising from her bed and striding around the apartment on occasion. On the night of July 16, 2014, however, the anniversary of her parents' marriage, her breathing became irregular. She seemed fine in the morning, so Hagood said "I love you" and went to the gym. When she returned, something had changed. Stritch opened her eyes again, more sleepily this time, and looked at her neighbor with a tiny smile. Hagood noticed that her feet were a little discolored, got onto the bed, and took Stritch in her arms.

"We love you, it's okay, I'm here, it's okay."

Stritch's eyes had closed. She was clearly fading.

Still, Hagood said, "I have to tell you, when she took her last breath, I was shocked. I was completely flabbergasted."

EPILOGUE

When the worst that can happen happens," Jean Kerr wrote in *The Snake Has All the Lines*, "it is even possible to be jaunty in the ashes." So it was with Stritch's death, which made headlines in newspapers across the country, including the front page of *The New York Times*, which anointed her "Broadway's Enduring Dame." "She got the obituary of a head of state," Greg Dinella said. And Broadway dimmed its lights in her honor for the traditional minute, which she probably wouldn't have thought quite enough.

She had planned and paid for her funeral years ahead of time: a private affair for about fifty people overseen by a priest who sang "I Feel Pretty." Her headstone, next to John Bay's, revealed her long-fudged birth year, 1925, and then just "Later."

For months afterward, English muffins kept arriving to colleagues and friends. And there were far more generous bequests. Along with rewarding her caretakers and staff members at the Carlyle, Stritch had donated hundreds of thousands of dollars to the Juvenile Diabetes Foundation and the Actors Fund. She had left money that marked both private relationships, like that with Pamela Myers, her costar in *Company*, and public ones, like a $10,000 check to Liz Smith, "to take Barbara Walters out to lunch." Her will, like her other scripts, was a highly revised, heavily annotated document, with laugh lines inserted.

Stritch may have reached "a final resting place," but she was far from gone, her memory continuing to provoke those who knew her and those who would discover her. The affectionate admirers might laugh or shake their heads ruefully, and even those leery tend to concede her wit, resilience, unusual forthrightness, and courage.

It was so much fun, she typed once of her adventures, *so wild, so freeing, so many silly sappy dopey ding-a-ling days and nights full of vodka and bikinis and stingers and sex and sunshine and ocean and Bain de Soleil and late dinners and late nights and night calls one after the other and sunrises and hangovers (not me) and Bloody Marys . . .*

For Dorothy from Kansas there was no place like home, but for Stritch home was no place, except when she alighted on the stage. "Honest to god, when I got into a play—even a musical," she said, "that was where I lived."

NOTES

ABBREVIATIONS USED IN THE NOTES

ESAL: *Elaine Stritch: At Liberty*, written with John Lahr. Versions consulted include bound typescript dated May 19, 2001, furnished by William Berlind; Broadway typescript dated February 2, 2002, is held at Billy Rose Theatre Division, the New York Public Library for the Performing Arts, New York City

ESP: Elaine Stritch Papers, 1925–2012, Billy Rose Theatre Division, the New York Public Library for the Performing Arts, New York City

GFP: George Furth Papers, 1932–2008, Billy Rose Theatre Division of the New York Public Library for the Performing Arts, New York City

HPP: Harold Prince Papers, 1954–1999, Billy Rose Theatre Division of the New York Public Library for the Performing Arts, New York City

JWKP: Jean and Walter Kerr Papers, c. 1920–1993, State Historical Society of Wisconsin, Madison, Wisconsin

LGJL: Transcripts of interviews conducted by Larry Grossman for the show that would become *Elaine Stritch: At Liberty*, in the John Lahr Collection, Howard Gotlieb Archival Research Center, Boston University, Boston

LHP: Leland Hayward Papers, 1920–1995, Billy Rose Theatre Division, the New York Public Library for the Performing Arts, New York City

LSP: Liz Smith Papers, 1934–2016, Briscoe Center for American History, Austin, Texas

NCC: Noël Coward Collection, University of Birmingham, Cadbury Research Library, Special Collections, Birmingham, England

NCR: Noël Coward Papers at the Noël Coward Room, Alan Brodie Representation Ltd., London, England

SAS: Elaine Stritch Room, Stella Adler School for Acting, New York City

PROLOGUE

4 *He had a respiratory infection*: Interview with Stephen Sondheim.

4 *"I don't know if I really have"*: LGJL.

5 *"shifting gears without the clutch"*: John Stark, "Alone in the September of Her Years, Elaine Stritch Beats Booze to Score a Comeback in a Woody Allen Drama," *People*, January 11, 1988.

5 *"You were a shining star"*: Interview with Clay and Elaine Kelly.

5 *Judy Garland's famous "Get Happy" sequence*: Interview with Vincent Roppatte.

6 *"phony" and "a shuck"*: Jeanne Miller, "Elaine Stritch on the 'Sickest Place in the World,'" *San Francisco Examiner*, September 20, 1971.

1. "THANKS FOR EVERYTHING"

9 *February 2, 1925*: Birth certificate, ESP.

9 *quickly encouraged bootleggers*: Larry Engelmann, *Intemperance: The Lost War Against Liquor* (New York: Free Press, 1979), 51.

9 *oft mispronounced "Job"*: Twelfth Census of the United States, Clark County, Ohio, June 1, 1900; city directory, Springfield, Ohio, 1912, www.ancestry.com.

10 *tires, gas masks*: B.F. Goodrich Company Records (1868–1990), University of Akron Libraries Archival Services.

10 *"he was all legs"*: Interview with Sally Hanley.

10 *seminal gossip columnist*: Walter Winchell, "On Broadway," *Orlando Evening Star*, April 16, 1947.

10 *"When you have a lot of relations"*: LGJL.

10 *"Elaine, that's my chair"*: Carol Kramer, "Elaine Good Company, Still Frieda Fun," *Chicago Tribune*, June 14, 1970.

10 *George's youngest sister*: Interview with Midge Moran.

10–11 *George worked for a textile mill*: Interview with Frank Moran, Jr.; Thirteenth Census of the United States, Springfield Township, 1910; World War I draft registration card, Springfield, Ohio, National Archives and Record Administration, June 4, 1917.

11 *A childhood friend of George*: Anthony Slide, *The Encyclopedia of Vaudeville* (Jackson: University Press of Mississippi, 2012), 100–101; and Frank Cullen, *Vaudeville Old and New: An Encyclopedia of Variety Performers in America* (New York: Routledge, 2008), 231–32.

12 *"a private room for ladies"*: Robert Wahls, "Footlight," New York *Daily News*, May 28, 1967.

12 *"He'd sit up till the last customer"*: Dorothy Kilgallen, "The Voice of Broadway," *Scranton Times*, May 27, 1955.

12 *Louis's wife, Sarah*: Interview with Lorelei Villarosa (wife of John M. Bolton).

12 *Mildred had neither need*: Yearbook, College of St. Mary's of the Springs, Columbus, Ohio, 1911–1912, *U.S School Yearbooks, 1900–1990*, www.ancestry.com.

13 *Mildred was the only young lady*: Interview with Midge Moran.

14 *The family lived in a series*: Interview with Chris Bolton.

14 *But the clerk botched*: ES birth certificate, ESP; George Stritch to Department of Health, State of Michigan, November 28, 1925, ESP.

14 *"When Elaine was born"*: Interview with Georgene Moran, ES's great-niece.

14 *a modest house at 2250 Tuxedo Street*: Fifteenth Census of the United States, Precinct 33, Detroit, Wayne County, Michigan, 1930.

14 *"They'd be talking"*: Interview with Elaine Kelly.

14 *At age five*: LGJL.

15 *The old vaudeville houses*: Dan Austin and Sean Doerr, *Lost Detroit: Stories Behind the Motor City's Majestic Ruins* (Charleston, S.C.: The History Press, 2010); see also www.historicdetroit.org.

15 *Along with many of his peers*: Interview with Bolton; Sixteenth Census of the United States, Ward 2, Detroit City, 1940.

15 *"Eighteen plus twenty-one"*: George Bulanda, interview with ES, April 2014, www.hourdetroit.com.

15 *Rudy and the peppier Biff*: Interview with Marianna Sterr.

16 *Net sales in the first six months*: "B.F. Goodrich Sales Higher," *Pittsburgh Press*, August 7, 1930.

16 *"My father was a self-made man"*: LGJL.

17 *"It was her way of supposing"*: Julie Keyes, "Behind the Scenes with Elaine Stritch," *Fairweather*, Summer 2013.

18 *George had concealed*: Interview with Clay Kelly.

18 *she kept a watchful eye*: Interview with Hanley.

19 *Mildred removed her wedding ring*: Interview with Midge Moran.

19 *"She was a very straightforward, glamorous woman"*: LGJL.

19 *"And I watched my father with him"*: Cleveland Amory, "They Say," *Minneapolis Star-Tribune*, September 8, 1968.

19 *"That afternoon I experienced"*: Unpublished notes on "Talent," ESP.

20 *"Elaine would get up and sing"*: Interview with Diane Wenger Wilson.

20 *"in a lovely suit of white trimmed with red"*: "'Ho-Hum,' Says Hills Colony in Post-Holiday Doldrums," *Detroit Free Press*, July 8, 1934.

20 *rubber bathing costumes*: Interview with Sterr.

21 *"give the old tootsies a pat"*: Ann Loges, "The Chatterbox," *Detroit Free Press*, October 15, 1939.

22 *"a couple of super-zanies"*: Helen C. Bower, "The Theater," *Detroit Free Press*, September 26, 1927.

22 *"If that's Elaine Stritch"*: Bulanda interview with ES.

22 *"Count on being regaled"*: Karl Krug, "The Show Stops," *Pittsburgh Post-Gazette*, August 24, 1931.

23 *"Remember how the girls"*: Len G. Shaw, "Bobby Clark, Now Trouping Alone, Recalls Early Days with McCullough," *Detroit Free Press*, April 18, 1937.

23 *"As a kid I was not particularly pretty"*: "She's a Million Laughs," *Daily Reporter* (Dover, Ohio), April 8, 1961.

23 *"because I was taller"*: LGJL.

24 *"a kind of unbelievable excitement"*: Unpublished notes on "Talent," ESP.

25 *demystifying alcohol in the home*: Marian Mays Martin, "Drinking By Parents Invites Their Children to Imbibe Too," *The Salinas Californian*, August 27–28, 1938.

25 *"seemed so elegant, so feminine"*: ESAL.

26 *"a vision in white net"*: "Who Goes Where: By a Passerby," *Detroit Free Press*, January 1, 1939.

26 *"Dance is this Friday"*: ES to Diane Wenger, January 24, 1941, ESP.

27 *"tinkling away for all its worth"*: "In Detroit Society: Music Box Gives Out Glad News," *Detroit Free Press*, December 23, 1940.

27 *Recently photographed dancing*: "That Fast-Stepping Lad at Right Is Cotton Price," *Detroit Free Press*, November 19, 1940.

27 *"Lately it seems"*: ES to Diane Wenger, March 8, 1941, ESP.

27 *"No kidding Diane"*: ES to Diane Wenger, May 3, 1941, ESP.

27 *"All of those gals"*: ES to Diane Wenger, March 31, 1941, ESP.

28 *"I'm so in love I could die"*: Ellen Brennan to ES, July 16, 1942.

28 *"Bill said he thought"*: Marianna Sterr to ES, October 13, 1941, ESP.

28 *"It scared me to death"*: Interview with Sterr.

28 *"When people spend a long time"*: Datebook pages, October 20–23, 1942, box 1, ESP.

28 *"so bad that I have quit drinking"*: Jack from Camp McCoy to ES, March 23, 1943, ESP.

29 *Her final marks*: Convent of the Sacred Heart, school records, box 1, ESP.

29 *"I passed Caesar on red wine"*: *The Dick Cavett Show*, November 9, 1979.

29 *"Take back the watch"*: Interview with Sterr.

29 *"I wanted to split"*: Thomas Blakely, "*Company* Gives Backers a Shot in Arm," *Pittsburgh Press*, August 16, 1970.

29 *"I was okay"*: Douglas MacKaye Harrington, interview with ES, 2010, www.hamptons.com.

30 *"One life wasn't enough for me"*: Miller, "Elaine Stritch on the 'Sickest Place in the World,'" *San Francisco Examiner*, September 20, 1971.

30 *"I wasn't too hung up on myself"*: Eddie Shapiro, *Nothing Like a Dame: Conversations with the Great Women of Musical Theater* (Oxford University Press, 2014), 6.

2. A HELLUVA TOWN

32 *Aside from the omnipresent nuns*: Author's visit to the building.

33 *"Excited and nervous"*: "As Told by Elaine Stritch Truth Is Funnier Than TV," *Detroit Free Press*, December 4, 1960.

34 *"He never partook"*: Judith Malina, *The Piscator Notebook* (London: Routledge, 2012), 11.

34 *"Piscator would get up"*: LGJL.

34 *"I was a girl raised at the convent"*: Ibid.

35 *"I was so taken with Marlon"*: Ibid.

35 *"Brando was not just an actor"*: Joyce Johnson, "Exit, Followed by Brando as a Bear," *The Telegraph* (London), February 5, 2006.

36 *"Whatever the normal emotion"*: LGJL.

36 *"Marlon reserves his favor"*: Anna Kashfi Brando and E. P. Stein, *Brando for Breakfast* (New York: Crown, 1979), 3.

36 *"the only thing that was foreign"*: LGJL.

36 *"every Saturday night"*: Earl Wilson, "It Happened Last Night," *Reno Evening Gazette*, December 10, 1960.

37 *"a tall redhead"*: Memoir notes, ESP.

37 *"two things: silence and distance"*: Ibid.

37 *remembers her describing being fully clothed*: Interview with George C. Wolfe.

38 *paddled wholesomely*: "Summer Showhouse," *Independent Record* (Helena, Mont.), August 19, 1945.

38 *"with bells on my fingers"*: LGJL.

38 *"It was a wonderful compliment"*: Ibid.

39 *"There were all these quiet songs"*: Ibid.

39 *"There was no light fare"*: Harry Belafonte, *My Song* (New York: Alfred A. Knopf, 2011), 68.

39 *"I had no idea what I was doing"*: LGJL.

40 *"The plot was"*: Alex Witchel, "The World According to Elaine Stritch," *New York Times*, April 11, 1993.

40 *"Her development in art"*: Erwin Piscator to Duchesne School, undated, SAS.

40 *"Within hiking distance"*: "Hotel For Women: New York City's Barbizon Hotel Is a No-Man's Land of Beauty and Talent," *Detroit Free Press*, April 18, 1948.

40–41 *"swung like Tarzan"*: "As Told By Elaine Stritch," *Detroit Free Press*, December 4, 1960.

41 *Elaine tried waiting tables*: Eddie Shapiro, *Nothing Like a Dame: Conversations With the Great Women of Musical Theater* (Oxford University Press), 6.

41 *"find a beautiful girl who can act"*: Annie Oakley, "The Theatre and Its People," *Windsor (Ontario) Star*, April 9, 1946.

42 *"He scared me to death"*: ES, notes for unpublished memoir, ESP.

43 *"I fooled them all"*: Ibid.

43 *"I thought Elaine was superb"*: Kirk Douglas to author, September 11, 2015.

43 *"I would have welcomed a tennis racket"*: ES, memoir notes.

44 *"You know, Stritch"*: Liz Smith, "Scoop," *Indiana (Pa.) Gazette*, March 14, 1998.

44 *"I was so anxious to brighten up"*: ES, memoir notes.

45 *"Your daughter is a fucking winner"*: LGJL.

46 *"the poor man's Sardi's"*: "The Press: Drugstore Paper," *Time*, March 9, 1942.

46 *"I didn't hang out with the gang"*: ES interview in documentary *Broadway: The Golden Age, by the Legends Who Were There* (2003), Rick McKay, director.

46 *"I'd rather talk to someone"*: ES, memoir notes.

46 *"tall, blonde, lovely"*: Walter Winchell, "On Broadway," *Courier-Post* (Camden, N.J.), January 12, 1948.

46 *"charmer"*: Walter Winchell, "On Broadway," *Daily Times-News* (Burlington, N.C.), December 22, 1947.

47 *"Watch for a girl named Elaine Stritch"*: Dorothy Kilgallen, "The Voice of Broadway," *Record-Argus* (Greenville, Pa.), November 15, 1947.

47 *"I felt, 'Well, I've had a lot of training'"*: LGJL.

47 *"a tongue-in-cheek commentary"*: "Show Stopper," *Cincinnati Enquirer*, February 8, 1948.

48 *"SHE IS TRULY SPLENDID"*: Virginia Perry to George and Mildred Stritch, December 19, 1947, ESP.

48 *"The Hartmans are the personification"*: Lewis Nichols, "About Two in the Wings," *New York Times*, January 11, 1948.

48 *"twosoming at the midnite movies"*: Walter Winchell, "On Broadway," *Tampa Times*, April 20, 1948.

48 *"We did most of our talking"*: Interview with Tony Monaco, né Tommy Morton.

48 *"WILL ARRIVE BY CAR"*: ES to George and Mildred Stritch, September 11, 1948, ESP.

49 *"I wasn't anybody who would have loved"*: Interview with Harold Prince.

49 *"As soon as I hit Broadway"*: LGJL.

49 *"I was really living"*: ES, memoir notes.

50 *"It's nice to have something lasting"*: "People: The Way Things Are," *Time*, February 23, 1948.

50 *"We were in our jammies"*: Claudia Cragg (daughter of Diane Hart), interview with ES, 2009; provided courtesy of Claudia Cragg.

50 *"They were sincerely backdoor Johnnies"*: Interview with Cragg.

50 *"trifling"*: Brooks Atkinson, "At the Theatre," *New York Times*, October 5, 1949.

3. "HEAVENS, THAT GIRL AGAIN!"

51 *"with the lingering, graceful gestures"*: George H. Combs, Jr., "It's All New York," *San Bernardino Sun*, July 12, 1951.

52 *"I never wore a bra in rehearsal"*: LGJL.

52 *"Miss Elaine Stritch"*: Whitney Bolton, "Looking Sideways," *Daily Press* (Newport News, Va.), February 12, 1952.

53 *a trumpet, penny whistle, and Wurlitzer*: Walter Kerr, "Merman: A Kid Who Wins All the Marbles," *New York Times*, April 12, 1970.

53 *"Anyone can get Marilyn"*: "Broadway: 10% For Glo," *Time*, January 26, 1959.

53 *"I have a terrible desire"*: Clarissa Start, "Likes Her Role as Madam Ambassador," *St. Louis Post-Dispatch*, October 16, 1952.

53 *"Elaine Stritch reminds me"*: "Ethel Merman to Keep Appendix," *Times Recorder* (Zanesville, Ohio), August 6, 1954.

54 *"Now I wish somebody"*: E. V. Durling, "On the Side," *San Francisco Examiner*, March 27, 1952.

54 *"Merman couldn't keep up"*: LGJL.

54 *"If you want to do musical comedy"*: Michael Riedel, interview with ES, *Theater Talk*, December 16, 1999.

54 *"Boys, as of right now"*: Brian Kellow, *Ethel Merman* (New York: Viking, 2007), 130.

55 *"You don't have to stay at the theater"*: LGJL

55 *After the ban was lifted*: Steve Cohen, "When the Music Stopped: How the ASCAP vs. BMI War Changed an Industry," www.totaltheater.com, December 2002.

55 *mistook her for another actress*: L. L. Stevenson, "Lights of New York," *Decatur (Ill.) Review*, January 24, 1948.

55–56 *"She had great parties"*: Interview with Helen Gallagher.

56 *she took some forty years*: "Update," Stritch interview with Frances Lear quoted in *Santa Cruz Sentinel*, May 7, 1991.

56 *"the off-again-on-again romance"*: Louella Parsons, "Louella's Movie-Go-'Round," *Albuquerque Journal*, November 20, 1951.

56 *"Take the line 'Walter Lippmann'"*: Charles Witbeck, "Brassy-Voiced Elaine to Try TV," *Press & Sun-Bulletin* (Binghamton, N.Y.), September 28, 1960.

57 *After Mass on Christmas Day*: Dorothy Kilgallen, "Snow and Ice Fail to Stop Elaine Stritch," *Muncie (Ind.) Evening Press*, December 31, 1952.

57 *"My understudy was in the wings"*: LGJL.

58 *And the few inches of snow*: "Third Storm Sweeps State, Tie-Ups Few," *Hartford Courant*, December 26, 1951.

58 *"ONE SCENE ONE SONG ONE SMASH"*: Mickey Rooney to ES, March 22, 1952, ESP.

58 *"She doesn't remove so much"*: Mark Baron, "*Pal Joey* Still Fresh, Charming," Associated Press, January 13, 1952.

58 *"Elaine Stritch, a comedienne hitherto"*: Wolcott Gibbs, "The Theatre: Fine Low Fun," *The New Yorker*, January 12, 1952.

58 *"Elaine Stritch winds up for a knockout"*: Walter Kerr, "The Theatre," *New York Herald Tribune*, January 4, 1952.

58 *"Dick was a little afraid of me"*: Michael Riedel, "Stritch Over Fifty Years from Understudy to Award-Winning Broadway Actress," New York *Daily News*, May 19, 1996.

59 *"Would you leave HIM"*: Leonard Lyons, "The Gossip of the Nation," *Philadelphia Inquirer*, February 7, 1952.

59 *the hotel tycoon Conrad Hilton*: Dorothy Kilgallen, "The Voice of Broadway," *Gazette* (Montreal, Canada), February 8, 1952.

59 *"asked me to marry him in front of St. Pat's"*: LGJL.

59 *"Ethel Merman's wheezing"*: Earl Wilson, "It Happened Last Night: Merman Disappoints Us—She Doesn't Collapse," *Delta Democrat-Times* (Greenville, Miss.), February 17, 1952.

59 *"Do you feel that MADAM"*: Leland Hayward to Leo Freedman, box 7, LHP.

59 *"Audiences more and more"*: Leo Freedman to Leland Hayward letter marked Friday, LHP.

60 *Hayward also solicited*: Telegrams between Leland Hayward and Edwin Lester, February 1952, LHP.

61 *"Elaine tried to get me to buy"*: Interview with Gallagher.

61 *"Oh yes, I went through the heavy veils stage"*: LGJL.

61 *"The problem is, Stritch"*: Interview with Frank Moran, Jr.

62 *She got her salary up to $1000*: Gloria Safier to Herman Bernstein of Leland Hayward Ltd., February 15, 1952, LHP.

62 *"the most dynamic, the most electric"*: Evelyn Peyton Gordon, "It's Been Many a Year Since Such a Gala Opening," *Washington Daily News*, May 6, 1952.

62 *Noting that Smith had a personal valet*: Herman Bernstein to Harry Essex, May 20, 1952.

63 *"WE WHO ARE ABOUT TO DIE SALUTE YOU"*: ES to Ethel Merman, as reported in Leonard Lyons, "Broadway Medley," *Philadelphia Inquirer*, May 13, 1952, ESP.

63 *"rosary beads and a double Courvoisier"*: LGJL.

63 *"I had quite a crush on her"*: Interview with Russell Nype.

63 *calling her "hammy"*: Letter from "Mrs. Ken" (full name unknown) sent by George Abbott to Leland Hayward, November 13, 1952, LHP.

64 *"Stop it! Right now"*: LGJL.

64 *"Is that coffee?"*: ESAL.

64 *"Every glass she poured me"*: LGJL.

64 *the older woman admitted*: Ethel Merman and George Eells, *Merman* (New York: Simon & Schuster, 1978), 190.

64 *"Kent was a gourmet"*: LGJL.

65 *"We went every place by train"*: Ibid.

65 *"I am supposed to ask you for OUR STAR"*: Harry Essex to Bernstein, January 12, 1953, LHP.

65 *"This life is no place"*: Start, "Likes Her Role as Madam Ambassador."

66 *"Miss Stritch, though gifted"*: Albert Goldberg, "*Call Me Madam* Makes Bow to L.A.," *Los Angeles Times*, June 24, 1952.

66 *the air-conditioning in the Imperial*: Douglas Watt, "Sillman Plans 3 New Shows; Lisa Kirk Up for Martin Role," New York *Daily News*, June 30, 1952.

66 *"Nearly all of them"*: Walter Winchell, "On Broadway," *Scrantonian*, June 29, 1952.

66 *"Dear Mr. Hayward"*: ES to Leland Hayward, letter from Biltmore Hotel in Los Angeles, LHP.

67 *"Who complained?"*: Leonard Lyons, "Broadway Medley," *San Mateo Times*, December 12, 1956.

67 *Conrad Hilton hosted an early buffet supper*: Invitation for July 29, 1952, ESP; Sheilah Graham, "Hollywood," *Pittsburgh Post-Gazette*, August 6, 1952.

67 *"We're a pair of entertaining boys"*: LGJL.

68 *"She was years too young"*: Interview with Liz Smith.

68 *"Elaine picked up that ball"*: Interview with Chita Rivera.

69 *"Handsome guy"*: Interview with Midge Moran.

69 *"She was just this wild character"*: Interview with Chris Bolton.

69 *"I think at the base of it"*: LGJL.

69 *"on tab"*: Jimmie Fidler, "Inside Hollywood," *News-Star* (Monroe, La.), August 24, 1953.

69 *"the long and serious romance"*: Dorothy Kilgallen, "Broadway Bulletin Board," *Scranton Times*, March 25, 1954.

69 *"There are two big fears"*: Leonard Lyons, "Elaine Stritch Has Two Big Fears," "Broadway Medley," *San Mateo Times*, June 24, 1953.

70 *"A woman walked out onstage"*: Interview with Dick Cavett.

70 *"flat-footed revival"*: "The Stage: Some Varieties of Comic Experience," undated, unsigned newspaper clipping in ESP.

70 *"Elaine Stritch deserves a paragraph"*: Walter Kerr, "Theater: On Your Toes," *New York Herald Tribune*, October 12, 1954.

70 *"Miss Stritch's non-expressive vigor"*: Harold Clurman, "Theater," undated clipping in ESP.

71 *invited on* The Ed Sullivan Show: ESAL; *The Ed Sullivan Show*, episode 8.9, November 14, 1954.

71 *"I almost died"*: LGJL.

72 *"How do you do?"*: George Eells, *Final Gig: The Man Behind the Murder* (San Diego: Harcourt, 1991), 107.

72 *Stritch walked into her bathroom*: LGJL.

72 *"I'm going to marry that girl"*: Eells, *Final Gig*, 108.

73 *"Think carefully"*: Ibid., 110.

73 *"Mother fell in love with Gig Young"*: LGJL.

73 *"It was so full of catechisms"*: Ibid.

74 *"She lost it Christmas shopping"*: Louella Parsons, "Hollywood," *Philadelphia Inquirer*, December 22, 1954.

74 *"I did not know how to drive"*: LGJL.

75 *"Who's Harold Clurman?"*: Ibid.

75 *"I remember her coming down"*: Interview with Midge Moran.

4. LEADING MEN

77 *Stritch was sitting*: LGJL.

77 *"young blonde girl of about twenty"*: William Inge, *Bus Stop* (New York: Bantam, 1955), 11.

78 *"Weighs like a hit"*: Leonard Lyons, "A Peculiar Play Pay-Off," *Quad-City Times* (Davenport, Iowa), January 27, 1955.

78 *"It was glorious"*: LGJL.

79 *"Why not like an Aronson?"*: Harold Clurman, *On Directing* (New York: Simon & Schuster, 1997), 58.

79 *"I just felt that I lived upstairs"*: LGJL.

79 *"At the first run-through"*: Celia McGee, "Backstage at a Hit: Memories Are Made of These," *New York Times*, February 18, 1996.

79 *"I drank so much beer"*: LGJL.

79 *"I have a very expressive body"*: Ibid.

80 *"designed for the at-home entertainment"*: Norman L. Johnson, "Publishers Entering Record Field Put the Emphasis on Show Business," *Courier-Journal* (Louisville, Ky.), February 22, 1956.

80 *"becoming a shadow"*: LGJL.

80 *"amicable cancellation"*: Earl Wilson, "The Midnight Earl," *Rapid City Journal*, March 28, 1955.

81 *"that kind of surly, sexy, Italiano"*: LGJL.

82 *"hand-holding"*: Walter Winchell, "The New York Scene; Man About Town," *Republican-Herald* (Pottsville, Pa.), January 16, 1956.

82 *"There was something very warm"*: LGJL.

82 *"What a moron"*: Ann Guerin, "If Ben Gazzara Gets Hung Up, the Analyst Is Always In: It's His Wife, Janice Rule," *People*, June 28, 1977.

82 *"With the Ben Gazzaras divorcing"*: Dorothy Kilgallen, "The Voice of Broadway," *Star* (Oneonta, N.Y.), February 7, 1956.

82 *"You stay away from my Benny"*: LGJL.

83 *"just said to me the other night"*: Ibid.

83 *"The real reason was that he was not as tall"*: Ibid.

83 *"The part was so terrible"*: Helen Eisenbach, "Seven-Inning Stritch," *New York*, June 12, 1995, 43.

83 With some excitement: Wayne Warga, "Elaine Stritch Creates Her Own Stir In Company," *Los Angeles Times*, May 16, 1971.

84 *"Up we go, up the few steps"*: LGJL.

84 Burt Lancaster: Ibid.

84 *"Well, Mother, I got a new boyfriend"*: Ibid.

84 *"I'm twenty-nine, really twenty-nine"*: Leonard Lyons, "The Lyons Den," *Des Moines Tribune*, September 25, 1955.

84 a psychiatrist named Dr. Weber: Memoir notes, ESP.

84 *"Not only am I late. I lie"*: ES, memoir notes.

85 *"We could have given forty awards"*: Arthur Gelb, "Popularizing the Tony Awards," *New York Times*, April 1, 1956.

86 *"You find you can't prove your worth"*: ES to George and Mildred Stritch, undated letter, c. 1956 (mentions being 31), ESP.

86 *"Truth of the matter is"*: Interview with Frank Moran, Jr.

87 he did want more yard space: Interview with Chris Bolton.

87 invested in four adjacent lots: Interviews with Frank Moran, Jr., and Midge Moran.

87 *"Ma Mil would take a bath every day"*: Interview with Sally Hanley.

87 *"She was crazy about Ben"*: Interview with Patricia Bosworth.

88 *"AND THEN SHOVE THEM UP YOUR ASS"*: A. E. Hotchner, *The Good Life According to Hemingway* (New York: Ecco, 2008), 60.

89 *"jerking him to his knees"*: Interview with Liz Smith.

89 *"Dearest Mother and Daddy"*: ES to George and Mildred Stritch, May 30, 1957, ESP.

90 *"Rock Hudson took me to lunch again"*: ES to George and Mildred Stritch, May 14, 1957, ESP.

90 *"But I didn't tell Elaine"*: Interview with Smith.

91 *"Had a dinner date with Rock"*: ES to George and Mildred Stritch, n.d, ESP.

92 *Using joking, affectionate signatures*: Liz Smith to ES, June 12 and 13, July 2, 1957, ESP.

93 *"I'm not promising"* and further quoted letters: ES to George and Mildred Stritch, mostly undated, ESP.

93 *"It was an interesting way"*: LGJL.

93 *"Hello, Elaine"*: Ibid.

93 *"Whappo"*: Ibid.

94 *"For Elaine, with thanks for laughs"*: Inscribed copy of *A Farewell to Arms* script; ESP.

94 *"I SINCERELY AND STRONGLY BELIEVE"*: David Selznick to ES, December 5, 1957, ESP.

94 *But Audrey Hepburn*: "Film Realism Too Much for Star, Lawyer," Associated Press, December 20, 1957.

94 *"A sense of deficiency and inconsequence"*: Bosley Crowther, "David Selznick's *A Farewell to Arms*; Hemingway Story Is New Film at Roxy; Rock Hudson, Jennifer Jones Are Starred," *New York Times*, January 25, 1958.

94 *"After changing my outfit"*: ESAL.

95 *"If I don't get the guy at the end"*: Earl Wilson, "It Happened Last Night," *Daily Gazette* (Janesville, Wisc.), November 22, 1958.

95–96 *"visited all the dives in Havana"*: LGJL.

96 *"I want to try the Actors Studio"*: Interview with Sharon Farrell.

96 *"You know, today she would be a big, huge star"*: Ibid.

96 *"There is this desire"*: LGJL.

5. "I NEVER KNOW WHEN TO SAY WHEN"

97 *"An actor either is there"*: Rome Neal, "The Thrill of Performing," January 22, 2004, https://www.cbsnews.com/news/the-thrill-of-performing.

97 *"gaggle of fast-living, fun-loving geese . . . was representing"*: Christopher Plummer, *In Spite of Myself: A Memoir* (New York: Vintage, 2012), 129, 291.

98 *"Perhaps the tinkling glass"*: Dorothy Kilgallen, "The Voice of Broadway," *Republican-Herald* (Pottsville, Pa.), February 4, 1957.

98 *"I could go to Hollywood tomorrow"*: Dick Kleiner, "The Marquee," *La Crosse (Wisc.) Tribune*, April 11, 1958.

98 *Stritch would mine the song*: ESAL.

99 *"The radioactive fallout from* West Side Story*"*: Walter Kerr, "West Side Story," *New York Herald Tribune*, September 27, 1957.

99 *"It is impossible to look to a critic"*: Arthur Laurents to Walter Kerr, October 6, 1957, JWKP.

99 *"her dream part"*: Kleiner, "The Marquee."

99 *"neo-gingerbread"*: Denis Hart, "Wittiest Woman in America," *The Guardian* (Manchester, Eng.), September 13, 1961.

100 *"Something was eating him"*: Susan Black, "Bon Appetit, or What's Eating Walter Kerr?" *The New Yorker*, December 24, 1960.

100 *though his original printed review*: Walter Kerr, "The Theaters: I Am a Camera," *New York Herald Tribune*, December 31, 1951.

100 *"Ever since I was first exposed"*: Dorothy Roe, "Husband-Wife Team Works Together on Broadway Hits, Child Rearing," *Eagle* (Bryan, Tex.), September 6, 1954.

101 *the editor Clay Felker*: Memo from "DB" to Carl D. Brandt, August 6, 1959, JWKP.

101 *"Ben asks only that the title"*: Leonard Lyons, "The Lyons Den," *Morning Call* (Allentown, Pa.), January 6, 1958.

101 *"You will not need luck with* Goldilocks*"*: Ben Gazzara to Jean and Walter Kerr, June 26, 1958, JWKP.

101 *"Composing at the mercy"*: Agnes de Mille to Walter Kerr, April 8, 1957, JWKP.

102 *"a very businesslike operation"*: Interview with Russell Nype.

102 *"borne aloft in a giant slice of silvery moon"*: Jean Kerr, typed draft of essay, "Out of Town with a Show," JWKP.

102 *"Think how it would gladden the hearts"*: Jean Kerr to Jean Kerr, 1958, JWKP.

102 *"We are all waiting with sated breath"*: J. Anderson to Walter Kerr, undated but later marked 1957, JWKP.

102 *"We are working frantically night and day"*: Jean Kerr to Carol Brandt, July 18, 1958, JWKP.

103 *"She was a very difficult person"*: Interview with Pat Stanley.

103 *"Walter gripes and grouses"*: Jean Kerr to Jean Kerr, August 26, 1958, JWKP.

103 *"The audience went out whistling the sets"*: Jean Kerr, "Out of Town with a Show," typed draft, JWKP.

103 *"This big, expensive musical comedy"*: Henry T. Murdock, "Faltering *Goldilocks* Fails to Dim Theater Hopes," *Philadelphia Inquirer*, September 7, 1958.

104 *"OPENED SLOPPY"*: Jean and Walter Kerr to Jean Kerr, September 3, 1958, JWKP.

104 *"She was the only one that knew"*: ES recorded interview with Kevin Kelly, Kevin Kelly Collection, held at the Howard Gotlieb Archival Research Center, Boston University.

105 *"How does an eminent critic"*: Noël Coward, *The Noël Coward Diaries*, ed. Graham Payn and Sheridan Morley (Boston: Little, Brown, 1982), 386.

106 *"I am going to be very, very honest"*: *Theater Talk*, December 16, 1999.

106 *"They say she simply isn't being allowed"*: Kilgallen, "The Voice of Broadway," September 17, 1958.

106 *"*Goldilocks *would be a delight"*: Julius Novick, "Goldilocks (review)," *Harvard Crimson*, September 26, 1958.

106–107 *"Elaine Stritch was quoted"*: Letter from Jean Kerr to Jean Kerr, 1958, JWKP.

107 *"Kitty Carlisle's husband . . . $70,000 worth"*: Burt Boyar, "Best of Broadway," *Philadelphia Inquirer*, October 17, 1958.

107 *"Goldilocks is a bountiful handsome musical comedy"*: Brooks Atkinson, "The Theatre," *New York Times*, October 13, 1958.

108 *"sweet party"*: Coward, *The Noël Coward Diaries*, 390.

108 *"Of course she was very put off"*: Interview with Nype.

109 *"Walter would have to go along with it"*: ES interview with Kevin Kelly.

109 *"the lone, whinnying exception"*: "Children Run Longer Than Plays," *Time*, April 14,
1961.

110 *"The years that I was working there"*: Interview with Joe Allen.

111 *"And Elaine is flying"*: Interview with Sally Hanley.

112 *"I wanted to see Don Ameche"*: Interview with Stephen Sondheim.

112 *"I had never met him before"*: John Bell, "Honest-to-God Talent," *The Sondheim Review*, Fall 2008.

114 *"I started bawling right there"*: LGJL.

114 *"I've been living a situation comedy all my life"*: Marie Torre, "She Tells How to
Adjust to TV Pace," *Democrat and Chronicle* (Rochester, N.Y.), November 1960.

115 *"When a woman drinks"*: Marguerite Duras, *The Lover: Wartime Notebooks; Practi-
calities* (New York: Everyman Library, 2017), viii.

115 *"In comic-strip language"*: Interview with Dick Cavett.

6. "SOMETHING VERY STRANGE"

117 *"a brittle, stylized, insignificant comedy with music"*: Graham Payn, *My Life with Noël
Coward* (New York: Applause Books, 1994), 165.

117 *"the person whose job it is to herd"*: Hugh A. Mulligan, "Noël Coward Launches
Musical—Stem to Stern," Associated Press, August 6, 1961.

118 *"complex about appearing on Broadway"*: Noël Coward, *The Noël Coward Diaries*, ed.
Graham Payn and Sheridan Morley (Boston: Little, Brown, 1985), 464–65.

118 *"like the cavalier with the silver rose"*: William Marchant, *The Privilege of His Company* (Indianapolis: Bobbs-Merrill, 1975), 121.

118 *"I foresee leetle clouds"*: Coward, *The Noël Coward Diaries*, 466.

118 *"episodic opportunities"*: Whitney Bolton, "Noël's Sail Away," *Philadelphia Inquirer*,
July 23, 1961.

118 *"It was a very strange part"*: Interview with Jean Fenn.

118–19 *"A musical of this type should be fun"*: Jack Gaver, "Noël Coward Keeping Busy,"
United Press International, December 31, 1961.

119 *"a house of strange enchantment"*: Noël Coward, *The Noël Coward Reader*, ed. Barry
Day (New York: Vintage, 2011), 504.

119 *"Everybody laughed"*: Interview with Grover Dale.

119 *"Then she shouldn't want co-star billing"*: Leonard Lyons, "The Lyons Den," *Montgomery Advertiser*, April 20, 1961.

120 *"Stritch, as I suspected"*: Coward, *The Noël Coward Diaries*, 475.

120 *"We're going to play a little game"*: Interview with Scott Griffin.

121 *"She'll use only Method actors"*: Walter Winchell, "The Broadway Lights," *Times
Leader* (Wilkes-Barre, Pa.), August 2. 1961.

121 *grubby and lacking in basic stage technique*: Coward, *The Noël Coward Reader*, 503.

121 *"I got nothing but laughs up there"*: Lyons, "The Lyons Den," *Morning Call* (Allentown, Pa.), December 12, 1955.

121 *"You're not supposed to be scarred"*: Whitney Bolton, "Actress, Like a Carpenter, Should Use Tools of Trade," *Valley Morning Star* (Harlingen, Tex.), December 18, 1958.

122 *"Life is a banquet"*: Richard Tyler Jordan, *But Darling, I'm Your Auntie Mame!: The Amazing History of the World's Favorite Madcap Aunt* (New York: Kensington, 2004), xvii.

122 *"I've got loads of dependents"*: Lyons, "The Lyons Den," April 20, 1961.

122 *"Isn't this weather godawful?"*: Interview with Maurice Bernstein.

123 *"Elaine had a lot of style"*: Interview with Fenn.

123 *"to her everlasting credit"*: Coward, *The Noël Coward Diaries*, 477.

123 *"publicity is the breath of life"*: Ibid., 476.

123 *"I loved the show"*: "First Lady Enjoys Noël Coward's New Musical Comedy *Sail Away*," Associated Press, August 18, 1961.

124 *"There's no question about it"*: Coward, *The Noël Coward Diaries*, 478.

124 *"exalted mummery"*: Marchant, *The Privilege of His Company*, 131.

124 *"has turned* Sail Away *into a one-woman show"*: Henry T. Murdock, "The Melody Lingers On," *Philadelphia Inquirer*, September 10, 1961.

124 *"The great voices should remain"*: Marchant, *The Privilege of His Company*, 133.

124 *"I felt bad"*: Interview with Fenn.

124–25 *"When you want to do something"*: LGJL.

125 *"that I almost cried"*: Coward, *The Noël Coward Diaries*, 479.

125 *"He's terribly chic"*: Earl Wilson, "Noel's the Rage of 'Divine' Elaine," *Philadelphia Daily News*, August 1, 1961.

125 *"If you go to the theater with Noël"*: LGJL.

126 *"Maurice, I know it's a ghastly hour"*: Interview with Bernstein.

126 *a dozen teasing telegrams*: Noël Coward to Elaine Stritch, October 2, 1961, ESP.

126 *"Oh no! Twasn't Adlai"*: Earl Wilson, "It Happened Last Night" *Morning News* (Wilmington, Del.), October 10, 1961.

126 *"Beautifully organized hell"*: Coward, *The Noël Coward Diaries*, 480.

126 *"A big, handsome, rakish vessel"*: Howard Taubman, "Noël Coward at the Helm; His *Sail Away* Opens at the Broadhurst," *New York Times*, October 4, 1961.

127 *"The new Noël Coward musical"*: Walter Kerr, "First Night Report: *Sail Away*," *New York Herald Tribune*, October 4, 1961.

127 *"Oh, I guess we missed this time"*: Interview with Joe Allen.

127 *Feeling snubbed and unrecognized*: Harrison Kinney, *James Thurber: His Life and Times* (New York: Henry Holt, 1995), 155.

127 *Enchanted by the show*: Interview with Chris Bolton.

128 *"It received the ecstatic raves"*: Coward, *The Noël Coward Diaries*, 482.

128 *"You must answer instantly"*: Earl Wilson, *Daily Press* (Newport News, Va.), November 27, 1961.

128 *"I was a kid from a small town"*: Interview with Grover Dale.

129 *chalet in Les Avants*: Coward, *The Noël Coward Diaries*, 504.

129 *"their egos have grown inwards"*: Ibid.

129 *"with someone I love"*: NCR.

129 *"The hullaballoo was considerable"*: Coward, *The Noël Coward Diaries*, 504.

129 *"It was crazy"*: Interview with Dale.

130 *"I want you to behave yourself"*: ES interview with Michael Low in the documentary *The Noël Coward Trilogy*, Part 1, 2001.

130 *"got fried and flung four-letter words"*: Coward, *The Noël Coward Diaries*, 507.

130 *"When Miss Stritch is absent"*: Robert Muller, "The Master's New Show Sails In, But Only Just," *London Daily Mail*, June 22, 1962.

130 *"And what about that Stritch girl!"*: Henry Sherek to Noël Coward, July 3, 1962, NCC.

131 *"By the end of the cruise"*: Interview with Dale.

131 *"a blouse from the Nile"*: Ward Morehouse, "Elaine 'Sails Away' With London," *Indianapolis Star*, August 26, 1962.

131 *"YOUR DEAR LITTLE BLONDE DAUGHTER"*: Coward to George and Mildred Stritch, June 26, 1962.

131 *"he told her she was too old"*: Leonard Lyons, "The Lyons Den," *Pittsburgh Press*, September 18, 1962.

132 *"Stritch, with all her talent and vitality"*: Coward, *The Noël Coward Diaries*, 525.

132 *"more or less"*: Elaine Stritch to Noël Coward, February 28, 1963, NCR.

133 *"Love you doll"*: Leonard Lyons, "The Lyons Den," *San Mateo Times*, March 14, 1963.

7. "WHAT A DUMP!"

135 *"'bitchy' and god knows what"*: Elaine Stritch to Noël Coward, March 1963, NCR.

136 *"The nylon curtains I shouldn't think"*: Anne Marie Ponsonby to George Stritch, undated (probably May 1963), ESP.

136 *"His new work, flawed though it is"*: Howard Taubman, "The Theater: Albee's *Who's Afraid*," *New York Times*, October 15, 1962.

136 *"The play at its best communicates"*: Walter Kerr, "First Night Report: *Who's Afraid of Virginia Woolf?*," *New York Herald Tribune*, October 15, 1962.

136 *"very good money"*: Elaine Stritch to Noël Coward, March 1963, NCR.

137 *"the johns did nothing but flush"*: LGJL.

137 *"By acting, I get it out of my system"*: Conversation with parents recounted to Leonard Lyons in "Best of New York," *St. Petersburg Times*, June 29, 1963.

138 *"Line? What's my goddamned line?"*: Interview with Eileen Fulton.

138 *Recollecting the incident*: Ken Marsolais and Rodger McFarlane, *Broadway Day and Night* (New York: Pocket, 1992), 89.

138 *"You're not playing the play I wrote"*: Leonard Lyons, "The Lyons Den," *New York Post*, September 19, 1963.

138 *"Stritch, as you know"*: Stephen J. Bottoms, *Albee: Who's Afraid of Virginia Woolf?* (Cambridge University Press: 2000), 149.

139 *"I want to get you with a cracking agent"*: Interview with Fulton.

139 *"Steve was so unhappy"*: Meryle Secrest, *Stephen Sondheim: A Life* (New York: Vintage: 2011), 157.

139 *"I went to hear Arthur"*: Elaine Stritch to Noël Coward, August 6, 1963, NCR.

140 *"was bowled over by"*: Anthony Page, email to author, December 13, 2018.

140 *"You know, I didn't know choices"*: LGJL.

141 *"It will work or it won't work"*: ES to Noël Coward ("as you said"), August 6, 1963, NCR.

141 *"They have made so many changes"*: Ibid.

142 *"I had a feeling it was out of Kafka time"*: LGJL.

142 *"a haunting Cole Porter ballad"*: Elaine Dundy, *Life Itself!* (New York: Little, Brown, 2002), 296.

142 *"the pictures"*: John Szwed, *So What: The Life of Miles Davis* (New York: Simon & Schuster, 2002), 242.

142–43 *"He thought I was great"*: LGJL.

143 *"the throes of completing the rehearsals"*: Frederick Brisson to Alfred S. Bloomingdale, October 11, 1963, Frederick Brisson Papers, Billy Rose Theatre Division, the New York Public Library for the Performing Arts, New York City.

143 *"Without prejudice, he was friendly"*: Page, email to author.

143 *"It was the atmosphere of total unworkmanship"*: LGJL.

143 *"It is an unsmooth and spotty journey"*: Barbara Bladen, "The Marquee," *San Mateo Times*, October 24, 1963.

144 *"Larry, you'll be stoned to death"*: LGJL.

144 *"because of Elaine's erratic performances"*: Sheilah Graham, "Inside Hollywood," *Paterson (N.J.) Evening News*, November 11, 1963.

144 *"You were very good"*: LGJL.

145 *"If I told you some of the things"*: "Actors: The Boy Prince," *Time*, December 6, 1963.

145 *"no longer close to the altar"*: Dorothy Kilgallen, "The Amusement Scene," *Philadelphia Daily News*, November 16, 1963.

145 *"WHO DO YOU HAVE TO BE"*: Mildred Stritch to Noël Coward, as reported in undated clip, ESP.

145 *"Some enterprising record company"*: Kilgallen, "The Voice of Broadway," March 4, 1964.

8. FROM "STAR MAID" TO "BARMAID"

147 *"People used to say"*: Interview with Liz Smith.

147 *"You're coming over a little bit butch"*: LGJL.

148 *"Leave your key under the mat"*: Ibid.

148 *"About same-sex marriages"*: Ibid.

148 *"They were friends or acquaintances"*: Interview with Frank Moran, Jr.

148 *"She has no sex"*: Liz Smith, "Celebrity Gossip," Tribune Media Services, September 16, 2011.

148 *"I've always had a kind of attraction"*: LGJL.

149 *"there's a little of all"*: "Elaine Stritch and Liz Smith in conversation at the Center," LGBTCenterNYC, YouTube, June 20, 2009.

149 *"The idea for instance"*: LGJL.

149 *"I was down in the dumps"*: Ibid.

150 *"Last billing? Terrific, I'm coming"*: LGJL.

151 *"I've never said this before"*: Pat Williams, "Elaine Stritch—Humor Only One of Many Talents," *Record* (Pocono, Pa.), September 6, 1967.

151 *"I was not a Judy Garland type"*: LGJL.

151 *"Upside-Down Diet"*: Lydia Lane, "Hollywood Beauty," *Traverse City (Mich.) Record-Eagle*, April 7, 1964.

151 *Anxious about returning*: LGJL.

152 *Someone had threatened*: "Bomb Threat Empties Theater," *Palm Beach Post*, March 17, 1964.

152 *"toasted tycoons"*: Yolanda Maurer, "PB Name Parade Marches On and On," *Fort Lauderdale News*, March 24, 1964.

153 *He sent a capacious Rolls-Royce*: Earl Wilson, "It Happened Last Night," *Courier-Post* (Camden, N.J.), June 17, 1964.

153 *"He was getting more attractive"*: LGJL.

153 *the frug*: Earl Wilson, "It Happened Last Night," *Progress-Index* (Petersburg, Va.), June 5, 1964.

154 *"Elaine, I can make a great stinger"*: LGJL.

154 *"I didn't think she was going"*: James Kaplan, "Café Society," *New York*, July 8, 1996.

154 *"Elaine didn't pay me anything"*: LGJL.

154 *"happily shaking up a stinger"*: Leonard Lyons, "The Lyons Den," *Pittsburgh Press*, August 14, 1964.

154 *"Bartending is a lot like the theatre"*: Robert Wahls, "Footlight," New York *Daily News*, May 28, 1967.

154 *"the place to go"*: Dorothy Kilgallen, "The Voice of Broadway," *Star* (Oneonta, N.Y.), July 23, 1964.

154–55 *"She was very nice to me"*: LGJL.

155 *"There is no doubt"*: Michael V. Gazzo to ES, November 30, 1963, ESP.

155 *"How long has Mike Gazzo"*: LGJL.

156 *"It seemed to me to fit in perfectly"*: Interview with Stephen Sondheim.

156 *"Elaine, why are you doing this?"*: Interview with Smith.

157 *"Put on your Sunday clothes"*: Lyons, "The Lyons Den," *Post-Standard* (Syracuse, N.Y.), December 24, 1964.

157 *Rodgers, chary after the experience*: LGJL.

157–58 *"It was all fun and games"*: Interview with Gary Pudney.

158 *"I thought, This is a big nothing"*: Interview with Daniel J. Travanti.

158 *"had eighteen thousand brandies"*: LGJL.

159 *"the new rage saloon"*: Kilgallen, "The Voice of Broadway," *Asbury Park (N.J.) Press*, February 24, 1965.

159   *"because I don't think a married woman should work"*: Earl Wilson, "Ursula The Upset," *Detroit Free Press*, February 3, 1965.

159   *"Elaine Stritch keeps telling people"*: Kilgallen, "The Voice of Broadway," *Glen Falls (N.Y.) Times*, September 2, 1965.

159   *"It looks as though"*: Kilgallen, "The Voice of Broadway," *Glen Falls (N.Y.) Times*, November 4, 1965.

160   *"Dorothy and Stritch"*: Lee Israel, *Kilgallen* (New York: Delacorte, 1979), 375.

160   *"That was the most natural"*: Robert Wahls, "Footlight: Fun Dame in Fun City," New York *Daily News*, May 28, 1967.

161   *"squired girls from the Best Families"*: Walter Winchell, untitled column, *Scranton Tribune*, December 12, 1965.

161   *"That was just one"*: Interview with Pudney.

161   *"Did you like Gary, Mother?"*: LGJL.

162   *"grim commentary"*: Margaret Harford, "*Teddy Bear* Is Grim Commentary on New York," *Los Angeles Times*, December 10, 1965.

162   *"cooked her own seaweed"*: LGJL.

162   *"I mean, she milked every line"*: Dick Shippy, "My Dear, What This Town Needs Is a Little Glitter," *Akron Beacon Journal*, June 11, 1978.

163   *"a revivalist"*: LGJL.

163   *"she didn't cow me"*: Interview with Jonathan Tunick.

163   *"Why Miss Stritch is not"*: Bernard L. Drew, "Wonderful Town Is Like Month in the Country," *Star-Gazette* (Elmira, N.Y.), May 30, 1967.

164   *"THAT'S WHAT YOU GET"*: Kent and Edith Smith to George and Mildred Stritch, July 16, 1967, ESP.

164   *"Guess who's not coming to dinner?"*: LGJL.

164   *"Ooooo, I've heard so much"*: Aileen Mehle, "Suzy Says," *Hartford Courant*, June 10, 1968.

165   *"I was about as aware"*: LGJL.

165   *"I was thinking that"*: Interview with Judith Ann Abrams.

165   *"I don't know, I hate to think"*: LGJL.

166   *"As a Noël Coward evening"*: Dan Sullivan, "*Private Lives* Revived," *New York Times*, May 19, 1968.

166   *"Now, you stay here"*: Interview with Eileen Fulton.

166   *For Stritch this came in the person of Lee Israel*: Unless otherwise indicated, the account of the Stritch–Israel relationship is based on a series of emails from Lee Israel to Jack Silbert, written between August 2012 and July 2014, courtesy of Silbert.

167   *after Israel removed her stockings*: Interview with Ray Barr.

167   *"They all love Elaine"*: Lee Israel, "Stritch: She Got Raves in *Private Lives* (and Was Out of Work a Week Later)," *New York Times*, June 23, 1968.

168   *"She was a character"*: Interview with Diana Baffa-Brill.

168   *"The biggest mistake of my life"*: LGJL.

168   *"I know more than you"*: ESAL.

9. "EVERYBODY RISE"

169 *"the acid inside the sponge cake"*: Anthea Disney, "This Lady's Dynamite," *Daily Mail*, January 17, 1972.

169 *"It's an absolute total departure"*: "Lee Jordan Interviews the Cast of *Company*" (sound recording), Columbia, at Rodgers and Hammerstein Archives of Recorded Sound, The New York Public Library for the Performing Arts, 1970.

170 *"It's Oh! What a Lovely War, about marriage"*: Handwritten meeting notes marked October 6, GFP.

170 *"Her voice comes from the absolute bottom"*: "Laraine and Allen," typescript, GFP.

170 *"Sarah Souse"*: Ibid.

171 *"practically jumped through the phone"*: "Lee Jordan Interviews the Cast of *Company*," 1970.

171 *"Every time you run into Elaine Stritch"*: Ralph Blumenfeld, "A Talk With Elaine Stritch," *New York Post*, June 13, 1970.

171 *the character had evolved*: Draft of "My Married Friends," March 1969, GFP.

172 *Sondheim was amused*: Emma Brockes, "Stephen Sondheim: A Life in Music," *The Guardian*, December 20, 2010.

172 *"Crinoline"*: Material on the composition of "The Ladies Who Lunch" from interview with Stephen Sondheim, unless otherwise specified.

173 *Playing the role*: Interview with Patti LuPone.

173 *an idea inspired*: Interview with Harold Prince.

174 *Sondheim said he came up with the idea*: Interview with Sondheim.

174 *Stritch would insist it was hers*: LGJL.

174 *"Everybody thinks I'm brassy"*: Jean Dietrich, "The Poor Little Stritch Girl Is Back," *Louisville Courier-Journal and Times*, August 16, 1970.

174 *"I told the Elaine Stritch wish"*: Typed meeting notes, February 24, 1969, GFP.

175 *"As a matter of fact"*: Interview with Barbara Barrie.

175 *"I told him the billing problem"*: Carl Fisher to Harold Prince, August 8, 1969, HPP.

176 *"We were all kind of edgy"*: Interview with Steve Elmore.

176 *"She said Hal Prince"*: Interview with Merle Louise.

176 *"Hal Prince took a big chance"*: Interview with Donna McKechnie.

177 *"A picture of it burns in my brain"*: Interview with John Cunningham.

178 *"a huge impression"*: Interview with Pamela Myers.

178 *"People were so afraid of Elaine"*: Interview with Teri Ralston.

179 *"She was not precisely an ensemble player"*: Interview with Prince.

179 *"She's playing too many things"*: George Furth rehearsal notes, March 13–April 2, 1970, GFP.

180 *"Wait till they try"*: Interview with Barrie.

181 *"first person to marry in a babushka"*: Interview with Liz Smith.

181 *a cost of $600*: Bill from Barbara Matera Ltd. to Carl Fisher, February 11, 1970, HPP.

181 *"This is what I'm going to wear"*: Interview with Barrie.

182 *"they would run on cue"*: Interview with Prince.

182 *"What happened to you?"*: Interview with McKechnie.

183 *"All the venom"*: Matinee notes, GFP.

184 *"Acid would melt"*: Kevin Kelly, "You're in Brilliant Company," *Boston Globe*, March 25, 1970.

184 *"unfortunately—and this"*: Frank Rich, "The Theatregoer: 'Company' at the Shubert Through April 11," *Harvard Crimson*, March 26, 1970.

184 *"She practically dropped her face"*: Interview with Prince.

185 *"Elaine Stritch, with her den-mother arrogance"*: Clive Barnes, "*Company* Offers a Guide to New York's Marital Jungle," *New York Times*, April 27, 1970.

186 *"Miss Stritch has what funny lines"*: Walter Kerr, "*Company*: Original and Uncompromising," *New York Times*, May 2, 1970.

186 *"Her sisters treated her like"*: Interview with Charlotte Moore.

186 *they lacked her feeling*: Interview with Chris Bolton.

186 *On opening night*: Interview with Vincent Roppatte.

186–87 *"My cab driver thought I was Phyllis Diller"*: John Wilson, "After 18 Hours, Just Tears," *New York Times*, October 25, 1970.

187 *"She didn't want a whole lot"*: Interview with Thomas Z. Shepard.

187 *"there was a bottle"*: Interview with Prince.

187 *"She had all afternoon to nip"*: Interview with Sondheim.

188 *"It was a cold show and a cold company"*: LGJL.

10. STOMPIN' AT THE SAVOY

189 *"men were smiling over Marilyn Monroe"*: The 25th Annual Tony Awards, March 28, 1971, ABC.

190 *"They were kidnapping dogs"*: Interview with Judith Ann Abrams.

190 *energetically plumping* Nanette: Walter Kerr, "Musicals That Were Playful, Irresponsible and Blissfully Irrelevant," *New York Times*, April 11, 1971.

190 *"If one of those other two broads wins"*: Interview with Helen Gallagher.

191 *"Long story short"*: Interview with Pamela Myers.

191 *"I'm Ted Chapin"*: Ted Chapin, *Everything Was Possible: The Birth of the Musical* Follies (New York: Alfred A. Knopf, 2003), 286.

192 *"They were the daddy figures"*: Interview with Barry Brown.

192 *"Somebody in the cast"*: Interview with George Chakiris.

193 *"She's hardly got room"*: Ibid.

194 *"spellbound, watching"*: Army Archerd, "Just for Variety," *Variety*, June 14, 1971.

194 *"In every marriage"*: The Dean Martin Show, episode 7.7, October 28, 1971.

195 *"People thought she was rude"*: Interview with Rip Taylor.

195 *"snappy black Cardin suit"*: Robert Downing, "World's a Stage to Elaine Stritch," *Denver Post*, undated clipping in ESP.

195 *her signature*: ES to Carl Fisher, December 7, 1971, HPP.

196 *"I mean, it's so American"*: Anthea Disney, "This Lady's Dynamite," *Daily Mail*, January 17, 1972.

196 *"most particularly, the irresistibly acidulous"*: Kenneth Hurren, "Theatre: Qualified Rapture," *The Spectator* (London), January 29, 1972.

196 *"Miss Stritch's whiskey sour voice"*: John Higgins, "Musical Life Begins at 35," *The Times* (London), January 19, 1972.

196 *Kotex and Cashmere Bouquet*: Interview with Barry Brown.

196 *"Get me out of here!"*: Interview with Richard Pilbrow.

197 *"She would come in after"*: Interview with Frank Bowling.

197 *"The Savoy doesn't take dogs"*: Interview with Harold Prince.

197 *"Right from the start"*: Israel Shenker, *The Savoy of London* (London: Chesler, 1988), 5.

198 *"We would party and party and party"*: Interview with Kurt Peterson.

198 *"The three of us watch"*: Interview with Brown.

199 *"Elaine is a performer"*: Wayne Warga, "Laurents' Novel Tells It Like It Is," *Philadelphia Inquirer*, May 21, 1972.

199 *"she wasn't a big enough name"*: Interview with Brown.

200 *"This is the Savoy"*: ES to Mildred Stritch (postcard), January 9, 1972, ESP.

200 *"And I went down"*: LGJL.

200 *"an island of entertainment"*: Walter Kerr, "2 People, 50 Numbers, 3 Cheers," *New York Times*, October 15, 1972.

201 *"drinking like a fish with her"*: Interview with Vivian Matalon.

201 *"She treated you exactly the same"*: Interview with Eric Deacon.

201 *"She told me about her life"*: Interview with Frances de la Tour.

202 *"I used to say to him"*: Interview with Matalon.

202 *the youngest of three brothers*: Interview with George and Jim Bay.

203 *"Who do you think you want to marry"*: LGJL.

203 *"He was warm and wonderful"*: Interview with Prince.

203 *"I know that is the most"*: Interview with Paul Gemignani.

204 *"May we have 'Rob Roys'"*: Tennessee Williams to ES (note card), n.d., ESP.

204 *"Her movement"*: Irving Wardle, "Miss Stritch Stars as the Barrom Wit," *The Times* (London), January 30, 1973.

205 *"Because I loved him"*: LGJL.

205 *"We pooled our rehearsal pay"*: ESAL.

206 *"Isn't this fucking ridiculous?"*: Interview with Matalon.

206 *"Everything everybody said"*: LGJL.

206 *"The real deep-down security"*: Ibid.

206 *"All these bartenders"*: Ibid.

207 *"I married Marlon Brando"*: Ibid.

207 *"I just felt like 'staying put'"*: ES, notes for unpublished memoir, ESP.

11. TWO'S COMPANY

209 *"Sex was not the big thing"*: LGJL.

209 *"'Christ,' she said"*: Jeffrey Bernard, "London Days," *The Spectator* (London), October 7, 1977.

210 *"He loved people"*: LGJL.

210 *"Is it a comedy? No"*: Mel Gussow, "Simon Traces Path from 'Flop' to Hit," *New York Times*, December 23, 1970.

211 *"Almost immediately"*: Stephen Greif, email to author, May 12, 2016.

212 *"she wouldn't wear the false fur coat"*: Interview with Luie Caballero.

212 *"All those kinds of expressions"*: LGJL.

212 *"Boy, was he El Square-O"*: Ibid.

212 *"a wisecracking female Pierrot"*: clipping from *Daily Telegraph*, n.d., ESP.

212 *"she paces her Manhattan apartment"*: Herbert Krezner, "Plenty of Jokes—But No Laughs," *Daily Mail*, n.d., ESP.

212 *"her angular body"*: Milton Shulman, "Compelling Stritch," *London Evening Standard*, n.d., ESP.

213 *"Stritchnine"*: Michael Billington, "Good Dose of Stritchnine," *Observer* (London), October 27, 1974.

213 *"There's a whole birthday cake"*: Interview with Vivian Matalon.

213 *"Congratulations"*: Barbara Hoffman, "Broadway's Poster Boy," *New York Post*, January 29, 2012.

213 *In a bar near Regent's Park*: Neil Stevens, "Sunshine All the Way for Stritch," *Showmail*, undated clipping in ESP.

214 *"What was that?"*: "IRA Bomb Rocks Office, 1 Dead," United Press International, December 18, 1974; interview with Matalon.

214 *"I don't think Elaine knew where Vietnam was"*: Interview with John Lahr.

215 *Stritch wrangled Sammy Cahn*: Interview with Stuart Allen.

216 *"My father had a serious problem"*: Interview with Marc Sinden.

216 *"noticed and admired"*: Tom Bolton to ES, August 2, 1975, SAS.

216 *"He was a party guy"*: Interview with Sally Hanley.

217 *"I'll be right over"*: Interview with Terry Hekker.

218 *irking the producers*: Felix de Wolfe to ES, September 24, 1975, ESP.

218 *"It should be noisier"*: Igor Cassini and Liz Smith, "Cassini Carousel," *Allentown (Pa.) Morning Call*, August 10, 1975.

218 *"I remember them in the lobby"*: Interview with Ellen Burstyn.

219 *"strange torrents of words"*: Dirk Bogarde, *An Orderly Man* (London: Penguin, 1983), 232.

219 *"Ah! Even the Lancaster goofs"*: Rex Reed, "With Resnais, It's All in the Voices," *Baltimore Sun*, August 15, 1976.

220 *"I am still haunted"*: Dirk Bogarde to ES, January 1, 1977, SAS.

220 *"As Elaine Stritch's lover"*: Pauline Kael, "Werewolf, Mon Amour," *The New Yorker*, January 31, 1977.

220 *"I looked like a Vogue model"*: Elaine Stritch, *Am I Blue? Living with Diabetes, and, Dammit, Having Fun!* (New York: M. Evans, 1984), 4.

222 *"Almost like an imaginary Mommy"*: Stritch, *Am I Blue?*, 105.

222 *"She disliked all the boyfriends"*: LGJL.

222 *"berserk" with joy*: Liz Smith, "Peopletalk," *Philadelphia Inquirer*, February 3, 1978.

223   *"Today the fashion"*: "Inflation, Changing Habits to Close Cabaret London Blitz Couldn't Shut," Associated Press, December 24, 1979.

223   *"I have a resentment"*: LGJL.

223   *"Truthfully, I really knew her only briefly"*: Interview with Angela Lansbury.

224   *"Eventually she took over"*: Interview with Peter Tear.

224   *"It has more punch and pulchritude"*: *The Stage*, December 6, 1979.

224   *"Miss Hellmanned her"*: LGJL.

225   *"I remember riding"*: Interview with George Bay.

225   *"I feel living in London"*: Lawrence DeVine, "Birmingham's Lady in London," *Detroit Free Press*, December 21, 1980.

225   *"I'm not saying goodbye"*: Interview with Victor Gower.

12. WHO'S THAT WOMAN?

228   *"formed by women who want to wear hats again"*: Alex Hamilton, "La Belle Le Beau," *The Guardian* (London), August 29, 1980.

228   *"I think you should stand up for Steinem"*: LGJL.

229   *"We became friendly very quickly"*: Interview with Terry Hekker.

229   *"I'm ahead of you"*: Earl Wilson, "Gossip," *Fort Lauderdale News*, October 8, 1981.

229   *"I got homesick"*: ES quoted in "People" column, *Boston Globe Magazine*, May 2, 1982.

230   *"I thought, Boy, I wish"*: Interview with Helen Gallagher.

231   *"If I'm involved in it"*: LGJL.

231   *"Like a movie from the 1940s"*: Interview with Donna McKechnie.

231   *"We all drank and smoked like Turks"*: Interview with Frank Bowling.

232   *"the thing that saved our friendship"*: Interview with Arlene Dahl.

232   *"Instead of Groucho"*: John Dalmas, "Groucho at Bay," *Journal News* (White Plains, N.Y.), August 8, 1981.

232   *"What are you doing?"*: Interview with Hekker.

233   *"You feel invulnerable"*: LGJL.

233   *"I made a few changes"*: Interview with Hekker.

233   *"Do you love me?"*: Ibid.

234   *"John never came to full bloom"*: LGJL.

234   *"A bad day at Black Rock"*: Nancy Cacioppo, "Enjoying the Pleasures of Her Company," *Journal News* (White Plains, N.Y.), October 14, 1984.

234   *"Now that I have lost John"*: LGJL.

234   *"How does it feel to be an authoress?"*: *The Tonight Show Starring Johnny Carson*, November 4, 1983.

235   *"simple hummable show tune"*: The 38th Annual Tony Awards, June 3, 1984, CBS.

235   *"I don't think I've ever done"*: Jerry Oppenheimer and Jack Vitek, *Idol: Rock Hudson* (New York: Villard, 1986), 181.

236   *"I hope it's just the punctuation"*: Interview with Teri Ralston.

236   *"I'm just glad I got out of there alive"*: Mike Cidoni, "Sassy Stritch Saves 'Cocoon' from Drowning in Sweetness," *Press & Sun-Bulletin* (Binghamton, N.Y.), January 6, 1989.

237 *"I got the job"*: LGJL.

237 *"I went to rehearsal every day"*: LGJL.

237 *"Geez, I sound like Lionel Stander"*: *Great Performances: Follies in Concert*, episode aired March 14, 1986, PBS.

238 *"She couldn't remember the words"*: Interview with Mandy Patinkin.

238 *"That was not the tempo"*: Interview with Paul Gemignani.

239 *"Standing ovation"*: Interview with Arlene Dahl.

239 *"Here's our friend Elaine"*: Interview with Marc Rosen.

239 *Newman . . . had been astounded*: Interview with Phyllis Newman.

239 *"It's almost, like—ascension time"*: LGJL.

240 *"For me to work with Betty White"*: Marc Peyser, "A Stritch in Time," *Newsweek*, February 10, 2002.

240 *"'Listen, I'm ninety-three'"*: Interview with Midge Moran.

241 *"Having my turkey"*: Shirley Eder, "'Crimes of the Heart' Actresses All Deserve Awards," *Detroit Free Press*, November 26, 1986.

241 *"All married to terrific girls"*: *The Tonight Show Starring Johnny Carson*, November 4, 1983.

242 *"end up sounding like Julie Andrews"*: Liz Smith, syndicated column, March 27, 1987.

242 *"Mr. Allen is calling"*: Kathleen Shea, "People," *Philadelphia Daily News*, December 29, 1987.

242 *"brilliant but difficult to work with"*: Woody Allen to ES, n.d., SAS.

242 *"Oh boy, Woody, I don't care what you say"*: Liz Smith, "When Elaine Stritch Tried Her Best with Woody," http://www.newyorksocialdiary.com/guest-diary/2015/liz-smith-when-elaine-stritch-tried-her-best-with-woody, July 20, 2015; see also further unpublished notes in LSP.

244 *"so smitten by her movie director"*: Liz Smith, "The Warner Power Struggle Gets Warmer," New York *Daily News,* July 5, 1987.

244 *She told an almost identical:* Christopher Kennedy Lawford, *Moments of Clarity: Voices from the Front Lines of Addiction and Recovery* (New York: William Morrow, 2008), 253.

244 *"So, I decided to pay Him back"*: ESAL.

244 *"I guess it would be impossible"*: ES interview with Kevin Kelly.

245 *"He didn't go out like a champion"*: LGJL.

245 *"I'm not going back there"*: Interview with Hekker.

245 *"Does anybody have a cigarette?"*: Interview with Midge Moran.

245 *"The ebullient, energetic Stritch clan"*: Smith, syndicated column, July 26, 1987.

245 *"If you could meet me that's fine"*: Interview with Hekker.

246 *"was the most dramatic thing"*: John Stark, "Alone in the September of Her Years, Elaine Stritch Beats Booze to Score a Comeback in a Woody Allen Drama," *People*, January 11, 1988.

246 *"I have to go back to AA"*: Interview with Hekker.

246 *"I'm not touching this one"*: Interview with June I.

13. ROLLING ALONG

247 *"I'm afraid I'm not going to be good"*: Interview with Michael Feinstein.

248 *"If you could go to such a planet"*: Shirley Eder, "Movie Camera Still Scares Elaine Stritch," *Detroit Free Press*, November 26, 1988.

248 *"Now, all of a sudden"*: Paul Willistein, "Stage Star Elaine Stritch Wrapped Up in a New Career," *Allentown (Pa.) Morning Call*, December 19, 1988.

248 *"She got taxed mightily"*: Interview with Terry Hekker.

248 *"When she drank"*: Interview with Elke Gazzara.

249 *"Everybody else was taking cabs"*: Interview with Barry Brown.

249 *"It was a little bit of a show"*: Interview with June I.

249 *"Over the years"*: Interview with Joe Allen.

250 *"Elaine was never sober"*: Interview with Tricia Walsh-Smith.

250 *"She was one of Elaine's handmaidens"*: Interview with Andre Bishop.

250 *"Elaine viewed Elzbieta as a peer"*: Interview with Scott Griffin.

251 *"I couldn't stand the bed"*: Interview with Maurice Bernstein.

251 *"Here was the thing"*: Interview with Michael Riedel.

252 *"with a realistic, 'gritty' documentary feel"*: Garth Drabinsky, *Closer to the Sun* (Toronto: McClelland & Stewart, 1995), 445–78.

253 *"The entire play"*: Clyde H. Farnsworth, "Blacks Accuse Jews in *Show Boat* Revival," *New York Times*, May 1, 1993.

253 *"Because that's always been played"*: Interview with Harold Prince.

253 *"Hal, she's very* urban": Interview with Garth Drabinsky.

253 *"I got an hour"*: Ibid.

254 *"You know, Garth"*: Interview with Larry Grossman.

254 *"Not logical, and I knew it"*: Interview with Prince.

254 *"What happened was"*: Interview with Drabinsky.

255 *"I'm not doing this"*: Ibid.

255 *"a Tasmanian devil in a box"*: Interview with Marjorie McDonald.

256 *"You give it up, Louise!"*: Interview with Michel Bell.

256 *"the show chronicles slavery"*: John Lahr, "Mississippi Mud," *The New Yorker*, October 25, 1993.

256 *"All right, kids"*: Interview with Bell.

257 *"driven Stritch to distraction"*: George Rush, "Morse: Out of Show for 'Show Boat'-ing?" New York *Daily News*, March 10, 1994.

257 *"He was a problem"*: Interview with Drabinsky.

257 *"My darling, angel, turkey"*: ES to Garth Drabinsky, January 17, 1995, ESP.

257 *"because Garth, my darling"*: ES to Garth Drabinsky, May 24, 1995, ESP.

258 *"I am Welsh"*: LGJL.

258 *He liked the idea*: Elizabeth Ireland McCann to ES, June 26, 1995, ESP.

258 *"She sent me the script"*: Interview with Hekker.

258 *"The greatest musical-theater performance"*: Interview with Bishop.

259 *"Elaine, I know this is very far"*: Alan Willig to Elaine Stritch, May 12, 1996, ESP.

260 *"No one was funnier than Gerald"*: Mel Gussow, "Gerald Gutierrez, Director, Is Dead at 53," *New York Times*, December 31, 2003.

260 *"You know, actors are so sensitive"*: Interview with Rosemary Harris.

260 *"I don't ever remember one person in a play"*: Brian Kellow, unpublished interview with Elizabeth Wilson, part 1, posted on followkellow.com, December 31, 2017.

261 *On opening night*: Gerald Gutierrez to ES (postcard), April 21, 1996, ESP.

261 *"that she had piled"*: Andre Bishop and Bernard Gersten to ES, April 21, 1996, ESP.

262 *"If you were twenty years older"*: Interview with Riedel.

262 *"How can one compare"*: Stephen Sondheim to ES, May 29, 1996, ESP.

14. HER TURN

263 *"I'm gonna buy a house"*: Interview with Midge Moran.

264 *"It's just what I wanted"*: Judith Miller, "For the Creative, Havens in Sag Harbor," *New York Times*, May 17, 1998.

264 *instructed his business manager*: Barbara Bryson to ES, September 30, 1997, ESP.

265 *"What the hell"*: Interview with Harold Prince.

265 *"She's tall and thin"*: Interview with Bob Kingdom.

265 *"my two favorite comediennes"*: Elsa Maxwell, "The News of International Society," *Philadelphia Daily News*, March 28, 1961.

265 *"After a week"*: Interview with Rick Borutta.

266 *"If I don't show up"*: Interview with Maurice Bernstein.

267 *"Elaine was not known to do duets"*: Interview with Larry Grossman.

267 *"I was just gobsmacked"*: Interview with John Schreiber.

268 *"Originally I had in mind"*: Woody Allen to ES (fax), April 15, 1999, SAS.

269 *"Always her. Every year"*: Interview with Garth Drabinsky.

269 *"Every time I got close"*: Interview with Julie Keyes.

270 *"Would you do that for me"*: LGJL.

270 *"If you go for the truth"*: Ibid.

270 *"I was not looking forward"*: Interview with Grossman.

271 *"She was exceptionally good"*: Interview with John Lahr.

271 *"pedal to the metal"*: Harold Prince to ES, December 23, 1999, ESP.

272 *"I don't think it will work"*: Interview with Schreiber.

272 *"a real Hattie McDaniel"*: Interview with George C. Wolfe.

273 *"It's a play"*: Emma Brockes, "I'm a Do-It-Myself Kind of Broad," *The Guardian* (London), July 26, 2009.

273 *"In the other show"*: George C. Wolfe to ES, January 8, 2001, ESP.

15. STRITCH, INC.

275 *"Well, I guess we're not going"*: Interview with George C. Wolfe.

275–76 *"She was in one of her all-white"*: Ibid.

276 *"John, I want to change"*: Interview with John Lahr.

276 *"The reconstruction means I had"*: "A Stritch in Time," *Newsweek*, February 10, 2002.

277 *"We're off to see the wizard"*: Footage in unfinished documentary, Rick McKay, director.

278 *"I was wrong"*: Interview with John Schreiber.

278 *Hodgman made headway*: Interview with George Hodgman.

278 *"Because Elaine was doing business"*: Interview with Lahr.

280 *"I am very, very upset"*: Michael Riedel, "Elaine Stritch !@#$% Furious Over CBS's Unkindest Cut," *New York Post*, June 3, 2002.

281 *"I wish I could forget"*: ES, notes for unpublished memoir, ESP.

281 *mawkish and sentimental*: Lyn Gardner, "Elaine Stritch at Liberty (review)," *The Guardian*, October 11, 2002.

281 *"In the last few years"*: Interview with Harold Prince.

281 *"I never saw her at ease yet"*: Michael Buckley, "Stage to Screens," *Playbill*, May 9, 2004.

281 *"What the heck?"*: Interview with Elke Gazzara.

282 *"Get that fucking thing"*: Interview with Sheila Nevins.

283 *"I think I really fucked up"*: Interview with Michael Feinstein.

283 *"I'm an out-of-work, broke actress!"*: Interview with Clay and Elaine Kelly.

283 *"She hated going out there"*: Interview with Larry Grossman.

283 *"But she didn't need steaks and chops"*: Interview with Greg Dinella.

284 *"30 Rock is not funny"*: Liz Smith to ES, May 11, 2010, LSP.

284 *"She talked about him"*: Interview with Liz Smith.

286 *"to mutual satisfaction"*: Interview with Carl Koerner.

286 *"I gave her to a certain degree"*: Interview with Lahr.

286 *"What next?"*: "Elaine Stritch—Rose's Turn," Kevin Brazil, YouTube, June 13, 2013.

287 *"Theater is an escape"*: Ibid.

287 *"Elaine had jazz inflection"*: Interview with Stephen Sondheim.

288 *"She was entirely wrong"*: Ibid.

288 *"She was trying to give back"*: Interview with Bernadette Peters.

288 *painfully showed*: Dave Itzkoff, "At the White House, Elaine Stritch Is At Liberty (To Forget Her Lyrics)," *New York Times*, July 20, 2010.

288 *"Why is this flower here?"*: Interview with Hunter Ryan Herdlicka.

288 *a list of her entrances and exits*: Box 6, ESP.

289 *"You break all the rules"*: Trevor Nunn to ES, June 28, 2010, ESP.

289 *Walking with her*: Interview with Donna McKechnie.

290 *"You have to understand"*: Interview with Michael Riedel.

290 *"Elaine, just use a music stand"*: Interview with Feinstein.

290 *"We were looking for people"*: Interview with Matthew Barney.

291 *"I need to go where my relatives are"*: Interview with Smith.

291 *"With me, Elaine would get very drunk"*: Interview with Scott Griffin.

291 *"I don't want to be"*: Interview with Terry Hekker.

292 *"They captured a moment"*: Interview with Greg Dinella.

292 *"this is not New York"*: Interview with Kim Hagood.

293 *"I hope to see you"*: Kirk Douglas to ES, November 13, 2013, courtesy of Kim Hagood.

293 *"I remember that girl!"*: Kirk Douglas to ES, December 11, 2013, courtesy of Kim Hagood.

293 *"Raising pigs or chickens?"*: Kirk Douglas to ES, March 10, 2014, courtesy of Kim Hagood.

293 *"You are a true romanticist"*: ES to Kirk Douglas, November 27, 2013.

EPILOGUE

297 *"When the worst that can happen"*: Jean Kerr, *The Snake Has All the Lines* (Garden City, N.Y.: Doubleday, 1960), 112.

297 *"She got the obituary of a head of state"*: Interview with Greg Dinella.

298 It was so much fun: ES, notes for unpublished memoir, ESP.

298 *"Honest to god"*: LGJL.

ACKNOWLEDGMENTS

I can't explain what higher power made me feel the urgency of writing Elaine Stritch's biography, but I am grateful to it, for guiding me vaporously back to a first love: the theater, particularly the musical theater.

Thanks to James Lapine and Frank Rich for the documentary *Six by Sondheim*, which I watched crying on a plane coming back from Europe after a failed stint as a fashion critic, realizing, No, *this* was what I really cared about. (To paraphrase Stritch: "And fashion doesn't seem the least bit upset about it.") Also to D. A. Pennebaker, Chiemi Karasawa, and the late Rick McKay, whose own documentaries animate this subject better than prose ever could. And to Frank, and Alex Witchel, for kind early steering.

My cousin Carol Fineman, who worked on *At Liberty* and knew Elaine well, got me a coveted seat at the "Everybody, Rise!" memorial and provided invaluable introductions, and her sister Nina Fineman gabbed tirelessly with me about subsequent discoveries. To the fabulous Finemans, "Stop it!" and "Shut up!" are compliments, and for this and many other reasons I adore them.

Stritch's longtime attorney, Joseph Rosenthal, alerted me to her bounteous archive, granted crucial permissions, lent priceless additional material, and took me to an elegant lunch at the Harvard Club. He also delivered me to her family in Birmingham and beyond, all of whom I thank profusely for their warm welcome, generosity of time and spirit, and trust in a stranger.

Every archivist and librarian who helped with research for this project is an angel, but extra thanks to the entire staff at the New York Public Library for the Performing Arts (aka heaven; seriously, scatter my ashes over the travertine plaza), especially

Annemarie van Roessel for early and tantalizing access to Stritch's papers and the unflappable guardians of treasure: Suzanne Lipkin, Jennifer Eberhardt, Jess Gavilan, Jeremy Megraw, and John Calhoun.

And to the many publicists and press representatives who fielded my nagging requests, particularly Tom D'Ambrosio, Merle Frimark, David Kalodner, Judy Katz, Rick Miramontez, Joe Machota and team, and Philip Rinaldi.

Maevefiona Butler gave leads and quiet encouragement, and Rob Bowman came through in the clutch. Eric Price drew a straight path to Harold Prince; Rick Pappas and Steve Clar paved the yellow brick road to Stephen Sondheim; and Denis Ferrara and Mary Jo McDonough sent me floating down El Rio with Liz Smith.

In London, my uncle Andrew Leigh, distinguished alumnus of the Old Vic and elsewhere, provided not only his hospitality and expertise but also tickets to *Gypsy*, *Follies*, and, most felicitously, Marianne Elliott's 2018 version of *Company*. There should really be a musical called *Kismet*. Oh wait, there is (1953)! And the music is by Alexander Borodin, so my mother, Veronica Leigh Jacobs, might actually enjoy it. Thanks to her for letting me watch *Sweeney Todd* on PBS when I was ten and taking me to *Sunday in the Park with George* when I was twelve.

The New York Times has been a part of my life since before I could read, and to have worked there for almost a decade is a source of ongoing gratitude and wonder. Thanks especially to the Stritch enthusiast Stuart Emmrich and to Choire Sicha, my old pal from *The New York Observer*, for granting time off. And to Scott Heller and Danielle Mattoon for theater assignments and shop talk.

Too many dear colleagues and friends encouraged, helped, or reassured to enumerate here, but thanks most especially to Miranda Purves and Ethan Hauser for the thoughtful close reads, Maria Russo for consultation on Catholicism, Kate Bolick for "spinster" insight, Sheelah Kolhatkar for feminist fortification, Katie Rosman for Detroit moxie, Julie Bloom for Parisian misery, Katherine Profeta for Fire Island dramaturgy, Peter M. Stevenson for first introducing me to the phrase "Another vodka stinger!," and John Koblin for courage. Also to Jeff Roth and Tim Sternberg for photo guidance and Simone Mandell for transcription help.

My agent, Todd Shuster, stayed loyally with me through years of ridiculous book proposals and helped immeasurably with one that finally made sense.

I suspect that Stritch would have been thrilled to have been set to paper and pixels by a publishing house of FSG's eminence. Thanks to my editor, Alexander Star, for his patience, faith, and humor, and to his diligent assistants Dominique Lear and Ian Van Wye, aka my new psychotherapist. Carrie Hsieh kept a torrent of words on track, and Trent Duffy saved me from innumerable instances of absolute humiliation and ridicule; any remaining errors are my fault alone.

Most of all, thanks to my funny, tolerant, and tuneful husband and children: beloved beyond words.

INDEX

PERMISSIONS ACKNOWLEDGMENTS

Grateful acknowledgment is made for permission to reprint the following previously published material:

Lyrics from *Goldilocks*, by Jean Kerr, Walter Kerr, Leroy Anderson, Joan Ford, copyright © 1958. Reprinted by permission of Samuel French, Inc., A Concord Theatricals Company. 235 Park Avenue South, Fifth Floor, New York, NY 10003.

Lyrics of "Rose's Turn," "Some People," and "Together (Wherever We Go)" from *Gypsy*, lyrics by Stephen Sondheim, music by Jule Styne, copyright © 1959 (renewed), Stratford Music Corporation and Williamson Music Co. All rights administered by Chappell & Co., Inc. All rights reserved. Used by permission of Alfred Music.

Lyrics of "The Ladies Who Lunch," "The Little Things You Do Together," and "Broadway Baby," written by Stephen Sondheim, published by Herald Square Music, Inc., and Range Road Music, Inc. All rights administered by Round Hill Carlin, LLC.

The author wishes to thank the following individuals and institutions: Sally Hanley and Joseph Rosenthal, for use of excerpts from the letters and writings of Elaine Stritch; Larry Grossman and John Schreiber, for use of excerpts from Larry Grossman's interviews with Elaine Stritch; Alan Brodie Representation Ltd., for use of the correspondence of Noël Coward; Jonathan Prude, for use of a letter by Agnes de Mille; Gilbert Kerr, for use of the correspondence of Jean Kerr; Peppi Masciandaro and Christopher Gazzo, for use of a letter by Michael V. Gazzo; Janet Gullixson, for use of the papers of George Furth; Sally Hanley, for use of a letter by Thomas Bolton; and Woody Allen, George C. Wolfe, Kirk Douglas, and George Hodgman, for the use of their own correspondence.